# SUGAR ALPHA

# SUGAR ALPHA

## The Life and Times of Señor Huevos Grandes

ROGER AND MELISSA NELSON

iUniverse LLC
Bloomington

**Sugar Alpha**
**The Life and Times of Señor Huevos Grandes**

iUniverse books may be ordered through booksellers or by contacting:

iUniverse LLC
1663 Liberty Drive
Bloomington, IN 47403
www.iuniverse.com
1-800-Authors (1-800-288-4677)

ISBN: 978-1-4759-8939-7 (sc)
ISBN: 978-1-4759-8941-0 (hc)
ISBN: 978-1-4759-8940-3 (ebk)

Library of Congress Control Number: 2013909455

Printed in the United States of America

iUniverse rev. date: 09/09/2013

# CONTENTS

# DEDICATION

This book is dedicated to my father, Roger Nelson, who inspired many by his outrageous and extraordinary adventures, and to all who dare to live the dream.

DEDICATION

# ADVISORIES AND ACKNOWLEDGEMENTS

The events depicted in *The Sugar Alpha Chronicles* actually happened. Some names, dates and locations have been changed to protect the innocent, the guilty, and the unindicted. Some literary license has been taken to fill in gaps and smooth out the narrative where the record was fuzzy or non-existent, however I was not the source of information. But the bottom line is: All of it is truth, most of it is fact—and the more outrageous and unbelievable any part of it seems, the more likely it is to be both truth and fact.

Another fact is that my dad and I wouldn't have been able to complete *The Sugar Alpha Chronicles* without a lot of help from people who wanted as much as we did to share his story with the world. First thanks, of course, go to my mom, Jeanie, who stood by my side through the entire project. And thanks to my dad's skydiver friend, DD Bartley, who transcribed the hand-written and typewritten pages onto a computer so we could actually do something with it when my dad finished his sentence.

Next, thanks to the friends and family members who recalled so many narrative pieces of that era, and the advisors who helped me track down various records. I also owe a debt of thanks to those who helped me find the police and court documents related to my dad's adventures, many of which were not computerized and thus physically difficult to find.

Thanks to David Barletta for the use of his photo of Sugar Alpha used on the cover.

Next, thanks to Ben Lowe, love of my life, business partner, and sounding board through good moments and bad as I put together *Sugar Alpha*.

Thanks also to my publishers, whose 2012 review notes and recommendations about *Sugar Alpha* were so pivotal in shaping its final form.

Which brings me to my next thank you; to Robin "Black Death" Heid, a longtime skydiver, pioneering BASE jumper, prolific and respected writer-editor, and a friend of my dad's—who had years before sent *Sugar Alpha* to him on a 3.5-inch disc, then died before they could ready it for publication. The disk ended up forgotten in a file box until Robin found it while looking for something else and called to ask me what was going on with it. He was happy to hear I was working on it, and he offered his services, but I told him I was almost done, thanked him for calling, and said I'd get in touch if I needed him—but I was sure I wouldn't.

Then I got the publisher's notes and knew I needed him after all, so I sent him an email. He was at that moment on a mountain in the middle of China, judging a wingsuit BASE jumping race that was being broadcast live to 100 million-plus Chinese and other Asians, an event that would have made my dad laugh at the Sugar Alpha audacity of it all. Robin said he'd love to help me get it over the finish line, so when he got back to the U.S., he checked out the publisher's notes, then tuned up the work my dad and I did to match their notes and recommendations.

My final thanks goes to you, dear readers, for trusting that *Sugar Alpha* was a good way to spend your time and money. I guarantee you won't be disappointed!

# FOREWORD

You are about to read one of the most rollicking, real-life adventure stories ever written: *Sugar Alpha*, the first half of Roger and Melissa Nelson's *Sugar Alpha Chronicles*, the original draft of which Roger write while doing time in federal prison for tax evasion and running a "Continuing Criminal Enterprise." Roger died in a skydiving accident before he could get it ready for prime time, so his daughter Melissa took the project to the next level, then enlisted me to put the finishing touches on this tale that will make you mad and happy and keep you amazed and utterly entertained from the first word to the last—which pretty much also describes the amazing man around whom the whole tale revolves.

Roger Nelson lived life out of the box. Whatever he went after in life, he injected into it big dreams and big ideas, always framed by those two big questions that are the Holy Grail for out-of-the box thinkers: "Why?" and "Why not?"

Roger went after three main things in life; sport parachuting and drug smuggling, two activities connected by a love for adrenaline, adventure and high-wire-without-a-net consequences if you make too many mistakes; and his family, the needs and wants of which were usually out of sync with and often diametrically opposed to the wants and needs of his other loves.

Let's start with parachuting, the arena in which I knew him—or knew of him—for close to 20 years. When he died in 2003 at age 47, Roger Nelson had more than 9,000 jumps, 100 hours of freefall time, multiple instructor ratings and a two-year stint as a director on the board of the U.S. Parachute Association. He was also a commercially-rated pilot with more than 10,000 flight hours.

Beyond the numbers, however, Roger left a legacy not only as one of sport parachuting's most dynamic, colorful and controversial characters, but as one who arguably accomplished more than anyone before or since to change the sport's thinking and practices so it could develop it into the amazing extreme sport community it is today.

He organized parachute centers more like ski resorts and hosted large skydiving "boogies" that were basically raves with airplanes and parachutes as well as the standard partying that went along with that. He engineered competitive skydiving innovations so far outside the box but still inside the rules that flummoxed event organizers disqualified his team the first year he did it only to . . . well, you'll learn in *Sugar Alpha* what finally happened.

Not long after that, Roger developed student training and equipment doctrine so outrageously different but so unassailably better than the status quo that it shook the souls of parachuting's "that's-the-way-we've-always-done-it" crowd and changed almost everything about how people now learn to skydive. And all along the way, his personality and personal adventures gave rise to stories told so many times around so many parachute center fire pits that they became legends and cartoons— except that, as it turned out, the more outrageous and unbelievable the tale was, the more likely it was to be true.

That's because Roger Nelson's second great adrenaline love was drug smuggling, a secret life he began living not long after he started jumping. He'd done low-level drug dealing in high school and, out-of-the-box thinker that he was, he noticed a lot of airplanes sitting at airports doing nothing when they could be in the air doing something productive. He also noticed that both pilots and skydivers seemed to like living on the edge as much as possible even if they weren't exactly *thinking* outside of the box—so he combined these two elements and his alchemy produced a gold mine of adrenaline, adventure, cannabis, cocaine and Krugerrands. Roger was unarguably a drug smuggler *par excellence* and one of the most innovative and methodical drug outlaws who ever ran a gig. As he did with parachuting, he challenged conventional wisdom and came up with ways to bring top-shelf weed into the United States that both satisfied his customers and boggled the minds of *federales* and fellow smugglers alike when they figured out what he was doing. It was not for nothing that he was known among drug smugglers as *Señor Huevos Grandes*.

But eventually the feds did figure it out and so, after a 20-year run as a full-time professional parachutist and 15 years of "pioneering outside the sport," as he sardonically put it to me in a 1997 *Skydiving Magazine* interview, Roger pleaded guilty to several drug and tax evasion charges, forfeited some a pile of assets and in 1987, surrendered to federal authorities for an extended, all-expense paid vacation as a guest of the United States government.

He was also trying to be less colorful; while he'd always had a not-so-noticeable spiritual side, Roger had in prison become bunkmates and close friends with disgraced televangelist Jim Bakker and, as a result, Christianity essentially replaced drug smuggling in the non-skydiving part of his life. Gone were the wild days and nights of partying and hell-raising, and the "pioneering outside the sport" recounted in *The Sugar Alpha Chronicles*. When reminded of adventures past, however, Roger acknowledged them cheerfully, as he did during our *Skydiving* interview when at one point I asked: "What was that story about you and Kong at Freak Brothers a few years back? Something about local whuffos (non-skydivers), a chain bolted to a baseball bat and a .357 magnum?"

"That wasn't at Freak Brothers," Roger replied without hesitation. "That was the Nationals—and it was a .44 magnum."

And then he died. Fortunately for us, *The Sugar Alpha Chronicles* still live, with all of their great storytelling, compelling characters, outrageous adventures—and object lessons about the lure of money and power, and the oxymoron that is "good government." As I said earlier, *Sugar Alpha* is a rollicking, real-life adventure tale about skydiving and pot smuggling and loyalty and brotherhood and pushing the limits a dozen different ways. I'll leave the second half of the *Chronicles* alone for now except to say that it's provisionally called *Charlie Bravo*, and it's a darker, more dangerous and disturbing saga about cocaine smuggling, personal betrayal and political corruption—and those high-wire-without-a-net consequences I also mentioned earlier.

Fortunately for Roger, the skydiving and drug smuggling that was so out of sync with and diametrically opposed to the wants and needs of his family did not in the end prevent him from being as successful a family man as he was a jumper and outlaw—and the unarguable proof of that is the children he and his wife Jeanie produced, all in the middle of the maelstrom that was his first two loves. I know both Melissa and Rook. I respect and admire them both, and every time I think of who they are and what they themselves have already achieved, I tip my hat to their father and mother and say, "well, done, Mom and Dad, well done"—and I know that praise would mean more to him than any accolades for his many parachuting or smuggling accomplishments.

In the end, Roger Nelson had everything he ever wanted except a longer life, and even on that score, he came out all right, too, at least according to the man whose face he saw so often during his 47 years.

"A long life may not be good enough," said Ben Franklin, whose name is synonymous in outlaw circles with the American $100 bill on which he appears, "but a good life is long enough."

Good thing for Roger that the first Franklin didn't say life had to be legal to be good.

—Robin "Black Death" Heid, Northridge, California, April 2013

# PREFACE

*The Sugar Alpha Chronicles* is a two-book tale about the life and times, crimes and adventures, of my father, Roger Nelson. It is a true and largely factual story, the original draft of which was written by my father not long after the epic skydiving adventures and audacious drug smuggling escapades chronicled therein. My father kept a meticulous log of events, so he was able to accurately recount them when needed. Of course, he also had access to the equally meticulous law enforcement records and court transcripts that resulted in the prison term he served effectively of what he once called "pioneering outside the sport" of parachuting, the prison term during which most of the *Sugar Alpha Chronicles* were written.

My father was released from prison in December 1992 after four and a half years behind bars. He then printed the original manuscript and let many of his friends read his story. He always knew how to captivate an audience with his stories, but the written manuscript still needed serious editing. Unfortunately for the manuscript (though not the sport of parachuting), my dad's focus was more on the future than the past, so he devoted his energy and attention to bigger parachuting projects and adventures and his incredible story sat on a shelf collecting dust.

Then my dad died in a 2003 skydiving accident, perhaps the last way anyone who knew him expected him to pass away, given his knowledge, experience and approach to the sport. His death reminded everyone that, no matter how good you are, danger still lurks every time you fly in the sky, and one day you may meet your end there, even if you're doing everything right.

My dad also died without completing *Sugar Alpha*, so the dust got thicker as our family sorted through the aftermath of his death and all the loose ends that come with such an event, no matter how well organized (or not) are the affairs of the departed.

In fact, three years passed before we even thought about *Sugar Alpha* again. That was when I decided to take a break from full-time skydiving to do some soul searching and self seeking—and when all family fingers suddenly pointed at me to finish the book since I would now have so much free time.

Those fingers pointed at me to move forward with the project because my immediate family and a few friends were privy to my mostly covert life as a writer. I'd been writing since I was 12 and counted among my works several dozen short stories, a number of articles for skydiving magazines, and a journal that spanned almost two decades.

Begrudgingly, I agreed to do it because I knew it was a story that needed to be told, but I also knew it would take my soul searching and self seeking in a different direction. There was a whole new world lurking in those pages, and I knew I had to be ready for it.

As a child, I knew only that my dad was away from home a lot, "working" for long periods of time, that he often came and went at night, that he regularly left and returned abruptly. I was in the first grade when the police first started knocking on our door, when they started calling the house, when men without uniforms but with badges would visit. Soon after these visits started, my pre-school age brother started asking: "Are they here to take Dad away?"

I wondered about that myself, and I remember one day when the police pulled us over and my dad very sternly warned my brother and me not to say anything, no matter what.

"No matter what," he said." If they ask you anything, say, 'I want to speak to a lawyer,' then we'll talk about it later." I was about eight, so of course I didn't know what the truth was even if they had asked, but I know now that my dad was trying to protect us from the trauma of being questioned by the police. At the time, however, it aroused my suspicion that either the cops were very bad people or my father himself had done something bad.

Another lesson my father taught us was, "It's better to get caught by me than by the cops." I understood that better when I was in my teens and being my father's daughter in certain ways, I won't further detail here.

I also remember that, about the time I turned 12, my dad had an adult conversation with me and told me that he might have to go away for a long time. By then, I'd heard rumors that my dad had done illegal things. I assumed it was probably drugs, but, as my mother had done when I was younger, I wasn't interested in being a detective. It always seemed better to enjoy him for what he was when he was with us, and to willfully know nothing about what he did when he was away.

That's why even holding *Sugar Alpha* in my hands was hard—and why even after I picked up the manuscript it took me 18 months to actually open it and read the first page: Reading it meant learning the whole truth about his life and his outlaw ways, about the good things he did as well as the illegal things that many people would and still do consider to be bad—very bad. It meant I would discover why he was gone so much during my childhood—and what he did when he was gone. It meant I would have to accept the fact that his family life—and that I myself—was not his first priority, even though he did the best he could when he was around.

Somehow, I sorted through the discomfort and resentment that grew in me as I read, even though it sometimes was so intense that the tears flowed. And don't misunderstand; the discomfort wasn't always from learning about his smuggling, about his lawbreaking, or about his sometimes ruthless behavior. No, sometimes it was from pride and admiration—the way he led his team to the Nationals, how he backed one teammate all the way to the podium, how he outfoxed the authorities so many times, how he treated his fellow smugglers and especially how he treated the people of Belize.

You'll get to know him too in *The Sugar Alpha Chronicles*, along with the rest of my family. You'll see how the two generations before me become parachutists, and get a deeper look into part of the drug smuggling world of the early 1980s as well as my dad's efforts to organize the biggest skydiving events of the time, from wild "Freak Brother" conventions to buttoned-down world records recognized by international sport organizations. And you'll find out how torn my father was between the clandestine, money-fueled and adrenaline-charged world of drug smuggling—and the sweetness and low-key routine of family life.

I was torn too as I read it, and as I added my own research and writing to the narrative, I felt the thrill of his adventures: flying around the world for his outlaw lifestyle, managing a successful skydiving business as well as being an internationally respected pioneer in the sport, and struggling to be a family man. Going through it all made me feel compassion for him and helped me to understand him better because I truly am my father's daughter; I too love jet-setting for skydiving events and just traveling to exotic countries (legally, of course, and under the real name on my own passport). He was a difficult man to love, but he was an innovator, a pioneer, determined to seek and achieve great things, all while maintaining his integrity and demanding nothing less than excellence from himself and everyone around him. So no matter how hard it was to understand him, Roger Nelson was an amazing man—and I am proud beyond words to say that he was my dad.

# PROLOGUE

## THE RULE OF THREE

Moonbeams cut through broken clouds over a calm Caribbean Sea and shined on a U.S. Coast Guard Cessna Citation jet flying four miles above the water, following an unknown aircraft running without lights toward the Bahamas.

"Almighty, this is Omaha," called the Citation pilot. "Suspect aircraft now sixteen miles southwest of Great Inagua, heading three-three-zero at 185 knots at nine thousand feet. Over."

"Roger Omaha," replied a voice reeking of authority. "Nassau is alerted and standing by. Almighty out."

Somewhere south of the Mason-Dixon Line in a remote farmhouse distinguished only by two towering antennas, a young, self-assured 30-something man, clean-shaven, with a full head of thick, untamed dark hair sat dressed in an old pair of jeans, with his favorite plain brown leather belt, and a faded blue skydiving t-shirt, presiding over a maze of sophisticated radios, listening to the Coast Guard transmissions.

Roger Nelson knew exactly what this meant—thanks to a Bahamian official he'd met and befriended when he'd bought part of a Bahamian island a while back.

"Almighty" was the code name of the American drug interdiction base station on the U.S. Navy base at Guantanamo Bay, Cuba. "Omaha" was equipped with tracking radar that could follow aircraft from high above, and he also knew the U.S. had given helicopters to the Bahamas to help chase down drug smugglers. Roger silently thanked his friend and keyed his mic.

"Whiskey Oscar, this is Papa. Are you with me?"

"Like you're sitting next to me!" answered a tense, excited voice.

Roger was relieved to have reestablished comms with Billy, the skittish, black-haired pilot of the 20-year-old Beechcraft Excalibur Queen Air being tailed by the Citation. They had planned to keep in contact every 30 minutes, each time changing frequencies to a lower band, both to improve clarity as their distance decreased and help lose anyone trying to listen in. The tail, however, changed Roger's plans. Hoping his gut feeling was wrong, he keyed his mike again.

"Have you seen Wendy yet?"

"Left her fifteen minutes ago, looking fine."

Roger checked a map on the wall and moved a marker just north of the Windward Passage, the strip of water between Cuba and Haiti.

"Slow down and turn to zero-one-zero."

"Copy slow down and turn to zero-one-zero."

A moment later, Roger heard the sound he'd dreaded.

"Target is slowing and turning through three-six-zero," said the Citation pilot.

"Whiskey Oscar, return to original course, and stand by. Over." Roger sighed, but his eyes glinted with resolve as the Citation pilot confirmed that his target had resumed its previous course.

"Whadda you got?" queried Billy's worried voice. Roger knew that at that moment the young, green pilot had completely forgotten the fatigue of flying 2,000 miles in 20 hours without a break, that time was stretching out for him, that he was probably mashing his face against the windows looking for his tail and seeing nothing but moon and stars, then looking behind him at the 1,500 pounds of Colombian marijuana baled and stacked neatly in the seatless, Visqueen-lined fuselage.

"What should I do? What do you think?" crackled his panicky voice over Roger's radio. "I'm gonna turn back, all right?"

"Relax," Roger said sternly. "Stay cool and quit trying to think. Nobody at Charlie's now anyway."

"O.K.," Billy replied but his voice did not sound okay, "but I'm gonna tune in their frequency, OK?"

"Not okay," Roger snapped. "Keep your discipline, you're all right. Above all, maintain contact with me. That is the key. Stay with me! We got options, and we're gonna use 'em. Got it?"

"Got it," said Billy in a still-tense but no longer panicky voice.

Roger cursed himself for letting such a novice fly this gig, but quickly ditched the hindsight scolding in favor of dealing with the situation as it was. Billy was normally a basket case flying over the ocean even without pressure. It was going to be a long night, but Roger had enough confidence for both of them—confidence in his planning and in his ability to execute it.

"Game on," he said out loud to himself. Roger had long ago learned the "rule of three"—always have three options—and the experience to know when to switch gears. In this case, it was time for Plan B. He keyed the mike on another radio.

"Panther team, come to Papa," he called calmly to his auxiliary team in Blairsville, Georgia—though he felt a thrill of anxiety as he did. His previous trips had always gone like clockwork, and the Blairsville backup crew had never done anything except collect its fee. "Panther team, come in. Over."

"Panther team copies Papa," replied a young voice Roger knew as Joel. "Over."

"Stand by for welcome mat," said Roger. "Over."

"Copy standby for welcome mat," answered Joel. "Over."

"Roger that," said Roger. "Stay close. Be ready. Out."

Roger kicked back in his chair. He knew his "just-in-case-boys" were now jangled with adrenaline and reviewing every piece of their part in Roger's carefully designed secondary plan. The veteran smuggler felt the adrenaline too; for the first time, he would see if he and his organization would measure up to a real threat.

Two hours later, Billy's periodic radio pleas for reassurance gave way to a far more measured voice on Roger's headset.

"Almighty, this is Omaha," said the Citation pilot. "Suspect plane turning three-one-zero towards Bimini. Appears to be heading stateside."

"Roger Omaha. Per Rampart, Cobra One and Cobra Two are staged in Opa Locka and West Palm awaiting dispatch."

Roger was puzzled by Almighty's involvement. Usually, the regional El Paso Intelligence Center (EPIC) handled drug, human, and weapon smuggling interdiction across the southern border. Maybe Almighty had only stumbled across the Queen Air and hoped to get lucky. If that was the case, the operation was not compromised, but Roger still needed to get Billy and his cargo safely on the ground—and with helicopters waiting for them in Florida, that validated Roger's earlier decision to change his plans.

Right on schedule, Billy dropped down to 50 feet north of Bimini and turned west. The Citation followed, reducing its own altitude to maintain radar contact.

Billy soon crossed the U.S. coastline and, as Roger expected, Almighty handed the mission off to EPIC, which dispatched the Opa Locka and West Palm helicopters.

Roger, tracking Billy's position by the Citation pilot's frequent situation reports, told him to fly towards Lake Worth, 100 miles north of Homestead.

"Bingo fuel," called the Citation pilot seconds later. "Breaking off the pursuit."

Roger pumped a fist in his farmhouse redoubt. By ordering Billy to fly low, he'd forced the Citation pilot to burn far more fuel, pushing itself through the thicker air so it could keep tracking Billy. His tactics had put the Coast Guard pilot in a box he couldn't escape.

EPIC launched a far less capable plane to continue the pursuit—a Florida-based Drug Enforcement Administration (DEA) King Air turboprop. It also initiated a rolling alert with state and local authorities as Billy neared their jurisdictions—knowing that smugglers typically traded fuel for cargo and landed near the southern coast.

These authorities were well practiced in coordinating their tactics based on this operational assumption—but Roger's plan was specifically designed to beat these tactics. Billy continued northward, away from the regular theater of smuggler operations. Better yet, they hadn't IDed Billy's plane so they had no idea of its range—or of the fact that Billy not only had fuel to fly far from the coast, he had a mission commander who knew what he was doing.

Roger radioed Billy and told him to program his Loran navigation system for the Plan B destination. A few minutes later, the Queen Air crossed into Georgia and the choppers broke off their pursuit, as they had fallen hopelessly behind the faster Queen Air. Now Roger and his crew faced only the DEA King Air and whatever short-notice ground support EPIC could muster—ground support without experience at coordinating with federal drug agents.

Still, Roger knew the King Air was a formidable threat all by itself because it wasn't just a surveillance plane with a pilot and a radio; it almost certainly had a six-man DEA "bust team" aboard, most likely comprised of armored, heavily-armed young guys eager to make their mark, but led by a drug war veteran who, like Roger, knew what he was doing. If Roger's Plan B didn't go off as designed, things would go to hell fast.

He didn't have long to wait for his answer. When the Queen Air was 20 miles from Blairsville, Roger knew Billy would pick up a low-powered marine band radio that was ideal for short-range communications and call the ground crew. Right on time, Roger heard the conversation over Billy's primary radio.

"Panther team, Whiskey Oscar. Over."

"Panther team standing by. Over."

"ETA ten minutes, Panther. ETA ten minutes. Over."

"Copy ten minutes ETA, Whiskey Oscar. Out."

Roger heard the excitement in Joel's voice and the fear in Billy's—and he was happy that during Billy's original briefing he'd followed the tried-and-true operational procedure of telling his twitchy pilot only what he needed to know.

Billy thought that he was only doing a test landing to see if he was still being tracked. He'd been told to expect ground support but nothing else except to *stay in the plane and wait* for further instructions because Roger knew that Billy might decide to run for it after he landed if he lost contact with Roger's stern but soothing voice.

"Whiskey Oscar, start your descent," Roger instructed. Then he heard the King Air pilot notify EPIC of an impending landing and the likely location—followed by an EPIC advisory that local law enforcement was enroute.

"Papa, Whiskey Oscar. On final."

"Copy Whiskey Oscar. Focus and relax. Focus and relax."

"Copy, Papa."

Meanwhile, the King Air pilot lagged higher up and farther back, hoping the gap would hide their engine noise and lure the ground crew into the open.

Down on the farm, Roger knew the DEA team would be locking and loading and as pumped with adrenaline as Billy and Joel and Dennis, the other Panther crewmen.

Back at the airport, Sheriff Hargrove Pattimore parked his personal car behind a small hangar and waited for several deputies to join him. He didn't know who was coming, but he relished the chance to cover his crooked tail in front of the feds. After all, he'd "rented" his facilities to several outlaw entrepreneurs in the area and it never hurt to bust somebody now and then, both for the good PR, and to put the outlaws on notice that using "his" facilities without payment was *verboten*—and these guys hadn't paid. Pattimore listened to the approaching airplane and wondered if he'd get a chance to steal the load anyway.

"One minute to touchdown," the King Air pilot reported to EPIC. "Is ground support in position?"

"Negative, Cowboy One. ETA unknown."

Roger laughed at this good news. Joel had already told him the local muscle was waiting on the other side of the airport, so that meant the locals were incompetent, corrupt—or both.

Joel and Dennis lurked in the tree line 1,500 feet down the approach end of the runway, two small dirt bikes nearby, pointed the other direction. Like Billy, the two 19-year-olds knew only their own role in the operation. Roger had recruited them through friends not for their smuggling knowledge or criminal background (they had none) but because they grew up hunting and fishing in northern Georgia and knew its woods like the back of their hands. Just as importantly, they knew from their hunting experience when to stay calm and still—and when to explode into action.

Now they were still, like panthers waiting to strike, as they watched the dark silhouette of the descending Queen Air and tightened their grip on the tow handles of their "welcome mats," two 16-foot-long trains of two 4x8-foot plywood sheets tied together and pierced with hundreds of nails.

Billy settled below tree level. He turned on his landing lights, bounced the plane in hard and quickly turned them off. The moment he rolled past the boys, they dragged their welcome mats onto the asphalt, laid them end-to-end across the runway, then ran back to the woods and climbed on their bikes. Joel clipped his radio to his handlebars.

Behind him, the Queen Air stopped halfway down the runway.

"Whiskey Oscar to Papa," called Billy, and Roger could hear the terror in his voice. "I'm down, landed I mean. I think they're on me, but I can't be sure. What do I—"

"Focus and relax, buddy," Roger commanded calmly, "focus and relax and *stay in your seat. Got it?*"

"Shit! Shit!"

"*Stay in your seat.* Got it?"

"Got it." Voice slightly calmer. "But what do I—"

"Just wait, Whiskey. Just wait."

Sheriff Pattimore thought he heard the landing but dared not move until his backup arrived. Still, he pulled forward enough to see the King Air's landing lights go on as the DEA plane dropped below the treetops—and cursed the tardiness of his men.

The King Air touched down lightly, then went dark again and the engines roared as the pilot reversed the props to slow down faster. Farther down the runway, Billy saw the King Air's lights go out.

"They're down! They're down!" he shouted into his radio. "I'm outta here!"

Billy jammed the throttles to the firewall, and the two 400-horse piston engines hauled the Queen Air down the remaining runway.

Behind him, the King Air ran over Roger's welcome mat. Nails shredded all three tires, and the crippled nose wheel dug into the asphalt, snapping the strut. The props gouged the runway and the plane screeched to a halt in a shower of sparks. In the forest near the runway, Joel and Dennis motored away, the sound of their dirt bikes drowned out by screaming turbines and tortured metal.

"Panther team to Papa," said Joel into his radio as he followed Dennis through the woods. "Mission accomplished. Over."

"Copy that, Panther. Great job. Out."

Joel turned off his radio and followed Dennis, a satisfied smile curling his lips.

The Queen Air lurched from the runway into flight, stayed low and disappeared into the night.

Back on the farm, Roger heard Billy yell into the radio.

"I'm airborne! All clear, all good!" Roger pumped his fist again. Plan B had worked. Now to Plan C. He turned to another radio.

Back at the airfield, Sheriff Pattimore mistook Roger's Queen Air for the DEA King Air making a go-around and gunned his car down the runway toward the crippled plane to make the bust and hopefully abscond with some product before the feds returned.

Over at the King Air, the DEA squad tumbled out of the side door, cursing and disoriented, dragging the pilot with them. One man tripped and fell. His submachine gun went off, sending rounds in Pattimore's general direction. The sheriff saw the muzzle flashes and assumed that the drug smugglers were shooting at him, so he swerved off the runway and stopped, then grabbed his radio and took cover behind his car.

"Dopers got me pinned down with machine guns!" he shouted into his radio. "I need backup *now!*"

He peeked over the hood and saw heavily armed men around the wrecked plane and knew he was dead unless he threw them off balance—so even though he was out of range, he emptied his service revolver in their direction, then scrambled to his trunk for his shotgun and extra ammo.

The pistol rounds had the desired effect. The DEA agents hit the ground and the team leader fired back at the muzzle flashes *he* had seen, then ordered his men to retreat into the treeline while he laid down more covering fire.

At that moment, Sheriff Pattimore fired multiple buckshot rounds toward the DEA, adding to the urgency of their retreat and the fury of the team leader's return fire.

The DEA team leader turned Pattimore's car into Swiss cheese. Fuel leaked, and Pattimore ran for the woods on his side of the runway. Moments later, another round set off the fuel and the car exploded into a fireball. War had arrived in rural Georgia.

Meanwhile, the Queen Air flew serenely through the moonlight, high above and far from the fray, headed for its original destination near Rockwood, Tennessee. Roger had calmed Billy down and bucked him up by telling him his flying had lost the DEA tail.

"I feel like Sky King," Billy had joked in response, confirming for Roger that the kid was back on a reasonably even keel.

The detour meant Billy would arrive near dawn at the airport on the edge of the Great Smoky Mountains, so when the horizon glowed on his right, he called Dave and Mike, the Rockwood ground crew waiting anxiously in a large white cargo van, already prepped by Roger on the new schedule.

As planned, Billy overflew the field at a high altitude so they could watch and listen for any following aircraft. After the Queen Air engine sounds faded into the distance, Mike confirmed that Billy was alone and called him in. Billy executed a quick, descending turn back to the airport and landed quickly.

Now the whole team was charged up for the climax, and feeling antsy at having to finish the job in daylight. They snapped on latex gloves as Billy taxied behind a hangar and, like a NASCAR pit crew, moved without a wasted motion and started working before the plane had stopped.

Dave ran into the prop blast and dropped the air stairs, then guided Mike and his windowless cargo van back between the wing and the tail, stopped it at the threshold and climbed into the plane. With the engines still running on both vehicles, Mike set the brakes, ran around the back, grabbed four 16-gallon fuel containers from the van and set them by the wing.

Then he started catching bales from Dave and stacking them neatly in the van so they'd all fit. As the two veteran smugglers unloaded the plane, Billy sat at its controls, wound up and twitchy—again acting like a trapped animal.

Less than six minutes later, the van was full and the plane was empty. With thumping hearts and sweating bodies, Dave and Mike eyed each other proudly, then Mike dashed for the driver's seat and Dave grabbed baby powder from his backpack and spread it on the bales to hide the smell. Then he shut and locked the doors, swept off the bumper, and gave Mike the "go" signal. Off went the van.

As Mike drove away, Dave checked his stopwatch: five minutes and 39 seconds, 21 seconds under the allotted time and just 16 seconds shy of their record. Then he plucked two fuel containers from the ground and poured them into the wing, being careful not to get shredded by the prop. He was done in a minute, repeated the procedure with the remaining fuel containers on the other wing tank, then tossed the empty containers inside the plane and jumped aboard.

"Hit it!" he yelled to Billy as he pulled the door shut and Billy taxied. Dave unslung his backpack, which had radios, a vacuum, and two crushed, empty coffee cups—the evidence of their presence.

Billy rolled onto the runway and gunned the engines and they were soon airborne. Dave put on a fresh pair of latex gloves and stripped the thick Visqueen liner that so perfectly fit the fuselage, stuffed it into a bag, sprinkled carpet freshener everywhere, then vacuumed the cabin until it was spotless.

"Is Mike clear?" he asked Billy when he was done. Billy's eyes bulged as he realized that he'd forgotten a key element of the final phase—making sure the van had made it safely to the interstate so Roger could coordinate the unloading at its next stop. He grabbed the marine band handheld.

"Hey, buddy, how ya doing?" Billy asked.

"Gee, thanks for asking," came the sarcasm-coated reply. "I'm good to go. Out."

Dave shook his head at the greenhorn pilot as Billy set down the marine radio and keyed his control wheel mike.

"Whiskey Oscar to Papa, all good to go. Over."

Down on the farm, Roger Nelson smiled at the news.

"Copy good to go, Whiskey. Good work. I'll see you tomorrow. Out."

Roger kicked back in his chair and looked out the window as the world woke up to a new day. He allowed himself a moment to enjoy the view, then turned back to his radios. The tricky part was over, but he still had one more thing to do before the gig was done.

"Tango, this is Papa. Over."

# CHAPTER ONE

## The Freak Brothers

Green water rippled around Carl Nelson Sr. as he paddled his canoe down the Fox River, steering from the rear so he could more easily navigate around rocks and snags in the meandering watercourse 75 miles southwest of Chicago. His eldest son, Carl Jr., paddled from the front; youngest son Roger paddled from the middle. Carl Jr. concentrated on paddling and helping his father steer the cleanest course down the river. Roger's attention alternated between the river, his paddling, his brother's developing muscles, and getting away with "accidentally" splashing him.

Carl Nelson Sr. was a war hero, though he wouldn't admit it and he didn't talk about it. Like many of those in The Greatest Generation, he knew that too many young men lay in foreign graves for those still living to make hay about what they did and lived through in World War II. The dead and their sacrifice deserved respect and gratitude, not grandstanding.

To that end, Carl proudly wore his 82nd Airborne Division pins and patches and his airborne wings on his hats and jackets, including the baseball cap perched on his head now. His fellow Americans instantly recognized these emblems of his service in the "All American" division, and that was enough.

Yet no word other than hero can sufficiently describe a man who willingly parachuted from an airplane into the dark night above occupied France, behind enemy lines, through enemy fire, carrying 100 pounds of gear, to fight the world's most feared military machine with no backup expected for days—and then only if the largest sea

1

invasion ever launched succeeded against the most formidable coastal fortifications ever built. That's exactly what Carl Sr. and thousands of his similarly heroic buddies did—and several thousand of them still rest in peace in quiet fields near the Normandy coast.

Carl's wife, sons, and daughter knew nothing first-hand about the horror of war, and this suited Carl just fine; he knew there was no glory in killing young men torn away from their youthful dreams to kill other young men just like themselves. Killing in war was a bloody necessity forced on a man by his government and he did it to save his buddies and himself more than "for duty and country."

At the same time, Carl knew there was something glorious and manly in facing down an enemy and conquering fear. If more such men existed, monsters such as Hitler could never have risen to power. People would rise up and say, "Enough!" More practically, such men would never live under the boot of life's ordinary bullies and bigots. This was the legacy Carl wished to pass on to his children before they reached adulthood. He just hoped there could be a way to do it without war and killing.

Then, as the boys alternated between paddling and splashing, Carl Sr. heard a sound and saw a sight that stirred his soul and reawakened long-dormant memories; three round military parachutes popping open in the sky.

They seemed to appear from nowhere, but Carl Sr. heard the faint sound of an aircraft and searched the sky until he found it, descending now, but still almost two miles above them.

"Would ya look at that!" he called out to his boys and pointed with his paddle.

"Cool!" they exclaimed. "Wow!"

The canoe drifted in the current as the Nelsons watched the parachutists descend and then disappear behind the treeline along the river.

"Wanna go check them out?" asked the father of his sons—but he'd already made up his mind as he dug his paddle into the water.

"No way!" snorted Carl Jr.

"Really?" said Roger. "Can we?"

Carl Sr. nodded.

"Can *we* jump?" Carl Jr. asked slyly, thinking he knew the answer.

"Maybe," came his father's unexpected reply.

"Cool!" shouted Roger. "Then let's go!"

And with that they all dug their paddles into the water, and flew down the river toward their pickup point, all horseplay forgotten, all splashing truly accidental.

Carl Sr., was at the wheel of the family car as they approached the grass strip and small hangar grandiosely labeled with a hand-lettered wooden "airport" sign. The boys peppered their father with questions.

"How much does it cost?" Carl Jr. wanted to know.

"Don't know yet, son."

"How do we learn what to do?" asked Roger.

"Not sure, but if they do it the way I did, they'll make sure you're in shape to do it, then teach you how to land and fall down without hurting yourself—it's called a PLF, a parachute landing fall. Then they'll teach you how to steer the parachute and what to do if the main doesn't open."

"But *then* what?" Roger persisted. "How do we actually jump?"

"With a main chute and an emergency chute and, for at least the first few times, you'll be attached to the plane by a 10-foot line that automatically opens the parachute when you hit the end of it. Pretty simple, really."

"And you did this, Dad?" asked Carl.

Carl Sr. parked next to the hangar and turned off the engine.

"A few times," he said simply.

"What happens if neither parachute works?" asked Roger.

"Then you have nothing to worry about. Just enjoy the rest of your life."

His father laughed. After a moment, Roger and his brother did too. Nervously.

When they got out of the truck, they saw three jumpers preparing to board a small, noisy, high-wing aircraft.

"You're just in time to see a jump," bellowed one jumper over the engine noise, a big guy past his prime but still plenty beefy. He looked like he might be in charge; at least he sounded that way.

"We usually charge for the show," he grinned, "but if you promise to pick up anyone who lands off the airport, we'll let you watch for free."

Carl Sr. grinned back and gave him a thumbs up.

3

"Doing these fellows a favor'll help us get in good with them," he said to his boys. Roger nodded knowingly. Carl was busy watching the jumpers.

The jumpers boarded. Big green military rigs and billowy jumpsuits filled the single-engine plane's passenger windows. The pilot waved, the engine roared, and the plane bounced down the grass runway, building speed until, with one last bounce it hurtled into the sky and turned almost graceful.

"Well," said Carl Sr., "let's find a good place to watch and see if we can spot them as they come out."

They laid down in the grass on the shady side of the hangar and watched the plane climb higher and higher until they could barely see or hear it. After a while, Carl Sr. shaded his eyes with one hand and pointed with the other.

"Okay, they're on jump run. Listen carefully and you'll hear the pilot cut the power so they can get out easier. Then watch for them."

The boys held their breath and, moments later, even the faint engine sound stopped.

"He cut it, Dad!" said Roger excitedly.

"There they go!" chimed in Carl Jr.

They watched three spots separate from the plane and plummet earthward faster and faster. Soon, the dots turned into tiny human shapes.

"Wow," Roger said quietly, enthralled by the spectacle.

"Too cool," added his big brother.

Carl Sr. just smiled, remembering old adventures and enjoying the new one he was having with his sons.

The parachutes cracked open, and true to the old paratrooper's expectations, none of the jumpers landed on target. One man had to pick his way through the bean field; Carl Sr. sent his older son out in the pickup to get the other two down the road.

When they returned, Carl Jr. nearly flew out of the truck.

"Dad! Dad!" he shouted. "They said I can jump! I can jump! I just need some money for lessons, and they'll let me use their parachutes and everything! I can start tomorrow!"

Summers would never be the same. The first few were the most fascinating and frustrating of Roger's young life. While his brother earned his "wings," as his father called them, Roger stayed grounded. The "club" had its rules, though the excuses varied.

"It's against the rules," the airplane's owner said flatly.

"But it's your plane," countered Roger. "You can change the rules."

"Sorry, you ain't old enough, kid," said one old veteran patronizingly.

"Our insurance don't cover you," said another—even though Roger knew that, while the plane was insured, it wasn't covered for jump operations.

"We'd have to stuff your pockets with rocks," laughed another, "or you'd land in Indiana."

"Get a haircut and we'll think about it!" he heard more than once.

So Roger ran errands in town, picked up jumpers who missed the landing area, fueled the airplane, and, eager for anything skydiving-related, learned to pack their parachutes. He learned the jargon and the gear and earned some money, but he never earned "a slot on the next load" no matter how hard he tried.

"Rules is rules, kid," they'd all laugh over beers at the end of the jump day.

And it wasn't just this club. On fair weather weekends, Roger, now old enough to at least drive, would drop his brother off at the "drop zone" or DZ, then explore the local area to find a club that would let him jump. By this time he already knew the training by heart, and he could pack as well as any jumper. He even lied about his age, but no one would give the skinny, long-haired jeans-clad kid a chance.

So Roger settled into a routine. On jump weekends, he'd pack and help around the DZ, making a few bucks and sometimes scoring a plane ride. If he was lucky, the pilot would let him take the controls for a while. In his first summer, Roger learned more about skydiving gear and aircraft than many of the jumpers in the club.

He also added to his earnings by selling bags of pot to the rule-keeping hypocrites who wouldn't let him jump due to his age. He sold them "ditch weed" dope he'd found growing wild in the Illinois countryside—dope he swore to them came from exotic places like California, Mexico, or Hawaii. And they believed it came from just such places because Roger wore his hair long, his jeans flared at the bottom, and he wanted the Vietnam War to end before he was forced to fight for something nobody believed in anymore.

He sold pot in the evenings around a BBQ grill while the jumpers told jump stories. From those Saturday night jump stories he learned about "style and accuracy," and "the Nationals" and the legendary DC-3, a plane these jumpers dreamed of, but hadn't ever jumped. And he learned about "relative work"—or "RW"—and how only damned fools risked freefall collisions trying to "fly" together in mid-air to make patterns in the sky.

He learned how the military would make a man out of him when he got his ass drafted. He learned about killing dinks and slopes and gooks—and what bullets, grenades, napalm, claymores did to human flesh, bone, and brains. And "Willy Pete," especially Willy Pete, the white phosphorous that burned when exposed to air, that burned underwater, that burned into flesh and all the way through it, and kept on burning until it burned itself out and not before.

And he learned how men burned up and worn out by war would smoke too much and drink too much, then vomit, pass out, and piss themselves in their nightmare-torn sleep. And as he learned, he wondered about a country that could turn youngsters like himself into men like them.

And thus Roger came to realize that only the air and ground and gravity were pure—and that he wanted to live his life there. And to get there, he would consort with these men, and learn from them, so that he could ultimately escape them and achieve his dreams.

And so it was that after an adolescent lifetime of waiting, there came the day when Roger could finally jump. He had found a place nestled in cornfields close to his home and far from the hypocrites and their stringent, silly rules. He jumped and he loved it. He embraced it, he *lived* it exactly the way he knew he would, and then he never looked back.

As soon as he passed through his basic training jumps, he did what he had ached to do since that first day at the first airport; jump with his brother. They became inseparable at the DZ, jumping, packing and partying together.

And learning. They learned from the former military men, from the pilots, and from each other, too. Questioning authority came naturally to them in the early '70s; they never wanted to just know "how" to do something; they also wanted to know "why do we do it *that* way?"

Parachute gear was one of their first areas of inquiry. They knew the mostly surplus military gear they jumped was heavy and unwieldy because the military always made gear to last for a long time in the worst conditions. And they knew the openings were rough because the military never planned for people to make more than a few jumps a year—not several every day.

So Roger and his brother experimented with ways to lighten their gear, make it safer and less prone to malfunction, make it easier on their bodies when it opened.

They also experimented in the air. They tried to fall slower, faster, move farther horizontally. They even tried something unheard of; maneuvering on their backs.

The "old guard" told them it was impossible—until they did it, eliciting more catcalls about their "freaky" behavior. So, naturally, they called their new skill "Freak flying."

The military jumpers who had created sport parachuting in the '50s and '60s found it hard to accept the new kids and their new ideas and new ways of doing things. As paratroopers, they jumped the gear they were given, jumped the way they were trained, and they were discouraged from asking the question that came so naturally to Roger and Carl: *"Why?"* As veterans, these men knew only one way, and they didn't try to change. They jumped old, heavy gear. They fell through the air "flat, dumb and happy" on their bellies. Sometimes the openings wrecked their backs. Sometimes they got hurt. Once in a while, one of them died. That's the way it was, and if you didn't like it, *take up bowling.*

Thus the more Roger and Carl experimented, the more new stuff they did, the more alienated they became from the "old school" boys. They didn't jump like typical skydivers, they didn't respect established skydiving authorities, and they sure didn't look like typical skydivers.

Moreover, they didn't care much for jump stories about the old days; they listened instead for word about innovations and ideas coming from California, America's skydiving Mecca, and so they searched for a DZ with at least a few jumpers like themselves.

They finally found it, in Hinckley, Illinois, not too far from where they lived. They found new mentors there, too, a new breed of "sky god" after their own hearts: long-haired, with a disregard for authority and no fondness for the military way of doing things.

They were the notorious members of the Midwest's only challenge to California's skydiving dominance: the exuberant, outrageous outlaws known as "The James Gang."

And there at Hinckley the legend began, on a fine blue-sky afternoon, when "Pops" Connor offered to provide Carl and Roger, and their buddy Cicero with some tips and then coach them through a jump. The young men were honored and supremely excited, but as they got ready, an old sky god named "Pirate" limped by on his prosthetic leg and invited Pops to round out a hot 10-way jump he was organizing.

"Thanks, but I'm already on a load," said Pops.

"Don't waste a jump on those freaky brothers," sneered Pirate.

"I won't," Pops assured him, then turned to his long-haired, wavy-haired, just plain strange companions and said with a grin, "All right, Freak Brothers, let's do it."

# CHAPTER TWO

## DEBRIEF

Roger looked away from the window and sat up in his chair. Yes, the tricky part was over, but at what cost?

He hadn't wanted to do the run from Colombia through the islands. First off, there was a lot of heat because of the television drug war waged around Florida by Vice President George H.W. Bush. Second, his well-honed sixth sense had given him a weird feeling about it. Finally, the whole trip was pretty much senseless because Roger had already shifted his farming operations from South America to the small Central American backwater of Belize, a peaceful, English-speaking nation 500 miles closer than Colombia. There, he'd taught his growers how to grow the much more potent *sinsemilla*—seedless—pot. It resulted in a stellar product that cost him a fourth of what he paid for Colombian and he sold it for twice as much at wholesale.

But his chief pilot, H.R. "Hanoi" Gibson, had set up a final trip to collect a debt owed to him by his Colombian associates, a trip that was delayed because it was late in the season and quality product was scarce. The Colombians had to go deep into the mountains to find the required quality, so during the wait, Hanoi went to Alaska to make a few legitimate bucks hauling salmon. Unfortunately, he died there when workers overloaded his airplane and it crashed on takeoff, leading Roger to use the inexperienced Billy for the run—and the resulting head-to-head with The Man had broken his multi-year streak of good planning and good luck.

This was where the as-yet untallied costs lurked. He and his crew had essentially hit a hornet's nest with a big stick. He knew the feds were pissed and would swarm in all directions looking for the guys who embarrassed them. He wondered which way they would swarm and, more importantly, whether he'd left a trail.

He put on his sunglasses, grabbed several rolls of quarters, drove to a pay phone, and called his California answering service. Prepaying for this service with money orders and using pay phones created untraceable anonymity, a key element of Roger's business operations.

Roger dialed the 800 number, gave the operator his extension, and picked up two messages. The first said: "Mike called." That meant "delivery completed." The second contained a coded callback number from the boys in Georgia. He placed a call to the deciphered number, and a pay phone rang.

"Joe's Pizza, we deliver!"

"Yes, you do," Roger replied, recognizing Joel's voice, still pumped from their adventure. "How'd it go?"

"Perfect! Blew all the tires, nose gear snapped, props hit, wrecked the plane. Then I guess after we left the place turned into a friggin' combat zone!"

"What do you mean, you guess?" Roger frowned. "What happened?"

"My dad knows one of the deputies," Joel said. "Dude told him someone cut loose from the plane after it hammered, sheriff shot back, then the other deputies showed up and they blasted each other half the night. Dude said sheriff thought he was fighting Cubans. Guess the feds thought they were fighting smugglers 'cause sheriff and his boys showed up in their own cars. What a clusterfuck!"

Roger heard laughter over the line, but this was not good news. The hornets would be even madder now.

"Anybody get hurt?" he asked, dreading the answer.

"Nah, but Dude said the feds turned their cars into Swiss cheese," Joel said. "Then the boys started flanking 'em, so they ran for the woods and kept shooting. Didn't sort it out until the local cops showed up in squad cars."

Laughter on the line again, and Roger smiled in spite of himself.

"Great work, guys." Roger said, "but be sure you lay low for awhile, you know? And remember—"

"Yeah, we know," Joel interrupted. "'Don't talk trash, don't flash the cash.' And just to make sure we don't, we're heading south to skydive until it's all gone."

Now it was Roger's turn to laugh.

"Good plan," he said. "Have fun and check back in a week."

"Will do. Blue skies."

Roger hung up, somewhat relieved. The feds and sheriff would be fighting with each other over the mess more than they'd be hunting him. His panthers had performed flawlessly and he knew they'd be cool afterward, too. They were still kids in age but they already lived like grown men.

Roger sighed. The same could not be said for Billy. No phone call would do for him. Roger needed to deal with Billy in person.

The noon sun beat down on Roger as he entered a small house in a modest part of town, carrying a briefcase. He heard snoring as soon as he got inside and saw Billy sprawled on the sofa, more comatose than asleep. He walked lightly down a hallway into the nearest bedroom, where he found Dave sleeping soundly, too.

He went back to the kitchen and started the coffee machine, then turned on the radio to a medium volume. He didn't want to bulldoze them, but they needed to get up and running so he could debrief them and move on to the next thing—the weekend was coming. He dropped his sunglasses on the kitchen table and sat down to wait for the radio and the smell of brewing coffee to do their work.

Roger was sorry he'd met Billy and sorrier still that he'd used him for a run. He certainly wouldn't do so again. Damn that Hanoi anyway, getting killed two days before the run, leaving him without a pilot—and prompting him to violate two of the rules that had served him so well over the years: Know when to say no to a run; and use only trusted, team-oriented people for critical slots.

Roger knew in hindsight that Hanoi getting killed should have killed the run too—and would have if it wasn't for Roger's two-edged personality trait of giving people a chance to prove themselves, even though they might not be up to it. It was a great trait for life in general, but a dangerous one in business, especially the smuggling business.

Billy had been flying jumpers at a nearby parachute center, dreaming as he did so of "getting one in" to become a millionaire—and dropping hints about it to certain people in the jump community. Those people had passed on his hints to Roger, and when Hanoi died, Roger focused more on figuring out a way to get the run done than he did on figuring whether he should do it at all.

So he let Billy fly, without knowing whether Billy fit the profile of a "Team Nelson" operator. Billy, for his part, jumped at the chance because he wasn't competent enough to put a run together by himself—though, in fairness, not many people were.

Twenty minutes later, the three men were settled into their chairs around the kitchen table, Dave sucking down coffee, Roger sipping his as Billy finished up his version of the previous night's run.

". . . and when that DEA plane spotlighted me on the runway, I held back until they hit the nails," he said calmly, in sharp contrast to his demeanor when it actually happened.

"Thank those guys in Georgia for me, will ya? They sure saved my bacon."

*And ours too*, Roger thought as he grinned, not at what Billy said, but on the look he knew would cross Billy's face if he heard a recording of his panicky *"I'm outta here!"* as he took off too soon from that Georgia runway, without knowing for sure that the DEA plane had been disabled.

"Yeah, I'll let them know," Roger said, suppressing the urge to tell Billy what a complete dickhead he'd been throughout the run. Roger knew that to keep Billy from becoming an after-the-fact danger to them, he had to feel good about what he'd done, and think that he was still part of the team so that he'd observe those two "end-game" rules that were so critical: "Don't talk trash, don't flash the cash."

So Roger smiled and congratulated Billy, then handed him the briefcase. Billy opened it and his eyes went wide as he surveyed the neat stacks of green that filled it.

"Wow," he said softly, more to himself than to his companions. "Just like the movies."

Roger and Dave rolled their eyes at each other, knowing that the mesmerized Billy wouldn't notice. Billy thumbed through a few stacks of Franklins, then snapped the briefcase shut and stood up.

"I think I'll catch a few more Zs," he said, and patted the briefcase. "With this. Thanks, man."

Roger and Dave watched him disappear into a bedroom, then drained their coffee cups. Roger put on his sunglasses and they headed outside.

"How do you think Billy's gonna handle this?" Roger asked as they got in the car.

"Like you would expect," said Dave knowingly.

"Great," Roger said, facetiously, and they both chuckled as they headed to the motel where Mike was staying. They both knew it had been a mistake bringing Billy into the operation but they were stuck with him now and could only hope for the best.

"Fortunately, your system is bad-ass enough to overcome some flawed parts and bad luck," Dave said. "Sure was nice to have those 'what-if' plans in place and ready to go."

"Extra gas never hurts, either," Roger added.

"Part of your plan, too, my man," said Dave, appreciatively.

"Still ended up being a lot closer call than we've ever had," Roger reminded him, and paused for a long moment. "Maybe I shoulda called it off after Hanoi went in."

Dave shrugged.

"Maybe, but you didn't and it worked anyway. Next!"

Roger smiled. Next is right, he thought to himself, though maybe not in the way Dave is thinking.

"I think it's time to reevaluate things," Roger said after they joined an already up and about Mike in his motel room. "Hanoi's gone, and we just kind of forced this last one through. I'm not happy with what happened in Blairsville and I think you ought to know what really happened."

"The way Billy told it—" Dave started to say.

"—made him the hero, I'm sure," smirked Roger. Mike and Dave traded concerned glances as Roger cleared his throat and became Billy— imitating the rookie's timid radio voice, and reenacting his imagined expressions and gestures. Roger crouched as if he were sitting in the pilot's seat, widened his eyes, and hyperventilated.

"Why aren't you telling me everything, Roger?" Roger said in Billy's high-pitched, frightened voice. "I'm all alone in this tin can of an airplane. I'm freaked out! Oh my Gawwwd!'"

Dave and Mike bellowed in laughter. They knew it was hard staying cool during your first run, but neither they nor one they knew had ever sounded *that* bad.

"I'm surprised he didn't shit his pants," Roger said in his own voice, shaking his head.

"How do you know he didn't?" Mike deadpanned.

They all laughed again, then they got serious again, with the eerie feeling hanging over their conversation that somebody could have been killed on this one, either one of them or one of their pursuers.

"If I hadn't been there holding his hand literally every moment of the run, we'd be cleaning up shit instead of collecting money," Roger went on. "I kept asking myself, 'why did I let this imbecile fly for me!?'"

"Everybody fucks up now and then," Mike said gently, "and you were long overdue."

"True enough but this one almost cost us big-time—and, my old and dear friends, it confirms what you both know: I'm also long overdue for getting out of this business."

Mike and Dave traded glances and sighed in unison at their old friend.

"Yeah," Dave said quietly, "we know."

"And like you said," Mike continued, "with Hanoi gone it just didn't work like it should. Makes more sense getting out than trying to find and train a new pilot."

"Who'd never measure up to Hanoi anyway," Dave added.

Roger was touched but not surprised by their understanding.

"It's been fun and easy working with you guys," Roger said, "and you know from how much I pay you that for me smuggling dope was more about the thrill than the cash."

"But with a young family and a thriving drop zone, it just ain't worth the risks any more, is it?" Mike said, finishing Roger's sentence for him. Roger nodded, but didn't say anything. He was afraid his voice would break if he did, and he didn't want his friends to see him blubbering.

There was a long silence filled alternately with meaningful glances and staring at the floor.

"Won't be the same without you," said Mike. "Aren't too many people like you in the world, especially in this trade."

"Thanks, Mike," Roger said, sure of his voice again, "but you hit it on the head. It just doesn't feel right any more . . . it's hard to explain."

"Then don't," said Dave. "We get it. Maybe hard for us to imagine being in your shoes, with everything going on at the drop zone and finding time for your wife and kids, but we get it—and no matter what you decide, we're with you, buddy."

"Aren't too many like you guys in the world, either," Roger said, "especially in this trade." He clapped his hands together. "So it's settled. I'm leaving as soon as we can sort it out, but I'll leave it in good order if you decide you want to carry on. So Mike, be ready to fly at the DZ mid-morning. Dave, I'm gonna give you a run for your money at team training tomorrow!"

Those words signaled the end of the meeting. Now it was time to play! They stood, shook hands and embraced, manly back-slapping embraces to hide their true feelings as this beginning-of-the-end began to sink in. Then Roger separated from them and looked at them with a twinkle in his eye.

"Before I go, though, I have one more run I'm thinking about."

Dave grinned. Mike smirked.

"Of course you do," said Mike.

"Details later," Roger smirked back. "Now let's go skydive!"

# CHAPTER THREE

## SANDWICH

Roger woke up to a loud alarm and bright sunlight streaming through the bedroom window. He tapped off the alarm and looked over to see his wife Jeanie still slumbering next to him. Then he looked out the window to see blue sky speckled with small puffy clouds, and trees swaying gently in a light breeze. A perfect day for jumping!

Saturdays were always busy at his drop zone outside of Sandwich, Illinois. First timers, experienced jumpers and competitive skydivers filled all the "slots" on every "load" flown by the drop zone's venerable but perfectly maintained airplanes: a single-engine, four-jumper Cessna 182, and a twin-engine, 40-jumper DC-3. After a week without "putting his knees in the breeze," Roger was rarin' to go.

On the other hand, he thought, as he looked at the angel face of his achingly beautiful wife, the quiet house meant the kids were still asleep and there was something else he hadn't done for a week either. He smiled. The DZ could wait.

He caressed her back until she stirred, then their eyes sparkled with the love they shared as they moved with the romantic magic of newlyweds.

Roger loved Jeanie. Only she could tolerate his dual life and unexplained absences without question. She wasn't oblivious to his "other" business; she simply willed herself not to notice and not to ask. She'd helped Roger during some of his early runs, but as time passed and their relationship grew, she wanted—no, *needed*—to know less and less about it: with young children, Jeanie couldn't afford to know anything about this part of Roger's life. If something went wrong, she had to survive physically and legally to raise their children. Nevertheless, Roger trusted her above all others. She would do anything he asked of her without question. For her part, Roger's safe return gave Jeanie the comfort and the answers she needed.

"You better get out to the airport," she murmured as they lay entwined, gazing out the window at the sunny day. The TV went on in the living room. "Besides, you won't get any more action here today."

"Mom!" called a young voice over the sound of the TV. "I'm hungry."

Rock music and a beach party atmosphere greeted Roger and Jeanie as they arrived at the beehive that was the drop zone on any good weather weekend, an unexpected ambiance in the middle of Illinois farm country.

They climbed out of their van by the DZ hangar and Roger paused to take a deep, lingering, sky-facing breath, eyes closed, sucking in and savoring the sounds and smells and feel of the one place on earth where he really felt at home.

When he opened them, he saw parachutes descending out of the blue and, high above them, the Cessna from which they jumped diving steeply back toward the runway.

He grinned at Jeanie and she smiled slyly.

"I'll leave you to your mistress," she said, and gave him a semi-chaste departure kiss, then headed for the office where she managed the operation. Roger watched her go, smiling slyly himself as he remembered their morning. Then he turned his attention to the other love of his life.

Parachutes lay stretched out in the hangar packing area just inside the open doors. Over in the "dirt dive" area, a cluster of jumpers practiced on the ground the formation routine they would perform in the air. It resembled a ceremonial dance that pulsed in a coordinated rhythm that the group repeated until it was smooth. Other jumpers wriggled into jumpsuits, strapped on parachutes and walked toward the loading area to wait for the Cessna, goggles, helmets and altimeters dangling from their hands. Still others lolled around the hangar drinking coffee, shaking off hangovers, waiting for friends. And at the manifest counter, staffers shepherded new customers to manifest so they could make their first jump, their faces alternately excited and apprehensive.

A car parked near Roger's van and a young man stepped out, his face uncertain. He looked around searchingly. Roger grinned.

"Friends didn't make it, did they?" he said flatly.

"Apparently not," said the young man. "Maybe they got lost." He frowned. "How did you—"

"Or they had a flat tire, or their grandma died," added Roger. "Or the goldfish."

The young man smiled in spite of himself.

"Guess this happens a lot."

"Every weekend," Roger said. "Ten talk, one jumps, so congratulations." Roger held out his hand. "I'm Roger." They shook hands.

"Stan," said the young man. "Stan Brown."

"Welcome to Skydive Sandwich, Stan. Let's get you in the air!"

Roger's enthusiasm was instantly infectious. Stan grinned broadly as they turned toward manifest—and even broader still when they passed a fit young lady kneeling on her partially packed parachute, tight butt in the air, toned legs spread shoulder width apart, halter-topped breasts sliding sensuously against the colorful nylon as she squeezed the air from its "cells" so she could fit it into the container attached to the other end of the lines.

"I love this sport already," Stan said as they both admired the scenery.

"Your friends snoozed, didn't they?" Roger said. "And just think; with a little training, you'll be doing that."

The two men chuckled at Roger's double entendre, then stopped at the manifest counter in front of Jeanie.

"I think we got a keeper," Roger said to her.

She smiled warmly at Stan, eyes twinkling.

"You ready to skydive?"

"Yes ma'am!" he said.

"I leave you in good hands," Roger said, slapping Stan on the shoulder. "Have a good one!"

"I'm sure I will," said Stan, who already seemed to be more alert and alive and loving life than he had when he first stepped from his car.

Roger walked away from the counter, smiling at Stan's already-underway metamorphosis; helping others to know the joy of the sky was second only to being there in the air himself—well, that and the thrill of smuggling. He paused by a human-size door on one side of the hangar and surveyed his smoothly-running legal business, a business to which he applied as much thought and attention to detail as he did his outlaw business. Past the jumpers packing, lounging and dirt diving in the hangar, outside in the morning sun, sat the Cessna with its prop turning as another load of four jumpers climbed aboard. Past the Cessna, the DC-3 roared down the runway and into the morning sky to cheers from the jumpers on the ground as the old but sturdy plane took off on its first load of the day, "Mr. Douglas" emblazoned on its side between blue and red pinstripes.

Hanoi had first brought the DC-3 to a small airport near Roger's home so Roger and his friends could jump whenever they weren't away on outlaw business. But the classic airplane and its thundering radial engines had drawn not only a lot of spectators but many people interested in putting their knees in the breeze too.

So Roger had scouted the area for a suitable site to start a commercial parachuting center and thus he had come to Sandwich. There, as he had done with his smuggling business, his strong leadership and out-of-the-box thinking led to a school that attracted both local and international customers, the latter of whom came because they heard through the skydiving grapevine that Roger's place was *the* place to go if you wanted to learn to jump fast—and well.

The drop zone soon prospered after the same fashion as Roger's "other" business. Moreover, it not only fed Roger's insatiable desire to fly his body through the sky, it served as perfect camouflage for his acquisition of multiple airplanes suitable for both jumping and smuggling.

Roger opened the door and walked outside into a scene out of dystopia movie. Behind the hangar was "Bagland," the DZ's campground, littered with battered cars, tents, trailers and pickup campers, punctuated by smoldering fires, trash cans, and a blizzard of empty beer bottles and cans. Several people lounged amid the chaos or wandered through it like battlefield survivors, sucking on morning cigarettes or policing up the debris and putting it in the cans. Some waved greetings to Roger while one skinny, long-haired young man bounced over to greet him.

"Hey bro', what's happenin'?" he said, grinning.

"You're happenin', Chris," Roger grinned back. "Been to sleep yet?"

"You kidding? Man, did we have a screamer last night! She rocked and rolled so long I got horny and played earthquake with my lady in the 'bago. When we finished the screamer was still at it, so I looked out to see who it was."

"Darlo again, I bet," said Roger.

"Yup," Chris laughed. "A bunch of Bags were sitting in chairs around her tent, listening to the show, so I grabbed a six-pack and a doobie and joined 'em. Man, she was *wailing*. We start cheering them until there's one really loud long scream and out staggers Dave. We give him a standing ovation and he said, 'Somehow she got her legs around my neck and tried to kill me!' Then Darlo's hand comes out the door and waves someone else inside. Dude, it was *epic!*"

"Well, I'm glad he survived the night," said Roger. "Our alternate's out of town this weekend."

"No worries, man," Chris said, slapping Roger reassuringly on the back. "We made sure he got to bed before the sun came up. Can't win the Nationals if you don't practice!"

"You got it," said Roger, approvingly, then looked around at the mess. Chris grinned again.

"And don't worry about that," he said. We'll have Bagland shiny before the next Three load goes up."

"Good man," said Roger, and he went back through the hangar door.

Inside, he saw Dave parked on a couch next to his packed-and-ready skydiving gear, slurping coffee. The rest of his Freak Brothers "10-way speed star" teammates were there too: Ardis, Barboni, Jeff, Kimmers, Kong, T.J., Tommy, Piras and Bob the flying cameraman, whose job it was to video the team with his helmet-mounted camera so they could study each training jump and try to improve their performance on the next one. Most were brighter-eyed and more alert than Dave, but Roger knew his teammate was always ready to rock and roll, no matter how hard he'd partied the night before—or how much the worse for wear he looked.

Roger smiled inwardly at his teammates; a wild, woolly and eclectic bunch, to be sure, but talented, focused, reliable and, above all, enjoyable to be around. They'd been practicing all summer and now had just four weeks to practice and prepare for their surprise assault on the reigning national champions, Team Magic from Perris, California.

Ten-way was competitive skydiving's drag race event and it was simple: Ten jumpers explode out the door into freefall in a tight bunch and make a hand-holding circle in the sky called a "star." Time starts as soon as the first jumper "shows" out the door to judges on the ground 9,500 feet below with high-powered, tripod-mounted binoculars called telemeters. Time stops when the circle is complete. Fastest time over six jumps wins. It was demanding and exhilarating, with little room for error; the difference between winning and losing was measured in tenths or even hundredths of a second.

"We're on the next load," Dave said to Roger, "so we'll need you for door jams after it lands." Then he stretched and yawned.

"Tired?" Roger asked.

"Not enough that you'll beat me!"

"I taught you that good, huh?" Roger smiled. "Better tighten your goggles if you really think you'll beat me in."

Dave laughed and went over to the coffee machine.

Roger weaved his way through the hangar, being unconsciously careful not to step on anyone's parachute lines, and lurking, always lurking, looking for someone who needed a hand, for something about someone's gear that wasn't quite right—for some little thing that could kill someone up there in the beautiful deadly sky above. It had happened before, and he knew it would happen again, but hopefully not on his watch. He sighed, lost in a distant thought. Not on his watch.

Everything seemed to be in order at the moment, though, so he made his way outside again onto the tarmac, empty now of airplanes.

Around him, jumpers began stretching out on the ground, shading their eyes and looking skyward. Spectators new to the DZ frowned at the ritual until they craned their necks to gaze skyward at the tiny white cross and faint but distinct rumble of Mr. Douglas passing 13,000 feet overhead. They realized it was easier to watch the action from their backs, so some of them joined the veterans to see the show. Suddenly, the rumbling engine sound stopped.

"They're out!" shouted more than one voice as black specks appeared in the sky behind the white cross and, like iron bits attracted to a magnet, drew together and coalesced into a flower-shaped pattern, then morphed into a different pattern, then another and another, the specks growing larger with each passing moment until Roger heard the sound of the skydivers whistling through the air. Then the specks became people and they split apart in a starburst maneuver that separated them enough from their companions that they could open their parachutes safely without fear of collision.

Explosions of color blossomed in the blue sky, followed an instant later by what sounded like shotguns being fired one after another until more than 30 canopies filled the sky and their pilots whooped and hollered all the way down until they converged on the landing area. They quieted then, focusing on landing softly without getting in each other's way.

After everyone was down, Roger went back into the hangar to gear up with his team and get ready to practice their exit from Mr. Douglas when it landed.

Another ritual started, casual but precise as each man first donned his jumpsuit, then his rig, then grabbed gloves, helmet and altimeter, and turning the knob on the latter to zero the needle to match the day's barometric pressure.

Meanwhile, the crowd outside the hangar was on its feet again, the jumpers going about their business, the spectators soaking it all in.

Then a few jumpers paused and looked low into the sky, drawing visitor eyes with them, toward Mr. Douglas as it wafted toward the runway, wheels down, engines droning softly at low power. The main wheels screeched sharply as the old plane touched down, then the tail wheel settled silently onto the asphalt. Within moments, Mr. Douglas slowed to jogging speed, black nose sticking proudly in the air, then pivoted on one main off the runway onto the tarmac and shut down at the loading area.

"Used to jump out of those in World War Two," said one old spectator proudly to no one in particular, an 82nd Airborne baseball cap perched on his head. "Called 'em Gooney Birds. Put 28 paratroopers or more than six tons of war gear in 'em."

"If you're up for it, you could jump it again today if you wanted to," said one young jumper. The old paratrooper snorted.

"If I can't do it in the dark with 100 pounds of gear on and people shooting at me, well, it just wouldn't be the same, son," chuckled the paratrooper.

"Wow," said the young jumper, suitably impressed. "That is hard core."

The old paratrooper nodded at the young man and walked slowly over to Mr. Douglas for a closer look as Chris trotted over to its jump door with a short ladder, followed by Roger and his teammates, bantering as they walked.

Chris leaned the loading ladder against the fuselage and the two pilots climbed out: Mark, a short, gremlin-shaped American who inherited Mr. Douglas when Hanoi died in Alaska; and his co-pilot Kristen, a tall, willowy Norwegian who looked like a fashion model. She smiled sweetly at the old paratrooper as she passed, and he stared after her as she and Mark went to the hangar.

"Sure as hell didn't have pilots like *that*," he said as he stopped next to Chris.

"And she's a badass on top of being some nice ass," Chris said. "Girl has three thousand hours and two thousand jumps."

The old paratrooper shook his head at this news as he watched the Freak Brothers climb aboard to practice their exit, banter suddenly stopped, game faces on.

"Seems like they're pretty serious about this," he said to Chris.

"More than that, sir," Chris said. "Right now, their only goal in life is to win gold at the national championships. All their money, time, and energy is on that. Hell, they even blow off chicks to get this right. Well, most of them, anyway!"

The Freak Brothers lined up inside as tightly as possible without any part of their bodies or gear hanging out the door. Dave and the Piras were first, the rest in a line angling across the narrow cabin to the opposite wall, where Kong stood ninth, with his left foot braced against the wall.

"Hot!" he roared.

"Ready!" Roger roared from behind him.

". . . GO!" the team shouted as one and they all lunged forward with tremendous force, almost ejecting Dave and Piras out the door, who strained to hold back the tide.

"Okay!" Roger said and everyone relaxed. "Nice one, team! Piras, good job holding us back so we can explode out the door. Remember that in the air and we are good to go. Next!"

They lined up again. The old paratrooper nodded.

"Don't look much like soldiers, but they act like 'em," he said.

"Really?" Chris asked. "You guys partied that hard too?"

"No comment, son," the old paratrooper said with a smile. Then he walked away to admire the rest of the Mr. Douglas.

"Be care—" Chris started to say before he realized that the old man skirted the propeller arc of the left engine like a seasoned jumper. Chris smiled and looked toward the hangar to see the rest of the next load parading toward the plane, Mark and Kristen leading, steaming coffee cups in hand. Behind Chris, the team climbed out of the plane, satisfied with its practice session.

"Okay," said Roger, "then turn left and dock on the first star you see. Oh yeah, and Piras, try to beat Ardis and Dave!"

"And Tommy," said T.J., the cool, calm veteran to the younger hothead, "don't fuck up."

"What, scared the youngster's gonna beat your ass to the star?" Tommy retorted.

"All right, all right," Roger interrupted with a grin, "save that fire for the dive."

Chris steadied the ladder as Mark and Kristen climbed aboard, followed by 25 other jumpers, then the Freak Brothers, who boarded last because they were first out. Camera flyer Bob rounded out the manifest. When he was aboard, Chris pulled the parking chocks from the main wheels, then grabbed the ladder and with a wave headed back to the hangar, followed by the old paratrooper, who moved with surprising speed to get clear of the plane, his face split by a big grin.

In the cockpit, Mark sat in the left seat, Kristen in the right, both wearing radio headsets. He slid open his window and leaned his head outside.

"Clear left!" he shouted and started the engine. The propeller turned slowly, then with a cloud of blue smoke and several compression coughs, the engine burst into rumbling life, vibrating the whole plane. Then Kristen opened her window, held her long hair in one hand and leaned out.

"Clear right!" she shouted and Mark repeated the startup procedure on that side. Another blue cloud and more coughs and both engines rumbled in unison. Mark adjusted the mixtures, then pushed the throttles forward and Mr. Douglas lumbered onto the runway. The high nose blocked most of Mark's forward view, so he looked out the side window to see where he was going. When he reached the end of the runway, he pivoted the plane on one main again, then stopped.

Kristen read off every item on the pre-takeoff checklist, Mark confirmed, then he looked back to make sure his passengers were seated. Happy with everything so far, they closed their cockpit windows, then Kristen pushed the throttles all the way forward and held them in place with one hand as the engines wound and Mark almost stood on the brakes. He released them a moment later and with both his hands and feet guided Mr. Douglas as it accelerated down the runway. A few hundred yards down the asphalt, he pushed forward on the wheel; the tail rose into flight position, the nose dropped so they could see where they were going, and Kristen flashed airspeed signals with her free hand.

A few hundred yards later, Mr. Douglas took flight.

"Blue sky!" shouted the jumpers as the wheels came off the runway. "Black Death!" they added as the Three gained altitude. Their lives now were one on one with the beauty and danger of God's natural laws.

Mark signaled Kristen with his right thumb, and she rapidly flipped handles and knobs on the floor and instrument panel to retract the wheels and do other transition chores. When she was done, they opened their side windows again, creating a cool draft for their passengers, and allowing Kristen to look out, one hand holding her sunglasses tight to her face, and confirm that the wheels had retracted. When she gave Mark a thumbs up, he pushed the headset intercom button on his wheel.

"Okay," he said to her, "you have the airplane." Kristen smiled her fashion model smile and took control of the legendary aircraft that was twice as old as she was, and like the practiced pro that she was, guided the sturdy old bird heavenward with a sure hand and a light touch.

Behind her, Roger turned on the stereo and the jumpers talked, napped, read books or sang during the 35-minute climb to jump altitude. Roger sat with Dave by the open doorway, soaking up the beauty of the countryside below as the slipstream whipped around them.

"How can you put words to the things you see in this sport?" Dave asked.

"You don't," Roger replied. "Things like this are meant to be felt, not described."

Roger searched the two rows of jumpers sitting with their backs to the fuselage on long collapsible bench seats, and the rest sitting on the floor between them, backs to the front of the plane, in between each other's legs, He searched for problems, for something that wasn't quite right, something that could kill or maim if it went out the door undetected.

He found one, a low-experience jumper whose eyes darted nervously about, even though they were many minutes away from exit. Roger went over and sat next to him.

"Johnny, right?" he said with a warm smile and extended hand. Johnny nodded and shook the hand. "Sometimes it feels like the first time all over again, doesn't it?"

Johnny nodded again, and took a long shuddering breath.

"The key is to relax," Roger said just loud enough to be heard over the rumbling engines. "It's not like you have to do much, you know—just fall, right? And we can all do that without trying, right?"

Johnny laughed.

"You said that the first time, too," he said, and Roger could see his words taking effect. "Falling is natural; just jump and remember what I practiced."

"You got it," Roger grinned, and jerked a thumb toward his team. "Same thing I tell those yahoos. Sometimes they forget too."

"Really?" asked Johnny incredulously. "They do?"

"I do too," Roger confided." The trick is to let that go and remember that you're ready. You know the routine, you practiced on the ground, now close your eyes and go over it again in your mind. And when you go out the door, don't fight the force; go with it and become part of the wind."

Roger saw confidence flare in Johnny's eyes and this time the breath he took was a centering one.

"Thanks, Roger. I got it now." Roger put a comforting hand on Johnny's shoulder.

"And if you forget the drill, just watch us before we go." He stood up and went back to his seat near the door.

As he sat, he looked at Kong, who clenched one formidable fist. Their eyes met.

"We're gonna take them out," Kong snarled, "and not to lunch!" Roger smirked at him, then turned to Kimmers.

"Awesome job on the radio campaign," he said. "I checked the schedule today; school's maxed out all weekend and into next week. Keep running this place that way and I'll have to give you a raise."

"Thanks for the warning," Kimmers laughed. "I'll try to do worse next time."

A few minutes later, talking stopped, the music and singing went away, the books were stashed, and everyone started doing their last minute gear checks and mental dirt dives. Roger glanced at Johnny and smiled: The young jumper's eyes were closed and his hands moved in an odd repeating pattern as he went over his dive, body relaxed, clearly in the groove and ready to go.

The Freak Brothers made their own final checks and adjustments and got to their feet. They formed a circle of right hands, each grabbing the thumb of the man next to them, and looked at their leader.

"Go slow," Roger said. "Don't rush it. We don't want to exit as fast as we can; we want to exit as together as we can. Then fly only as fast as you can fly perfectly. Kong, give us a good count so nobody's late." They all looked into the center of the "hand star."

"Hot!" roared Kong.

"Ready!" roared Roger.

". . . GO!" the team shouted as one, at the same time moving their hand star up and then down breaking it with a growl. They moved loosely into their lineup and started psyching themselves up for launch. Roger looked forward and saw Kristen looking back at him from the cockpit and all the other jumpers on their feet, ready to go. He also saw Johnny watching the Freak Brothers like a hawk. Roger winked at him, then took off his sunglasses and stuck his head out the door to line up the direction of flight with the exit point. He pulled his head in and held up one finger.

"One minute!" he shouted.

Roger looked at Kristen and slashed a knife hand across his throat. Kristen tapped Mark and the pilot pulled back the throttles, muting the thunder of the engines and softening the air blast in the door.

Roger waited a few seconds, then nodded at Bob the camera flyer, who backed out the door until he was completely outside except for his hands gripping underhanded at the top of the door. He sighted his helmet camera on the line up as the team jammed into launch position.

"Hot!" roared Kong.

"Ready!" roared Roger.

". . . GO!" the team shouted as one and exploded out the door.

Outside, they entered a new dimension of awareness in the hurricane force winds. Kimmers and Jeff linked hands first to create the base, the target in the center of the group upon which the other eight would converge in two opposing lines, one above the base, the other below.

The jumpers built their lines smoothly and quickly, with Dave and Roger docking almost simultaneously to complete the star. An electric wave surged through them as they realized it was maybe their fastest build ever because they were still flying in the slow, sloppy air that came before they reached "terminal" velocity of 120 miles per hour at the 12-second mark.

Roger counted to five, then nodded to key the team to create the next formation. They built several different patterns until they hit their breakoff altitude of 3,000 feet, then did their starburst separation move and opened up their canopies. The noise of freefall was replaced by the near-silence of canopy flight as Roger's parachute opened—at least until he put on his sunglasses.

"We're gonna take 'em out!" Kong bellowed from nearby, then dove his canopy radically towards the ground. Roger picked out his landing spot and cranked a hard turn to quicken his descent too, then flattened out and wafted to a feather-soft tiptoe landing.

He looked skyward and watched Tommy land screaming beside him as Chris pulled up to them in a golf cart already loaded with Kong and Ardis.

"Man, we were *smokin*!" he shouted as they climbed aboard. "What do you think the time was?"

"Let's see what the video says," said Roger quietly, but he had trouble keeping a grin from covering his own face.

Jumpers on the ground cheered when they went into the hangar, knowing from their rough estimates that they'd seen something special.

"Sub-ten, I think," said one as everyone sat or stood around a big TV screen on one hangar wall and waited for Bob to run the video. He loaded it and handed Roger a stop-watch and remote, then plopped down on "his" chair next to the video player.

The Freak Brothers screamed as the tape began with their explosive, seamless exit, then quieted as they watched everyone dock. When Dave and Roger closed the star the whole room went up in a roar of excitement.

"Beat ya!" said Dave triumphantly as Roger quickly rewound the tape.

"What's the time?" someone asked.

Roger ran the tape again. Dave was right; he was a hair faster—but they were all fast.

"I got it at eight point nine!" Roger said quietly, and the room erupted again and the Freak Brothers high fived all around.

"We're gonna take 'em out!" Kong bellowed above the din, and several others screamed along with him.

"No one's ever done faster than nine in a competition," Ardis said to Kimmers, tossing her dark hair proudly.

"Looks like we have a chance to be the first," he answered.

Roger turned off the tape and let the celebration die down, then handed the remote and stop watch back to Bob.

"Pack up," he said flatly. "We're wasting daylight." Then he walked outside to see how the rest of his operation was going.

Four parachutes were descending toward the landing area after jumping from the Cessna, one spiraling wildly closer and closer to the ground. At the last moment, the jumper planed out at high speed and narrowly missed colliding with a lower jumper who was making a normal approach.

Both veered to avoid a collision; both tumbled to a stop. Roger ran over to the low person, a young woman he recognized as Shelly, who had 200 jumps and was quickly turning into a very good skydiver. She saw him coming and almost cried.

"I'm so sorry, Roger," she said. "I didn't see him."

"I saw him," Roger said, all traces of good humor erased from his face. "You okay?"

He helped her to her feet, and she tested her legs and ankles.

"Everything seems to be in order," she said.

Roger gave her a comradely hug and a slap on the back. "Might have been different if you hadn't done a flat turn to avoid him. Nice work," he said, giving her an emphatic thumbs up. "Well done."

"Thanks, Roger," and Shelly beamed at this praise from the master. Then he about-faced and marched over to where the wild one was gathering up his parachute—Patrick, another gifted young jumper, but one who thought he knew a lot more than he did. Patrick grinned sheepishly, but Roger was having none of it; he grabbed the kid by his harness, lifted him off his feet and threw him to the ground, then stood over him, eyes flaming, lips curled into a snarl.

"You almost killed her,' he growled so quietly and coldly it sounded like a curse in church. "Now get your butt over to the school and watch the basic canopy control video, then write me a report hitting the ten key points—and then I'll think about whether you can jump again this weekend. Are we clear, Patrick?"

The now-scared kid nodded mutely. Roger pulled him to his feet and pointed to Shelly.

"Apologize to her first," he said, as Patrick picked up his parachute again, "and if you do this again, I'll give you to Kong."

Patrick went from scared to terrified at this news and walked over to Shelly.

Roger turned his back on the scene and walked grimly back to the hangar, eyes still smoldering, lips still snarling.

He walked by several stunned spectators and several knowing jumpers to a door at the rear of the hangar. He opened the door on a dark room and shut it behind him without turning on the light.

"What the heck is that all about?" one new jumper wondered aloud to Jeanie at the manifest counter.

A small tear welled in Jeanie's eye as she looked at the closed door.

"Long story, hon," she said softly. "Now let's get your waiver signed."

# CHAPTER FOUR

# JAMAICA

Roger dropped Jeanie off at home after another busy weekend at the DZ, then drove to a local pay phone and called a number that rang in a bank of pay phones at O'Hare International Airport. Someone picked up after one ring.

"Hi buddy, you comin'?" said a voice.

"It all depends," answered Roger, recognizing the voice as Mickey. "What's up?"

"Well, I got this hot date," Mickey answered with the rest of the code, "and my car broke down. I was wondering if I could borrow yours."

"I guess, but only if you don't have any other options."

"Thanks man," said Mickey's noticeably happier voice, "and don't worry, I'll fill it up when I'm done and take real good care of it."

"We can talk about it."

"Hey, do you know anyone who can chauffeur me?"

Roger shook his head. This was getting worse by the minute. "You want me bring the date too?"

"C'mon, man, you know I wouldn't ask if it wasn't important. Very special lady we're talking about here."

"Okay, I'll pick you up at 10 p.m. at the usual place," Roger said and hung up without waiting for an answer. Then he leaned against the phone booth wall and pondered his options. Lending a plane to his old friend and partner was sketchy enough, but the only "chauffeur" he had at the moment was Billy, which made the whole proposition sketchy times ten—at least. Still, he knew how Mickey operated, and he owed him a favor, so Roger decided to feel it out for a while before he made a go-no go decision. He sighed and picked up the phone again.

Shortly thereafter he parked in front of Billy's house and walked into a wave of amateur excitement. Billy had $100 bills scattered around his living room and hooted at Roger as he entered.

"You're here to plan another one, right?" he gushed. "Well, I know a bunch of guys who can help us and they'll do it cheap. I know how to set it up so we can make even more money! It'll be a—"

"Sit down and cool it," Roger said coldly, and pointed a damning finger at the almost-deranged young pilot. "Have you said a word about this with anybody?"

Billy didn't sit.

"Not yet, but I know a pilot I can use, and I got a lot more thought out," he boasted. "I'm not gonna sit around and do nothin'—not after I've found such an easy way to make big money. Let me tell you how I—"

Roger poked him so hard in the chest that it knocked him into a chair.

"Sit. Down," he hissed, then leaned over and got in Billy's face.

"You found nothing," Roger said. "I hired you to be one piece of a big puzzle I spent half a decade building, getting the right people, and spending half a million bucks on the gear to do it right." He picked up a Franklin and waved it in Billy's face. "This is chicken feed, and you will not only never earn more than chicken feed if you keep acting like this, you *will* end up dead or in prison."

"So you're saying it's your way or no way?" Billy asked, resentfully. "That nobody's smart enough to do this except *you*?"

Roger pressed his finger into Billy's chest.

"What I'm saying is that you need to relax and learn before you go off half-cocked," Roger said intently. "You know about one percent of what you think you know and what you think you know is about one percent of what there is to know—and one of the main things there is to know is when to wait and when to go."

The two men stared at each other for a long moment, then Billy dropped his gaze to a Franklin lying on the floor.

"This pilot was my flight instructor, Ralph, and he's real cool," he said. "I know he can do it." He looked at Roger. "I thought you could help me. Those guys down there already know me. They'd work with me. I got the money, and that's all it would take."

Roger stared at Billy, shaking his head in frustration. Billy was serious, clueless and not listening to a voice of experience and success. A very dangerous combination. Roger knew he'd made a mistake bringing Billy into the operation and literally created a monster by letting him fly "just one run." He'd have to play Billy delicately from now on and hope he started learning before he did something really stupid that endangered all of them. He backed off and sat in another chair.

"Billy, let me tell you something, and please let this sink in," Roger said in a patient tone. "You're a great pilot or I wouldn't have invited you to join us, and you proved on the last run that you can keep it together even when the pressure's intense, all right?"

"Damn straight," Billy said haughtily, but Roger noticed that under the bravado Billy's body language had softened a bit.

"But it's not just about cowboying up when things get tense," Roger went on. "There are a lot of ballsy dead guys and prisoners out there. And it's not just about making money, either. That's a great part, but it's more important to first make sure nobody gets hurt—and that you get away with it *clean*! I'm not sure I even want you flying for me again if you keep thinking you can recreate my years of experience and gear with your flight instructor and five hundred Franklins. Doesn't work that way. Capiche?"

"I'm listening," Bill said sullenly, but with even less bravado than before.

"I'm not saying you're not capable of doing it," Roger continued in the same patient tone. "I'm saying that if anything goes wrong, you'll remember this conversation and wished you learned a lot more before you tried to do a run yourself. I recommend that you learn what you can from me, and part of that is flying a few more runs for me or somebody else before you try one on your own. You get what I'm saying?"

Billy looked down again at the scattered Franklins and tapped his toes on the floor for a long moment, then looked again at Roger, noticeably more subdued.

"Okay," he sighed. "I get your a point. I know I need to learn—but I also know I'm ready to *work*, to get back in the mix soon, so give me some ideas. Show me how to take the next step."

Roger breathed an inward sigh of relief; he seemed to be getting through at least a little bit. He leaned forward and plunged into the next phase.

"The first thing I want you to know," he said, pointing at the scattered money, "is that what you have in your hand is just that—it's *in your hand*. You'd be way better off playing poker or craps in Vegas than gambling it on an operation you don't even fully understand. The odds of winning are better in Vegas and the consequences of failure are even better than that: you can't get busted, you won't crash, and you probably won't get shot. See what I mean?" Billy's eyes narrowed at this summation and Roger knew he'd finally gotten Billy's full attention.

"You're right, man," Billy said. "I guess I got carried away, but this stuff's got me all hyped up. I can get *rich!*"

"Yes, you can," Roger said, "but only if you don't get busted—which means, you talk about this to nobody. *No. Body!* That's the agreement we made, and I expect you to keep it. Not even your flight instructor—and why is that?

"Because everybody I tell will tell ten people," Billy recited, "and every third one of them is a cop."

"That's right, so if you want the gravy train to keep flowing, you keep your mouth shut and what else?"

Billy looked sheepishly around the room at the scattered Franklins.

"Don't flash the cash."

"Okay, then," Roger said, concluding the lesson, "now listen up. There may be a run coming up very soon for you—a friend needs a pilot. Are you interested if it comes together?"

"How much can I make?"

"You already have an idea what the going rate is, so is that a yes?"

"Yes."

"Okay, I'll let him know."

"Let me go with you."

"Calm down, Roger Ramjet," Roger said soothingly, "but stay here in case I need to see you again tonight—and no calls or conversations with anyone, right?"

"Sarright," Billy said and saluted his mentor.

Roger arrived at O'Hare still worried about the loose cannon he'd brought into his operation. He knew he'd made some headway with

Billy, but as far as him becoming a professional smuggler, the kid didn't even qualify yet as a work in progress; at the moment, he was just work. He hoped hooking Billy up with Mickey would both retire his debt to his old friend and keep Billy safely occupied for a while.

Mickey climbed into Roger's faded green Ford pickup truck at exactly 10 p.m. After a few quick glances in the rear view mirror and one slight backtrack around the Mannheim Road cloverleaf, they pulled into Café La Cave, Roger's truck contrasting sharply with the parking lot full of luxury cars. Two parking attendants opened his doors.

"Roger, good to see you," said one. "How are you tonight, sir?"

"Never better, Sammy, and you?"

"Can't complain," he said, and grinned as Roger handed over his keys. "I'll leave it right here in front so I can keep an eye on it for you."

Roger and Sammy chuckled at his jest.

Inside, the tuxedoed maitre d' grabbed Roger with both hands and welcomed him, then shook Mickey's hand more formally.

"I'm sorry, sir, but I've forgotten your name."

"Mickey."

"Yes, yes, of course, forgive me," he apologized. Turning back to Roger, he said, "I wish I knew you were coming. I would have had your table ready."

Roger looked into the main dining room and saw a flurry of waiters preparing his corner table.

"Put us in the bar if you need to, Gus," Roger said.

"Don't be silly," he frowned. "You're family!" As they walked to the table, each waiter greeted Roger by name, causing more than a few well-dressed patrons to wonder why two t-shirt-and-jeans-clad ruffians were getting such royal treatment. Several more regular customers, however, nodded their own subtle greetings; they knew that the elegant Café La Cave with its great food, unique ambiance and its gracious customer service was one of Roger's favorite indulgences, even if his "business" attire was out of the ordinary.

Gus soon reappeared with the sommelier, who carried a magnum of Dom Perignon, courtesy of the house. The sommelier filled their glasses and left the magnum in an icer. Two waiters took their positions a respectful distance away and made sure no need went unattended. Bill, the headwaiter, came over with greetings and started to recite the specialties until Roger held up a hand.

"Bill, why don't you order for us?" he asked. "It all sounds too good to decide."

"I know just the thing," Bill said, bowing slightly, and disappeared into the kitchen.

When they finally had some privacy, Mickey looked bleakly at Roger.

"Man, what a bummer about Hanoi," he almost moaned. "I can't believe he died in a plane crash. That guy didn't fly 'em, he wore 'em."

Roger shook his head sadly.

"That's what happens when you trust someone you shouldn't," he said. "They were boat guys; first time they ever loaded an airplane."

"Jesus," said Mickey. "What a helpless feeling he must have had, not being able to make her fly."

They fell silent, thinking about the man they'd both known for so long and who had been such a big part of their lives, adventures and fortunes. Then Roger remembered his champagne glass and raised it high. Mickey raised his next to it.

"To Hanoi," said Roger soberly.

"To motherfucking Hanoi!" snarled Mickey softly.

They clinked their glasses together loud enough to draw looks from nearby diners and drank their glasses in one long pull. Roger refilled their glasses and looked Mickey in the eye for a long moment.

"There's something missing without him," Roger said. "Half the fun was watchin' him laugh at the impossible. I heard him in my head after this last one: 'Just finished one that grew a tail, and boy what a nightmare. I really thought they had us this time but in the end, no worries!' And I'm telling you, I would've felt a lot better if Hanoi was driving, that's for sure."

"The whole business is changing," Mickey said. "Hard to find anyone but short-sighted amateurs who bring us a lot of heat."

"So you already know I've been thinking about quitting," Roger went on, "but now I think I'm really gonna do it."

Mickey looked at Roger in amazement. They had started smuggling together in the mid-'70s out of Florida. Their first load had been just seven pounds, but their last venture together had earned them an island in the Bahamas where they both built beautiful homes. They'd never had a failed mission, never even had a real close call, and, unlike so many former partners in the business, they had split and remained on good terms.

"Right," snorted Mickey. "How many times have you said that—have *we* said that? And what about that thing you were putting together in Central America?"

"Hanoi was going to fly it," Roger said simply.

"But you said it was a gold mine and no one else was working it."

Roger stayed silent and Mickey saw he was getting nowhere. He backed off with a slight laugh.

"All right, Hanoi is irreplaceable." He leaned forward and dropped his voice. "Okay, here it is. My man in Jamaica has a load of primo stuff I can get for near nothing, but it has to move now—*right* now—but it's too much to haul in my Cessna 210 so I was hopin' you'd loan me yours."

Roger pondered for a moment. "And?"

"I'll give you fifty grand and a hundred pounds on the back side." Roger laughed.

"Some deal. I risk my highly-equipped plane to make a hundred grand—if you make it. The extra fuel tanks alone make it worth twice that—and where will I be if you get busted or the plane gets hot? I can do much better myself."

"Man, how can you take advantage of a desperate friend?"

"Save it for someone who doesn't know your rap. You buy into half the plane, I'll do it for half the load."

"Man, what kind of deal is that?!"

"The only one you'll get."

Mickey took a long drink from his glass as the waiters interrupted with their appetizers. After they'd retreated, Mickey leaned forward again. "Listen buddy, I know where there's a Cessna Titan we can get for one seventy-five. Guy'll take trade-ins, so you put up your Queen Air, I put up the 210, done deal."

"What can it do?"

"It's a dream plane. I swear Cessna made it from the ground up for smuggling. It'll go eighteen hundred miles with a ton of cargo and fly from twenty-five hundred feet of dirt. Don't make 'em anymore, and not many available. We ought to jump on it."

Roger popped an escargot into his mouth and pondered while he chewed, then drank some champagne and smiled at his enthusiastic companion. Nice way to lose the Queen Air, which was a burden to hide when it wasn't working.

"Okay," Roger said. "That works for me."

Mickey grinned slyly. "You provide a driver and turn it and we have a deal."

Now it was Roger who snorted.

"You know my problem with that. First off, I can't turn that bush you call ganja, and second, I just told you how I felt with Hanoi gone."

"Me too," said Mickey glumly. "I'd planned on him doing the run, I was all set—and then I couldn't get a hold of him and didn't know why he didn't call back until you gave me the news."

Roger looked at Mickey as his enthusiasm faded. "Then maybe it really is time for both of us to just hang it up. What do you think?"

Mickey shook his head and looked wistfully at Roger. "Love to, man, but I need a couple more to pad the cushion before I head to the island and go fishing. And hey, you obviously know a driver. Who did your last one?"

"He's the main reason I want to call it quits," Roger smirked. Mickey frowned, not sure what Roger was getting at.

"Look, I'll turn it if you let him drive."

"Only if you go with him." Roger said firmly. "Otherwise, forget it."

"What? Is he afraid of the dark?"

"You know him!" Roger said.

"Oh man, now you're scarin' *me*."

"Seriously," Roger said, "the dude can fly. He just can't *think*."

Mickey sighed and weighed the news as he ate an escargot without even tasting it. "I'd fly it, but there's no time to get comfortable in the plane. Let me meet him and see what I think of him."

"Okay," said Roger, as he reached for the Dom again, "but first things first."


"You used trash compactors?" Mickey said incredulously as they motored down the freeway toward Billy's house.

"Had to," Roger replied. "That *sinsemilla* was so bulky we couldn't fit as much as we could carry. We pressed it into twenty-pound blocks, so that helped but without the seed weight we still ran out of room. The buds are sugar coated and full of red hairs. Everybody loves it. The first load not only sold itself, but I got front money on the next one. Hanoi and I pulled three loads outta there."

"Sounds like the discovery of a lifetime—and not something you'd retire without milking a lot more."

Roger's grinned at how well his friend knew him.

"Well, we were planning to do one last load, a DC-3 full of Hawaiian *sinsemilla*."

"Hawaiian?" Mickey said, eyes wide. "How?"

"Guy I know there shipped me a thirty-gallon drum of seeds. First crop's already in. Be ready in November."

"Wow. Imagine Sky Train stuffed with Hawaiian," Mickey mused, then frowned. "Well, not any more, but still, you can't let a plan like that die. Why not use Mr. Douglas instead?"

"Out of the question," Roger sighed. "When Hanoi crashed Sky Train, I wrote off the trip. Not on my radar any more." He glanced at Mickey, his eyes showing fatigue. "So let's talk logistics about the one that is."

"I have the people, and we're getting the right plane. Trust me, this is an easy one as soon as I get a pilot."

Roger did trust the way Mickey operated and knew his track record, so he weighed that against Billy's limitations and decided it could work.

"All right, I'm in. But here's the deal. I'll turn you on to this guy but if you go with him, he's yours from then on. Not my responsibility."

"Agreed."

"When do you want to go?"

"Soon as you're ready, I make a call. I was thinking of the Georgia strip after a refuel on the G-H logging road."

"Who's refueling?"

Mickey took a deep breath. "The Bushman."

The name curled Roger's lip into a snarl.

"You're letting the *Bushman* handle that?"

"He's done it before. He's cool."

"He wasn't cool when I tried to unload the 206 in Ocala. He was hiding in the bushes."

"He was scared, that was his first one. He's been right there since then."

"Billy and the Bushman," Roger muttered, almost angry with himself for letting it go so far without calling it off. But I'm doing an old friend a favor, he thought, and he's running the show and he's always done it right before. He blew out a huge breath and flashed Mickey the devil-may-care grin so familiar to those who knew him.

"Okay, Mickey. Sure. What could possibly go wrong?"

Down on Grand Bahama, the Bushman muttered in his beard as he looked at trenches dug across the logging road Mickey wanted to use as a landing strip. They were too deep to fill in without a backhoe and Bushman had no access to one, much less a legitimate reason to fill in the trenches.

"Fuck me for a Catholic," he swore as sweat started pouring from his head. He looked up and down the road from where he stood. Trees grew close to the road in both directions, too close for an airplane to land. One direction seemed less dense than the other, so he headed that way, then paced off the width and length he thought the plane would need for landing and takeoff, then counted the trees inside that rectangle.

When he finished, he shook his head forlornly.

"Fuck me for a Rasta. I gotta get some chainsaws."

It was past midnight when Billy ushered them into his house. Roger noted that there were no Franklins lying around and the whole place looked shipshape, like it belonged to a serious person. He smiled his approval at the young pilot, then introduced him to Mickey.

"You guys could be brothers," he said, noting the similarities between them, and indeed, the two of them hit if off from the start. As Roger mediated their discussion, he noticed that Billy grew more confident as the conversation went on. Things were going smoothly until Mickey said:

"Forty K for the run."

Billy sneered. "Is that all? For a pilot like me?"

"You're right," Roger said, smiling at Billy even as he wanted to smack him upside the head. "Pilots like you *are* hard to find, and that's why you're getting the usual rate even though Mickey'll be flying right seat with you. You'll be getting paid to learn—and learn a lot—so I think it'll be well worth your time, don't you?"

Billy looked down at the floor.

"Impress me," Mickey said, "and I'll make it up to you on the next one."

Billy looked up, grinning, and shook Mickey's hand.

"Deal!" Billy said.

*If there is a next one*, Roger thought to himself.

The next morning, Mickey and Billy flew the Queen Air to Memphis and met with the aircraft broker who owned the Titan. Billy, trying not to leave prints, clumsily tried to open the cabin's rear door without using his fingers. The broker turned to an embarrassed Mickey and laughed.

"What do you call him, 'Knuckles'?"

"Nah, he just doesn't want to smear his fingernail polish," Mickey joked back, hoping to deflect the broker's attention for Billy's amateur hour antics. The broker said nothing more about it, and focused instead on the bonanza he was reaping in getting two good planes for one.

The deal went off without a hitch and they flew the Titan back to rendezvous with Roger in Illinois. On the way, Mickey told Billy they'd leave the next day, then kept him in sight as much as possible to make sure he didn't blab anything to anybody.

On Grand Bahama, the Bushman watched smiling as his three Bahamian crewmen made fast progress on the trees near the road section he'd picked out, chainsaws roaring, bodies sweating. They'd been at it just one hour and were already almost 25 percent done. No worries.

Then one saw went silent and the crewman walked over.

"Chain is done, monn," he said matter-of-factly. "I need another."

Bushman stared at him.

"You need another *what*?"

"A chain, monn," he said, raising the saw to Bushman's eye level. "They get dull—must be resharpened or replaced."

"Fuck me," Bushman muttered, shaking his head once more.

Roger watched the Titan circle the field and land. Its long nose made the mid-sized twin-engine seem larger than it actually was, and he noticed beefier, after-market main gear struts and brakes. *Finally*, he thought, *a nice surprise and not a nasty one for this run*.

He got another nice surprise when he opened the door; a plush and mint condition eight-seat executive interior. Mickey grinned as he walked aft, crouching in the low cabin, and patted one soft leather seat.

"We could fly this to Europe after the run and party, don't you think?"

"Let's see how the run goes first," Roger said, game face already on, studying the layout. "Let's get going."

They rolled the plane into a hangar and stripped out the seats and oak tables. Then Roger lined the interior with a tightly fitted layer of Visqueen to protect it from contamination. After that, they loaded several items for Mickey's people in Jamaica, then Roger fueled the wing tanks and Mickey programmed their destination into the Loran computer. When everything was set, Roger drove Mickey and Billy to a nearby motel. The two smugglers spent the night going over the mission plan while eating pizza and watching cable movies.

The next morning, the Bushman sat drunk in his favorite Grand Bahama bar, signaling his bartender, who shook his head.

"Monn, you need a shower and a shave more than another drink," he said gently. "You too liquored and too smelly and you scare away my other customers. C'mon, monn, give me a break."

"Jess pour me one more and I leave," Bushman said, banging his glass on the bar.

"You said that two drinks ago, monn. Sorry. Besides, must you not return to the work you do that makes you so smelly?"

Bushman looked blearily at the bartender, finally defeated.

"Work . . . ah yes . . . still much work to do." He left a Hamilton on the bar, oozed off his chair and wobbled out the door.

That night, Roger watched the Titan disappear into the darkness as he swallowed his misgivings and convinced himself that the run was a good move. He knew Mickey would be a good babysitter and coach for his problem child, and was confident Billy would return as a wiser and better pilot—and one who could maybe even start thinking a little, too. He thought back to his own early days and how long night flights on a smuggling run made people very close, made them talk about things, think about things, that they didn't talk or think about when operating in the real world in the light of day. He knew that as his two business partners flew non-stop to Florida to refuel, then on to the Bahamas taking turns flying and sleeping, that they would indeed become like brothers.

The following noon, the men made the turn around Cuba and approached Jamaica. Mickey pulled a marine band radio from his flight bag, alligator-clipped it under the instrument panel and turned it on. When they passed over the coast, he keyed it.

"Lucky Duck to Marley, over," he said.

"Yah monn, Marley here," came the clear answer from a Jamaican voice Mickey knew to be Winston's, his ground chief. "We ready and waitin' and da harbor clear."

"Roger out."

Mickey set down the radio and directed Billy towards the clandestine strip.

"That's it there. Land if we see a truck with the hood open by the approach end of the runway; if we don't, something's up and we fly to Kingston."

Billy nodded and smoothly dialed in the landing as if he'd been to the runway a dozen times already. Mickey noticed and smiled to himself, then searched for the truck. He found it, hood open, exactly where it should be, and held an upturned thumb into Billy's field of vision.

"Good to go," he said to confirm the gesture.

Billy greased the plane onto the runway perfectly, and Mickey slapped him on the shoulder as he got up from his seat.

"Nice work, man. Very nice."

Billy just nodded as Mickey went aft and dropped open the door while they were still rolling. The ground crew jumped aboard before the plane stopped and with a rush of energy unloaded the equipment Mickey had brought them and began throwing the packaged goods aboard. Mickey quickly arranged them to keep the weight and balance right as Billy set the brake and climbed out through the pilot's door.

"Here!" said Winston, already up on the wing, and gestured for Billy to hand up several gas containers. Winston poured as fast as Mickey stacked and both the fueling and the loading were completed at almost the same instant. Billy climbed back into the cockpit and Winston handed him a piece of paper.

"Give this to Mickey so he can call me when you make it."

"Thanks man, I will," Billy said, smiling, but when Winston turned away Billy's face went cold and he pocketed the paper as Mickey pulled the aft door shut and locked it.

Mickey climbed in the right seat as Billy taxied the plane quickly to the runway end, wound the engines until the brakes no longer held them back, then raced down the runway and back into the air, engines humming, the rush of loading fading away.

"Damn good work, Billy, "Mickey said proudly. "You really are a good pilot."

"Thanks, man," Billy smiled, "and you're a good guy to work for—really got your shit together. Everything's planned out to a T."

"Only way to fly," Mickey grinned back, then turned his attention to the Loran.

The Bushman's crew frantically chopped down trees, two with chain saws, two with axes. A broken chain saw sat on the roadway near their van.

"Fuck me for a sailor," Bushman said as he set down his axe and wiped sweat from his face, counting the trees they had left to cut. He'd already narrowed the width of the runway and some of the stumps stuck up almost waist-high. The other axe man paused near him and surveyed the remaining work.

"We never get it all done, monn," he said, exasperated. "Why we not start sooner?"

Bushman glared at him through still-bleary eyes.

"Shut up and cut, monn."

Mickey relaxed as they circumnavigated Cuba and shot through the Windward Passage into the Bahamas. The whole run was going like clockwork and Billy was proving to be more pilot and less problem than Roger had led him to expect. Hell, he even liked the kid.

"Even with this detour," Billy observed, "I get to see more land than my last trip."

"Yeah, it's a big pond between Colombia and here," Mickey replied.

"Has anyone ever made a run directly across Cuba?"

"I know a few scammers who made it by getting down in the trees but it scared the shit out of them and they never did it again."

"Sure would save a few hundred miles."

"Not worth it. One guy told me a MiG got in front of him and almost melted off his windshield with the afterburner. Castro's crazy."

Billy checked his gauges, then dialed back his power and tweaked the fuel mixture. Mickey frowned a question. Billy tapped the instrument panel clock.

"Tailwind. We're ahead of schedule," he said. "Better to slow down to miss the sunset tourist traffic and stay in sync with our refueling time."

Mickey's eyebrows arched.

"Good thinking, kid. Good thinking."

The Bushman had quit thinking; he was exhausted, unable to swing the axe another stroke. His crew was still working feverishly to finish, but unless Mickey was late, they wouldn't get it done. Then his radio squawked.

"Maverick to Goose, over," said Mickey's voice.

"Fuck me for a Cuban," the Bushman muttered. "Right on time as usual." He looked at his unfinished business and hoped it would be enough. He keyed the radio.

"Goose here, Maverick," he replied. "You are clear in front of the van."

Mickey frowned at the odd instruction and scanned the terrain below until he understood what the Bushman had meant. He saw the trenches, the van further up the road toward the trees than planned, and saw the stumps where Bushman and his crew had cleared them. All this he saw, but none of it he mentioned to Billy. The kid had enough to think about getting it in there.

"You didn't tell me it was this narrow," Billy said as he settled the Titan into a short-field approach.

"Guess it looks wider when you're in a 210," Mickey lied.

Billy repeated his Jamaican landing, greasing the twin onto the narrow road with just feet to spare on either end of the wings.

"Fucking excellent, Billy," Mickey blurted in relief. "Didn't think the runway would be that sketchy," he added truthfully.

Billy stopped quickly and the two men stayed aboard with engines running, watching as the Bushman and his crew replenished the wing tanks from 5-gallon containers. They didn't notice that the heavier-than-a-210 Titan sank into the rough roadway as it gained fuel weight. When the refueling was done, Billy peered ahead.

"Don't know if we can make it off before the trees, man—can't they drag us back a hundred yards or so?"

"Already on it," Mickey grinned, as he looked out the cockpit window at Bushman hooking a line from the van to the tail tie-down ring. "Standard operating procedure on this run."

They made it 50 yards before the plan bogged down in a low spot. The van's tires dug it into the dirt too. Bushman unhooked the line and gestured to Mickey that they could do no more. Mickey acknowledged, then turned to Billy.

"That's all we get," he said. "You got this?"

Billy blew out a centering breath as he scanned the soft, short runway and with a now-sweaty palm pushed the throttles forward. "Let's see what she can do."

When Billy released the brakes, the Titan didn't budge. He shot a glance at Mickey who sat, teeth clenched, sweat rolling down his face.

"SOP, huh?" Billy said, and then the plane broke free and started down the road.

Halfway down, branches started slapping both wingtips. A hundred yards later, the left wing hit a stump. The plane veered off the road but Billy stomped right rudder to bring it back and it kept building speed.

But not enough. They weren't yet at takeoff speed but it was either fly now or hit the trees.

"All right, here we go!" Billy said, and pulled the plane into the air with the stall horn blaring. It flew for a moment on sheer momentum, then settled back toward the ground. Billy chopped the throttles and hoped he could stop before they hit the trees.

It was a vain hope. The mains hit the road, then the right wing hit a tree and the Titan cartwheeled into the forest strewing parts and fire through the trees, then plopped down right-side up and started burning. Bushman and his crew jumped into the van and raced towards the huge cloud of black smoke that rose from the wreckage.

Mickey and Billy were conscious and little injured, but they were trapped; their cargo blocked the aft door and flames blazed around them outside the cockpit.

"No choice, man!" Mickey shouted. "Gotta go!" Billy threw open the door, and they dove through the flames, singing their hair and blistering their skin in the intense heat. They hit the ground and ran toward the Bushman's van. Seconds later, the flames reached the right wing tank and the wing exploded, hurling wing pieces and blazing fuel in all directions.

The Bushman stopped and stared at the wreckage as they climbed in. "Fuck me for a Catholic," he said softly.

Roger checked his answering service a few hours later. The first message was bad.

"It crashed, monn," said a panicky Bahamian voice. "Halfway house need to talk to you right away."

The next message had the number. Roger called and got all the information he could, then picked up Dave and Mike and made a plan.

The next day, Dave boarded a jet carrying new IDs for Mickey and Billy. When he got to Bahamian customs, he handed a Franklin to their usual officer, who backdated the entry stamps on the documents. Soon after, Dave handed them over to the Bushman at a pre-planned meeting point, then returned to the States and updated Roger.

After Dave left Roger's house, Roger went out in the back yard and stared into space, adding up the good and bad of the situation.

No deaths, limited injuries. Good. No short-term bust headed their way so far. Good. Lost a plane and cargo. Bad. Generated more heat. Bad. Long-term bust status unknown. Bad. Two weeks until Nationals and now I have to deal with this. Bad, he thought. Very bad. For the first time in as long as he could remember, Roger felt his shoulders sag under the weight of it all.

# CHAPTER FIVE

## SUGAR ALPHA

### *Summer 1982*

Gloomy clouds had hung low over Skydive Sandwich most of the Saturday following Billy's crash, dropping rare June rain on the Illinois farmland. Most of the Bags slept in, but several clusters of hopeful weekend jumpers trickled in, always looking skyward as they got out of their cars, then trudging into the hangar, gear bags over their shoulders, to wait on the weather. Once inside, they talked among themselves, worked on their gear, drank coffee or read newspapers. Some just staked themselves a snoozing spot on a couch or out-of-the-way corner of the hangar and asked for a 30-minute-to-takeoff wakeup call.

The gloom mirrored Roger's mood as he pondered the recent past. First, choosing Billy, then the tail, then going ahead with Mickey, and now the crash. His long run of good luck and smart thinking seemed to be over and he wondered what might next go wrong. The post-crash cleanup had many moving parts and it was still in progress. Worse, the jury was still out on Billy. Worst of all, his confidence in both Mickey and himself to get it right was shaken. Then Kong's voice boomed over the hangar.

"Don't worry, man, we're gonna take 'em *out!*"

Roger snapped instantly from his funk as he grinned at his fierce friend and the rest of the team—the one bright spot in his life besides Jeanie and the kids.

The Freak Brothers, of course, had trained the whole morning, with minimal input from him. They'd watched and discussed video of previous jumps, brainstormed about lineup engineering and dive mechanics. And they talked about the head games and mental landscape of national-level athletic competition. Some team members were veterans, but others were new to competition, and with the Nationals just a few weeks away, the jitters were already creeping into the corners of their minds.

"Just remember that the Nationals are like the Wizard of Oz," Roger said, in support of Kong's declaration. "In your mind you make it up to be this big scary thing, but it's only a little man behind a curtain. Right now that may not register because you're not there, but you'll know what I mean once you're there. So right now, you've got to trust me when I say, we're doing fine. We're right on schedule. Perfection is unreachable because you can always do better. If we do our best, we should outperform the other teams, and they'll call us the winners. Our objective is to keep improving right through the meet. We want to make our best jump on the last round of competition."

Roger could see that his words calmed his comrades, but they were jittery for another reason too; they only had a few weekends left to prepare, and this one was rapidly wasting away. Roger felt it too, and sighed as he glanced at the grey blanket wrapping the sky outside the open hangar doors.

"Yo Roger," he heard someone say behind him. He turned to see Mark gesturing toward the open personnel door on the west side of the hangar. Through it Roger still saw the grey blanket, but there was a hole in it—a big hole—and it was coming their way.

"Soup starts about three grand," Mark said, guessing Roger's mind. "I can scrape it and build up airspeed as I head in, then pull 'er up into it about a mile out and let you figure it out from there."

"Get us four?" Roger asked, crossing his arms.

"More or less. Take off in forty."

"Good enough," Roger said, and turned to his team, half of whom were already reaching for their gear, jitters replaced by game-face grins.

Except for Ardis. Ardis was never jittery but she was almost always more cautious than her testosterone-fueled teammates. She walked to the personnel door to see for herself, reeking of skepticism as she stopped just outside, hands on her lean hips, squinting skyward through the still-falling rain. Then she looked over her shoulder at her teammates as they geared up, laughing and joking, then back again at the sky.

"Sucker hole," she said to herself. "We never learn." Then she chuckled and walked back inside to get her gear too.

Forty minutes later, Roger gave each team member a high-five and a smiling, confidence-building look in the eye as they boarded the half-empty DC-3. Knowing the weather conditions weren't entirely favorable, each one flashed back a cocky grin—except for Ardis, who was last on and arched a questioning eyebrow at him. Roger's smile faded slightly and he winked in acknowledgement of her concern.

His smile returned as she disappeared into the plane. Gender equality was a great thing about skydiving; if you could do it, you were in, regardless of sex. Still, that didn't mean men and women were the same. Men tended to be confident and then get cocky. Women tended to build their confidence slowly—and with that came a truer sense of their abilities and limits—and those of the cocky guys too. It was one reason he'd picked Ardis for the team. There were guys who flew as well as she did, but she was seldom full of herself like the guys almost always were, including himself—and that was good for the team. More than once, Ardis had reality-checked them about jumping in marginal winds or other sketchy weather, or just telling them it was time to stand down when they'd worn themselves out to the point of lessened productivity and heightened risk.

Roger listened to her, too—well, mostly, anyway, but definitely more now than at first, after several of her cautions had been ignored, only to prove correct, much to the pain or at least embarrassment of the boys.

Even Kong, who feared neither God, man, nor devil, didn't argue with Ardis when she put her size 5 foot down.

Roger followed his reality checker aboard and walked to the cockpit.

"Same plan?" he asked Mark as he pre-flighted the bird with Kristen.

"We'll know for sure when we get there," said Mark.

Roger nodded and slapped the pilot on the shoulder and went aft through the seated jumpers again, then stood near the door facing them as the plane rolled.

"We fly to the cloud base, then decide whether to jump or not," he shouted over the engine noise to everyone, his eyes checking every face. "And don't worry if the team goes and you have reservations about the altitude. If you don't feel safe, ride the plane down. No jump's worth getting killed over."

He checked the faces again, then, satisfied for the moment, and kneeled near Ardis.

"It's still a sucker hole," she said quietly, as up front Kristen pushed the throttles forward and Mark steered the DC-3 down the runway, engines roaring, light mist spraying into the fuselage through the open door.

The tail came up and the mains lifted from the ground.

"Blue sky!" shouted the jumpers. "*Black Death!*" they shouted much louder, and they were sky creatures again, climbing toward the grey blanket.

Roger looked over to his reality checker and patted her knee.

"Don't worry, Ardis," he said quietly. "We're on the same page here. There's no judging and no pressure if we don't jump, and it's too close to Nationals to heal up if someone gets hurt doing a low one."

"It's still a sucker hole," she said just as quietly.

"That's right, and the only way we know if we can get enough altitude and hit the hole is by going up and seeing for ourselves. I'll even make you a deal; if you say no, we won't go."

"Oh gee, no pressure there," she growled, "but it's still a sucker hole." She eyed Roger coldly for a moment, then flashed a smile, "so we better go fast."

Roger laughed out loud and tousled her thick hair.

"God I love this team!" he said to no one in particular.

Soon after, he felt the plane level out and he checked his altimeter: 3,200 feet. Wind whipping his hair, he took off his sunglasses and knelt by the door, then stuck his head out to check their approach as the plane went in and out of the cloud layer's ragged bottom. He smiled at what he saw and stood up, then gestured for Ardis to join him at the door.

"Hole's over the DZ," he shouted above the wind noise as she looked out the door. "What do you think?" Ardis checked her altimeter.

"We need four," she said.

"We'll have that when we get there."

Ardis arched her eyebrow at Roger again.

"You guys," she said, then signaled to the team to take up their positions. They all whooped and lined up. If Ardis was good to go, then they were too.

Roger looked up at Kristen, sitting sideways in her seat waiting for his signal, and pointed one finger upwards. Kristin repeated the signal for Mark. A moment later, the DC-3 accelerated, then zoomed into the clouds for a few seconds and leveled off again.

Roger checked his altimeter: 3,800 feet. He glanced at Ardis.

"Blue sky," she said, then turned her attention to the lineup. Roger grinned and took his place at the back of the line as it tightened up for exit. He glanced at Bob, who wore his rig and cameras, but wouldn't be jumping into possible rain with them. Instead, he'd film their exit from inside. Roger high-fived him, then tapped Kong.

"Hot!" roared Kong.

"Ready!" roared Ardis.

". . . GO!" the team shouted as one and exploded out the door into a pelting blast of stinging rain that rippled over their goggles, but the exit was among their best ever, so they could see each other. Still, they flew more by feel than by sight and their star was halfway built before they burst from the clouds and saw the ground already rushing up at them. Their altimeters needles were well into the yellow warning zone when Dave and Roger closed the circle and they immediately shook off their hand grips and flew apart to deploy their chutes.

Roger and Kong had the same idea: track farther and open lower to give the others more space higher up. It was a good plan—except that they both tracked the same way and deployed dangerously close together. Roger grabbed his risers to steer his still-opening canopy away from a collision. Kong's parachute opened, but Roger's maneuver made his streamer for several seconds. It gave him separation from Kong but he opened less than 1,000 feet above the dirt—lower than pattern entry altitude. He had little time to set up his landing and zoomed across the grass at high speed. He flared, but his parachute ran out of lift before it ran out of forward speed and when he set his feet down to run out the landing he slipped on the wet grass and tumbled to a stop amid much laughter.

He stood up and saw skid marks all over his jump suit, a bad-landing badge he'd have to wear all day. Chris pulled up alongside him in the golf cart, face grim.

"You almost killed yourself,' he growled quietly and coldly in a perfect Roger Nelson imitation. "Now get your butt over to the school and watch the basic canopy control video, then write me a report hitting the ten key points—and then I'll think about whether you can jump again this weekend. Are we clear, Roger?"

They stared each other down for a long moment, then laughed as one while Roger climbed into the cart, wet canopy bunched in his arms.

"Did Patrick see it?" Roger asked.

"Everybody saw it," Chris chuckled.

"Tell him his next jump's on me and I'll—" Roger said, stopping short as he realized that the windsock had turned 180 degrees since they took off. Then he realized something else and turned toward the end of the runway to see Mr. Douglas on short final—for a downwind landing. He grabbed the radio from the cup holder.

"*Abort*, Mr. Douglas! *abort*," he shouted as he watched Mark float the DC-3 over the threshold toward a mid-runway touchdown so he wouldn't have to taxi as far.

No response, no change in flight path. The DC-3 touched down as Chris reached over and turned the radio on.

"*Abort-abort-abort!*" Roger shouted again, but it was too late. The plane rolled out and the tail dropped. Roger gestured for Chris to follow the plane, then they watched helplessly at the tail waving side to side as Mark tried to stop his beloved machine before it reached the end of the runway.

He failed. The Three skidded all the way to the end, then up and over a small hill and out of sight. Roger and Chris heard the sound of breaking trees and crumpling metal.

Chris and Roger followed the tire tracks over the hill, expecting the worst, as Roger got out of his gear and put on his sunglasses, and Mike trailed behind them in the drop zone's pickup.

"We're okay," Kristen yelled from the rear door as they approached the plane, its tail wheel dug so deep into the grass that she stepped out of the plane without jumping, gear pins in hand. "Mark's freaking out about Mr. D, though."

Chris grabbed the gear pins from her, crawled under the plane's belly, and pinned the landing gear in place. Mark stuck his head out from the pilot's window and mumbled as he surveyed the damage. Several trees were smashed against the wings; one had, remarkably, passed between the nose and engine without hitting the propeller. He shook his head disgustedly and pulled his head inside. Moments later, he too stepped from the rear door onto the wet grass and looked sharply at the windsock. It was back to the way it was when he took off. Mark looked at the others, bewildered.

"What the hell happened?"

"Wind swung one-eighty when you were on final," Roger said quietly, and gestured at his stained jumpsuit. "Got me too."

"Yeah, all you gotta do is wash that," Mark said as he ducked under the wing and between the trees to see how bad it was. He looked up at the nose and pointed where a now-broken-off tree had smashed right in its center. "Now look, I went and hit a tree." Mark sank to the ground in grief. Roger turned to Mike and Chris.

"Leave me the cart, take Kristen with you and find somebody who can tow this thing outta here." He pointed to some approaching jumpers. "And take them too. We don't need gawkers."

The others climbed into the pickup as Roger turned back to Mark, who still sat disconsolately on the wet ground, oblivious to his now-soaked jeans.

"How could I have been so stupid?" he said. "Now I'm ruined; no insurance, no money to fix it. I saw it'd be close but I was too late to lift back off. Stupid, stupid, stupid."

"Come on, get up," Roger said as he laid a hand on Mark's shoulder. "Stupid is how you look sitting there looking like you peed your pants."

"How do you know I didn't?" Mark shot back. Roger laughed.

"Okay, maybe you're not so stupid," he said, and helped Mark to his feet, the evil mood now broken. Roger cupped one hand behind Mark' neck. "Hey man, be thankful you didn't end up like Hanoi. We all make mistakes."

"Yeah, but this one just wrecked my plane and reputation. I'm screwed!"

"Hey, *Hanoi* is screwed," Roger persisted, "so get over it. You're not only still alive, nobody got hurt and your plane isn't even totaled. You have a lot to be thankful for, my friend, so let's stay positive and figure out how to solve this."

Inside, though, even as he bucked up Mark, Roger was as numb and forlorn as the DC-3 pilot. *Well, now I know what went wrong next,* he thought, *and now I'm the one who's screwed on the most important thing in my life right now . . . the Nationals are lost before we even got there if I don't hurry up and find another—*

"Yo boss," Chris's voice intruded on Roger's reverie. "Look what I found!"

Roger turned to see a fertilizer truck with 10-foot-high tires bouncing over the small hill, Chris standing on the driver side running board. It stopped next to Roger and the cab door swung open.

A young man in overalls climbed out, chewing a piece of straw. Roger recognized him as a neighbor he'd seen watching the DZ action from his porch or from his tractors as he worked the fields around the airport.

"Hi Roger, I'm John," he said, extending a hand. He and Roger shook. "Figured you might need a hand when it went over the hill."

Roger's mood brightened as he looked at the massive rig, while Mark hung his head in shame.

"Looks like you can pull her out with that pretty easy," he said.

"Most likely," said Farmer John. "Let's have a look."

The two men walked around the Three. Mark sat down in the rear door, still nursing his bruised ego and broken attitude.

Farmer John eyeballed the scene, then checked the hill angle, stomped the wet grass with a boot and chewed on his straw. Mark joined them as he ruminated.

"Cut down a few trees, drag away the broken ones and jack that tail outta the mud and it should pop right out," he said after a few moments.

Mark sighed in relief as he heard Farmer John's verdict. Roger smiled and slapped him on the back.

"Phase One complete," he said. "Only one way to go from here, man; onward!"

Mark finally cracked a smile.

"You're right and I'm good to go from here. You go take care of your team."

When Roger drove back to the hangar, he parked the cart next to Mike, who sat in the DZ pickup listening to music. He turned it off and joined Roger in the cart.

"Man, I can't believe this," he said in a low voice. "That's two crashes in less than a week. What the hell's going on?"

"Good luck meets bad luck. Coulda been a lot worse."

"True, but I'm sure glad that you're the boss. I wouldn't want to deal with all this."

"Neither do I, but that's the hand we have to play."

"Kristen told the team everyone's okay, but I didn't want to go in there yet and have to look at those faces."

Roger flashed the confident smile he knew he had to show, not just to Mike but to everyone from this very delicate moment forward. As he had with Mark, he had to use all his leader skills to dampen the team's despair and refocus them on their mission.

"Thanks for waiting, Mike," he said, "and those faces'll be fine in no time. We'll figure it out. You know we always do."

Mike laughed as he got out of the cart.

"Can't argue with that, buddy."

They walked into the hangar and the team's blue mood struck them like a wave. Mike sat down with them while Roger stood in front, looking from face to face.

"Three weeks 'til Nationals and no more practice," glowered Kong when their eyes met. "We're out of it."

Roger said nothing, just moved on to the next face. Some were bummed, some were angry, all were looking to him for leadership. He looked last at Ardis and, true to form, she did not have an "I told you so" expression on her face; in fact, she was the least agitated and most unreadable of them all. He smiled at her.

"Once again," he said, "Ardis made the right call and I should've listened to her and because I didn't, we now have a problem."

The boys shifted uncomfortably but several of them also nodded appreciatively at the girl in their midst. Then they looked back at Roger and his smile was gone, replaced by the hard face and jutting chin that always appeared right before he challenged someone or something.

"Time to check your composure," he demanded, and he looked straight at Kong. "You guys got any composure? Huh? We've been practicing all summer, kicking butt all summer, and we hit one speed bump and you whine that it's over?"

Several team members dropped their eyes and heads, still bummed but also not a bit ashamed at their behavior. Kong kept his eyes locked on Roger's, still glowering. Then Ardis looked at her teammates.

"Roger doesn't think it's over, so I don't either," she said quietly. "He's our captain, and I have confidence in him. I think getting us another DC-3 by tomorrow is a bit much even for him, but he and all of you can count on me being here by 7:00 a.m. next Saturday morning, ready to go. That's the commitment I made, and that's the commitment I'll keep. And I'll be here tomorrow too—just in case!"

"And you know," chimed in Jeff, "that was a hell of a jump we did in the rain and clouds. We closed it about two seconds out of the cloud—"

"So that puts it at nine seconds, give or take," added Dave, completing Jeff's thought. Then Kimmers jumped in.

"Even if we don't get any more practice," he said, "when we do a jump like that I can't believe anyone's gonna beat us, practice or no practice!"

Kong's glower turned to a snarl and he winked at Roger.

"Rain, clouds, low altitude—no problem!" he boomed. "If we can handle that, we can handle Nationals. We're gonna take 'em out!"

Roger held out his hand. They all jumped to their feet and formed a circle of right hands, each grabbing the thumb of the teammate next to them, and looked at their leader.

"You know I will find a way to get us back in the air," Roger said, "so do your part and keep your heads in the game. Make this situation the event that leads to victory in three weeks and from this day forward our new motto is 'onward!'" He looked into the center of the hand star.

"Hot!" roared Kong.

"Ready!" roared Ardis.

". . . GO!" the team shouted as one, at the same time moving their hand up and then down breaking it with a growl.

"Okay, now let's go get Mr. Douglas," Roger said, outwardly unchanged but internally much relieved at the change in attitude. *I love this team,* he thought.

"I'll handle it," Kong said. "You go find us another ride." He turned to go, then stopped and looked back. "But first, follow your own advice and put your feet up on the desk for a few minutes, yeah?"

"Yeah," Roger said, and gave Kong a thumbs up as he walked off to gather a crew to help Farmer John drag the plane out of the trees.

Roger went into his office, followed by Mike and Dave and, as Kong had directed, put his feet up on the desk, took a deep breath, and closed his eyes. Dave and Mike followed suit and stretched out on the sofas for a quick recharge.

Minutes passed as Roger cleared his mind and let his body relax, trying not to think of anything in particular. Mickey and Billy kept popping into his thoughts, though—how they were making out . . . how much heat there was . . . his conversation with Mickey about Belize and Hanoi . . . the—

Roger sat bolt upright, startling Dave and Mike.

"What?!" exclaimed Dave.

"Y'okay?" asked Mike. "What's up?"

Roger grinned his leader-confident grin and this time he felt it in his own soul too.

"Sugar Alpha," he said quietly.

"How?" asked Mike. "He has an airshow contract."

"Not any more," Dave said. "Firestone cancelled it."

"After he painted it in their colors?" said Mike. "That sucks."

"Wife wants a divorce, too," Roger added.

"Poor guy," said Mike, "but he hates the business. Can't use it for that again."

"Weren't using Mr. D for that, either," said Roger as he thumbed through his Rolodex, "so maybe he'll haul us for a few weeks."

Dave and Mike traded expectant glances as Roger dialed the number and kicked back again in his chair. Roger and Mickey had once owned Sugar Alpha, so named because its registration number was N85SA. They'd used it early in their smuggling days, then sold it to Paul Feden after he landed an airshow contract at an amusement park owned by Firestone. Now the gig was done, and the marriage was done, so maybe Paul was interested in making some changes. He heard the phone pick up.

"This is Paul."

"This is Roger. Want to put Sugar Alpha to work for a few weeks?"

"Depends on the work. What's up?"

"Got a team that needs to practice for Nationals and Mr. Douglas just ate some trees."

"Bad?"

"No, but it'll be a month before he's running again."

"How soon do you need it?"

"Tomorrow." Roger heard a hearty laugh on the other end of the phone.

"How many loads a day?"

"Ten or more on the weekends, two or three on Friday evenings."

"Twenty plus?" Paul blurted. "Didn't know you were that busy!"

"It's the team working the Three because I'm really serious about being the first team from the Midwest to win ten-way at the Nationals, but, yeah, biz has really taken off."

"For ten a day, I maybe could be there tomorrow."

"Thanks, Paul, but Thursday will be fine. Then Rumor Control will make sure everyone knows that we're back in business."

"Well, I'm sure we can make this work, Roger. Just one thing—do you have a Cessna or something we can get back and forth in? We can't just relocate there on five days notice."

"No problem, you can use my Aztec."

"OK, deal. I'll have her up there Thursday. By the way, was Mark scheduled to fly at Nationals?"

"Yeah."

"Then I'll call and see if I can get that slot too—but do me a favor, though."

"What's that?"

"Tell Mark I hate profiting from his misfortune, but better me than a stranger and let him know I'll help however I can to get Mr. D back in the air as soon as possible."

"Sure. I'll let him know."

"How's Jeanie doing?"

"She's doing fine and keeping real busy."

"Wish I could say the same. You're the first good news I've had for ages. First I lose the air show, then they sold the airport to a cargo outfit so I have to shut down the DZ, and yesterday I found out the divorce is going through. Sure don't want to lose that woman but it looks like she's gone and without the DZ, I gotta sell Sugar Alpha too. Are you interested?"

Roger's heart jumped at the notion as his Belize conversation with Mickey echoed in his head, but now that he'd taken care of his team, he was all business again.

"Not really," he lied. "I'll leave getting all greasy to you guys that love wallowing in DC-3 blood."

"So far I'm only telling a few friends, because I want to keep her in the jump circle. "I'll make you a good deal. She's got to go."

"I'll think about it," Roger said, "and I'll definitely pass the word and see if I can get you some leads. Thanks again. See you Thursday."

He hung up the phone and turned to see Dave and Mike already high-fiving.

"Woohoo!" said Mike. "Maybe our luck's turning!"

"As long as things go like that for our friends in the Bahamas," Roger cautioned, but he was smiling too. After all the trials and tribulations of the past few weeks, this mountain of a potential problem had not only just evaporated into thin air, it provided an opening to put his retirement run back in play.

"All right," Roger said, getting up from his desk and heading for the door. "Let's go tell the team."

Thursday afternoon Sugar Alpha made its Sandwich entrance at 250 miles per hour about ten feet off the landing area grass. Paul had replaced Roger's custom paint job with Firestone's corporate colors, red and white. On either side of its fuselage and under its wings blazed the name "Firestone" in letters several feet high.

Roger and a few dozen DZ regulars watched in awe as the plane pulled up into a climbing barrel roll to 2,000 feet—and then two people jumped out and opened their canopies. Everyone on the field was hypnotized as the pilot circled for landing, then cranked the big bird 90 degrees right off the end of the pavement and touched down on the threshold. Ordinarily hard to impress, Roger shook his head in admiration.

"Never seen anyone make a DC-3 dance like that," he said to Mike.

"Make you forget all about Billy," Mike whispered.

"Don't remind me," Roger said. "I'm trying to enjoy myself here."

As Sugar Alpha taxied in, Roger drove the pick-up over to help unload the tools and parts all veteran DC-3 operators carry. Sugar parked alongside Mr. Douglas, where Mark and his helpers labored to remove damaged parts.

Mark's mood darkened as he watched Sugar Alpha shut down. He threw down a wrench and stalked into the hangar to sulk. Kristen just shook her head as he went, and kept on working, her striking Nordic face streaked with grease.

"Do you think bringing in Sugar Alpha will take the wind out of Mark's sails?" Mike asked as they got out of the pickup between the planes. "May take him longer to get it running again."

"To tell you the truth," Roger smirked, "I think he'll get it done in half the time now."

Roger lowered the door and welcomed Paul to the airport with a backslapping hug.

"Welcome, my friend," he said. "Now introduce me to your pilot."

A fit young man whose face shared Roger's mysterious grin and confident eyes stepped through the rear door and extended his hand.

"Roger, meet Andy," said Paul. "Andy, Roger."

"Honor to meet you, man," said Andy, and it was clear from his body language that he meant it. "Paul's told me awesome stories about you."

"Some of them may even be true," Roger said disarmingly, "and the feeling's mutual, Andy." Roger let go of Andy's hand and ducked his head inside the fuselage for a moment, then withdrew it grinning broadly. "Where do you keep your balls in there? I thought I've seen it all, but I never saw anyone do that with a Three. How much stress does that put on the plane?"

"None," Andy grinned back, "if you know what you're doing!"

Roger knew immediately that he and Andy would get along great.

Chris drove up in the cart with the two jumpers, and they greeted Roger warmly.

This is Don and Linda," he said to Chris. "Old friends from Paul's side of town. Why don't you find them lockers in the hangar and send Mark out."

Chris nodded and drove off as Roger, Mike and Andy unloaded Sugar Alpha.

Mark reappeared as they were checking out Mr. D's injuries, and stood obstinately silent as Andy and Paul discussed the wing root damage. Then Andy flashed Mark a sunny smile and held out his hand.

"Nice to meet you, Mark. I'm Andy."

"Hi," said Mark, taking the hand without enthusiasm. Andy and Paul both ignored the slight and gestured toward the pickup.

"Roger told us about the damage," said Paul congenially, "so I brought some parts that may work for you."

"And we'll both be happy to wrench for you whenever we're free, man," added Andy. "I hate looking at bent airplanes, especially Threes!"

"And Mr. Douglas is one of the greatest Threes flying," Paul continued, "so we're honored to help however we can to get him back in the sky."

Mark was taken aback by their generosity and good cheer and embarrassed by his rudeness.

"Thanks, guys, I don't know what to say," he mumbled. "I'm sorry I—"

"Forget it," Paul interjected with a dismissive wave. "I'd be pissed off at the world for a month if I was in your shoes. Beer's on me tonight, okay?"

"Us too?" asked Mike. Roger elbowed him. "Just kidding," he wheezed.

Everyone laughed and even Mark relaxed. Roger walked to Sugar Alpha with Paul and Andy to inspect the interior.

"Nice work, guys," Roger said. "Mission accomplished."

"Meant every word," Andy said, and climbed aboard. Paul held up Roger for a moment.

"You'll soon notice that's SOP for him," Paul said.

"Already have," Roger replied.

"He's a good egg, and absolutely the best pilot I've ever seen, myself included."

"Praise doesn't get any higher than that," Roger grinned and the two men joined Andy inside.

The next day at noon, the Freak Brothers 10-way team gathered at the airport, more excited than they'd been since acing the jump right before the crash, and thanked Roger more than once for bringing in Sugar Alpha.

"Thank me by winning Nationals," he replied.

"And I apologize to you and the team for doubting you, brother," Kong rumbled, humbled but unbowed. "We're gonna take 'em *out*!"

Minutes later, Sugar Alpha roared into the Illinois sky with 14 excited jumpers aboard, "Blue Sky! Black Death!" echoing over the engine noise.

The first exit through the slightly different door was clean and as Roger cleared it he flared and looked back for a moment. When he turned back to the star he was right on top of it and desperately de-arched and opened his body wide to avoid a hard collision. To his amazement, he finished decelerating just as his grips completed the circle.

An electric thrill went through the team, and they all kicked and screamed with excitement, then some flipped upside down while still holding on, funneling the star. They tumbled joyfully on top of one another, then separated in good order and finished the jump without incident.

They gathered happily in front of the big screen, only to discover that they had one more "new-door" adjustment to make.

"Didn't get it," Video Bob said glumly. "Hit my ring sight on climbout. Sorry about that."

"Oh man, you got to be kidding," said Tommy. "That was our best time yet!"

Others on the team started fussing. Even Ardis frowned in disappointment.

"Composure check!" Roger said above the grumbling, and everyone quieted immediately, realizing how foolish they were acting over a video from their miracle-find airplane.

"Well, we know what we did," Kong rumbled, "and if we're as good as we think, we'll do it again."

"And again and again," Paul added as he sauntered into the hangar. He stopped in front of the screen.

"Don't sweat it," Kong said. "Time only counts when the meet starts and until then we live on magic—*Sugar* magic!"

The team cheered his words.

"I felt it from the moment Roger called," he went on. "I needed this gig and you needed me and Sugar Alpha needs us all because you are destined to win! There's something going on here that I've never felt before. Now pack up and let's go again. We're burning daylight."

The team dispersed to repack while Chris worked with Video Bob to re-zero his camera sight.

Mike squatted over Roger's partly packed parachute.

"Mickey and Billy'll be at O'Hare at eleven p.m. tomorrow," he said quietly. "With Paul and Andy at your house, where should I take them?"

Roger thought for a second.

"I better pick 'em up. We'll get a motel in Aurora." Mike nodded and turned his attention to his own repack.

Two jumps later, the team was finished for the day and well-satisfied. They knew they'd be rotating through all the different DC-3s at the Nationals, so jumping today from Sugar Alpha—and performing well after a short layoff boosted their confidence that they could maintain their level no matter what plane they drew.

"Competition is a mental experience," Roger said to them at the end of their last debrief. "It's a mind game between the teams. If they feel they can't beat you, they'll try to break your confidence. The best thing to do is stay together and lean on each other for support. We'll be the best team there. Don't let anyone get you to doubt it—and if they try, tell Kong and he'll talk to 'em."

"Yeah, and then we can *all* visit them in their private hospital rooms," he growled as everyone laughed at the thought of Kong "counseling" another team about playing head games with the Freak Brothers.

Roger related this last bit of camaraderie to Jeanie as they lay in bed after tucking in their guests on the downstairs couches and checking on the sleeping children in their rooms. She smiled at her husband and tousled his hair.

"Really proud of you, honey," she said, "but not surprised. It's always something to watch you solve a problem when you set your mind to it, no matter how big or unexpected it is. I'm telling you, if your teammates respected you before, they're way past that now. They will literally follow you anywhere."

Roger kissed his wife and snuggled against her.

"Thanks, sweetheart," he said. "It seems to have worked out okay, but I gotta tell you, for a while there, I didn't know how I was gonna do it."

"I know," Jeanie said sweetly, "but I knew you would. That's why you're so good at this."

Those were the last words they spoke until they fell asleep quite some time later.

# CHAPTER SIX

## REGROUP

Roger pulled up to the O'Hare airport terminal tired but content after Sugar Alpha's successful first weekend. Plane, pilots and team had all performed flawlessly and, as he'd predicted, the Mr. D crash had in fact brought them all closer and imparted more focus and urgency to their training. As he watched Mickey and Billy walk up to the van, he figured that if the other crash on his plate worked out even a fourth as well, everything would be fine. They got inside wearing stocking caps and sheepish grins.

"Welcome back, road warriors," Roger said warmly.

"Thanks, man," said Mickey as they shook hands. "It was close. If you saw the plane you wouldn't believe we lived." Then he removed his hat and exposed his singed hair and a large bald spot. "Doc cut it off to dress a wound."

"Must've turned some heads coming through Customs," Roger said as he pulled away from the terminal. "Did you pick up any weird feelings?"

"You think that's bad, check this out," Billy piped in, pulling up his shirt to expose his bandaged abdomen.

"Took his shirt off before take-off because it was hot," explained Mickey.

"I didn't know what hot was until we had to jump through fire to get out! I'll never do that again."

"Well, I'm happy I can still give you guys some grief," Roger said as they left the airport grounds. "Sounds like one for the movies. Now back to my question—do you think you picked up any heat?"

"No, at least, not coming back," Mickey answered carefully.

Roger's head snapped around. He knew Mickey well enough to know that when he chose his words carefully, there was a big "but" on the way.

"But, I have some good and bad news," Mickey went on.

Roger flipped on the radar detector and headed west toward the suburbs, taking a moment to center himself for Mickey's big but, then he gave his companion a "go ahead" glance.

"Cops got there before the guys could get the plane off the road," Mickey said. "Only recognizable part was the tail, and they dragged it into the woods, but they didn't have time to bury it so the cops found it."

Roger clenched his teeth but said nothing. This was not starting out well. Mickey saw Roger's jaw muscles twitch and tried to build up some sympathy.

"I'm sorry man, but we almost got killed." Then he patted Billy on the shoulder. "Woulda died for sure without the job Billy did salvaging that mess. He saved us."

Mickey's gambit worked—Roger relaxed and nodded his approval at Billy, who smiled proudly.

"Wouldn't have happened if *Stumpy* had done his job," Mickey added.

"Stumpy?" asked Roger.

"The Bushman's new name." Roger's mouth dropped open as he attempted to talk, but Mickey interjected, "I know, I know, we can talk about it later."

"Jerk left the runway half full of trees," Billy snarled. "No way we could take off, especially after the mains sank into the road."

"What do you—" Roger started to ask.

"Had to use a different road," Mickey interjected.

"Any other bad news like this?" Roger asked sarcastically.

"We bought the police report," Mickey said. "It was no problem."

"What did they have?"

"The 'N' number, data plates, the incident report . . . that sort of stuff. Nothing they can trace back to us."

"Any other good news?" Roger asked stonily.

Mickey sighed and sat back, chastised.

"I knew he'd be pissed off," Billy whispered to him, but Roger heard.

"Yeah, you know everything, don't you, Billy?" he snapped, then turned on the radio and looked straight down the dark road.

Silence reigned until Roger dropped Billy off at his home a few miles from the airport. Then Roger told Mickey about Mr. Douglas and Sugar Alpha as he drove another 20 minutes to a motel. Roger registered under a new alias, and the clerk gave him a key for a third floor room. Needing an escape route from fire or feds, Roger asked for and received a second floor room. The "fire" excuse satisfied the clerk.

When they went inside, Mickey turned on the TV and set the volume slightly louder than normal. Roger checked the window behind the drapes and pulled them shut, then they each flopped on a separate bed and propped themselves up with pillows.

"I'm sorry man," Mickey started, "but—"

"Yeah, yeah, let's get past that." Roger interrupted. "I don't want to talk any more about all the bad luck I've been having."

"*We've* been having."

"*We've*! Man, two hundred grand!" Roger paused, "Oh well, what can we do? The good news is you made it back, and I'm glad to see you again." Mickey sat up and held out his hand. Roger slapped his into it, and they shook. Mickey yelped.

"Not so hard. I'm still messed up!" Both men started laughing. The heavy mood dissipated quickly.

"OK, so where do we go from here?" Roger asked.

"Glad you asked," Mickey replied, grinning. Roger rolled his eyes.

"Should have known you had something worked out."

"I told Jamaica Winston what happened, and he said he'd forget the debt if I did another run."

"Thought it was all gone," Roger said as Mickey grinned.

"You're smarter than that. You know how it works. They'll tell you anything to get you down. Besides, I don't think he has anyone else."

"Well, that's sure nice of him, huh?"

"I do feel we owe him something for being so understanding, don't you?"

Roger shrugged and readjusted his pillows so he could lay back against the headboard and stretch out his legs.

"So you want to try it again."

"Been thinking about it. When I got back to Florida, I met the Cookie Monster since he was going to unload us, and he's still into it—says he's got it all set, with buyers waiting. Then I called a plane broker and he had a Twin Bonanza for twenty grand, so I bought it with the expense money and sent Billy up to get it. I felt I owed you that, and Billy told me he could handle the trip alone."

"You believe that?" Roger asked. Mickey nodded emphatically.

"He did do a good job on the last one—and not just flying. He did some good thinking too, some deliberate, some on the fly. I don't know what went down when he as with you, but the guy I saw is ready to solo. So basically, I have the whole deal regrouped without you having to do a thing."

Roger stared at the TV without seeing it, then sat up and swung his feet off the bed onto the floor. He looked intently at Mickey.

"Right now, my priority is taking the team to Nationals and winning 10-way. We're leaving in two days. After all that's been happening, I don't want anything to screw it up. It's been a real bitch keepin' it together, and the team deserves it." Mickey sat up on his bed and looked just as intently at Roger.

"So do you, man," he said, "so cool, no problem. Like I said, I got it together. Go ahead and go, just keep in touch with your service in case I need you, but as far as you're concerned, this whole deal is on autopilot."

"So was the last one," Roger shot back. Mickey hung his head. Roger put a comforting hand on his friend's shoulder. "Listen, I'm not trying to discourage you, but losing the Titan hurt and with Nationals starting this week, I can't properly do a trip or even help much." Roger stood and walked over to a chair. He pulled it out and put one foot on it. "I can't understand why I'm letting you drag this one through the islands with all the heat down there. There are some weird omens about that. I think it's the 'Triangle' or something." They both laughed.

"I got it all set," Mickey assured him. "Let me turn this luck around while you go and kick ass skydiving. I'll bang it out this weekend, so don't worry. It'll go sweet!"

Roger gave Mickey a startled look and then sat down in the chair.

"That's the same thing Hanoi said to me the last time we spoke, two days before he crashed. Then Billy got his job, the trip grew a tail, we met the sheriff, and I've had two planes crash on me in the last week! It makes way more sense to run up the Gulf or bust through Mexico."

Roger flopped back onto the bed. Mickey got up and leaned against the wall.

"Well, then you have to put it together, and it can't wait until the Nationals are over," Mickey said. Roger pulled the pillow around his head and moaned. "So it's better to stick with the plan we have. You go skydive, I'll handle the run. The momentum's there and you know as well as I do that the chances they'll pick us up are one in a thousand— maybe even more now because rumor has it the DEA bent its King Air."

Roger didn't confirm the rumor; he wanted to stay on task.

"It's just that, lately, I've been making some piss-poor decisions on the spur of the moment, and those are the ones I usually make best!"

"That's right and from what you told me about the *Sugar Alpha* deal, it seems to me that you're back on track. Plus, we just made it up to Grand Bahama without any heat, and—"

"All right, man," Roger interrupted. "Enough with the sales pitch. Go ahead and go for it!" They shook hands, sealing the deal.

"And hey," Mickey added, "we won't recover everything on this one, but we'll get all the debts paid off and have the cash to finance the next one—you know, like using Sugar Alpha to do that DC-3 trip you and Hanoi were planning."

Roger shook his head at his friend's never-say-die enthusiasm.

"Yeah, you already know what I'm thinking, but let's do this one at a time."

"Yeah, right," Mickey said sarcastically. "You've never ever scammed anything *one at a time*."

"What I'm saying is let's wait to see how it goes for you."

"Goes for *us*, partner."

"Goes for *us*. Then we'll take it from there. But you're right. It's crazy how Sugar's fallen back into our hands, and she'll be flying at Nationals, so I'll get an even better idea of how she's flying."

"I'll betcha she's still plumbed for the extra fuel tanks," Mickey said, his mind jumping. "If that 'T' fitting's still on the fuel line, no more dragging them through the Bahamas. She'll go anywhere non-stop! The pieces are really falling together for us."

"Seems that way," Roger said, "but let's just see how the next one goes. We're down to the last of our cash. We might be more strapped than we'd like, if you know what I mean." Mickey grinned slyly at his partner.

"Hey man, remember your own rule—don't you be thinking anything but *positive*. Let's get this one done and then do the Belize trip. You pitch, I catch. We put the two groups together and won't need anyone else except a pilot." He paused, "And I'll make you a promise. When it's done, I'll retire with you!"

Roger again stared at the TV, again seeing nothing on the screen, until a smile spread slowly across his face. He turned to Mickey.

"Okay, but we gotta make one rule. No more Bahamas, for anything. We keep that as our retirement playground paradise. Deal?" Mickey nodded solemnly and they shook hands again. "Everything else, I'm behind you all the way. I've been hesitating since Hanoi went in, but I'll start poking the stick in the fire and see what's happening down there. Then we can make the run and retire this year, again."

"All right bro," Mickey said, smiling broadly. "Don't worry about me, you just blow their socks off at the Nationals, and I'll hit your phone service when we get back. Now let's see if I can get a flight out tonight. I've got a lot to do."

Roger's mind raced as he lay in bed after taking Mickey back to O'Hare and driving home late that night. Every time he started to doze off, he thought of another piece for his Belize puzzle and wrote it down in a notepad on a table next to the bed. Finally, with the sky outside showing the first hint of dawn, he gave up and climbed out of bed.

Less than an hour later, he was inside Chicago's 312 area code with his sack of rolled quarters and direct-dialed Belize. A sleepy voice answered, a voice Roger recognized as that of his lieutenant, George.

"Hey George, what's happenin'?"

"Roger boy, how are you?"

"Real good, my friend," Roger answered sincerely. "I appreciate you asking. How are you and the family?"

"My wife and I are very well, and the girls, you wouldn't believe how big they've gotten. They are even more beautiful than their mother. Time is passing so quickly. It won't be long before they'll be leaving us, so I been spending a more time with them. They're getting to that age where I gotta keep an eye on those Latin males. Can you believe my oldest will be graduating this fall?"

"Amazing! I hope I'm still invited to the graduation party."

"Oh Roger, it would be such a pleasure to have you. It would mean much to us all."

"Well then, you can count on me being there."

"Our home is always open to you. Please plan to spend some time. I'd like to take you diving. The water is so clear and beautiful."

Roger smiled into the phone. Everything was on track. The "girls" would be ready for harvest on schedule.

"My friend, I got to get going. Call me at the duplex at midnight my time."

"No problem. Extension six?"

"Or three if six is busy. Talk to you tonight." Roger hung up and wrote the numbers in his note pad. They represented pre-arranged radio frequencies.

He visited several more phones and spoke to the necessary people for a Belize run. He needed to put a plan in place before his midnight ham radio call to George. The calls confirmed everything. The crop was in fact doing well, the buyers were clamoring for a quality product, and combining Roger's group with Mickey's covered all the personnel slots except for pilots. And Sugar Alpha had flown back into her rightful place for the run.

That fact, however, set a warning bell clanging in Roger's head. Using Sugar right after it had flown at his own airport violated all the other precautions he'd taken to cover his tracks. Still, it felt right to go forward. Everything was coming together so smoothly.

Roger drove to another phone and called an Arizona-based group he knew to find a pilot and from the tone of their cryptic conversation, he thought he'd found the solution so he arranged to meet them in two days in Muskogee, Oklahoma, when he and the team arrived for the Nationals.

Content with the day's progress, he headed back to the peaceful farmlands and the farmhouse where he stashed his loads. There he found Dave and Mike in the barn building a dividing wall between the driver's compartment and the cargo space of a van.

"Where you thinkin' of landing it?" Mike asked after they'd gone into the house for a break and Roger briefed them on Belize and using Sugar Alpha for a run that would go through Mexico or the Gulf, not through Florida.

"Not sure yet," Roger said, "but if we can find a place west of Texas, we can make a land crossing in Mexico. Otherwise, we'll run it through the Gulf. Either way, it'll be ten times safer than Florida, and I'd rather not use an airport since we can stuff Threes into a lot of fields and dirt strips. And how about you guys—any locations you can think of to scope out?"

"The Edna field outside Tulsa might work," said Mike. "Can't say for sure if it's big enough because I never worked a Three, but it's certainly out in the middle of nowhere!"

"Okay, we can check it out during Nationals," said Roger. "In fact, if you guys are caught up with the checklist, I'd like you to get going tonight and start checking out some sites around the Texas, Arkansas, and Missouri borders, then meet Friday in Muskogee."

"How about Muskogee?" Dave asked. Roger laughed.

"Been used too many times. This is gonna be a special, custom run, so let's be original."

"How soon do you think this will come together?" Dave asked.

"Couple of months. We got a lot to scope out and put together yet. Mickey's doing a run with Billy flying that'll give us the money we need to buy Sugar Alpha."

"What the hell is Billy doing flying another load?" Mike asked.

"Mickey liked how Billy handled himself on the last one."

"He *crashed*!" Mike exclaimed.

"That was the Bushman's fault," Roger said. "Besides, Mickey made the call and he's doing the whole run, so put that out of your mind. Right now, our priority is winning 10-way at the Nationals, right?"

"Right!" said Dave and Mike together.

"Let Mickey do his job while we do ours and then we'll think about Belize," Roger said as he unrolled several aviation charts and spread them out on the floor. "Until then, limit yourselves to a little scouting and a lot of skydiving."

Then the three men got down on the floor and hunched over the maps like kids checking out letters to Santa.

Down in Florida, Mickey was conducting his final preparation for the Jamaican run—confirming there were no "bugs" on the airplane. The day before, he'd scheduled a tour through the radar room in the Federal Aviation Administration's Miami Center facility, telling the operator he was a skydiver pilot who worked with Miami center and wanted to see how things looked from their point of view. With professional courtesy, they accepted. Then Mickey arranged to have Billy fly circles around a VOR while he was there.

Now Mickey strolled through the dark rows of radar screens, glancing at his watch to confirm his timing. Mickey had done this drill with other planes previously so he knew the facility. He looked around, drifting toward the controller working the screen that covered Billy's pre-arranged flight path. When he reached it, he introduced himself to the controller, a friendly man who was proud that a pilot was interested in his work. He returned Mickey's interest by asking about jump operations as he monitored the planes in his coverage area.

"How do you distinguish the commercial traffic from the recreational?" Mickey asked.

"By the squawk and data strip. The commercials are handed to me before they come into the scope, so I know they're coming. When they enter my coverage, the guy next to me has them give me a call, and I confirm their position, altitude and airspeed." He struck a key on the keyboard and isolated one "blip" with an enlarged rectangle near it. "That's the data block."

"Where's the VOR on the scope?" Mickey asked.

The controller punched another key and pointed it out. Mickey acted impressed.

"Wow, that's pretty cool," he said as the controller paused to speak to a series of aircraft and he watched a blip on the screen flashing the ID "1201"—Billy, flying the pattern as planned.

"Looks like one of yours," the controller said, catching Mickey off guard.

"Whaddaya mean?" he asked, a lump rising in his throat.

"A jump ship by the way it's circling, or else a student pilot. You know, that's a VFR code we use for you guys."

Mickey breathed a sigh of relief and, with his mission accomplished, he turned the conversation casual again.

"Amazing. I guess you get a real feeling for the traffic rhythm from where you sit."

"Yeah, you get used to it."

"Bet you're good at video games," Mickey laughed.

"Not a chance! Last thing I want to do after a full shift here is stare at another screen."

"Makes sense. Well, thanks for your time. Hey, ya know if you ever want to come out and make a jump with us . . ."

"No thanks!" the controller laughed. "This is close enough right here."

Back at the airport, Mickey found Billy inside a small hangar talking to the "Cookie Monster," a bulky man with shaggy hair who rarely shaved, and who got his name from always sniveling, stealing, or bargaining for every dollar he could get. He was constantly jumping connections and trying to maneuver himself into deals—kind of like Billy, Mickey thought. The word "money" quickened their pulses but froze their brains.

Mickey had deliberately kept them apart, but they had inevitably met when the Cookie Monster arrived at the hangar with fuel barrels for the run and the two of them unloaded them. The way their heads snapped around when they saw him coming, Mickey figured they had not only spilled their guts to each other, but probably started plotting a run of their own using everyone else's assets.

"Tail check went fine," Mickey told Billy. "No worries there. Cookie, why don't you run Billy over to the store so he can fill his cooler, then drop him at his motel and we'll see you on the flip side."

"Will do," the unkempt man said. Mickey watched them saunter over to the Cookie Monster's equally unkempt car, knowing that their association would probably bear bad fruit at some point. But there was nothing he could do about it. Billy was his only pilot at the moment, and Cookie his only unloader.

At the grocery store, Billy shopped while the Cookie Monster trailed behind, scheming.

"You're flying, I'm unloading," he grumbled. "Seems we're doing the whole run."

"Yeah, and Mickey and Roger are making all the money," Billy agreed. Cookie grinned as he heard the resentment in the pilot's voice.

"All we need is a connection, and we're in business," he continued.

"I got a lot of them," Billy boasted. "I've been runnin' trips to Colombia and Jamaica, you know. Got phone numbers and everything." The Cookie Monster grinned wider.

"Why don't we just tell Mickey we want more bucks? What's he gonna do? He can't do it without us!"

"Not on this one, man," Billy cautioned, knowing he couldn't yet back up his talk. "It's too late for that, but when we finish this one, let's see what we can do."

"Sure, okay. The next run then," Cookie agreed.

When Cookie dropped Billy off at the motel, they exchanged phone numbers and shook hands on their new partnership, then went their separate ways, each harboring schemes for the future.

Mickey picked Billy up just before sunrise the next morning and reviewed the plans one final time, then Billy climbed into the plane and put on a heavy old flight jacket he wore up north during the winter. Before Mickey closed the cabin door, he saw Billy shudder, so he smacked him collegially on the shoulder.

"You've done this trip before so nothing's new except that this time you'll have a decent landing area for your refuel," Mickey chuckled. "So don't worry, buddy. You're a great pilot. Remember, radio contact ten minutes out." Mickey shook Billy's hand, shut the cabin door and walked away, hoping things would go better than last time.

Billy recited the pre-flight checklist out loud, palms sweating, heart pounding. "Relax, man," he also said out loud. "It's all good. You can do this."

He taxied tensely and felt his heart wind up as he powered up the engines, then let out a deep breath and released the brakes. The plane rose effortlessly into the sky and with it rose Billy's spirits. He hooted and hollered, thankful that nothing horrible had happened on takeoff, confident again now that he was back in the saddle.

Billy arrived at the same Jamaican strip at almost the same time before noon and, just as before, the Jamaicans quickly loaded 1,300 pounds of cargo aboard the plane while he and Winston refueled it.

"Have Mickey call when you make it, monn," Winston said, flashing a bright smile as he swapped out an empty fuel container for a full one, "and I bet you have no more trouble this trip!"

"Hope you're right, man. I don't need any more adventures like that one."

"How soon can you get back to do another one?" Winston asked. Billy frowned at the unexpected query.

"How many more can you do?"

"As long as you keep on jammin' monn," he said, dreadlocks flying in the prop blast. Billy hesitated for a moment, then seized the moment.

"If Mickey can't get back down, would you load me?"

"Mickey's good people. If you're working with him, I'm sure to work with you. You get my number from Mickey and give me a call."

"Already got it."

"Then get yourself back down here, monn. It'll be gone soon!"

"Deal!" Billy said as they finished filling the last wing and jumped off.

With a big smile, Billy shook Winston's hand and zipped up his heavy leather jacket, which elicited another laugh from Winston. He climbed into the plane, and the crew pushed the door closed. His hands and face started sweating as soon as he sat in the cockpit, and his knees shook as he reached the end of the runway and advanced the throttles. The plane lunged forward down the strip, and the moment it leaped into the sky, Billy's stopped sweating and shaking.

"Fuck man!" he scolded himself, laughing. "You gotta get over the takeoff!"

The trip went fast as Billy thought about running his own operation. He figured out how much he would make on the first trip, then a second and third. Before he'd made the turn around Cuba through the Windward Passage, he was an imaginary millionaire, a smuggling mastermind with the Cookie Monster as his right-hand man and his Illinois friends on his payroll. His remembered the movie *Scarface* and pictured his own South Florida mansion with servants and fancy cars. It didn't occur to him that the Cookie Monster had the same kind of dream, but with their profit positions reversed.

Billy crossed the Florida shoreline and made a climbing turn to make his plane appear on radar as a southbound target. Then he flew towards the Vero Beach airport and did a touch-and-go landing to break out of radar coverage again and checked his tail.

Soon after, he landed in a grass field alongside a highway obscured by a tree line near Christmas, Florida. He shut off the engines and before the propellers had stopped turning, Mickey and the Cookie Monster were unloading the plane while the Bushman sat lookout in the bushes. Nine minutes later, Mickey followed the Cookie Monster off the field on a 50-mile journey to the stash house in a quiet Florida sub-division. Billy gave them a 15-minute head start, then fired up the engines and took off back to the hangar. He still sweated the takeoff, but at this time his knees didn't shake.

They unloaded the Jamaican weed at the stash house, then Mickey nodded to the Cookie Monster.

"Let's make sure now that we got our terms straight," he said. "Look over each bale, and make sure you like it."

The Cookie Monster did just that, first cutting the burlap on some, then feeling the firmness on others, and filtering through the contents on still others. One by one, he accepted each bale and set it in a separate pile. Then he went Cookie Monster on them.

"How about three pounds per bale for paper weight?"

"We just weighed them out at one and a half!" Mickey protested.

"Hey, I'm gonna have weight loss and spillage, and I'm sure I'll find a rock or two."

"I got the time," Mickey riposted, knowing his unloader-buyer's *modus operandi*. "We'll go through each one and make sure there's no rocks, and if you wish, we can weigh the paper on each one."

Seeing that his tactic wasn't going to work, Cookie tacked another direction.

"C'mon, man. Give me a little slack so when my people come back to me with weight discrepancy, I can give them a fair deal."

'Okay, three pounds for paper and that's it."

"But what if—"

"Enough, goddammit," Mickey said testily. "I just took twenty bucks a bale off the price for nothing, so be happy and shut the fuck up, all right?"

"Hey man, no need to get intense," Cookie said soothingly. "Just trying to look out for my customers." He held out a hand to Mickey and they shook. "Deal."

"Deal," Mickey confirmed. "Thanks for your help. See you next time around."

"Sure thing," said the Cookie Monster, grinning as they said their goodbyes and shut the door behind them as they left. The smile evaporated.

"Not if I can help it," he said out loud. "Who needs you when I have my own pilot?" he said as he pulled out a humidifier out of a closet and turned it on. He laughed out loud as he poured each bale onto a large plastic sheet and misted them with a spray bottle to increase the dope's weight and cheat his buyers.

# CHAPTER SEVEN

## NATIONALS

### *July 1982*

A caravan of motor homes and vans carrying Roger's family and the Freak Brothers 10-way team arrived for Nationals at a former Air Force base near Muskogee, Oklahoma. Hot weather and waves of descending parachutes greeted them as they set up camp in one corner of the huge open space that made Muskogee such a perfect site for a parachute meet. Meanwhile, Jeanie and several team wives and girlfriends headed to town to check in to their hotel.

As others completed the set-up chores, Roger and Kong went to the registration office for the competition paperwork, with multiple delays to chat with friends, and one scouting stop at the concession trailer to hear rumors about the hottest 10-way teams. As usual, they heard about old and new teams from California, which had a reputation for fielding the best 10-way competitors. The Freak Brothers, on the other hand, were viewed as "the rookie team with a string of lucky practice jumps," which naturally angered Kong.

"The pressure's all on them," Roger reminded him cheerfully. "We're expected to lose, but those guys *must* win to live up to expectations and their own egos. So, c'mon, now we know the lay of the land. Let's get to registration."

Kong was still grumbling when they ran into two Magic team members, Bob the tall, athletic captain, and Mark, one of the team members, built more like a string bean.

"Good afternoon, Roger," said Bob formally, while looking at Kong as if Roger should have a leash on him. "So this must be the Kong I've heard about for years."

"Kong, this is Bob, Magic's team captain. Bob, meet Kong," Roger grinned.

Kong stuck out his hand and shook Bob's with a bone-crushing squeeze and a smile. When Bob's face changed from a cocky smile to pale white, Kong released him and held out his hand to Mark, who decided the better part of valor was to wave hello instead.

"So, you guys got a full team together this year?" he asked, trying to ignore his still-hurting hand.

"Yeah," said Roger, "we don't need to find somebody here at the last minute."

"How's practice been going?"

"We ought to do better than last year, but we're gonna need every practice dive we can get if we're gonna give you guys any heat."

"Well, you guys *are* from Chicago," Bob grinned.

"What's that supposed to mean?" Kong snarled.

"Well, as they say, there's always next year," Bob smirked, and he and Mark walked away laughing.

"Should've ripped his arm off instead," Kong muttered. "What an asshole!"

"Nah, just giving us a composure check. He knows darn well we have a practiced team that's ready to compete. Maybe they're a little insecure."

"That wimp looked at me like I was a newbie," Kong said, "but I'll bet he remembers me every time he takes a grip for a while."

Roger laughed and slapped Kong on the back as they walked into an old building that served as the registration office, where a pretty young woman who seemed to know them efficiently and happily took care of their needs.

"Who the hell is she?" Kong asked outside, his interest clear.

"Name's Kelly," Roger said. "I'll introduce you tonight but now let's focus on our team meeting."

When they all sat down inside Roger's big motor home, they told different stories of what they'd heard and who they had seen. Roger also checked out each one to get a feel for how they were handling the competition pressure that was already building. Everybody seemed fine except for Ardis. She sat quietly, hiding it well from everyone except him—he could tell she was feeling the pressure, and didn't want to let the team down, which of course added to the pressure. He'd have to keep an eye on that.

"I ran into Koska from the East Coast," Tommy said, "and he told me Magic's been funneling practice dives! They've cranked out some fast ones but they're not consistent."

"Word I heard," added Kimmers, "is that if we're nailing our exits 'as rumored,' we might have a chance and give 'em a run."

"That'd be great," rumbled the Piras. "People say Magic's been mocking us."

"There are a lot of mixed stories out there," Roger cautioned. "Don't pay attention to any of it. What counts is how we jump, so our plan remains the same: Stay focused, do our best, and let the judges tell us who won."

"That explains why Bob was so obnoxious," Kong snorted. "I *really* should have ripped his arm off!"

"Kong introduced Bob to his 'grip' when I introduced them," Roger explained, to a chorus of chuckles and mumbled variations of wish-I'd-seen-that, "but Magic is hot, let's not take that away from them. They wouldn't be champs if they weren't. Besides, we want to beat them at their best. It wouldn't be as good if one of them walked into a ditch or something," Roger looked over at Kong pointedly, and the team howled at the thought.

"Okay, okay," Kong said, grinning wolfishly, "but after the meet . . ."

Roger looked on, content that the session had relaxed his team, although Ardis still seemed a little out of sync with the rest of the mood.

"One more thing," Roger said. "We're all Freak Brothers. A lot of those sky gods come out of drop zones where everything's about them. But that's not what the Freak Brothers are about. We don't bump low-timers off loads so our team can get its practice jumps in. We don't sell them gear then leave them to learn on their own. We build up our low-timers." Roger made eye contact with Ardis. "We train up our low-timers, so we'll have more friends to jump with in cool competitions like this. We can win this thing if we keep our heads together by maintaining our vibe, not just our cool. There's a lot of bad vibes out there, but I want to make sure none of it comes from us. We don't want to sound like them. We're better than that. Got it?"

Roger made eye contact with each member of the team and held it until they acknowledged his words.

"Now go out and have some fun. Dinner tonight and dirt dive tomorrow at seven."

As everyone stood to go, Roger pointed to Jeff.

"One more thing. Be sure you're in uniform at all times for the duration of 10-way," he said. "Jeff has them."

Several howled in protest until Jeff handed out the "uniform"— black-brimmed hats with a Freak Brother patch to go with whatever else each of them wanted to wear. They laughed at the rigid flexibility of it all as they filed out of the motorhome.

Roger stayed in to sort through the paperwork for a few minutes, then he headed out too, but his mission was much different. He needed to get in touch with Ron and Jim from New York to discuss his next venture, so he went looking for them under cover of a casual hi-how-are-you stroll through the various camping areas. While so engaged, he ran into Logan, another jumper he knew was in the business.

"Roger! How've you been?" Logan said enthusiastically, and gestured him into his own motor home. "Come on in and grab a beer."

"Hey man, good to see you here," Roger replied warmly as they sat down inside and cracked open a pair of cold ones. "We pulled in an hour ago. Just cut my team loose."

"That's great. Listen, I've heard from a friend you've been pretty active lately, so I was hoping to see you here because I may have some business for you."

"To business and ten-way!" Roger said, holding his beer up for a toast, and to give him time to digest what he just heard—something odd, something a bit out of sync in Logan, something he couldn't quite put his finger on.

"We have a trip going down soon," Logan said. "Think you might be interested in working it?"

"What's cooking?"

"Colombia, I hope. Last trip fell through. We had some problems."

"Like what?"

"Had to deadhead back," Logan replied, "When we got there, no product. Pissed me off! At least they had someone meet us with fuel, or we would've had to leave the plane."

Roger was surprised to hear that a group with Logan's rumored experience and connections would have the kind of trouble that usually happened only to amateurs.

"How did that happen?" he asked, without revealing how fishy this was all starting to sound. Logan's eyes didn't hold the scammer's conspiratorial sparkle, he didn't seem to want to make eye contact, and he looked uncomfortable.

"Well, from what I understand, our main man got popped for not paying the army. We always sent the money down, but apparently he was pocketing it and apparently the Major nabbed him. We haven't heard from him since—I think one of his underlings screwed everything up."

"That really sucks," said Roger sympathetically, but inside he was debating whether Logan was acting like this because he was embarrassed, or his confidence was shaken—or something else.

"I was curious," Logan said suddenly, "if you had something going I could work into?"

*Something else!* Roger concluded. *Red flag time—first this guy wants me to turn a load for him, and now he wants to work on one of mine.* Roger still didn't know for sure what was up, but he knew one thing for sure.

"Things have been pretty dry on my end," he lied, then added truthfully for good measure: "Besides, I've been way more interested in winning ten-way. But who knows? Nationals'll be over in a week, so I'll ask around then to see if something's happening, and in the meantime, keep me up on Colombia."

With that, Roger drained his beer and left, so paranoid about the encounter that he headed straight to his motorhome to think things over—where he discovered that the people he'd been looking for had already found him. Several backslaps, bear hugs and fresh beers later, they got down to business, starting with Logan.

"Watch out for him, man," said Ron after Roger had recounted their meeting. "He got popped about a month ago. Saw his plane on the news, but they never IDed the people, then suddenly the story disappears with no record of arrest or court hearings."

"One of my friends," Jim added, "told me he tried to introduce some Fed-lookin' guy as his 'cousin'."

"So for now I think we should just assume old Logan crossed to the dark side and steer clear of him. Glad to hear your antennas were working."

"Amen," added Jim.

"Thanks," said Roger, "me too, and along those same lines, this place is a bit too busy to talk about the stuff we mentioned on the phone, so why don't we get together tonight at your hotel?"

"Room three-four-eight," Ron said, and both New Yorkers stood up to go. "Nine p.m. work?"

Roger nodded.

Later that night, the team and its supporters met for dinner at a local restaurant. Roger liked getting the team together as often as possible for meetings and meals to keep up the team spirit and communications. Food and drink seemed especially to help the atmosphere by making it seem to be more fun than obligation.

"Now, listen," Roger said after the appetizers were about half gone. "This is competition. This is where the weak are separated from the strong, so let's be strong. This is also not a time where we try 'new' things. We stick with what we know because that is how we practiced."

"Yeah, and let's make sure," Kimmers added, "we keep our lines of communication open about anything that's happening in the line-up, exit or freefall."

"And one last thing," Roger said. "You can do what you want, but I highly recommend that to go out there and be at our best to perform, we need to lay low during competition. Keep cool around others, and get enough sleep."

"Aw, man!" cried Tommy.

"Kong, that goes for you too!" laughed Dave, as everyone left the table and went their separate ways. Only Ardis lingered.

"I'm not sure I'll sleep much even if I go to bed right now," she confided to Roger and Jeanie. "The anticipation is really buzzing me." Jeanie smiled at her warmly and Roger laid a hand on her arm.

"Noticing is the first step toward calming yourself," he said, "and remember that going to sleep's like going out the door—center yourself with some deep breaths and relax." Ardis smiled at the analogy.

"Interesting way to look at it," she said as she got up. "I'll give it a try. Thanks and see you in the morning."

Finally alone at the table, Roger turned to Jeanie.

"Thank you so much for being here to support me through all of this. It means so much to me."

"I know you've been restless," Jeanie said, "about the team, about Mr. Douglas, about the business. I just hope that you're making the right decisions out there. You don't want—"

"Hey, El Presidente!" came a sudden growling intrusion.

Roger turned to see Kong returning to the table, gesturing over his shoulder towards the lounge entrance at Kelly, the pretty girl from the registration office. Roger laughed.

"Go. Go do your thing," sighed Jeanie, resigned to yet another interruption.

"Sorry, honey," Roger said, and kissed her. "Team business."

Roger went into the bar with Kong and directly to the young lady's table.

"Mind if we join you, Kelly?" he asked.

"Sure, Roger," she said. Kong sat down and Roger introduced him, then excused himself to buy a round of drinks.

"Bring those two a screwdriver and a Long Island ice tea," Roger said to the waitress as he handed her a Grant, "and keep them coming until this is gone." Then he handed her a $10 tip and slid unnoticed out of the noisy bar to Ron's hotel.

He entered a room drenched in pot smoke, with MTV playing loudly on the television.

"You wouldn't believe the run we just finished," Ron said after they finished some small talk. "Everything had gone down like a cold beer. I had a tailwind going each way and scattered thunderstorms all the way from Colombia to the Texas coast. We broke the ADIZ below the oil rigs at sunrise and stayed there cruising about two eight zero following the contour of the land. The old Howard was singing and then Jim taps me on the shoulder and casually points out the window."

"Man, you should've seen his face!" said Jim as he exhaled a cloud of smoke and laughed.

"I look out and see the nose of a Phantom and the smiling face of some young National Guard kid," Ron continued. "Scared the shit out of me! He snapped the mask back on his face and suddenly two more Phantoms descended and stacked a formation above him. Then they broke off and each took a side on us!"

Jim shook his head in wonder as Ron took a hit off a joint.

"The guy first waved at me and dropped his gear," Ron continued. I waved back and shook my head 'no'—I wasn't gonna land!"

"He turned to me and said, 'I haven't flown three thousand miles to give up now,'" Jim interjected, "and then he dropped her down so low he was kicking up dust."

"I look over at the kid," Ron continued, "and he comes down with me. Then he gives me this big smile and flips his thumb up—he wants me to lead the formation up and over the trees. I think if he hadn't been smiling I would've shit. So I just keep going and about forty-five minutes later—"

"A long forty-five minutes later!" Ron added.

"The Phantoms form back up alongside of us, and the leader looks at me and points to himself and then the ground, and then each one fucking *salutes* us and then they roar off!"

"We spent the rest of the trip trying to guess what happened," Jim said, "and expecting them or some others to reappear. I think we ran them out of fuel down low like that, but it also seems like they liked us."

"Spooked the hell out of me, though!" said Ron, "so I made a couple of extra diversions as precaution and flew to the LZ paranoid as hell. I certainly would have felt a lot better if it was dark. Anyway, it went off without another hitch."

"Man, what a rush!" Roger exclaimed. "Don't you think they IDed you?"

"I taped on a set of fake tail numbers" said Jim, "but how many Howard 500s are flying anyway?"

"My baby never had such a good cleaning," Ron added. "We steamed the whole trip off the belly and shampooed every stitch of the interior. I just knew we would be getting a visit, but nothing happened. I can't help thinking the kid in the Phantom wanted us to get in and was just checking us out. I've heard stories that the military only cares about foreign invasion. As fast as we were going, we had to look like some type of fighter on radar. I hope we never know. I can tell you one thing for sure, we'll never go back to that unloading site again!"

Roger laughed and then they got down to new business.

"Belize? I heard that place is unorganized," Jim said after Roger briefed them on the situation there. "What about fuel? What about an airstrip? To lift a good load we gotta have at least forty-five clear."

"We got the green one-thirty octane we were pulling from Mexico."

"Now you're talking," Ron said. "That'll give us another thirty or forty horse."

"As for the strip," Roger continued, "there's a couple of places you'll be happy with." Ron and Jim grinned at each other.

"Figures," Ron said to Roger. "If anyone could get things coordinated there, I would have to say it would be you."

"So, when do we go?" asked Jim.

"Couple of months."

"Damn," Ron groaned. "We're ready to rock and roll."

"Sorry, don't have all the pieces yet," Roger explained. "Besides, this trip'll be one for the record books."

"Growing, packaging, hauling and selling a Three load of quality *sinsemilla*," Jim said admiringly. "Yeah, I should say so!"

"So it's cool," said Ron. "We were just hoping you're ready now because, well, you know *we're* ready!"

"Then can I count on you?"

"In a heartbeat!" they said in unison.

"One more piece of the puzzle done," Roger said as he shook both their hands to bind the agreement.

"Keep in touch, though, man," Ron said. "We might have something happen in front of yours. Nothing for sure. Since we lost our landing spot, we were thinking about doing a kickout. But hey, enough about that? How's that rookie team of yours gonna do?"

"Pretty impressive for rookies," said Roger.

"Rookies, my ass," laughed Jim. "Wish we could stay and watch, but we're outta here in the morning."

"What? And miss all the excitement?"

"Those Phantoms were enough excitement for a while," Ron chuckled. "We just came to see you and find out what's up."

"And what's up sounds fucking *epic*," Jim exclaimed. "Just thinking about it's excitement enough for me."

"So you go kick some ass up there for us," said Ron. "We'll be in touch."

Jeanie and the kids were already asleep when he got back to his room. He took a moment to savor the scene. Jeanie lay on her side, back to the door, breathing slowly and steadily, exhausted from the day. His daughter, not yet in pre-school, slept sprawled across the matching double bed next to the window and humming air conditioner, looking small, innocent and perfect with big blond curls framing her soft face. Roger quietly put down his keys and walked over to brush her cheek gently with his kiss, ashamed that the smell of pot might invade her sweet dreams. His son, just turned two, slept fitfully on a nest of blankets at the bottom of his portable playpen between the beds. He'd long since learned how to escape its confines, but it comforted Jeanie to put him there at night when away from home. Roger lay across his bed and fell asleep still dressed.

In another room, Piras plotted. Like Roger, he knew Ardis was not handling the pressure of the Nationals stage well and he worried that all their hard work would go down the tubes if she flailed in the air too, so he was taking steps to fix the situation he was certain would arise by doing the only thing that made sense to him—find somebody better and steadier. The solution now sat before him, a young, talented and currently unattached skydiver named Michigan.

"So what's going on?" Michigan asked as they each nursed a cold one. "Rumor is you have all ten."

"Yes, yes we do," Piras said, "but there's this girl on the team and, well, she could make it or break it for us."

"Has it always been that way with her? I hear you guys are pulling some really good times."

"We are, and she's been solid all summer, but she's been all tensed up since we got here. We'll see how the practice jumps go, but I think I already know—and here's the thing: If everyone's solid, we can *win*, and I know you could replace her without skipping a beat, and we could at least add you as our alternate."

"What does Roger think about all this?"

"Haven't spoken to him yet—wanted to see if you were interested first, then feel it out with some of the guys before I went to Roger and the rest of the team."

"You really think the gold's in reach, huh?"

"I'm feeling pretty good about this team. I just have my doubts about Ardis."

"I'd be up for playing for a gold medal."

"So you're in?"

"Yeah, man. If Roger and the team agree, I'm in."

When the Freak Brothers began dirt diving next to Sugar Alpha the next morning at 7 a.m., they discovered that Paul had stenciled "Freak Brother Express" in large black letters above the plane's door. The gesture helped boost their pride and even their confidence as they boarded for their first on-site jump, but true to Piras's expectations, Ardis flailed. Roger shrugged it off as pre-competition nervousness. When it happened again on the second jump, only worse, Roger walked in with her from the landing area.

"Something bothering you?" he asked gently.

"No," she said, "I just choked."

Roger put his arm around her shoulders, and smiled supportively.

"Ardis, I have faith in you, so have faith in yourself. You just gotta go out there and believe you can do it."

"I don't know what's going on up there, Roger. Really I don't."

"It's okay. Don't let all this hype get to you. Shake it off and just do the same thing you've done all summer—kick ass up there, girl and don't let today get the best of you!"

"I'll do my best."

But she didn't. On the last practice jump of the day, she flailed on the ride to altitude, her confidence faltering so much she couldn't bring herself to even look out the door, then followed that with her worst jump of the summer. Piras had been right, but he kept quiet and let the team's concern reveal itself at their post-practice meeting, which took place in a circle of lawn chairs between the team motor homes.

"There's no doubt things could have gone better," Roger said, setting the tone, "but there's nothing to worry about. That's what practice is for. It's always a little difficult getting adjusted to a new environment; tomorrow's another day. Don't forget, we want to do our best jumping during the meet, not in practice. The best dive is reserved for the last dive, right?"

The Freak Brothers nodded, though not with a lot of enthusiasm.

"And the most important thing is to not freak out and start making a bunch of changes," added Dave. "Stay with what we know."

The nods now were more emphatic in their agreement.

"If Roger's not worried, neither am I," said Barboni, "and we all coulda done better today, not just one or two of us." Kimmers jumped on that remark and looked pointedly at Ardis.

"And that means you, girlfriend," he said warm, his eyes twinkling. "Don't feel bad about today because, you know what, you helped me by taking the heat. I mean, I was afraid *I'd* be the one to screw up!"

"So was I," said Dave.

"Me too," rumbled Piras.

"Man, we sure got those other teams fooled now!" Tommy chirped, and the dour mood was broken—the Freak Brother vibe was in full flower again—well, almost.

Piras smiled to hide his true feelings—he no longer had any confidence in Ardis and thought Roger's idea that she'd be the first woman to win a gold medal in 10-way was a pipe dream that would cost all of them the win. But he knew better than to buck the team mood at the moment.

The next day, the team made two more sub-par practice jumps before breaking for lunch. Ardis had done better, but she was still not up to speed and her confidence remained fragile.

During the break, the event organizers called all team captains to a meeting, so Piras seized that moment to start politicking with the more experienced and respected teammates. When they agreed with his concerns and proposed solution, he invited the whole team to Roger's motor home to talk about it.

"Ardis, I'm sure you understand why we called this meeting," Piras began. "Clearly, our inconsistency has put our competitiveness into doubt."

"Nice way to put it," she said glumly, then looked steadily at her teammates, "but he's right. I'm sorry, guys. I'm just not feeling it, and it's screwing up the team."

"You understand then," said Jeff in a compassionate whisper, "that we need to make a decision now." He glanced at Piras, who nodded his thanks for the assist.

"Yeah," she said in a small voice, and hung her head, "I do."

Every other team member took a deep breath; it was time to start the execution.

Then Roger walked in, smiling and holding more competition paperwork, and wearing a newly-issued wide-brimmed blue and white hat with the word "Captain" on it. But the smile died as he looked at

Ardis and instantly knew what was going on. He wondered who the ringleader was, so he ended that speculation with a question.

"Anyone care to fill me in on what's going on?"

Everyone looked at Piras, including Roger, who waited patiently to hear what he had to say.

"We all know practice hasn't gone well," added Kong, "and we all agree something should be done—and now that you're back, Ardis wants to address the team." Roger nodded and sat down, surprised not at what was happening but that Piras was leading. He took off his sunglasses.

"You all know that I'm one hundred percent behind the team," Ardis said softly, "and would do whatever it takes to see us win—and after the last couple of jumps, I don't think I can handle the pressure." She bowed her head, wiped her tears, took a deep breath and went on. "We all know that there are more talented jumpers than me here looking for a team, guys who won't let the pressure get them, who can do a better job, so . . . for the good of the team . . . I . . . I am resigning, so Michigan can fill my slot."

Ardis handed her team hat to Roger, then stared at the floor and tried to wipe her tears, but they came too fast. Roger deliberately made eye contact with each member; everyone looked unhappy, uncomfortable, and unsure—except for Piras, who looked steadily at Roger, certain that he was right. Roger soaked it all up and then he took a deep breath, knowing the team's future depended on how well he did his job during the next three minutes.

"Well, Ardis," he started, "no one can doubt your loyalty to the team, or the sincerity of what you say, but as far as I'm concerned there isn't a more qualified person in the country, let me correct myself, the world, who can do a better job in your slot. To replace you now with anyone would be a disaster."

"But Roger," interrupted Piras, "we all talked it over and we all think she's right. We aren't gonna have a chance if—"

"*All?*" Roger challenged. "Do I or do I not count as part of this 'all' you're speaking about?"

"Well, of course you—"

"And I had no part in this so-called agreement, and as long as I'm the captain—"

"Enough with this diplomatic shit!" Piras spat. "We can't win with her, and she agrees—it was her decision to quit!"

The two Freak Brothers stared each other down for a long moment.

"I find it hard to imagine that she came up with this decision all by herself in the time that I've been gone," Roger said icily. "As far as I'm concerned, Ardis is as much a part of this effort as any of us."

"Forget it man, we came here to win," Piras shot back.

"Kong?" Roger asked sternly of his old friend. "Kimmers? Tommy? Dave? Anyone?" Torn between team loyalty and their desire for gold, they felt ashamed and looked towards the floor, refusing to look Roger in the eye.

Roger let the silence soak in, then calmly removed his new "Captain" hat and tossed it into Piras's lap.

"Well, if that's the way it's gonna be, and Ardis is no longer a part of this team, then I pass the captain's position to you. I'm resigning so I can jump with Ardis."

There was a collective gasp. Everyone knew that without Roger, the team had no chance for gold. Piras frowned and stared at the hat in his lap like it was a cobra. Ardis stared at it, too, in open-mouthed shock.

"Yeah," said Kimmers, his eyes going from dead to twinkling, "you know, we're a family as much as a team, and things wouldn't be right if it wasn't whole." He took off his team hat and tossed it in Piras's lap. "Hey Ardis, can I jump with you and Roger?"

Ardis's lower lip quivered at his gesture.

A moment later, six more hats landed on Piras's lap or in his face or fell on the floor at his feet. Only Jeff still wore his. Jeff looked at Piras with the same compassion in his eyes that he'd had earlier for Ardis in his voice.

"Every team I've ever jumped with were brothers," he said quietly, "and this team has been the strongest brotherhood I've ever felt until this meeting started." He paused and respectfully handed his own hat to Piras. "And now that it's ending, I feel that brotherhood again. Ardis, you need a diver?"

Piras sat buried in Freak Brothers hats, his plan in ruins, but his fierce team loyalty intact. He fished Roger's hat from the bottom of the pile and flipped it back to him.

"You're the captain and the team has spoken," he said firmly. "It's all or none and if you'll still have me, then let's get this done."

"Can't you fucking count?" Kong growled as he snatched his hat from the floor. "All or none means you too, dickhead."

The motor home exploded in laughter as foes became friends and family again. Everyone retrieved their hats and then Roger handed Ardis hers. Everyone quieted as she stuck it on her head and wiped her last tears away.

"Fuck all of you!" she said in true Freak Sister fashion. "I'm gonna leave you in the dirt, so you better get your act together. Like Barboni said yesterday, we all need to get better. There ain't gonna be no prisoners!"

The Freak Brothers were astonished for a moment by this hard-core outburst from their most genteel teammate, then delighted.

"Holy Jesus," T.J. laughed. "There ain't no keepin' her down now!"

Then they all converged on Ardis, kissing, hugging and backslapping her until she almost fell down. Only Piras stood back, uncertain, looking alone.

Ardis, of course, saw it, and dragged Piras into her arms.

"I love you man," she said loud enough for everyone to hear. "You did what you thought was best for the team."

"That's right," Roger said, "and now we're stronger for it, so thanks man!"

"That deserves a hymn!" Kimmers announced. Everyone nodded and raised their middle fingers to Piras.

"Hymn, hymn!" they howled. "*Fuck him!*"

Then they converged on Piras and repeated the group therapy, though with rougher hugs and backslaps and no kisses.

This time Roger held back, watching, satisfied as the team re-made itself before his eyes into an even stronger, more focused unit than it had been when they got here. Now he was more certain than ever: they really could win. He put his sunglasses back on.

"Ain't gonna be no prisoners," he heard Kong roar over the other voices. "We're gonna take 'em *out!*"

An hour later, the Freak Brothers boarded a DC-3 for their first practice jump since the meeting. Minutes later, Ardis performed as promised and burned into her position well before everyone else, wearing a fierce warrior face, eyes spitting fire as she focused on Roger's count. Her performance had put pressure on the others, and they'd turned in their best jump so far—and the fastest jump of the day.

Their accomplishment did not go unnoticed. Many other teams and observers has seen it, including Bob and the rest of Magic, who were amazed by what they saw through their binoculars. Bob was concerned enough that he found Roger afterward and asked if he could lurk their next jump.

"Team decision," Roger said. "Let me get back to you after debrief."

After repacking, debriefing and prepping for their last practice jump of the season, Roger brought up Bob's request. Several team members shifted uncomfortably, others looked thoughtful.

"What do *you* think?" Kimmers asked.

"I don't want to say no because it certainly seems like we got their attention," Roger said. "If we decline, they might see it as a lack of confidence and it'll boost their morale."

"So you think giving Bob a first-hand look at the rookies," said Dave, "might do the opposite?" Roger nodded, and several guys nodded with him, grinning wolfishly.

"Let him come," said Ardis quietly, then added more loudly, "but tell him to bring his sunglasses 'cause we're gonna be blazing!"

The team laughed and agreed, and Roger felt another piece fall into place. Not only could watching them in the air shake up Bob, the added pressure of having him along would be a great way to make this last training jump more intense and help them prove to themselves that they were ready for the upcoming battle.

"We're gonna take 'em out!" the team roared as they split up to ready.

When Roger stopped at the Magic camp and invited Bob along on his way to the plane, he could feel the team's cocky attitude and he saw Bob flash an evil grin at them as he shouldered his gear and followed Roger.

When they boarded, Roger turned a matter-of-fact gaze on his adversary.

"Don't push me on the exit," he instructed. "The tail of the line-up is fragile, so stay off my back and give us a couple of seconds, then don't enter until we're complete."

"Will do," Bob agreed and they shook hands. Roger knew there was no way Bob could follow him in the air, but he hoped to build some false confidence in his adversary and at the same time make it even harder for him to get to the formation.

On jump run, Roger took his place at the end of the lineup and felt Bob hugging his backpack despite his agreement not to—so with confidence in the team's performance and in his own, he decided to protect the exit by leaving space between him and Kong in case Bob tripped him accidentally or on purpose.

The team blasted out the door and the first nine completed an incredibly fast circle just as Roger docked, leaving Bob far behind.

Roger had counted to three when Bob crashed into the formation and blew it—and whether by accident or design, he had hit Kong directly, then spun off below everyone. Roger quickly scanned the carnage make sure everyone was conscious and okay, then watched Kong dive after Bob and, like a hawk swooping a rabbit, grab the Magic leader by his backpack, spin him around, and wrap his legs around Bob's head.

Kong squeezed Bob's head as they burned through opening altitude and the rest of the team deployed their parachutes until Bob bit Kong hard on his inner thigh. Kong screamed and released him. Bob pulled instantly; Kong deployed two seconds later.

Bob had opened high enough to fly his canopy back to his camp. Kong landed well short, much to Bob's advantage. Kong stripped off his gear and tore towards the Magic camp as soon as he landed. From the air, Roger saw Kong's equipment lying in a pile still partially inflated, so he landed between the Magic camp and his raging teammate.

"What the hell?" shouted Roger.

"I'm gonna kill him!"

"Gonna take on the whole team?"

"That asshole did it on purpose! We cranked one, and he tried to take *me* out."

"Relax, man, where's the team gonna be if you get yourself thrown in jail?"

Kong settled down and grimaced as he rubbed his leg.

"Bastard bit me."

"No kidding?" Roger chuckled. "Where?"

Kong peeled off his jumpsuit and they inspected the damage. On his thigh was the perfect imprint of Bob's teeth and a trickle of blood. Roger knew Kong was getting mad again.

"C'mon, let's get your gear and get packed up." Roger ordered.

T.J. met them back at team area, grinning from ear to ear.

"Man, you scared the shit out of him!" he exulted. "He's locked in his motor home looking out the window. What the hell happened?"

"Look!" Kong said and showed T.J. the bite mark on his thigh. Kong was still raging and Roger knew he could infect the team with his mood, so he had to stop Kong cold to keep the Freak Brother vibe intact. He stepped between Kong and T.J. and eyed his friend sternly as several other teammates gathered around.

"In order to get you to forget this and get it behind you," he said, "we're marching over there to make peace." Kong's eyes bulged in shock.

"Are you kidding? He bit me and wrecked our jump, so now I'm gonna wreck him!" With that he went in his camper. When he came out a moment later, he was wearing his shoulder holster and jacking a round into the chamber of his .45. Then he put it into the holster and grinned fiercely at Roger.

"Okay, let's go," he rumbled.

"Well, that certainly looks silly!" Ardis giggled. "Could you please get your act together?"

His teammate's giggle bit Kong harder than Bob had. His rage evaporated.

"At least let me scare him," he almost whimpered to her.

"You've scared him enough for one day," she said gently but firmly.

"Here, wear this," Jeff threw an Army field jacket at Kong to cover his hardware, then Roger and Kong walked off through the maze of campsites, Ardis trailing. The team filtered in several directions so they could watch Magic's humiliation without pressing the issue by being too close.

When Roger, Kong and Ardis got to the Magic camp, they met team member Alan outside Bob's motorhome. He looked quizzically at Kong, who looked odd wearing a heavy jacket in the Oklahoma heat.

"We came to make peace," Roger said, Kong next to him, Ardis discreetly behind.

Alan's eyebrows arched, but without hesitation he knocked on the motorhome door and went inside. Moments later, Bob emerged cautiously, keeping his eyes locked on Kong.

"Hey, I'm sorry," Bob blurted out earnestly. "I didn't mean to hit it like that but you guys were falling much slower than I'm used to, I just couldn't stop." Roger extended his hand.

"Apology accepted," he said, and they shook hands. Kong still glared.

"I'll give you a pass for the moment and trust Roger's judgment, but you got some more persuading to do for me." Roger smiled inwardly at Kong's natural flair for keeping people off balance with his fierceness.

"I guess the next thing is for you to apologize to the team," Roger said, moving the discussion along. Bob hesitated.

"But you better get moving while I'm still willing to accept it," added Kong. He turned his back on Bob and stalked away, the bulge under his jacket showing clearly. Ardis saw Bob's eyes widen as he noticed it and stepped close to him.

"Thanks, Bob," she said kindly. "It's best not to let him stew about it."

She smiled sweetly and then, with Roger alongside, followed after Kong. When they were out of Magic earshot, Roger looked approvingly at his genteel teammate.

"That's the best good cop-bad cop routine I've seen in a long time."

Ardis winked and gave him a Kong-like snarl.

"No prisoners," she said quietly.

Bob's apology to the team was formal, gracious and even good-humored and ended with him wishing them luck in the morning's competition. Bob departed to approving nods and as Roger watched him walk away, he knew he'd made multiple good decisions in how he'd handled the whole affair. His own confidence rose too; after all the bad decisions he'd been making lately, it seemed as if he had his mojo back.

At seven the following morning, the judges drew the jump order and the Freak Brothers were delighted: they were first. They eagerly headed off for round one, where they were joined on the tarmac by three other teams. As first to exit, they boarded last and sat near the door, then lounged silently as the DC-3 climbed toward the 8,000-foot exit altitude, though Roger could see competition jitters infecting even his most experienced teammates. He felt it himself, and it was a feeling he loved. He smiled at his teammates, then nodded at Kong to commence their psychological warfare routine.

They started making eye contact with everyone around them, flashing relaxed, friendly, confident smiles that contrasted sharply with the many inwardly-focused faces around them, some who clearly struggled with their composure.

When they finished that, Roger glanced at his altimeter and, with the whole team's eyes on him, gave a head nod. Per the well-established routine they had sharpened all summer, they all stood simultaneously. This unexpected team discipline caught the eye of the other competitors, just as it was designed to do. The Freak Brothers formed their circle of linked thumbs, and awaited Roger's final words to psych them up. Unnoticed behind them, the other teams straggled to their feet to get ready too.

"Just another skydive," he said. "Don't over amp. Go slow. Be smooth. All we want to do is stay in it. *We* set the pace for the others to beat. *We* put the pressure on them. *We* are ready. *We* earned the right to perform respectably. Now let's go out there and show them who we are. God be with us."

With that, their fists all squeezed tighter and they sang out the exit count in perfect rhythm, then took their places in line as they had so many times before. Roger looked toward the cockpit and saw the copilot hold up a bright red dustpan—the "stand-by" signal.

"Stand by!" he shouted to the team.

The co-pilot flipped the dustpan; the other side displayed two black "Xs."

"Exit, Exit, Exit!" chanted the other teams. The signal charged each Freak Brother with a burst of adrenaline. The adrenaline gave them tunnel vision, and their bodies automatically followed the familiar routine. As Video Bob took his position outside the aircraft door, they tightened up, belly to back across the fuselage.

Next, Roger slapped Kong's shoulder.

"Hot! roared Kong.

"Ready!" roared Ardis.

". . . GO!" sang the Freak Brothers and in one second they vanished out the door. As Roger dove out after them, the other teams rushed over to watch. They saw a smooth dive, though not their fastest.

With whoops of excitement, the Freak Brothers descended under canopy as the DC-3 circled around for another pass to drop the next team. Friends and family greeted them on the ground with cheers and hugs.

At camp, Roger felt relieved to get past the first round. With five more jumps to go, Roger needed to bring the team back down a bit. He called them into the motorhome to debrief.

"Magic's on jump run!" someone shouted from outside before he could start—and several team members started to leave to watch.

"Hey, let's finish our debriefing," Roger said, stopping them cold. "Let them take care of themselves. We've got five more rounds to concentrate on before what they do makes any difference." The team settled back into their places, but their minds were eight thousand feet above no matter what Roger said.

In the plane, Magic burst out into its victory chant, then lined up and rolled out the door. Things went wrong right away. Several team members were sucked into the vortex that follows each skydiver as they blast through the air at more than 100 miles per hour and the formation funneled. The Californians found themselves in a scrambled mess that doubled their normal build time—and after their first round of competition, Magic's reign as the country's undisputed 10-way speed star champions had already ended.

"Funneled!" shouted the helpful outside voice, and Roger heard the Freak Brothers family cheering Magic's agony.

"Okay," he conceded. "We're not gonna be able to concentrate until we know for sure. Let's go!"

With the efficiency of a team well rehearsed in rapid exits, they flew out the motorhome door in time to see the team open their parachutes—and hear silence instead of the screams of delight. They landed near their team area and walked to their camp with their heads hanging.

Except for two, who landed near the Freak Brothers camp and walked over to them.

"We want to apologize for the things that were said and the hard feelings between our teams," said one.

"It did not reflect all of Magic," said the other. "We had no part of it. You guys are real good, and we're rooting for you all to win."

The Freak Brothers appreciated this display of class and everyone exchanged handshakes and pledged friendship. Then the Magic men began the long walk back to their camp, their heads hanging low now, too.

"One down, several more to go," Kimmers said quietly, and the rest of the team nodded. They knew that Magic might be out of it, but the quest for gold had just started.

As each round continued, the race for victory tightened until only three teams remained as medal contenders: "Visions," another well-respected team from California; the "Beerhunters," also posting great scores; and the Freak Brothers.

As expected after their first-round funnel, Magic was out of it; their new exit technique had failed. The "podium" teams, however, were turning faster times each round, and pushing each other closer to the edge of the envelope. The Freak Brothers remained in the lead, and the pressure that came with it concerned Roger.

"Don't let the fact we're in first change our battle plan," he told the team during their fifth jump debrief. "It still takes six dives to win, and we still have one to go. Now is the time to go slow and take advantage of the slight lead we hold. Don't make any mistakes. The reason we're still in the running is because we've just gone up and done *our* skydive every time. Let's not beat ourselves!"

Visions was a few seconds back, almost assured of bronze, and not likely to win either gold or silver. The Beer Hunters, a pick-up team that included most of Synergy's former members as well as a few former world champions, trailed by a bit more than one second. The Freak Brothers just needed a clean, smooth final round to win. The Beer Hunters needed a record time to overtake them—or they needed the Freak Brothers to choke. And lurking in the minds of both teams was the fact that a minor mistake could drop either team out of gold contention clear down to third.

As the Freak Brothers anxiously awaited the call for their final jump, the judges postponed the meet due to a strong haze that would have obscured their view of the action from the ground. This left the teams to stew overnight and broke their jumping rhythm.

Roger sat alone with his wife while his kids stayed at their hotel room with a babysitter from town. He knew he could always bounce his ideas off his wife or just share his feelings. Just as she had a knack for comforting nervous students, she had a knack for building Roger's confidence, too.

"Ah, Jeanie. Why couldn't we get this over with today? All the momentum is with us. This could really hurt."

"Yes, you're frustrated," honey," she said firmly, "but so are the other teams. They have to deal with this too, so don't you even *think* about losing your drive here. It's not just the team that's come this far and gotten so close. You got a whole family of people who are a part of this effort, wives and girlfriends and the whole drop zone. It's been months of preparation and sacrifice for us too! We keep the whole show running while you guys are off practicing each weekend. What's another day?"

Roger sighed and grinned at his wife.

"I'll tell you, sweetheart, just because you don't say much doesn't mean you're not a badass supporter. I know you put in a lot more effort than words and there's never a day that I don't remember it and appreciate it."

"Really," she said, a touch of skepticism coloring her tone.

Really," he said, and pulled her close and embraced her tightly. Closing his eyes, he let the tremendous load on his mind escape for a moment and for a moment there were no thoughts of Mickey's status, the boys in Belize, Hanoi, the Blairsville investigation, the crash on Grand Bahama, the missing pieces yet to be resolved with Ron and Jim and most of all, the temporary delay in the 10-way championship. At that moment, there was just Jeanie and her loving touch easing his pain and reenergizing him for the fight.

He felt the tension leave his body and mind, and the timeless moment ended the instant he regained his clarity. He released his hold on Jeanie and walked out of the motorhome and called a team meeting.

"We're scheduled for seven a.m. takeoff," he said after they'd assembled in their lawn-chair circle. There was some grumbling but not much, and Roger waited patiently for it to dissipate.

"The judges made it clear that if anyone's late, it's a forfeit," he continued, "so I have three things to ask of the team. First, don't get arrested! Second, get some sleep, and make sure everyone staying in a hotel has a ride to the DZ. I want no one coming in alone. Third, be sober and as ready as you've ever been in your life and tomorrow we win gold."

He stuck out a fist with thumb extended and they did a pre-jump circle. Roger nodded at Kong.

"Hot!" roared Kong.

"Ready!" roared Ardis.

". . . GO!" roared the Freak Brothers, and with that they went their separate ways, both anxious and confident about what the morning would bring.

101

That night before Roger turned in, he paid a visit to Dave. His question was answered when the door opened to reveal Mike sitting with Dave, both grinning broadly.

"Found a sweet spot, man," Mike said by way of greeting.

"All right, I could use some good news."

"Here's some more," Dave said. "Mickey left a message telling me to say 'Hi,' and he'll see you soon."

Roger smiled at the news and gave both men their customary slapping handshake, all of them relieved to know that Mickey and Billy had completed a successful run.

"And don't forget, man," Dave reminded Roger, "you're the one who said things were turning for the better."

"So what do you think'll happen tomorrow?" Mike asked.

"We're gonna take 'em *out!*" Roger said fiercely.

At seven the next morning, the three top contending teams boarded the plane ahead of a team that would place no higher than fourth no matter how well it did, but which could still plummet in the rankings if they flailed. So each of the contenders high-fived them as they passed by and climbed aboard, offering encouragement and kind words as they went. After they got aboard, they had kind words and good vibes for each other too. They had all been humbled by Magic's surprise downfall, and their respect for each other had increased as their times had dropped.

The ride to altitude was quiet and calm. Right before jump run, the Freak Brothers all stood and created their traditional circle and waited for Roger's final pep talk.

"One more jump," Roger said, "one more where we take our time. No one rushes except the last person to enter. Everyone else lays a perfect target. We're in the lead because we've made the fewest and smallest mistakes, so let's keep it that way, and let me be the one to stop the clock. And whatever happens, I've never been more proud of any team as I am of you." As he spoke, he could read the sincere smiles of confidence and pride they shared. The pressure grew steadily in the circle of hands as they built up for the final performance. Roger knew in his heart they were ready. "Now let's show the world who we are and *give them one to remember.*"

They aggressively chanted their exit count and broke the circle. They formed their line, the co-pilot signaled Roger and Roger tapped Kong.

"Hot!" roared Kong.

"Ready!" roared Ardis.

". . . GO!" roared the team and a second later they vanished out the door.

Roger hit the air with an intense natural high and stretched out bigger than he ever had before. He caught all the energy he could from the prop blast, then rotated his body in line with the forming circle. As he caught sight of the others, he saw each member converging rapidly from every direction—and realized he was closer to the formation than he'd ever been before and was closing much too fast. He instantly extended his arms and legs and cupped as much air as he could with his body to slow down before he smashed into the star. Out of the corner of his eyes, Roger saw Jeff and Kong close in on each side and an eyeblink later he docked, completing the fastest star the Freak Brothers had ever made. An emotional wave went through the group and excitement built as Roger counted off three seconds in what seemed to be slow motion. When Roger hit five just to make sure, they all kicked their legs for joy and screamed so loudly they could actually hear each other in freefall. Their victory seemed assured.

After they opened, they flew their canopies in a pre-planned formation, each jumper landing in turn in the pea gravel target, emphasizing for everyone the obvious pride they had in their achievement.

Alerted ahead of time, ABC's *Wide World of Sports* filmed the team's reactions as supporters swarmed the landing area. In the frenzy of congratulations, one of Roger's staunchest allies from Connecticut poured a magnum of Dom Perignon over his head on national television. As Roger cleared the bubbly from his eyes, he saw Jeanie standing a few feet away so, grinning from ear to ear, they ran to each other and embraced.

For a few seconds, Roger stood oblivious to the hysteria surrounding them. The moment lasted only a few seconds, but he knew the feeling would last forever—and the network got its money shot.

The ecstatic team worked its way back to camp, loudly recalling the precious moments of the jump.

"Man you should have seen it!" glowed Kimmers. "It was magical man! Magical!"

"Did you see Roger, man?" enthused Kong, grinning for once instead of growling. "He came in like a fucking *rocket*! I thought he was gonna take *us* out!"

"I can't believe that skydive!" Tommy shouted, goose bumps pimpling his skin. "It was the best ever!"

"This is the best team ever!" Ardis mumbled, barely able to speak, her eyes spraying a shower of tears.

Then came the familiar overhead sound of a DC-3 on jump run, and the crowd quieted as everyone looked skyward or headed to a nearby tent with TV monitors. The Beer Hunters were next, the only team with even an outside chance to spoil the Freak Brothers victory party.

In the plane, the Beer Hunters had watched the Freak Brothers' exceptional jump and knew they had to go all out to win. They psyched themselves up, tapped into their hidden reserves, and blasted out the door.

In the tent watching TV or outside watching the sky, supporters for both teams waited intently. Roger held a half-uncorked bottle of champagne while waiting for this jump to confirm their victory. He heard the judges start the clock the instant the team appeared onscreen.

With amazing speed, the Beer Hunters formed their star with just one left to dock. As the spectators sat on the edge of their seats, the final man sailed into the picture and hit the formation with tremendous speed, deforming the circle almost to the point of tearing it apart.

"Seven-point-five seconds!" someone called out as, somehow, the jumpers absorbed the impact and kept the star together as their man broke into the circle to complete it and hold it for the required time before breaking off and tracking away.

Beer Hunter supporters erupted into the same frenzy Roger's team had experienced just a few minutes ago. If anybody had doubted that these people weren't poised, veteran competitors, no one doubted now.

Unsure of the exact time, Roger pushed the cork farther into the champagne bottle with his people and waited quietly, wondering if the dream they held in their hands had just slipped away, and their summer of joy shattered before their eyes. They had witnessed an awesome performance, but had that spectator shout of "7.5 seconds" been an accurate call by a disinterested party or been wishful thinking by a partisan?

Roger looked over his team and their supporters and saw the pain on their faces that he felt in his soul.

"Hey, keep your chins up," he said. "We got much to be proud of and nothing to be ashamed of. We performed to the best of our ability and peaked on our last jump. We followed our plan perfectly."

"They sure did fucking crank one, though," rumbled Kong.

"That's right, but it ain't over yet! They had to do more than crank one to beat us, though—they had to be *blazing*! So I'm going to the scoreboard to wait for the posting and I'm taking the champagne with me. If any of you want to drink it with me when we get the good news, then come on."

Every Freak Brother wanted to drink it with him, so, united, they walked over to the small office, guessing at all the possible outcomes.

"Well, second place wouldn't be that bad," Jeff said out loud to himself.

"Are you *kidding*?" chided Piras. "Second place means you're the first place losers!"

"And it's like Roger said," Tommy added. "It ain't over yet."

"Okay, okay," said Jeff. "We concede nothing until the final results are in!"

Roger smiled at the banter. He knew the unofficial times meant nothing, but he also knew the meet was close, and he knew that the Beer Hunters had in fact cranked one. All that remained was to see if they'd blazed their way to victory.

Shortly after they arrived at the scoreboard, they watched their official score get posted—8.3 seconds, confirming what they'd all felt in the sky; their last jump had been their fastest jump ever and the fastest jump of the competition.

"Roger was right," shouted Piras. "We peaked on our last jump!"

The team regained some enthusiasm and high-fived each other for their final showing, all of them also hoping that it would be enough. Roger felt better, too, and asked someone to calculate what time the other team needed to beat them.

"They need 7.6 or better to win," said Paul. "If it's 7.7, we tie."

Relieved to know it would indeed take a blazing, record-shattering jump to beat them, Roger still fretted about the unofficial 7.5-second call, and also wondered when the judges would credit the last jumper's entry into the formation. *Would they count as they should, from the moment the jumper broke grips and completed the circle—or call it from the moment of impact?*

Roger watched a runner for the Beer Hunters take off to report the Freak Brothers' record time. Soon, the rival members themselves arrived and joined the waiting crowd, some of them carrying champagne, too. The teams respectfully congratulated each other, but both wanted so badly to win that they couldn't bear to mingle.

Roger looked around. One team would leave the tent walking on air; the other would leave crushed. Some of his closest friends would celebrate for days; some of his other close friends would cry in their beer for weeks. He already knew the agony of defeat. He wanted this time to feel the thrill of victory.

He saw the scorekeeper appear, working her way through the traffic with a big smile to post the last time of the meet on the board. Kong was the first to see it.

"Seven-point-*nine!*" he bellowed, and Roger felt his hand reaching for the champagne cork even as his mind recalculated the number one more time just to make sure—and it came out the same as before.

"We won!" screamed Piras in Roger's ear as he popped the champagne cork and then the noise became so deafening he could no longer hear individual voices.

Some moments later, the Beer Hunters captain approached Roger and congratulated him with the dignity of a real gentleman. He thanked Roger for the fine competition and sadly departed. Then it really hit Roger; his dream of a lifetime had been realized; they had won the meet. Then he smiled and looked for the most genteel member of the Freak Brothers. Ardis would have her gold medal.

That night, scores of people gathered for the awards ceremony under a big circus tent. Banquet tables and folding chairs filled the area. A stage occupied one end, a podium front and center on it. The meet director and a few judges lined up along the front of the stage preparing for the ceremony. Roger sat with Jeanie and his team, savoring it all and enjoying the happiness of his friends and teammates far more than winning it for himself.

The chief judge took the stage with microphone in hand.

"First, we'd like to thank everyone for attending," she said, and the room started quieting. She waited a few moments and then went on. "The teams showed some real competition, and it was a pleasure and exciting to judge. So, without further adieu, let's get on with the awards ceremony. In third place, Visions!"

The Californians walked up on the stage and took the third-place podium step. One by one, the judges placed a bronze medal around the neck of each team member. The crowd cheered after the final medal placement, and the chief judge waited patiently until they quieted again.

"In second place, and owners of a new U.S. Nationals record for fastest ten-way star, the Beer Hunters!" The crowd, which had witnessed the fastest-ever ten-way speed star in competition, let loose a wild cheer. "In case you haven't heard," the chief judge continued with a smile, their time was seven-point-nine seconds, almost half a second faster than the old record."

The Beer Hunters smiled and casually took the second-place podium step. Although they hadn't won, they glowed with pride in setting a new record.

When the judges finished placing the silver medals around the team's necks, there was another sustained round of cheers and applause, then the chief judge grinned at the crowd.

"And now, the moment we've all been waiting for. In first place, and our new national ten-way champions, the Freak Brothers!"

Everyone jumped to their feet and cheered in appreciation of the achievement they had all seen. The Freak Brothers had a few old hands but were in fact comprised of mostly rookie skydivers, especially when compared to the jump numbers and meet experience on the teams they had just challenged and beaten. On top of that, they were from the Midwest and they had whipped the vaunted Californians at their own event.

As soon as the crowd's screams and whistles dissipated and all the gold medals were handed out, the chief judge made a final announcement.

"As most of you already know, the Freak Brothers briefly held the Nationals record for the fastest star—eight-point-three seconds, a record that lasted all of six minutes, if I recall correctly." Cheers and laughter interrupted her for a moment, then she continued. "But what not all of you may know is that one member of the Freak Brothers also made history today, so we would like to specifically recognize Ardis for being the first woman to win a gold medal in ten-way speed star competition."

More cheers and whistles and howls of delight greeted Ardis as she stepped down from the first-place podium step and stood alone at the front of the stage as the chief judge presented her with a beautiful flower arrangement. Wearing a summer dress, with her hair down and sporting a touch of makeup, Ardis looked more like the cute girl next door than a world class skydiver, and she played that part too, alternately crying and laughing in joy at the fun and wonder of it all. Then she led the three teams off the stage in a final shower of applause.

The team started partying in earnest, and Roger wanted so much to join in and lose himself for the night, but his mind had already shifted to Belize. Mickey was back, Ron and Jim were committed, and it was time to move *onward*. The dream-of-a-lifetime victory of that day already seemed like ancient history.

# CHAPTER EIGHT

## BILLY "BOB"

Before Roger left Oklahoma, he held a business meeting in his hotel room with Dave and Mike. Mike told him of the "sweet spot" outside the town of Enid, and Roger told them to scout the surrounding area and learn the movements of the locals, then get maps and find back road access in and out of the location.

"I won't have time to see the place myself, so lay out your strategy of entering and exiting with a load and devise an alternate plan," he said. "When you finish that, Mickey wants you guys to go to Birmingham and get some birth certificates. We're gonna need new IDs for the gig. Mickey and I need at least two and pick out some for yourselves. If it feels right, get extras. You've done this for Mickey before, right, Dave?"

"Yeah, it's a piece of cake," Dave nodded. "Should take less than a week." Mike looked puzzled. "It's easy, man." Dave went on. "We go to the library and look through the micro-fiche for newspapers around the time we were born. Find the obituaries, get some names that match our looks of kids who died within a year of birth. Pick the ones that list all the information on surviving relatives, like mother's maiden name, place of birth, that sort of thing. Filter out the best one and memorize all the data, then go to the Department of Health and ask for the birth certificates. Sometimes they quiz you a little to see if you're the person you're asking for, but last time, I gave them enough info they skipped the twenty questions and gave them to me straight up."

"Why Birmingham?" Mike wanted to know.

"I don't know," Dave shrugged. "I guess some guy turned Mickey on to it, and that's where he sent me. You could do it anywhere but this place is so cool. Last time I got four different ones in one day from the same lady!"

"The important thing," Roger interjected, "is to get the ground work done in the library. I worry about you spending too much time in a government building. If you get the chance, cool, but don't push it if it doesn't feel right. Once we have the info, we can get mail drops, and for five bucks a copy they'll mail them up."

"Why do we need so many?" Mike wondered.

"You can never have too many birth certificates," Roger answered. "I never use the same one twice. Some I use to build a full set of IDs, and that's all you need to get into Belize, Mexico or anywhere in the Caribbean. Others I call throwaways and use for immigration entries. In this business, the Feds don't catch you, you catch yourself. All that fancy TV stuff is BS. The DEA guys mostly just sit at their desks waiting for some police department to call with some guy spilling his guts, or they stumble across a sloppy operator—and leaving a paper trail is the worst kind of slop."

"Some people counterfeit them and say they work just as good because there are so many different kinds of birth certificates anyway," Dave went on, "but I like the idea of there being a record of the person actually existing somewhere. Once you have it, building the ID set's easy. Hell, one time I went to a swap meet, and some guy had a picture ID machine, so I got a bunch that matched the certificates, then used those bogus-looking things with the birth certificate and got a Florida driver's license. With that, everything else was cake."

"Amazing," Mike muttered, shaking his head at the ease of it all.

"Okay," said Roger, handing them each a stack of cash for expenses, "I'm not sure where I'll be. I got a lot of running around to do. If something comes up, leave a message on my service. In fact, leave one every day just to keep in touch. If it's something real important, bang one out to Mickey too."

The two men walked out of Roger's room, leaving him alone and, for the first time in months, with nothing to do. He flopped back on the bed and enjoyed it for five minutes, then grabbed his bag and closed the door behind him when he left.

"It's all good, buddy," Mickey said to Roger back in Illinois a couple of days later. "This trip went as smooth as the other one went rough. Actually, it went off quite well, considering."

"Quite well considering the nervous pilot, idiot Bushman and greedy Cookie Monster?" Roger grinned.

"I took some precautions after the last trip and everything went routine. Nothing happened out of the ordinary."

"I expected nothing less from you," Roger said. "Still, it's a relief and definitely good news after all the drama of the last few weeks."

"Good thing you won the meet or I wouldn't be speaking to you now." They laughed comfortably together. "Seriously," Mickey added, "congrats on winning the gold, buddy. Helluva'n accomplishment."

"Thanks, man, it was something, alright and as it turned out, the biggest challenge of the week was keeping Kong from killing somebody."

"So it was no different than any other week," Mickey deadpanned.

"True, except this time somebody took Kong out in freefall, then bit him on the leg."

"No way! Then what?"

"Well, let's just say it took a woman's touch to keep Kong's .45 in the holster, but nobody went to jail or the hospital so it was all good."

"Oh, man!" Mickey laughed. "What a trip—and everyone I run into says there's a whole new vibe out there now that somebody finally beat California's streak."

"Yeah, it was pretty special, so thanks for taking care of things while I did that."

Mickey leaned forward, all business again. "I found a broker who cashed us out of the plane, so we didn't have to worry about stashing it or me getting tempted to do another Jamaican run. Plus now we got a few more bucks towards the next one, so how about it—you ready to run Sugar Alpha to B-ville?"

"Whoa, Nellie, we don't even own her yet," Roger protested.

"And I spoke to Blind Jeff about flying her," Mickey added, ignoring that little detail, "and he's hot to trot!"

Roger smiled inwardly. Roger knew Blind Jeff well. He'd worked with Hanoi and him on many trips and he knew that Jeff could fly anything from small singles to four-engine transports as long as he had on his Coke bottle-thick wire rim glasses. But Roger already had the pilots for Belize.

"Moving and stashing a plane the size of Sugar draws heat," Roger said, "and I had some reservations about using her after having it at the airport anyway, so I talked to the guys with the Howard 500. It can't haul as much, but it's lower profile."

"Yeah, I heard about that paint job," Mickey laughed. "Anyway, nothing's cast in stone with Jeff. I just ran the idea past him 'cause he has a lot of Three time."

"Buying Sugar from Paul without raising his suspicion might be tough, too," Roger added, "especially now that Nationals is over and Mr. D will be back up in a few weeks, but I got to admit it's a nice back up if something falls through."

"I also spoke to Terry," Mickey continued, "but he's too high and mighty to do a pot gig now that he has something going with the Colombians. They sent him to a Texas flying school, and he connected with some guy named Jotham King."

Roger shook his head unhappily.

"That's crazy, man, thinking about strangers for a load like this. Those are the guys the Feds love the best. How does he know this guy is cool?"

"Same Colombians sent him to the school too. Believe me, I know these guys," Mickey said defensively. "Won't be no funny business!"

"That's what you said about the Bushman," Roger snapped. Mickey looked hurt for a moment, then let it pass and continued his train of thought.

"Anyway, Jotham knows Tony, who did three Merlin trips into Norman's Cay in the Exumas for Joe Lehder. Then he did something stupid and they cut him out."

"Lucky he's still alive," Roger reflected. He'd known Tony since he was an egghead student at the University of Tampa, flying jumpers for Mickey on weekends. Mickey finally introduced him to smuggling, and he slowly became a monster; ballsy but talented. Roger respected Tony's piloting abilities. However, when Mickey kept expanding the group, Roger bowed out, and Mickey and Tony became partners. Tony flew, Mickey unloaded.

Then Tony met the Colombians and jumped the connection, cutting Mickey out of the loop and ruining their relationship. Roger had no doubt Tony now worked with some major players in the cocaine trade and made a great deal of money.

Mickey, on the other hand, was still importing marijuana, which suited Roger. He disliked the cocaine trade, even with its big profits, because the heat was higher and people in the business were nasty and violent. With them, getting busted was the least of your worries. It was a good way to end up dead.

Mickey thought Roger was pondering the deal, so he sighed and leaned forward.

"Look, man, I don't like sub-contracting the plane, but this is your deal, so what's it gonna take for this gig to put a smile on their faces?"

"Nothing firm yet," Roger answered. "I just said I'd make them happy. They think we can haul around five thousand pounds and carry fuel for fifteen hundred miles. I question if we can get that much in before we cube out because that happened on all the previous trips."

"I know some guys flying *sinsemilla* out of Mexico in a Lodestar at forty-five hundred a pop," Mickey said. "Pretty much the same size, so why not start with that and figure it?"

Mickey and Roger rounded down to an even four thousand pounds and did a projected cash flow to determine the bottom line. They smiled at the results.

"Okay," Roger said, "plenty of room for Ron and Jim's cut."

"Man," Mickey marveled, "can you imagine what a Three would do if this is what a couple of tons works out to?"

"Yeah, and with a Three we'd have lower expenses," Roger conceded, "and the extra weight would all be gravy, but these numbers are fine, and all we got to do is pitch and unload. Now, since the load is easier and smaller, we need to cut down on staff, for money of course but mainly for the exposure, so I'll get rid of Billy, and you dump the Bushman."

"Hey come on man," Mickey frowned, "I owe the guy!"

"I don't."

"He did a great job on the last one."

"Great, so now he's one for three. Listen, I'm not going to have Jim and Ron risk their asses with someone who doesn't have his shit together. How would you like it?"

"Hey man, I'll be running the ground crew."

"If it was just our gig, no problem, but it's not. I told you from the start that this will be a class act or nothing. I will not compromise it with *any* weak links. Isn't about friendship—this is business. I don't care how close you guys are."

Mickey chewed on his lip for a long moment, studying Roger's face, but the set of his long-time partner's jaw made it clear that there would be no negotiation on this point.

"Okay, then that's the way it'll be," Mickey sighed. "I'm not gonna argue with you."

"Good," Roger said in a clipped tone, "but listen, I don't want you going through this unhappy. We got to be on the same wavelength for this one." Mickey waved Roger off and smiled.

"No. No, man," he said, "I'm good, and I mean it. You're right. It's just gonna be hard to swing the ax, that's all. But I'll handle it. There'll be other things for him."

The two men smiled and shook hands.

While Roger and Mickey were planning the Belize run, Billy and the Cookie Monster had set up their own. They planned out their virgin run using Mickey's connection, Winston, and Mickey's cash that Cookie still had from their last load. Their thinking was that, since Mickey still owed them for the trip they just completed, they were entitled to the first money back.

"Besides," Cookie had said to Billy as they discussed it, "we'll replace what we spend after we get back and I'll give Mickey the runaround on his dough until then. Nobody'll ever find out."

They'd planned to use Mickey's plane, too—until he sold it, which threw a monkey wrench into the plan. Cookie was undeterred, though; he approached an older fellow he knew who owned a Cessna 210 and negotiated a deal that gave the owner a bigger than usual cut, conditional upon on a successful shipment. The pieces had fallen together quickly, so they were both jazzed and Billy quickly called Winston and scheduled a pickup for the following day.

Then they scrambled to meet the deadline without luxuries such as a back-up plan or radios, using everything they could from Mickey's playbook, including the same landing site. Only at the last minute did Billy realize that he hadn't thought of how to carry extra fuel for the six-passenger, single-engine plane.

"What are you talking about?" Cookie smirked. "More than enough for this run in the wing tanks, and every extra gallon costs us thousands in product!"

"Cooks, you gotta trust me on this," Billy pleaded, knowing from his first run with Roger how extra fuel was critical to success. "More dollars from extra product sounds great, but it doesn't mean shit if you splash because of weather, or a tail, anything that stretches out the run."

"You're overreacting, buddy," sneered Cookie. "This trip was cake before, why won't it be cake now?"

"Because you seriously never know what could happen out there!" Billy persisted. "Plus we're using a smaller plane. We gotta have extra fuel over extra product. That's my vote, or I don't fly."

"Christ, Mickey's cautiousness is rubbing off on you," Cookie muttered, but he paused and pondered the situation, then smiled at Billy.

"So, you uhhh, know how to put on this auxiliary tank?"

"Aw shit!" Billy exclaimed. "No, I don't." Cookie laughed out loud, but Billy had convinced him that extra fuel was a good idea, so he helped him jerry-rig an internal fuel tank using tools and a plastic fuel tank they had laying around. They sweated profusely and cursed much as they tightened everything down and tested it briefly to make sure it worked. A few hours later, Billy took off on his first operation as an entrepreneur, hands still sweating, knees still shaking until he was airborne. But he smiled as he soared into the blue and wiped his sweaty palms on his pants.

"Much better this time. Much better," he said out loud.

Billy had the last trip fresh in his mind, so making his way back to the mountainous road in Jamaica was easy. He recognized all the inbound landmarks, and he decided to leave the internal tank untouched to save the extra time it would take to refill it for the ride home.

The loading and refueling went routinely. Unfortunately, Billy had based his estimate on how much weight the plane could carry, not how much product would fit into it. Several hundred pounds still sat on the ground as Winston's crew pushed the last bale inside.

"Whatsa deeel, monn?" Winston asked, one eyebrow arched questioningly.

"Sorry man," he said. "I thought it would all fit."

"The way you talk, monn, I thought you have a bigger plane. Mickey, he always know exactly how much, monn."

"Well, uh—" Billy, stalled as he made his way back to the cockpit.

"You leave me here holding my dick with four hundred pounds, monn," Winston growled, his easygoing mood evaporating. "I am not so hoppy right now. In fact, I'm downright pissed you leaving me with so much extra risk."

"Oh yeah, I'm *real* sorry about that. I am," Billy fidgeted, "but I gotta get going. I mean, you said you had plenty, you said to keep on rolling, so we're *rolling*. I'll just come back tomorrow for another one and we work it out, right?" Billy backpedaled, zipping up his leather jacket.

"I'll remember *this* one, monn," Winston said, "and we shall see if there *is* a next time." Winston turned his back on him and walked away, hustling his crew to put the pot back in his van.

As he flew home, Billy recalculated their profits based on the eight hundred pounds he had aboard instead of the twelve hundred pounds they'd planned on, and the profits still fueled his imagination with thoughts of hot cars and hotter women. Then he snapped out of his daydream as a sense of foreboding intruded.

Nervously, he checked his watch every few minutes as time seemed to pass more slowly than he expected. Finally, he saw the haze of the Cuban coastline.

"Aw shit!" he screamed. "Fuck!" Seeing Cuba meant he'd made a significant navigational error. His knees began shaking and his palms started sweating as he remembered Mickey's MiG story and pictured fighters shooting him down, saw himself surviving the crash only to be eaten by sharks.

He shook his head to ward off these thoughts and dropped below radar coverage, leveled off at two hundred feet and watched whitecaps ripple beneath his wings. Rough water, he noted, but he was good to go now.

He worked his way east, undetected, through the Windward Passage and towards Bahamian waters. However, the distractions had sidetracked his fuel management procedures and, once clear of Cuba, he remembered to check his fuel, where he realized he'd almost exhausted his main tanks.

He reached beneath his seat and opened a valve on a black rubber hose, then rotated his fuel selector handle, relieved that he'd caught the error before starving the mains—and even more relieved that he'd convinced Cookie Monster to add the extra tank. Still, he couldn't shake a growing sense of impending doom. The sight of Cuba had destroyed his confidence, and he flew onward, wide-eyed and anxious.

Fifteen seconds later, Billy's fears were confirmed as the Cessna's engine sputtered and stopped. His whole body tensed, and he put a death grip on the yoke. He sat frozen, trying to think through the reason for the stoppage. *He had only switched to his reserve fuel!* He thought, and quickly switched back to the factory tanks, hoping to undo the damage.

But he was too late, and too low. The heavily loaded plane sank towards the whitecaps as he struggled to maintain altitude and restart the engine, but he stalled it and the plane smacked into water and broke apart, spitting metal and marijuana bales in all directions.

The impact threw Billy into the water with the rest of the wreckage and, shocked he was still alive and conscious, Billy swam frantically away from the already-sinking plane.

Then he started sinking too, his heavy leather jacket dragging him down. With his last strength, he squirmed free of it and kicked upward until his head broke through the rough chop. He gasped for air and sucked in seawater and sank again. He grabbed the bottom of a nearby bale and dragged himself to the surface again and clung to it like a leech.

Finally, he had a moment of calm as he bobbed up and down amid the debris. *At least the water's warm*, he thought, *and I'm okay*, though as he floated he became aware that his head and right ankle throbbed from injuries. He hoped he wasn't bleeding.

He watched the 210's tail slide beneath the waves, another smuggling plane claimed by the Caribbean, soon to be followed by its pilot. He was sure he'd soon be shark bait whether he was bleeding or not—or maybe he'd just drown in the rough water.

A second bale bumped him from behind and he almost died of fright until he realized what it was and grabbed it, then tied the two bales together with their twine and climbed aboard. He sighed in relief at being aboard the crude raft and safe at least for a while from sharks.

Billy spent the next hour bobbing up and down, wondering how long it would take for his raft to become waterlogged and sink. His head and right ankle still throbbed. The waves kept him soaked. Still, he had moments to reflect on what had gone wrong.

*What happened to the fuel?* he asked himself. *It was a good decision to build the tank, but why didn't it work?* he wondered as he watched the sun draw closer towards the horizon. Then it came to him and he pounded the wet bales in helpless fury.

"The vent!" he wailed to the mocking sky. "I forgot to put a fucking vent in it. No wonder it wouldn't flow. Aw shit. Fuck!"

Then, as he wailed and cursed, he saw a white ship approaching like a mirage from the north, a wide orange stripe cutting across its hull. He waved frantically to catch its attention.

"I don't give a shit what happens, God," he shouted at the sky, "just please, *please* don't let me become another doper lost at sea."

As if in answer to his profane prayer, the ship turned toward him. He saw an American flag flying from its mast, some white uniformed sailors along its railing, and a big gun on its bow. The United States Coast Guard.

Billy had never been so glad to see The Man in his life and laughed hysterically as the very people he had hoped never to encounter were now his ticket to life.

In a final effort to save his ass from jail, Billy jumped from the bales into the warm water and swam as fast as he could toward the oncoming ship, where caring hands dragged him aboard a Zodiac inflatable that had been lowered over the side and was then winched back aboard—just as the sun dipped below the horizon, hiding the remaining evidence of his misdeed from view.

A Coast Guard medic steered Billy into a small room off the main deck and checked out his vitals and examined his swollen ankle.

"A sprain," he said. "Nothing broken." He looked at Billy's head. "Any dizziness, sir?" Billy didn't respond immediately. "Sir?"

"Oh, you mean me?" Billy laughed. "No, I'm fine. Hurts a little, but I'm okay. In fact, I'm great now that I'm on this ship."

A stern-looking young officer entered and surveyed the scene.

"Sir, this is Captain Johnson," said the medic. "He'd like to ask you a few questions." Before Billy could answer, the medic disappeared out the door. Captain Johnson held out his hand and they shook.

"Welcome aboard, sir. What's your name?"

"Dave . . . Dave DeWolf."

"Well Mr. Wolf, how the *hell* did you get yourself all the way out here?"

"I was out deep sea fishing . . . and my engine quit, and my boat has a tendency to take on water, so I'm down there trying to fix the engine and next thing I know I'm out to sea and sinking. I tried to bail 'er out but—"

"You didn't call for help?"

"Well, I been meaning to fix my radio, but, you know . . . anyway, I'd been floating for a while on a few pieces and, well, you guys saved my life!" Captain Johnson studied Billy for a long moment before speaking.

"That's quite a story Mr. DeWolf. You're lucky we found you. We had a report of a plane going down earlier today and were following up on that call."

"Thank God you found me!"

"That's our mission, sir. You'll need to sign a statement about what happened before we put you ashore, but until then, let's get some food in you and dry out your clothes."

"Great, thank you!" he said and saluted the captain to the best of his ability. Captain Johnson smiled at Billy's lame salute, then left the room and was replaced a moment later by another polite sailor, who ushered him down to the officer's mess.

That same night, Mickey received an unexpected phone call on his special line. It was Winston.

"Hey buddy, what's happenin'?" Mickey asked cheerfully.

"You tell me, monn," said Winston, and Mickey could tell instantly that the always-happy Jamaican was not happy at all.

"Tell you about what?"

"Tell me all is good."

"All is good, but how about you?"

"Your little friend took off early today with his date."

"Friend? Date? Today? What the hell's going on?"

"We drop Mary off and I think you are her date, monn, but it look mebbe like we have a cheater. I felt so when he left early."

"Damn it! I gotta get to the bottom of this. I'll call you as soon as I can clear this up. Sorry, man, sorry."

"Me too, monn, but we fix it, yes?"

"You bet your ass I'll fix it. Talk to you soon."

Mickey hung up, pissed and worried about what Billy had done. Not sure what to do next, he called Roger.

The next morning, Billy signed a bogus statement and hit the street. He called the Cookie Monster and they met a few miles outside the city. Cookie listened to Billy's story and didn't believe him—he figured Billy would do exactly what he, Cookie, would do if he had the chance—stash the load and stiff his partner.

The following day, Billy showed Cookie a newspaper story of his rescue by the Coast Guard, so Cookie accepted Billy's claims. Now they had to explain it all to Mickey, Roger, Winston—and the owner of the plane. They agreed that Billy would break the news while Cookie scrambled to collect as much money as he could. On the way to Illinois, however, Billy got cold feet and decided to call instead. Mickey wouldn't talk, so he had to follow through with a meeting at a motel outside Chicago.

"Trying to pull a fast one on us *already*?" Roger said icily as he sat cross-legged on the bed, staring at his double-crossing pilot as the still-rattled Billy told his tale.

"No, no!" whimpered Billy. "We were going to give you a cut, I swear. We were gonna do it like partners. It's just that, well, it didn't go as planned."

"What you *did* was jump our connections and try to do it all yourselves behind our backs," Roger said.

"And then fucked it all up royally!" Mickey snapped. "You fucking money-hungry amateurs!"

"I tried to tell you," Roger continued. "I tried to tell you to be patient, to learn the business, but you wouldn't listen and you couldn't wait."

"And now you fucked up for all of us." Mickey added.

"C'mon Mickey, you understand, though, right? I'm your *man*."

"*My* man? You jump *my* connection and cheat me, put *my* connection in danger. I don't think so, Billy. I don't have any *men* who act like that."

"So you bobbed in the ocean until the Coast Guard picked you up?" Roger said. "You really expect us to believe that?"

Billy showed them the article. Roger read it and then sat back in his chair, staring at Billy.

"How nice, Billy . . . Bob. Yeah, that's what we'll call you from now on—Billy Bob, the floating pilot. You know, I can't blame this on you because I knew you were a . . ." Roger bit his tongue. "Now, you're a hot potato for all of us."

"Hey, I'm the one who almost died!" Billy "Bob" whined. "And I almost died when Bushman screwed up too. If I didn't know better, I'd think you guys were trying to take me out on purpose. But hey, I forgive you, and I want to work this debt off, just to show you I *am* still your man."

That was the last straw for Roger and Mickey. They looked at each other, amazed at Billy Bob's babbling, and without a word or even a look at him, got up and left, shutting the door quietly behind them.

"Aw shit," Billy Bob whispered to himself. "Fuck."

Outside, the two men climbed into Roger's truck and sat staring through the windshield for a long moment.

"And here I thought our luck was turning," Roger said quietly.

"Your retirement plan is looking better and better," Mickey said bleakly. Roger started the truck and they drove out of the motel parking lot.

"Except now we got *another* debt with Winston and who knows how much heat Billy drew," Mickey sighed.

"You really think he might make us pay for Billy Bob's load?" Roger asked. Mickey just shrugged. "And I wish I had a better handle on the heat. I mean, the story he gave the Coast Guard . . . does he really think they bought it? And then he says he wants to work the debt off. What is he, nuts? And I wonder what he's going to tell the two-ten owner? I hope I never see that idiot again—reminds me what a fool I was for getting him involved."

"I got a feeling Cookie was the main instigator, though."

"Maybe, but Billy Bob didn't need much instigating, I can tell you that. That's why I warned you about him." Roger just shook his head in disbelief.

The men sat deep in thought struggling to form a plan as the dark highway streamed around them, largely deserted this late at night. But they'd been in tough spots before, so while the truck cab atmosphere was intense, it was pretty relaxed. Mickey turned towards Roger and smiled.

"You know, I think Winston'll be satisfied if we only pay him for our last load," he said. "I've done too many good gigs with him for the relationship to sour now. They really did crash on the Titan run, and we had nothing to do with the last one."

121

"Well, you got to get that straight with him," Roger said, "but if there's some confusion, we owe the guy."

"Agreed," Mickey said, "and, regardless, when things get rolling later, we'll throw something at him for the ones that didn't make it. Sound good?"

"Yes, it does."

"Okay, good. He's gonna meet me in Miami tomorrow afternoon and I'll get something worked out." Mickey looked at his glowing watch dial in the dark cab. "Cool. I can get back and catch Cookie Monster and get some money while it's still there."

"Never liked Cookie Monster," Roger muttered, "and never met Winston, so I'm gonna let you sort out this mess, and while you're doing that, I'm gonna go to Belize and see what's happening. We've lost too much momentum with all these setbacks. It's time to pick up the pace and get back on track. If we keep things moving, we'll at least stay well ahead of the Feds even if they are sniffing around Billy Bob. One thing for sure—no more Jamaica. Too much bad luck on that route, although it did serve one purpose—it put to rest the discussion about why the next team needs to be cream only."

"Agreed," said Mickey, and they smiled at each other.

"All right, then," said Roger. "Let's hope things are about to get better—way better."

They went into the airport together and continued planning while they waited at Mickey's departure gate, then checked their messages before separating.

"Hey man," Roger said to Mickey. "I just got a message to call Tony."

"Really?" Mickey said, arching his eyebrows at the news and heading for his gate as the final call announcement echoed through the terminal. "Let me know how that goes."

Roger walked back to a pay phone and dialed Tony's callback number.

"Hey man, what's up?"

"Oh man, am I glad to hear from you. I just finished up a serious run, and I'm rolling in it. You sure you don't want to step up to the big time? I'm sure I could set you up, you know—leave those hippie stoners in your dust."

"Not interested."

"You sure? With your connections, we could really set up some good trade."

"Very sure."

"Yeah, well, your loss. Look man, you know of any opportunities for a guy to 'invest' some cash? I'm open to anything, really: new 'ventures' or maybe something blue chip. Know of anything?"

"Not really."

"Well hey . . . I know you've got a guy with the Midas touch. Can you at least set that up for me?"

"Yeah, I suppose. When will you be up?"

"Hey, that's great man. I'll be up in a few days. And let me know if you hear of anything else won't you?"

"Yeah, I can do that."

"Ciao man."


On the flight south, Mickey wondered why Tony called Roger. He pounded down several drinks to help him mellow out and tried to use an attractive stewardess as a distraction. Mickey reflected on his falling out with Tony, on Billy Bob's backstabbing, and then on Roger's integrity to exorcise the worst scenarios clouding his mind.

When he got off the plane at his first stop in Orlando, Mickey went to the closest pay phone and retrieved his messages. His first call went to Roger.

"Hey, what's up with Tony?"

"He's been workin' and wanted to know if I wanted in. Sounded like he'd clicked off a good one. *You* know what I told him. Then he asked if I had anything he could invest in—so I said I'd help him buy some gold."

"Man, it does sound like something big just went down. I'll bet it's got something to do with that thing I told you about with Terry."

"Like I said, I said I'd help him buy gold because I haven't done anything with him for a couple years. Why would he call me now?" Mickey laughed.

"You may think you're operating secretly, but the word's out that you're working. Hell, just the fact you're not in touch with these guys makes them gossip."

"Anyway, he said he'd be up in the next day or two."

"Watch out for him man, he's a real snake. If you cut a deal with him, he'll want all the money and do nothing for it. His loyalty is only to himself."

Roger heard the pain in his friend's voice over past betrayals.

"Thanks, but you can calm down. It's just that since we're stockpiling alternatives, I think it would be nice to have some cash sitting in reserve in case Cookie Monster does it to us again. You know what I think of Tony. If I have to work with him, I'll eat him alive in the negotiations. You know that's my specialty. I'll have his greed so worked up he'll take any arrangement just so he won't miss out." Mickey laughed again.

"That's my partner," he said proudly. "So I'll handle Cookie and I'll also call Terry. He just left a message so I'll let you know what's happening. Later!"

Mickey smiled when Terry answered the phone, remembering the sloppily dressed, overweight Minnesota farm boy who'd grown up with Hanoi. They'd learned together to fly and skydive at a small airfield near their homes and Terry had flown the first Sugar Alpha loads from Colombia to the Bahamas for Roger and Mickey. Like many in his profession, though, his greedy side had led him to enter the emerging cocaine trade and its higher wages.

Mickey recalled how Terry's frumpiness contrasted with Tony's slick manners and ability to manipulate others that helped him rapidly advance in the trade. Tony had first conned Mickey into picking him instead of Terry as a partner after Roger left. As his reputation spread, Tony then broke into the cocaine trade well before his pot smuggling peers, hosing Mickey along the way, but he'd also established a reputation as a good source of information on the latest smuggling methods and, as his "Tony the Snake" nickname suggested, for other personality traits too.

"Had some friends from Wisconsin who were running three and four kilos at a time out of Bolivia by sewing it in the comfort pad of hiking backpacks," Terry said after Mickey asked him what was up with Tony. "It was the finest quality anyone had ever seen locally, and I wanted a piece of the action so I proposed that we make direct flights into the States instead of taking commercial flights. They liked the idea, so I told Tony, who instantly saw an opportunity."

"You shoulda known better," Mickey said bitterly.

"No shit, especially after what he did to you, but I thought I could keep an eye on him so I told him Jotham was interested and had a Cessna 310 equipped with really big tanks. So we made a three-way deal, but then we were worried flying through the Andes—man, those fuckers are *big*—so we hooked up with your old pal in San Cristobal—"

"Esteban?"

"Sí. He's on the border so we could fly around the mountains instead of through them, then refuel there. It was a sweet plan, and we all chipped in money, and used the amount we all risked as the formula for our investment return."

"Apparently the trip went okay," Mickey speculated.

"Damn straight," Terry said proudly. "Tony and me landed in the high desert kinda low on fuel, but we loaded 67 kilos no problem, refueled no problem, out here into your favorite logging road no problem. Then I had this bright idea that we should leave the load on the ground for a day in case we were detected coming north, and we all decided to have someone more expendable fly the final leg, so Tony had his younger brother rent a Cessna 172 and fly it to Florida."

"Where Tony scammed you all, right?" Mickey guessed.

"It had all gone so smoothly," Terry said glumly, "but yeah, Tony ended up screwing all of us and taking almost all the money. Fucker used the weeks between the shipment's arrival and its cash return to scam us, plus he took advantage of us being scattered around. He was so smooth we couldn't even figure out how he cheated. Hell, Jotham even threatened him but he just laughed it off; he knew we weren't hard-core enough to do shit except stamp our feet and never work with him again. What a fucking dick. We barely made back our investments. It was like we fucking worked for fucking minimum wage for Christ's sake." He paused. "I sure do miss doing business with trustworthy partners, man, so I want to help you with your next load."

"You want me to share my dinner when there's only enough for my family?" Mickey asked, thinking back to how Terry's greed had led him to dump Mickey cold when coke money floated in front of him. "Well, there's no dinner tonight anyway, so I'm sorry, buddy, but there's no deal." Terry sighed, then changed the subject.

"I was talking to Kojack at the Grave Yard in Great Harbour and do you know what he told me?"

"What?"

"You remember Operation Grouper last year?" Mickey nodded. "Well, the secret source that set up more than a hundred people is your attorney's cousin, Travis Miller! That's the campaign that kicked off the South Florida task force Bush runs."

Mickey sat back, stunned. Travis Miller's cousin Parker and his uncle Alvin Miller were the attorneys who set up the secret corporation that owned his Bahamian property.

"Shit!"

"There's more. While we were talking, a friend came in and told us Pindling has promoted Howard Smith, the last Great Harbour cop, and who is now the assistant police commissioner, to head the Bahamian Strike Force. Can you believe that? You know how dirty he is! All the officers working with Smith are being moved up through the ranks and repositioned. They're setting up for the loads to get bigger and making some serious money handling the trans-shipments. Kojack asked Smith about the Bahamians working with the South Florida Task Force and he just laughed. With Smith heading the Bahamian task force and Pindling running the country, it sure sounds as if the fox is guarding the hen house, huh? Our friend said that the Americans are fools buying the same line we were sold in the Vietnam interdiction. Now the former head of the CIA at the time that same CIA coordinated the opium and heroin smuggling out of Indochina, is our Vice President and overseeing America's new drug task force."

Mickey shook his head at the news. He knew Kojack was an emerging smuggler who had the customs and immigrations officials at Great Harbour in his pocket. The news about Howard Smith being repositioned signaled that things were about to get really active in their beautiful country. But he didn't have time to digest it all.

"Sorry, man, thanks for the poop, but I gotta jet," he said abruptly.

"Thought you said nothing was going on," Terry said petulantly.

"No man," laughed Mickey as he lied, "I got a flight to catch. Gonna do some fishing at the house."

"Sure, man," Terry said. "Just remember your old friends when some big fish show up, wouldja?"

"Of course," Mickey said cheerfully. "Thanks for getting in touch."

Mickey hung up the phone.

"Holy fucking shit," he said under his breath, then headed out for his appointment with the Cookie Monster.

They met on the Cookie Monster's doorstep.

"Come in, man," Cookie said solicitously. "I know you're mad but let me explain before we even get started. I'm so sorry. I really mean it. I let greed get the best of me this time. It made me stupid. I made bad decisions. Mickey please, you have to forgive me." He thrust a huge pile of cash into Mickey's hand. "Here! Almost all of what I owe you."

Mickey was so surprised at the amount that he couldn't help but smile.

"Okay, asshole," he said harshly. "You're forgiven—as long as you tell me how you got this much together."

"Mickey, you're the man! You're the man!" Cookie said, slapping Mickey heartily on the back.

"And you're still a selfish, greedy, thick-headed fucking *idiot*," Mickey replied in a gentler tone.

"I know, man, I know, but I tried to be smarter afterward," he said, beaming proudly. "I broke our last load up into smaller lots and bypassed the big buyer so I could make enough money to cover the fuckup. That's most of what I owe you—and I'll have the rest tomorrow."

"Really."

"No shit, man, tomorrow. I worked hard to make it right, man, 'cause yeah, I'm a little greedy, but that's all—I'm not that bad, right? C'mon Mickey, we're friends."

"Watch your words, Cookie, and watch your back while you're at it too. This greedy streak'll bite you in the ass one of these days. But thanks for the money, I appreciate it, but I gotta go. We'll hook up tomorrow for the rest."

"Sure thing, Mickey. You da man!"

Mickey walked away, shaking his head at the unexpected pile of cash. He was almost even! That was a big relief as he climbed into his car and headed for the airport for his flight to Miami to meet Winston.

"Okay, monn, 'tings be cool wit' us now," Winston told Mickey as they sat in a bar near the airport. "You respond quick to come and you put cash in my hand. You a good monn to work wit', wit' out these troubles. When you come back for more?"

"I've got to reorganize a bit," Mickey hedged. "You know, replace a few people, change some procedures. Neither of us can afford to have any more screw ups like this."

"Yaa monn, I knew 'tings were strange on dat last one," Winston agreed. "No call from you. You always call. So I knew it's not yours, but I go ahead anyway, so my fault as much as anyone. I don't hold you responsible, monn. It's hard to find the good people, and I want to do more bizzness wit' you."

"Cool," Mickey said, exhaling in relief. "I'm glad we cleared this up. You know I'd never leave you hanging."

"Or bring half a plane for a whole load," Winston grinned, and they laughed together at their situation, sealing the deal on their renewed relationship.

"I'll be in touch," Mickey said, "and talk details then. Thanks, my friend."

Mickey managed to surprise Roger with the news that the Cookie Monster had made good on his debt.

"Congratulations," Roger said. "That's the first time in a long time something happened that I didn't expect."

"Same for me," Mickey laughed. "Hell, he even came through the next day with the rest, as scheduled, no snivels. Almost asked him if he'd started going to church or something."

"And Winston?"

"Says Billy Bob's debacle is on him as much as it is on us so we're clear on that one. We still on for New Orleans?"

"Yeah. Now I can get something going when I get down."

"What do we need?"

"Fifty."

"All right. See you then."

Roger hung up and drove to the drop zone, where he told his staff he was burned out from Nationals and was taking a few days off.

"Take more than a few, buddy," Kimmers said cheerfully. "Take a bunch. We'll hold down the fort and hopefully have Mr. D. back up before you get back."

Roger embraced everyone within reach and left with a big smile on his face. *Belize or not,* he thought as he climbed into his truck, *I do need a break from that scene."*

Roger met Tony the next day at the county airport shortly after the pilot arrived in his King Air, gym bag in one hand, a briefcase in the other. As soon as they hit the road in Roger's truck, he unzipped the gym bag to reveal five kilos of cocaine, distorted football-shaped objects wrapped in brown contact paper and clear cellophane.

"Can you turn them?" he asked, a gleam in his eye. Roger waved him off.

"Don't have an outlet, don't want one," he said curtly. "You know how I feel about that stuff."

Unperturbed, Tony grabbed his brief case and spun the combination dials. He popped the latches and exposed tens of thousands of dollars. Roger smiled.

"Seems you've been doin' pretty good"

"Fuckin' A."

Tony then bragged about his latest ventures as Roger drove along the interstate and listened attentively to the bizarre stories. He liked it when other smugglers ran on at the mouth. That way, he didn't have to say anything about his own activities and, almost as importantly, he learned a lot about the Feds and their tactics by hearing what happened to the other guys. The things Tony had gotten into most definitely surpassed Roger's pot runs, but Tony had also exposed himself to multiple strangers, a blatant violation of Rule Number One in Roger's successful smuggler's code: Go only with who you know.

"How long will it take to get the gold?" Tony asked after he finished his story.

"Soon," Roger sighed, glad the brag marathon was over. He pulled into a Denny's and dropped Tony off, then visited Harris the bullion dealer with the briefcase in hand.

The deal had been pre-arranged, so when Roger handed Harris the briefcase, Harris handed him a strong plastic box Roger knew was filled with stacks of South African Krugerrands.

"Let me know if the count is accurate," Roger said.

"Will do," said Harris, as he scribbled out a receipt and handed it to him. "If it's off either way, we'll take care of it next visit."

Roger was back to Denny's before Tony was served. He handed the pilot the box and receipt, and they settled down to eat lunch.

When they got back on the road, Roger retraced their route back to the airport.

"What's your rush, man?" Tony asked. "Let's do the town—or is married life keeping you tame these days? C'mon, what's going on?"

"Not just married life, man," Roger said, "kids too. They take a lot of time and I love every minute I spend with them. Wish I was there more, actually."

"You a family man!" Tony snorted. "Never thought I'd see *that* day!"

When Roger pulled up to the King Air, Tony's demeanor changed from devil-may-care to downright nervous.

"Look, man, I was counting on you to turn this toot," he said earnestly. "I can't take it back with me."

"Why not?" Roger asked casually, but he was instantly on alert at the transparent attempt to force the dangerous powder on him. "You brought it here with the money."

"It's different going into Florida than it is coming out. Come on, man, you've got to help me. You got to know someone who'll take it."

"No!" Roger barked, "and I'm pissed you're trying to pull this on me. What were you thinking?"

"I'll drop twenty-five K off the price." Roger just glared. "Fifty." Roger said nothing. Tony waited for several seconds, then gave up.

"All right, but I'm serious; I can't take it back to Florida. I got a friend in Jersey who wants it, though, so will you hang onto it until I can get back?"

Roger stared daggers at Tony for a long moment, then another of Roger's two-edged personality traits kicked in: giving people the benefit of the doubt, even though they didn't deserve it. It was another good trait for life in general, but another dangerous one in the smuggling business.

"Okay, fine," Roger said reluctantly, "but I'm not responsible for anything except putting it back in your hand as soon as you come back here."

"Unless you try to turn it," Tony grinned.

"You don't have to worry about that," Roger said with his devilish grin, "and you come *here* to get it. I'm *not* taking it anywhere for you either. Got that?"

"Got it," Tony nodded. "We're cool."

They shook hands and Tony climbed into the sleek twin-engine turbine and fired it up. Roger watched him taxi to the runway and gun the engines.

"Tony the Snake," Roger muttered as he watched the King Air take off. "Tony the frigging snake."

Roger left the airport on one back road, then took several more until he stopped on an isolated section bounded on both sides by thick woods. He carried the bag 100 yards into the trees, walking delicately so as not to disturb the foliage, until he reached a fallen log. He moved it carefully and exposed the top end of a plastic tube. He unscrewed the sealed end, revealing several stacks of Franklins. He placed the packages on top of the money, resealed the tube, replaced the log, and walked out of the woods a different way.

The next morning Roger prepared for his trip to Belize. He reviewed his notes, then grabbed a gray Cordura bag packed with clothes, a roll of duct tape, and several rolls of quarters, and headed for the local shopping mall.

There, he made reservations to Belize via New Orleans with TACA International using the name on one birth certificate. Then he went to a toy store and bought two large bags of simple toys: rubber balls, plastic soldiers, and small dolls. Next was Radio Shack, where he bought several hand-held two-meter radios, spare batteries, miscellaneous parts, and a VCR. Then he stopped at J.C. Penney and picked up two dozen pairs of blue jeans, and two pairs of quality cowboy boots.

He took his goods out to the truck, where he poured the toys into a box in the bed, placed the electronic gear in the center, and duct taped it closed for the trip. Then he stuffed the clothing into the Cordura bag and drove to O'Hare, where he parked in the long-term lot, shuttled to the terminal, paid cash for a round-trip ticket and checked his bags. He looked at his watch. He had time for a quick walk to his gate to make the final boarding call. *Good timing*, he thought. *Good sign.*

Roger and Mickey met in a New Orleans motel room, where they started their meeting by counting out their money.

"We finally got ourselves above water again, but that's it," Mickey said. "Whatever you do, be careful. It's been tough keeping this in our hands."

"Hopefully, it'll grow into a lot more this time," Roger grinned.

"Hopefully," Mickey grinned back.

Mickey set out $50,000 in $5,000 bundles. Roger put his tennis shoes in his bag and took out one pair of the boots he bought. Then he unbundled the money and held a layer around his lower leg while Mickey taped it in place. They repeated the procedure on the other side, then Roger slipped more inside the boot on the bottom, and carefully squeezed his foot into it.

"Glad you brought mostly hundreds."

"Been there!" Mickey laughed as he watched Roger walk around the room to see if he moved naturally and without obvious discomfort.

"How much more do we have?" Roger asked as he bent over and straightened his tight jeans over the boots.

"Ten. All in twenties." They broke the blocks into $1,000 stacks and placed eight of them along the elastic of his underwear and one in each pocket. Then he stood in front of the mirror, checking for odd bulges. Satisfied, he looked at his watch.

"Time to tell them I'm coming," he said, and they left for the airport.

Roger called Belize from a terminal pay phone.

"*Hola*," said the voice of an elderly woman that Roger recognized as the mother of George, his contact.

"*Hola*, Mama," Roger said. "Is George there?"

"*Hola*, Roger!" she said happily. "No, George he in the bush two more days, but he say if you call tell you we have warm welcome, *sí?*"

"*Gracias*, Mama," Roger said. "I see you soon. I am on schedule as George and I talked."

"*Excellente*, Roger!" said Mama. "We make sure he knows. See you soon!"

Roger hung up, feeling comfortable that a messenger would be dispatched to George announcing his arrival.

Mickey and he carried the bags and box to the ticket counter, where Roger told the agent he had reservations, and handed her his birth certificate when she asked for proof of citizenship. She handed him his ticket and pointed urgently toward his gate.

"They're boarding now, sir," she said. "Please gate check your bags and please hurry," she smiled. "You don't want to miss your flight!"

"Thanks, miss," Roger said and with luggage still in hand, they quick-stepped down the concourse to the gate.

"Good luck, my friend," Mickey said as they handed their gear to a gate agent. "I'll see you soon."

"Thanks, man," Roger smiled. "I'll be in touch." Then, in his customary fashion, Roger boarded the jet last and they locked the door behind him. Moments later, the jet backed away from the gate, and he was soon airborne for Belize.

# CHAPTER NINE

## B-VILLE

Roger admired the view from his window seat as his southbound commercial flight to Belize took him across the Yucatan Peninsula. Shortly after they began their descent, Chetumal Bay's contours helped him locate the Mexican city of Chetumal on Belize's northern border. After he was oriented, Roger noted landmarks until they landed 15 minutes later at the international airport just outside Belize City. Roger had already crisscrossed this small country of 8,867 square miles several times by both land and air, but he tried to add to his knowledge every time he visited.

Anti-aircraft guns under olive drab camouflage netting greeted the airliner as it crossed the airport's threshold and rolled up to the terminal, and humidity blasted into the cabin as the door opened. The passengers were already sweating when they walked down the stairs onto the hot tarmac.

The other passengers covered their ears as they made their way toward the old building, a former military terminal, but Roger stopped for a moment to watch a British Harrier jump jet hover 50 feet off the ground on the other side the runway, rotate 180 degrees, then bounce its nose wheel off the ground and accelerate vertically into flight.

He smiled at the sight, then turned his attention to the ground crew as it unhurriedly unloaded the plane. One of the baggage handlers walked over to Roger.

"Welcome to Belize, *Señor*," he shouted over the engine noise with a broad grin that exposed big, tarnished teeth highlighted by one large gold cap in front. His dark face accented his sincere smile. "Your baggage tickets, *por favor?*"

"Here you go, Buddy," Roger shouted back as he produced the tags. "Nice to be back."

Buddy pushed a small hand cart to the plane's open cargo door, then waited while his co-workers unloaded baggage, watching until Roger pointed out his bag and boxes. Buddy retrieved them and wheeled them over.

"George is waiting in the circle," he shouted, "I take these to him and tell him you be right out." Roger nodded and pointed to the VCR box.

"That one's for you!" he shouted.

Buddy looked at the side of the box and cracked a wide smile.

"Thank you for remembering, Roger, my friend," he shouted. "You the only American I know who does these things."

Roger slapped him on the back as Buddy looked beyond the passenger line to see if any of his associates were watching. Satisfied that the coast was clear, he vanished behind a door of long black rubber strips into the cargo area. The line continued moving slowly towards the immigration desk.

"What is your business in Belize?" an officer sternly demanded of Roger when he reached the desk.

"I've come to dive the beautiful reefs your country is so famous for."

"How long?" the officer challenged.

"About a week."

"What hotel?"

Roger gave him a bogus itinerary, miles from his true destination.

"Return ticket."

Roger showed him his round-trip ticket, verifying the length of his intended stay and confirming his intention to leave.

"Next!"

Roger moved to next table to claim his baggage. Buddy had long since taken his position by the terminal's customs exit. When Roger presented himself at the desk, Buddy caught the inspection officer's attention and nodded discretely toward Roger. Roger identified his bag and the officer placed it on a narrow table. Roger unzipped it himself.

"Do you have anything to declare?"

Roger shook his head.

The officer pretended to look into the bag but he mostly kept his eyes on Roger.

"You may go," he said, nodding his head toward the exit. Roger smiled and shouldered his bag and walked directly out the door where Buddy waited.

"I need forty dollars, twenty for each station," Buddy whispered. Roger saw George sitting nearby in his bright red pickup and motioned for Buddy to follow him over. When they reached the driver's window, Roger gave Buddy five $20 bills.

"Here, give forty to each, and keep twenty for yourself."

"You don't, you don't need to—" Buddy stammered.

"Then please give it to your wife, and tell her I said hello," Roger interrupted.

Buddy flashed a bright smile as he slid the money into his pocket.

"Thank you so much," he said, and returned to work.

George gave Roger an enthusiastic handshake as he slid into the truck, then eyed him seriously.

"Roger, you don't have to pay them," he scolded gently. "I take care of the officials already. And you don't even know Buddy's wife; why do you give her twenty?"

"Listen man," Roger chuckled, "I know how tough it is down here for you folks. Everyone's just trying to survive. These people are working with us, so it's nice to make sure they're taken care of, and that way they go an extra mile for us some time when we need it."

"*Sí*, but they know they've been paid," George countered. "I don't want them thinking they can take advantage of us."

"I'm sure you took care of them," Roger grinned, "but better we err in their favor, not ours."

"True thing you say," George conceded. "Everywhere I go, the *ganjaneros* fight to work for you. Everywhere, they want to do us favors. You remind me of my father, *hermano*, and I know he would be proud that I work with a man such as you."

"*Muchos gracias*," said Roger, "now let's go say *hola* to Mama." George grinned and put the truck in gear.

As the lush countryside streamed around them, Roger thought of his companion. George was a third generation Belizean from the Ramirez family. His Spanish grandparents learned that hard-working countrymen earned their British superiors fortunes, leaving them only with callused hands and poverty. His parents encouraged him to use his intelligence so he might one day rise above hard labor. His mother's love encouraged him to study, and he became fluent in Spanish, Mayan, and English. His father traveled occasionally to outlying farms to purchase sugar cane and excess produce, and thus did George visit the country's northern villages. There he met the people, learned their ways, learned to negotiate—and built lasting connections. His father's consideration and respect for these people, and his gifts of food and money, made him a welcome friend among the thatched-hut peasants. Even with these advantages, though, George's five-foot-eight-inch frame was marked by scars from childhood labor and hardships—which underscored for Roger the need to be generous with the Belizeans whom he knew were nowhere nearly as lucky as George.

They passed clapboard houses set up on stilts above the flood plain as they approached Belize City, then crossed the Haulover Bridge over the Belize River just upstream of where it emptied into the Caribbean after its meandering path through the country from its origins in the country's Maya Mountains. On the other side of the river, age-streaked homes mingled with newer cement block structures. As they crossed the flat coastlands nearing the city, George broke the silence.

"We need to get a Land Rover from Smitty," he said. "I told him you were coming, so he said we can have one on credit. I'm tapped out of cash, so we're going to have to take care of him on that. Manu's there now picking one out. He'll drive it to Orange Walk for the re-supply."

Roger reached into his pocket and handed George $2,000.

"Here, no crew chief of mine walks around without a few bucks in his pocket."

"Thank you, Roger," that's a big help."

"No problem," Roger nodded. "We'll update all the accounts tomorrow, okay?"

George nodded, and a few moments later they crossed the Belcan Bridge over Haulover Creek and entered the narrow streets of the city's poorer Southside area. Wooden buildings in need of repair stood alongside gutters overflowing with raw sewage that emptied into the smelly Belize River. Old and poverty-stricken, Roger had no doubt this district was a tuberculosis breeding ground, but he also knew that a police tail would stand out in sharp contrast; the police here did not like being seen in beat-up vehicles when doing undercover work.

George stopped at a gas station to fill up, taking care to inspect his truck before they went into the bush.

With tanks full and all fluids replenished, George and Roger doubled back to the more open spaces of the west side. They took Central American Boulevard a short way, then turned into a dirt alley by Smitty's auto rental. Smitty's son was the first to see Roger, and he called his name from a second-story window.

Smitty came out with a bottle of beer for each of them. They exchanged hellos and started talking business. Roger paid the charges George had racked up, and left a deposit for another Rover. George inquired about his partner, and Smitty's son directed them across the alley to the parked rentals where Manu's feet stuck out from under a vehicle.

Manu, a skinny man of African descent with childlike features that hid his 30 years, had teamed with George when they first approached Roger. Tired of working for unreliable Americans who had trouble finding buyers for their substandard ganja, they saw in Roger a trustworthy partner who not only treated people with respect but also acted like a real businessman. Roger in turn had liked them too, seeing their seriousness and discipline, and soon shared with them his vision of growing a superior product that would change the dynamics of their market. Manu and George loved Roger's plan and agreed to work exclusively for him to make it happen. In return, Roger got reliable men on the ground that knew local families from whose ranks they could recruit and train growers.

Their equal partnership quickly hit a snag; Manu would take his payments and skip out on the work—at least until his money ran out, leaving George and Roger to take up the slack. Still, Roger admired Manu's fluency in English and Spanish as well as his considerable mechanical talents—a critical resource when working in the bush—so rather than bouncing him from the partnership, Roger put George in charge of the pair. Manu then got paid only as his completed his tasks. His work ethic quickly improved, and the arrangement now worked smoothly.

Manu crawled out from under the Rover covered with dirt and grease. Roger offered his hand, but Manu waved him off, showing a greasy hand. He handed Roger his beer instead, and Roger drank the cool beverage to show his appreciation for the gesture. The truck and the

Rover were soon ready. Manu washed up, and they headed back up the Northern Highway towards Orange Walk, avoiding the road's notorious potholes.

Roger enjoyed people and their history, and George made perfect company for the three-hour trip. With independence less than a year old, Belizeans, and George in particular, felt a tremendous pride in their new nation.

"Belize has been raped and plundered for hundreds of years," George said. "First, it was the *conquistadores*, who stripped the people of their gold and silver. You may have heard of their great treasure fleets and of the British buccaneers who hunted them? It was a pirate who founded Guatemala from which our country came. The Spanish had no interest in establishing settlements.

"And then they came after our resources, the Spanish and British. They made laws restricting trade and imposed their cruel tyranny on us. They built only the roads necessary to extract raw materials and transport them to the sea." George turned to Roger and grinned. "Even then we had smugglers who defied the great powers. Treaties among the powers brought the pirating to an end, and the British buccaneers converted their pirate ships into cargo hauling vessels to join the commerce. They built small settlements of African slaves and, together with repressed Mayan and Mestizo Indians, they did their master's grueling work. The poor Mestizos, they fled to Belize from the Spanish in the Yucatan. We became a melting pot. But our Latin pride and the African desire to rid themselves of their slavery aided our long struggle against the wealthy white masters.

"Once the land was stripped of its timber, we used the bare ground to plant crops for the absentee owners. They cared nothing for us."

George occasionally interrupted himself to point out a Mayan ruin or potential landing strip.

"German Mennonites seeking religious freedom immigrated here. They brought their skills and knowledge in agriculture and dairy farming with them. They were the first Europeans to not treat us as animals.

"The British conscripted the black Belizeans to do their fighting in World War II. This injustice flamed our desire for independence and, in 1964, the British allowed their last crown colony on the American mainland to self-govern, though only as a member of their United

Kingdom. In 1973, we changed our name from British Honduras to Belize and, finally, on September 21, 1981, just one year ago, the deeply rooted Catholic people overcame the tyrants, and our country won its independence!"

Roger knew about this last event. He had arrived in Belize just after its independence to evaluate the country as a potential marijuana source. During his stay, he'd actually heard a speech by Prime Minister George Cadle Price, the "founding father" of Belize, in which he told his people to help themselves raise their standard of living, which had been devastated by the falling price of sugar. In his address, he told them, "If you can't feed your family growing corn and cane, then grow something you can." Squeezed by the rich multi-nationalists on the world's sugar market, the Belizeans had to produce a more marketable good. Without the U.K.'s restrictions, trade began to flourish, and Roger realized that Belize was the place for him.

As they weaved down the neglected road, testing the limits of the truck's suspension, George changed the subject to the farm's progress.

"The plants are strong and healthy. The leaves, Roger, they're bigger than my hand!"

"I thought those seeds would give us plants like 'Jack and the Bean Stalk,'" Roger said. "Fertilizing them the way I showed you will give us the buds we want."

"Even the Mennonites are amazed. They want to buy our seeds, but I won't give up even one."

"As soon as we harvest our seed crop, we'll have more than we can use, so don't be afraid to give some out. It would be good to have others producing good bud. It makes a better demand in the States."

"No, Roger we are going to plant every one," George said, shaking his head in disagreement. None will go to waste. I want to do like you said before we started. I want to grow the best buds in Belize. Besides, Roger, we need them all for another reason."

Roger looked sharply at George. He could tell by the suddenly sad tone in his voice that something was up—something bad enough that George hadn't said anything about it until now.

"Your government has caused us a problem," George said. "It said we must fight drugs in order to get the benefits of the Caribbean common market, so the Prime Minister allowed helicopters from Mexico to spray some of the fields with something. We go there first so I can show you what happened."

They turned off the highway onto a dirt road just south of Orange Walk and parked next to a gravel quarry. Normally, they would hide the trucks in the thick vegetation, but there was none; all the trees were dead, dying or sickly, their leaves fallen or deathly yellow.

Roger's jaw muscles tensed as he looked at the carnage.

"Paraquat," he hissed. George nodded.

"And not only does it kill and hurt the plants," the Belizean went on, "it poisons the water and the food. The U.S. forced the Mexicans to spray it on their own fields, but when the Mexicans saw what it did to their land, they demanded it be stopped, but they had some left over, so the U.S. had them spray it on our fields."

"Jesus," Roger muttered as he became aware of buzzing and walked over toward the sound. There among the ruined bushes lay a young goat, dead and rotting in the sun.

"Our animals are sick, the vegetables are dead, and the peasants in the area are weak," George went on. "The newspapers came out loudly against it, and we have been told that the operation is over, but that your DEA is upset because only a few plots were sprayed. One of them was ours, but it was a small field so that is not so bad, but we will have to start it over again."

Roger sighed in disgust, still too upset to speak. He walked away from the dead goat and scanned the ruined field and surrounding vegetation.

"I'm so sorry," he said quietly to Manu and George, "and I apologize as an American for this terrible thing done in my name by the U.S. government. Put up some signs as soon as you can, will you, please? Signs that warn people of the danger so they will stay out and not drink the water or try to salvage the food or plants in the field." Then he turned on his heel and marched back to the truck, eyes angry that this newly independent nation was still being ground into the dirt by a colonial power.

They drove into the town of Orange Walk. It was a rich town by Belizean standards, but by American standards it looked more like a town from the old West, its dirt streets filled with Mennonite growers who had come out of the bush, seeking buyers for their vegetable and marijuana crops. To them, it was an open-air market of free enterprise all done for their family survival.

They stopped in the park square. George gave Manu some money to buy supplies, then he and Roger drove to George's house on the edge of town and pulled across a grass field next to the Coca-Cola factory. George's seven small children came running out of their house to greet Roger. George lit up proudly as he watched his children jump on Roger like a favorite uncle. Roger in turn acted like one; he pulled his box of toys from the truck and gave each one their choice. Soon balls were bouncing and Frisbees flying as the children happily entertained themselves.

"Roger, you're more than a brother to me," George said. "The day I met you changed my whole life. I am so proud to work with you and so happy that my family loves you."

Roger reached behind his neck and took off a gold chain and cross he had worn to get it through customs.

"This is for your wife, for putting up with you," Roger grinned.

Then he handed George a box with the other pair of cowboy boots. George saw the Tony Lama label and was so overwhelmed, he couldn't look Roger in the eye; he blindly bear-hugged him instead. Then they walked to the house and Roger gave his wife the cross and chain, not as a form of payment but as a token of their friendship.

Roger had cemented their relationship the year before when he sent down the red F-250 four-wheel-drive pickup. When George had received this unexpected shipment, he told Roger he would take good care of it for him.

"Take care of it for yourself," Roger had replied, "It's yours."

After a quick lunch, George dropped Roger off at the Chula Vista Hotel, conveniently above a gas station just north of town in Trail Farm, so he could get some rest. They had a big day ahead of them.

The next day, George handed Roger a blue knapsack he'd left on his last visit. Inside, Roger found his calculator, pen flashlights, and miscellaneous survival items. He took it back to the truck while George spoke to the hotel's owner. Roger reached into the box of toys and put the four radios in his pack, along with handfuls of toys.

The men went back into town and started buying a few additional supplies for the boys in the bush. They had lived on very little for a couple weeks while waiting for more cash. They loaded up with nylon bags of flour, rice, and beans, then made a final stop at a bakery, where George bought several dozen loaves of bread and placed large blocks of ice in coolers on a few bottles. They met Manu back at the square and loaded more basic staples and containers of water and gas into the truck.

"I checked some buds coming in from the fields," Manu told them, gesturing toward some of the farmers. "My eye is now trained for the quality the Americans want and there is nothing I see that compares with what we are growing. We have no competition in looks or bite here."

Only the previous year, Roger had taught the farmers something they had barely noticed the difference, between the male and females plants. He showed them that the female plants grew a pistillate flower with distinguishable white hairs, were generally smaller, and produced the highest levels of THC, especially if the male plants didn't pollinate the females. The male plants grew taller, had yellow and green sepals, and boasted clumps without hairs. Roger showed them how to delicately harvest the males a week or so prior to the females to prevent pollination.

During that first trip, Roger had also identified the harder working men who would support their families any peaceful way they could. Unlike most Americans, who never ventured beyond the whorehouses when they came to buy, Roger journeyed deep into the country's jungles and grasslands to personally meet and work with the people. In addition to giving them tips on growing, Roger taught them about health, hygiene, and world events. These expeditions into the heart of the nation convinced Roger to start a co-operative farm with the dedicated Belizeans. He saw clearly that by organizing their efforts and bringing in the right seed and equipment, they would earn more than they needed to survive; they could actually prosper—and so, of course, would he.

The heavily loaded vehicles bumped down dirt roads past Mestizo and Mennonite villages, bound for their hilly base camp in the Edenthal area bordering Mexico along Orange Walk District's northwestern corner. George led the way. Manu followed far enough behind to avoid George's dust cloud.

The jarring ride soon aggravated Roger's money-crowded feet so much he couldn't take it any longer. He removed the most burdensome one and peeled off the tape along with the hair on his leg. George heard the ripping sound and laughed at the grimace on Roger's face.

"Ha ha! Oh, Roger, you should wait until we pass the Blue Creek police station before you do that."

"Sorry, man," Roger said, flexing his toes and ankle. "I'd rather get busted than wear this another minute, much less two hours." He placed some of the money inside an inner pouch in his pack and handed $15,000 to George.

"Give this to the guys when we get there," he said, glad to be rid of it.

"Roger, that's way too much!" George said, startled at the size of the stacks.

"No, that's way too little."

"You don't understand," George countered. "If you pay them this much now, they'll go into town and expose themselves and the farm."

"Fair enough," Roger said, "so let's do this. Go to the village and leave something with their families instead. Their wives will manage it better than they will, right?"

"Ah, yes, Roger," George laughed, "that is a good idea—and we have to stop there to pick up a water pump anyway."

News of the famous red truck's arrival spread quickly through the village as soon as they arrived in San Felipe to pay the families the wages their men had earned. When Manu caught up, George gave him a radio and sent him southeast to the camp near Indian Church where his men were setting up plots for the future. Manu and his Rover rumbled off, trailing a cloud of familiar Belizean dust.

Roger and George loaded up the pump, then went to a cluster of dirt—floored, thatched huts where three of their workers lived. Livestock wandered freely through the one-room, bamboo abodes as the men entered and loudly announced their arrival, scattering chickens in every direction. George walked out of the hut to the rear yard and spoke to one of the grandmothers in Mayan. Roger returned to the front with his bag hanging from one shoulder and found himself facing a crowd of dirty, barefoot children. He smiled at one young boy, and the boy hid behind the leg of another.

Roger unzipped his bag, took out a ball, and began bouncing it to himself. Then he grabbed it in his hand and stooped down eye level with the child. Catching his smile, Roger rolled the ball slowly over to him. The boy grabbed it happily with both hands. The other kids closed in a little more, and Roger tried some of his Spanish on the small tribe.

"*Hola, niños. Como esta?*"

"*Quieres un naranja?*" a little girl replied.

"*Na-ran-ga?*"

"*No, no! Nar-an-HA. Orange.*" The little girl annunciated each syllable for Roger. As she corrected him, the children erupted in laughter, slightly embarrassing Roger. He sat in the dirt and opened the bag of toys. Soon he had the young lads hanging on him, waiting to choose one. Roger stood, feeling pleased with himself and even happier for the kids. His young Spanish instructor came over and gave him an orange.

"*Cómo te llamas?*"

"*Mi nombre es Rosa,*" Rosa grinned and ran to play with the other children.

George finished his business, and they headed to another hut. A boy came to George at the door and tugged at his sleeve.

"The elder asks if Mr. Roger has time to speak."

George looked over to Roger, who'd heard the request.

"Of course. Let's go."

The boy jumped into the back of the truck among the supplies and pointed the way to the elder, who sat in a chair on the porch of a raised plank board house in need of paint.

It was Francis, who Roger had briefly met on his last trip, a man respected by the other villagers and who acted as the village's mayor.

Francis stood up and invited the two inside, where his wife gave them each a glass of water and left them to their privacy.

"Mr. Roger. Your presence is changing my people," said Francis. "Can I ask you something, Mr. Roger?"

"Certainly Francis. And please, call me Roger."

"Roger, why do you choose to come to such a poor town, a poor country? Listen, I have lived here all my years and seen many changes. I've thought about what you are doing and its place with our people.

"Long ago I closed my eyes when we grew sugar cane for rum. The government said this was good, but we have had much trouble with rum and drink. Now, no one buys our rum, so we grow what we can sell even though it is against the law. Such things must be because we are poor. With so little money, we are forced to cross the river and buy our goods in Mexico. To survive we must break the law so our people can eat. But these drug laws are made for your country, which has much. We are blamed for the drug problem because we grow, but we grow what we can sell. When we grow our fruits and cane, sometimes we have good markets and sometimes not. If we do not, then our hard labor rots back into the earth, and we do not eat. We gain nothing and the rich nations say this is better. But better for who, those with much?"

"Not sure who it's better for," Roger said honestly, because he really had no idea why America's drug laws were like they were. He also wondered where Francis was going with his commentary.

"We are a poor nation," Francis continued, "one that has received little recognition for all we have suffered. So how is it Belize does not have a drug problem and the countries with plenty do? Since the past we have won many victories that have earned us dignity and self-respect.

"Now you have helped us to be independent from the markets we cannot control and do not understand. In little time, you have brought a chance for us to have better things, but who benefits? Here we have no government except in the towns. The villagers are simple people who are living simple lives. We have been left alone because we are so few with so little. Having little is the price we pay for freedom. It is better this way. When there is wealth in abundance, those who have much come to control."

"I think you say the truth very well, Francis," Roger said. "What you say is true all over the world."

"That is why I have asked you here, Roger," he said, "to help you understand the Belizeans and for a favor. Please, no matter what you do, do not import violence to our country. The Nicaraguans, Salvadorans, and Guatemalans come to Belize seeking peace. They flee from what your country has done to theirs. America brings to these places things for war, and now they have war. Your government denies involvement, but Central Americans still die. I fear one day the U.S. will come here and do the same.

"I have heard there are many guns at your camp. The young men in the village speak of owning one some day. The children hear, and they repeat the same. Since television has come to the house with electricity, our young crave the things they see from America. Our close family binding is damaged by longing for material items, and many move to the city in pursuit. You must realize your influence on the children and the people who see you with many things. Your actions can steer them right or wrong. I ask you to do the former. I have learned you are different from others like you. You are honest and good to the people, but if you bring weapons, one day you will be gone and the weapons will remain. We must not forget why the refugees are here."

Roger waited respectfully for several moments before he replied.

"I realize all the other countries growing pot are full of guns and pain, but that is not the case yet in Belize. Your police don't carry guns, and your army doesn't control the trade. Your government is still young and trying to learn how to govern, but Francis, as I already said, your words are true, so I am afraid. Your troubles will come when America imposes its will upon you. Our government blames others for our problems because it cannot expose the fact that it is our government that is the problem. We offer money to other nations, and they impose hardships upon people like you. When your government accepts our bribe money, it's only natural that lower officials do the same. If I am in business with people, with the farmers, they cry foul. But the black market is the truest form of free market, because it supports the people. Our governments operate with double standards, where their personal ends justify any means they can get away with. In Belize, it's an outright pocket payment, and in the U.S., our politicians take positions of wealth after they leave office. Government is supposed to serve the people, but it actually imposes suppression and injustice. This creates poverty and forces people into black markets to survive. Government-created poverty is the worst for the people, and it is the greatest root of crime and violence, much worse than drugs could ever be. Please understand it is not the American people who do this but the powers that run the government. We are taught to accept what we are told. Our submission will one day make things much worse. You are right, we will pay for this with our freedom, and . . . ."

A runner breathlessly interrupted, "The *policia* are here searching houses. Someone has told them goods from Mexico have come."

"Come on, Roger," George hissed, "let's get out of here. If they see us with the supplies, they will know it's for the *ganjaneros*."

"Go straight away," Francis interjected. "This boy will show you the safest way from the village."

Francis and Roger briefly locked eyes as Roger stood to leave. Roger meant to show humility and understanding through his eyes. He couldn't tell if Francis got his meaning, except maybe for the respectful nod he received from the elder as he went out the door.

The little boy ran through the back of the house and through the dusty roads. Roger and George kept pace with the little boy who ran proudly around the back of the little village to the red truck.

They got out of town without incident. George thanked the boy as he jumped from the truck, and Roger tossed him a bunch of bananas in appreciation as they drove off.

"It makes me mad when the police steal food from the peasants," George told Roger.

"They do that?" Roger asked, shaking his head. "Well, if the old man is right and that's their biggest problem, then their problems are small. We need to arrange a working relationship with the cops so they leave the villagers alone."

"No, no, Roger. We only need to make them pay one time for them to realize we will take no more." Roger smiled at George's determination, but he shook his head.

"If they revolt with arms, then the police will carry guns," he explained. "If they are brave enough to enter the homes and steal food now, how much more courage will they have if they carried guns? You gotta go to South America to understand, it's better the way it is. George, Francis is much smarter than we are about this."

"Well, we need guns to hunt, and to protect the camp. I always carry mine."

Roger thought again what Francis said and he weighed his next words.

"George, if I've taught you anything, I hope it's that the secret to survival is to not let anyone know what you're doing or what you've got. If you organized a resistance, it would expose a growing power, and the government will form a force against it. Believe me, this place is sweet the way it is. We've got it made. The trade is still small, and the farmers are unorganized. One day, it will change, but for now we should enjoy it. George, promise me that you won't forget that our progress is only temporary and you won't get crazy with your guns."

"I understand what you're telling me," George said, giving him a long, sober look. "I promise, neither I nor any of the crew will act except in self defense."

"Good," Roger said. "It's the only way to go."

The men drove down the open flatlands along the Blue Creek, passing the lone police station where the raiders were based. On the Mexican side of a narrow bridge, several homes lay scattered across the hillside. Driving quickly, they left more dust in the air as they went westward through rising terrain to the Mennonite settlement of Tres Leguas.

Beyond the first house on a ridge just outside the settlement, Roger saw the fuselage of an old Lockheed Constellation converted for storage by an enterprising farmer. The decades-old hulk bore witness that somewhere nearby there had once been a long landing strip. Following the dirt road that closely paralleled the Mexican border, they came upon a family of Mennonites in a horse-drawn cart. Roger pulled out his camera to take a picture, but as soon as the people saw the device, they hid their faces in their hands, and Roger quickly lowered the camera feeling embarrassed that he had violated their privacy. He held out his hand and gestured an apology as they moved past.

The Mennonite's religious lifestyle fascinated Roger. Their white shirts and suspendered black pants brought to life a time long past. They believed in doing everything in its most natural way and that modern innovation was the downfall of man. Roger wondered if they were right. He knew little of the people except what he observed and what some outcasts of the group had told him.

George spotted one Mennonite man talking to another as they sat in an old flatbed truck by the settlement. These were George's friends, outcasts who had violated their culture by driving trucks and tractors.

"This is the guy who's building the airfield," George said, pointing to one of them, "Jacob. And they've both been growing and selling too."

As George pulled alongside, the men looked in the back at the supplies, and one leaned in the window of the truck.

"Hi, Jacob," George said. "Anything going on?"

"No. Nobody's been by here. It's been real quiet. Heading back?"

"Soon. Do you remember Roger?"

"Yeah, from last year. Hello Roger." He stretched out his hand to greet Roger.

"Jacob, I hear you got a strip that's pretty long. Is it one you built?"

"No. Oh no. This one's been back there for many years. I think the last time it was used was in the sixties."

"It's perfect," George said. "Long enough, and close so we won't have to haul the load on any dangerous roads."

"When can we look at it?" Roger asked Jacob.

"Whenever you're ready."

"As soon as we get back from delivering the supplies," George said. "Tomorrow mid-afternoon okay?"

They nodded and George continued up the road. Roger grinned at George.

"Glad we can check it out," he said. "Can't trust a non-pilot's word about a runway, no matter what they think they know."

"You have trouble with that in the past?"

"Just once, but it was big trouble. I'll never do that again."

The road deteriorated rapidly as they drove on past a small, scattered Mennonite village. Soon the road became a two-rut wagon trail. Soon after that, it became a footpath. When it became impassable for the truck, George turned off into the trees and parked. Roger handed him a radio and he punched in the frequency monitored by the men in the bush. A few moments after the second call, their response came back, and George told them to bring horses and men to haul the supplies.

Roger arranged his bag for the hike, then looked up at a sound outside the truck and saw three shotgun-toting Belizeans standing next to his window. He tapped George on the shoulder and George got out to greet them with hugs and smiles and backslaps. Then he gestured for Roger to join them.

"Roger," he said as soon as Roger stepped from the truck, "these are my brothers Rubin and Hector, and this is Juan. He lives in San Felipe. Juan's a great runner and can go for many miles. He's our back-up radio. They are guarding the entrance to camp so no *banditos* come upon us."

Roger smiled and shook their hands.

"George, these two are your brothers? They don't look anything like you!"

George laughed as he handed them a loaf of bread and cold drinks, a bushman's luxury. While they waited for the others, George refueled the truck from a 55-gallon drum and checked its fluids. He took out a map when he finished and oriented Roger on the route they had traveled.

"See, the road had officially ended near the settlement," he said. "The ruts we followed are a peasant's crossing into Mexico. Jacob and Pedro, the other Mennonite on the flatbed, they picked the location for the farm because it's so close to Mexico we have an escape route if there are any problems."

"Sounds great, George," Roger said. "Good work."

"Thanks, man," and Roger could see George's pride at the compliment.

The carrying party arrived then, eight men and a pair of pack horses emerging quietly from the jungle. The short, black haired men with coffee-colored eyes and somber round faces smiled excitedly when they saw the supplies, and a moment later were even happier when Rubin and Hector handed them cold beers.

George, Roger, Hector and Rubin first loaded the horses with the heaviest parcels while the eight growers rested and quaffed their beers, then they filled each man's pack with a decent load. George picked two of the new arrivals to stay with Juan to guard the trailhead, then they started up the hill into the jungle.

Half an hour later, they passed a guard at the outer perimeter of the camp, a mile and a half into the jungle, and shortly thereafter reached the camp itself.

Roger surveyed the settlement of crudely made hammocks and makeshift Visqueen tents stretched between trees on the well-trampled ground. A small natural spring bubbled over a circle of rocks and trickled down an incline into a clearing at the edge of camp. He saw a fairly neat garbage dump and latrine downhill from the camp, and far offline from the stream. Aerial searchers could find it if they knew more or less where to look, but Roger was satisfied that it would probably elude casual observation.

The hikers dropped their packs, unloaded the horses, and stowed the cargo in wooden crates under thick trees that protected it from the elements. Rubin then picked the strongest growers go back downhill and get the rest of the shipment. When one of them balked at the additional hike, Rubin whispered in his ear.

"More cold beer down there, too, *amigo*." The man's frown disappeared and he dashed to the front of the group as they left camp.

"Works every time," George said to Roger with a grin.

The growing team consisted of 12 in all, a huge operation for Belize. The group had emerged from Roger's frustration on previous trips, when he'd been forced to travel from one end of the country to the other to put together a single ton—due both to small operations and such poor crops that he rejected most of what he inspected.

His searching time had not been a waste, though; through his travels, he met the most qualified growers and George had recruited them into the present operation. Each man was proud to be a part of the well-equipped co-op and of its productive yields, and each knew he was learning invaluable knowledge that he could use for his own plots when this commitment ended.

And they were extremely well-equipped, especially for Belize. Each time on previous trips, Roger and Hanoi had sent generators, pumps, and other gear for the plantation on every plane. They hadn't deadheaded to the country a single time. Now, with the operation fully scaled up through Roger's smart leadership and intricate planning, they were preparing the largest single shipment of Belizean *sinsemilla* in the country's history.

Much remained to be done, of course. The growers were now expert at working jungle pot farms, but they were also rookie smugglers and unaware of the mission's magnitude. Roger counted on the veteran help of his main men, George and Manu, to make sure each team member could handle his assignment the day the big plane landed. It would be a big challenge, but Roger was confident the operation would succeed.

He toured the facility and saw the yet-to-be-used processing stations. The first contained three stretcher-like devices made from long, straight trees holding apart several layers of chicken wire. George explained that this was where the dried tops would have the "sheesh" shaken from them. Slightly downhill from that were four trash compactors mounted on a plywood floor and protected by a heavy olive drab tarpaulin. The machines made a 12 x 18 x 18-inch, 20-pound block, an ideal size for handling, transporting, and selling stateside. Continuing down the gentle slope, the men walked along the spring-fed stream to the final station on the treeline. There he saw gardening utensils, machetes, and fertilizers.

George called over Paco, the head grower who Roger knew from San Felipe, and the three ventured into the clearing for a preliminary field inspection. They passed through the grower's vegetable garden, then entered row upon row of a well-cultivated crop. Roger knew the growing stages and was quite impressed with what he saw.

"What are your watering and fertilizing procedures?" he asked Paco.

"I let the plant tell me when it's ready for each," he said. "These are different than the Mexican I grew." He stopped next to a ten-footer and brushed aside the thick branches, exposing a huge main stalk. "These plants will get much bigger, so I don't want to rush the flowers. If we let the plant determine when to bud, we'll get much more than if we use potash now."

Roger knew Paco was right, both from the obvious health and vigor of the plants, and what he knew from his Hawaiian source: the seeds came from 20-foot trees grown from multi-year hybrids. He was delighted to see that Paco knew exactly what he was doing.

The rest of the supplies arrived as they wandered around the patch, and the three returned to camp just as the others finished storing the goods, so Roger gathered the growers together for a meeting. Before talking, however, he unzipped his Cordura bag and handed each man two pairs of new jeans that were exactly his size. Most of them stripped off their dirty old pants and donned their new denim on the spot, chattering happily among themselves and thanking Roger with smiles, nods and gracious words. When they settled down, Roger stood in front of them.

"My friends," he said, "I am very happy with your work. You built a good camp, and everything is in the right place. And the crop. It is—"

A nearby gunshot interrupted him.

Roger frowned as he watched the men quickly run off toward the sound, showing no fear or even concern. He looked at Paco, who was smiling.

With no sign of intimidation the men hurdled through the brush under the canopy of trees.

"Our hunter has been hunting *jabalí*," he said, "and I think he got one."

"Wild boar?" Roger asked.

"*Sí*, and the others go now to finish him off. With that and the new food, we feast tonight, yes Roger?"

"*Sí*," Roger said, smiling. *I really need this*, he thought. *I need this for my soul.*

Several minutes later, the growers returned proudly, carrying the dead hog. Roger noted that they all wore knives that Roger had previously sent to them, and one man was already putting his to work dressing and cleaning the main course. The others gathered around a young man Roger assumed was the hunter as he told the story of his hunt. When he finished, Roger went over to him and shook his hand.

"*Excellente, señor*," he said appreciatively.

"*Gracias, don* Roger," he said respectfully, and as he bowed, Roger noticed that he still wore old blue jeans. He counted heads and realized there were now 13 in all.

"I'm sorry I didn't bring jeans for you," he said, then turned to George. "How long's he been here?"

"We just brought him on to hunt for us."

"Well, he sure did his job today." He turned back to the hunter. "*Amigo*, next time I come down, I'd like to bring you something. What would you like?"

The hunter looked at George for guidance, unsure how to talk to the American.

"Go ahead," George prompted. "Answer him."

"I would like boots like yours," he replied confidently.

Roger looked down at the man's bare feet, then his own, then he pulled a pair of socks from his bag and handed them to the hunter. The young man took them, frowning in uncertainty at what Roger was doing.

Then Roger sat down and yanked off the expensive Tony Lama and handed them to the hunter.

"See if they fit," he ordered. The hunter instantly sat down and put on the socks, then pulled on the boots. They fit perfectly and the smile that spread across his face lit up the camp.

"*Gracias, señor*," he said happily. "*Muchos gracias!*"

The rest of the growers celebrated the hunter's good fortune as the young man stomped around the camp in his stylish new footwear.

Roger was at least as happy as the hunter; now he could put his comfortable sneakers back on, which he did, then kicked back under a tree and watched the show.

He saw the camaraderie of his growers as they sliced vegetables and made flour tortillas on a hot piece of metal over hot coals. The joy they took in preparing their feast showed him how such simple things were the most valuable. He could see what Francis was getting at when he told him about not wanting the children to become materialistic. Roger saw how happy these people were before he brought them gifts and a hefty salary, but he also saw that new jeans, cold beer, and fresh meat also made them smile.

Roger struggled with the paradox between his gifts and a relaxed life not spent in pursuit of material wealth. *Were they not already happy in their simplicity? Americans are not generally happy in their wealth, so how can bringing money and gifts benefit these people?*

Roger meant for his gifts to hopefully buy their loyalty, *but wouldn't this disrupt the simplicity Francis wished for his people?* This was just a different world, a different world that held different perceptions. He wondered if their generous salaries would lure them to seek the white man's toys in Belize City. Then he thought about the Mennonites. These people knew of but rejected the temptation of modernization. Finally, what about himself? Did he place too much value on his own fast-paced life of airplanes, boats, islands, and suitcases full of money? Roger took a drink from his bottled water, watched his team prepare dinner, and pondered which lifestyle was correct, if either.

Later that evening, the group sat in a circle on stumps, enjoying the spread. While the growers looked on, Roger hesitantly tasted the wild boar, then bit firmly down on it, crudely tearing a hunk with his teeth. He ignored the toughness and concentrated on the taste—and was surprised to find it very good.

"*Bueno!*" he said, and the growers applauded his pronouncement and went back to their own meals. Then Paco passed him the armadillo they had shot before Roger arrived, cooked in its shell. *Armadillo on the half shell,* he thought. *My God, this thing's a rat in armor!*

Roger didn't know what rat tasted like, but armadillo wasn't bad and he thanked his companions for sharing it with him.

"*De nada,*" said the cook, then smiled slyly. "Roger, I would like you to try my favorite, *habenero.*"

"Is that a pepper? Well, I really do like spicy and hot food."

The cook placed a small piece of the native *habanero* on some rice and Roger ate it. Instantly, his mouth felt like he had swigged battery acid; he spit everything out and tried to breathe. He tried to say he'd never tasted anything so potent, but he couldn't talk. Fresh beads of sweat joined the perspiration already rolling down his face. His eyes filled with tears and he stuffed tortillas in his mouth to dampen the burning.

It didn't help. Nothing helped. The growers roared with laughter as he tried to regain his composure.

"I'm so sorry, Roger," said the cook, laughing with the others, "but you said you liked hot things."

Roger's mouth finally calmed down, but he was done eating for the night. He had truly lost his appetite.

A mellow atmosphere fell over the camp as they sat around the fire with full bellies.

"Roger, what is life like in America?" one grower asked. "Is it great?"

"Great is a word for those who want to believe doing something or having something makes you better than others," Roger said thoughtfully. "For some of you, your fathers are most happy when they have lots of chickens laying eggs. For others, it's a good harvest. I'm an American, and seeing how you live, I can't say America is great, or even better. It's just different. Here you live in peace, free to do what you want in a natural environment. You are so different from the Mennonites and the other people who've settled here, but you all live in harmony and neither of you looks down upon the other. In America, we preach unity but segregate the minorities. One day that will all explode if things don't change, and then living in Belize will be much better."

"You mean this is better, living in the bush hoping one day to have a house and a truck?" asked another. "In America, doesn't everyone have these things?"

Roger listened, flashing back on Francis's words and he thought about his answer.

"First of all, no, not everyone in America has a house, or even a truck. Second, don't be fooled into thinking that having fancy things makes you happy. Yes, you can have fine possessions and be happy, but you must weigh more than the package. Nothing is better than God, health, and freedom. When we rate a temporary pleasure over things that last forever, we have lost sight of value. Don't underestimate what your parents can teach you. Good people only come from good stock, just like the plants we grow. Our plants are special because they come from special seeds. With lots of love and care, the plants thrive, but if they are neglected, they wither and die. As with you, you must let your parents teach you the things of life. So take advantage of the values you learn from them."

"You mean Belize is better than America," another asked, "but you still want to live there with all those things you have?"

The question threw Roger off because he had never realized that his philosophy was hypocritical.

"For me, I must say that as bad as America can be, I still feel it is the best place for *me* to live. It is my home, and that is what I'm used to. We must not forget that all things are temporary and power corrupts. If we don't keep watch on the government's actions, we will pay like the Nicaraguans. Americans are being lulled to sleep by chasing possessions. They don't realize the struggles that go on every day around the world. The most comfortable ones don't want to know there are people like you struggling to feed your families and happy when no one is sick. The fancy things you ask about have captured their minds, distracting them with materialistic pursuit. I guess what I'm trying to say is we all look through different eyes and have different goals. Being Belizean is the same in that respect as anywhere. We must always be happy with what we have rather than unhappy with what we don't have. When you obtain fine things, never allow it to change who you are. Remember these humble times."

"Roger, what other places have you traveled to?" Rubin asked.

"All over the United States and Mexico. Some other places too."

"What's it like being able to travel, Roger?"

"It's nice to see how other people live. It gives you a new perspective into your own life, and you get to see new things. And it makes going home even nicer."

"That sounds so great," Rubin said. "I can't wait until I can travel to new places. I have dreams about taking a jet plane to the United States."

Roger stayed with the party until fatigue and alcohol overcame everyone. Alongside the fire they prepared a bed for him by laying the horse blankets over a pile of sticks to soften the ground. Drifting into sleep, listening to the dwindling crackles of the fire, Roger pondered the questions they had asked. Never before had he been in a position to share his experiences, nor had he openly admitted his feelings to himself.

Roger woke up in cool shade that rapidly became humid light as the sun rose and the day began. He rolled his shoulders to stretch out the soreness from the ground as the camp began rustling with life. He took out a small portable electric razor and shaved. The growers laughed at him for it, but if things turned sour, Roger didn't want to look like he'd been in the bush.

After a hearty breakfast, the oldest growers assigned chores and the crews went to work. Roger's first inspection of the field had been brief, so he looked forward to a better look as George gathered Paco and Ramon, the most knowledgeable growers, and soon after they resumed the tour.

As they walked from one plot into another, the plant heights kept increasing until Roger stood beneath 16-foot pot trees with flourishing, six-foot colas that strained to hold the bud-laden branches. Their unmistakable aroma saturated the air. Roger walked in awe among the flowering plants.

"I can't believe how full these are," he said, as he grabbed a branch to closely inspect the glistening red hairs, feeling the hearty girth of the cola. Moist resin oozed between his fingers.

"Feels like flypaper," he said to a clearly proud Ramon as he pulled it to his face and sniffed the female's potent aroma. "Excellent, man, totally excellent."

He stepped back to gaze towards the top, still amazed by its massive size.

"How much older are these than the ones near the camp?" he asked Paco.

"Two weeks," he said, and Roger's eyebrows arched at this news. "These plants were sown two days before the full moon. That is the best time to start. It will give us nearly twice the yield as the others. The majority of the crop is from this planting."

Roger was intrigued by Paco's knowledge. His talent was evidenced by the farm's abundance. Roger followed him deeper into the mist.

"We stroke the long branches upward and knock off the yellow rain leaves," Ramon said, "and of course, the rows are planted north and south so they produce more."

"How long will it take to bale five thousand pounds?" Roger asked Paco.

Paco consulted Ramon in Spanish for a moment before answering.

"The amount you wish is much larger than we are accustomed to."

"And so are these plants!" added Ramon.

"Our guess is that each one will bring four pounds of dried bud," Paco went on. "In this field alone, we have over one thousand trees, and the largest patch is behind that hill. The answer depends on the rains because we will easily have over ten thousand pounds if all goes well.

This field should be ready very soon. We are only making them cry out more against the sun. When the rains end, which is soon, we bring in the last. That should be two or three more months. We have several more men coming in for the harvest. So we need half that time for the amount you need."

"Good," Roger said. "That'll be about right to get everything ready on my end too."

As they walked back to camp, dwarfed by the towers of legendary herb, Roger was quietly elated. The operation was running as smoothly as he'd hoped and the results were better than he'd expected. Now for the next piece of the puzzle.

They rested awhile before hiking back to the trucks, so George drew up a list of needed supplies and refilled their canteens. A relief team carrying food and radios for the watchmen at the trail head went with them and traded stations with their counterparts.

George and Roger drove back onto the road and a mile past the Mennonite settlement to the turnoff for Jacob's white, well-maintained two-story house. The tall thin bearded Mennonite came out to greet them, his children following him onto the porch but no further. His oldest boy had a green pet parrot perched on his shoulder, and they all stared at the visitors as Jacob got in the truck.

They headed east for a while, then turned onto a dirt road that ended at a private drive blocked by a locked gate. Jacob got out, punched in the combination, and waved them through. They cleared a small knoll and approached an apparently deserted house. Jacob looked out as they slowly drove by to see if anyone was there, then instructed George to pull across the grass and behind an old barn.

Roger looked around doubtfully. He saw nothing that resembled an airstrip among the rolling hills.

"You sure there's a mile-long airstrip out here?" he asked Jacob.

"Absolutely," Jacob said confidently, unconcerned by Roger's obvious doubt as he directed George's truck through a narrow pass between two small hills to a long valley hidden from the road.

A tremendous view of the Mexican mountains a mile away opened up in front of them, accented by an old hangar off to one side. Several broken-down buses and trucks blocked the runway. George parked near one end of the strip and they got out to walk. Roger looked down the deceptively narrow stretch and realized that this *had* been an active airfield. The crumbling blacktop needed repair, but it *was* blacktop, not dirt, and it could certainly handle the Howard.

The men fanned out into the waist-high grass growing through the cracks, looking for holes or obstructions. Roger walked the clear center and counted his steps. At the end of what he considered the usable length he had paced around 5,000 feet—almost a mile, just as Jacob had said. Recounting the steps back he noticed that the hill, which conveniently hid the strip from the road, was also a potential takeoff hazard for a heavily loaded plane.

"Which way's the prevailing wind?" he asked Jacob. Jacob pointed toward the unobstructed Mexican border. Roger nodded.

"Perfect," he said, and looked around the valley again, soaking it all in. "So who built this and what did they use it for?"

"Can't say," said Jacob. "All I can tell you is that no one's used it for many years, and certainly not for the purpose you have in mind."

They returned to the truck and Roger drove up and down it three times to re-check the length and test the smoothness. It came in at 1.1 miles and it was actually pretty smooth.

"We'll have to cut this grass down, though," he told Jacob. "Can't have anything dinging the props or slowing down the takeoff roll."

"Sure thing," Jacob agreed. "I can take care of that for the right price."

Roger grinned at the negotiating tone that instantly appeared in Jacob's voice and they spent the rest of their return drive haggling good-naturedly until they settled on a healthy figure that included some Mennonite loading help.

When they got back to Jacob's home, his blond-haired brood was playing in front of the house. Roger thought of the toy stash in the back.

"Is it okay if I give your kids some presents?" he asked. Jacob was surprised at the request, but he smiled warmly.

"Thank you, Roger. Yes, you may," he said. "It would be a blessing."

Minutes later, Jacob's kids were playing as joyfully as George's children had two days before—and Roger was just as happy watching them.

They took their leave of Jacob and went to San Felipe, where Manu waited at the edge of the village. Manu spotted their truck and hailed them on the radio. George pulled up next to the Rover parked on the side of the dirt road.

"The Blue Creek police came through here and cleaned these people out," he said, clearly upset. "They took *everything*—even stuff clearly marked from Belize. None of the people are asking for anything, but they're really hurting."

"Let's go talk to Francis," Roger said, controlling his anger. He hated bullies, really hated them, and bullies with badges were the worst. When they met up with Francis, though, Roger soon learned why he was so respected in his village.

"It was a small price to pay for the wisdom we all learned," he said calmly as he confirmed Manu's account for Roger. These are new police transferred from Punta Gorda in the far south. They are unlike the local police, who only took contraband." He smiled a little and his eyes twinkled. "Next time, we will be better prepared. They will find that we are a very poor village that has only empty shelves."

"You are a wise man," Roger said quietly. "It is an honor to know you. Please let me know how I can help." Francis shook his head slowly.

"We are a proud people and do not seek charity," he said. "Besides, Roger, you must keep your presence here secret from them, and if you help us they will know that—how you say in America?—something is up."

Roger smiled in spite of his grim mood, and shook hands with Francis as they got up to go. As soon as he got outside, though, he stuck a wad of cash in Manu's hand and told him to follow them back to Orange Walk, load the Rover with whatever he thought the villagers needed, and get it back to them before dark if possible.

Roger checked into the Chula Vista Hotel again when they got back to Orange Walk and reviewed their trip and past accounts while Manu went shopping. The hotel was very simple, but it was the best Orange Walk had to offer. It was pretty clean, for one, and, best of all, it had an improvised shower stall rigged in the corner. The building included a small but good restaurant below Roger's room, plus the adjoining two-pump gas station, over which the owners lived.

Roger approved George's past expenses, and they planned out remaining payroll and aircraft loading details. Roger decided to personally handle the stacking inside the plane so it was distributed properly and wouldn't shift in flight. George would supervise the bale throwers from the truck, and Manu would help the co-pilot refuel.

Roger chose three of the growers to help him, and George picked four. They also planned to place one of George's brothers as a lookout on the hill above the road. The total crew came to ten at the plane, plus the pilots and lookout.

Roger leaned back and visualized the operation. He calculated an estimated ground time of no more than 20 minutes. While waiting for Manu to return, they exchanged dreams for the future and casual small talk. Roger didn't tell George of his retirement plans. He wanted to see how things worked out first. If all went well, the organization should survive without him. He did tell George that the money was tight for the time being and asked him to be conservative. George, being honest and frugal by nature, agreed without hesitation.

One of their radios squawked. It was Manu.

"I'm just coming into town," Manu said. "Dude was blown away by what we brought. Tried to turn it down with that same charity speech, but I told him exactly what you told me to say—"This is only fair for all that your men have done for us in the bush." So he took it and said to tell you thanks."

"Great," Roger answered. "Good job. See you at dinner."

Manu filled in Roger on the Indian Church project over a delicious home-cooked meal of chicken *mole* and at Roger's favorite "mom and pop" restaurant, whose owner ran a black market currency exchange and was always happy to see Roger and his American money.

Indian Church was an abandoned village south of San Felipe that lay along a series of narrow fresh water lakes. With a year-round water supply, they hoped to farm during the dry season. Manu already had their youngest crop growing there to test this idea.

"Good work," Roger said to Manu around a mouthful of *mole.*

"That'll bring in a lot of cash if it works," added George, "because we'll have product when no one else does."

"Next thing," Roger went on, "I want you to charter a plane so we can get coordinates and landmarks on the Tres Leguas site for the pilots. I also want to over fly the farms to see how exposed they are from the air and, if we have time, try to find that abandoned strip at the Gallon Jug settlement on the west side of the district. I'm tired of slogging through the bush looking for it."

The next morning, Manu went back to Indian Church while Roger and George returned to Belize City. When they got there a few hours later, Roger went to the government telecommunications building and left a coded message for Mickey that everything was on schedule. Then they drove to the Belize Municipal Airport on the water's edge on the north side of town, and chartered a British-made Islander from Belize Aero, which they had picked over the other FBO because it had an air-conditioned office—a sign of a more professional, better-run business.

The Islander was the only available plane at that time, but Roger was more than happy with it because it was a rugged, high-wing, fixed-gear twin-engine turbine in which Roger logged many hours flying jumpers.

His next order of business was feeling out the young pilot, Romero, who needed to be a trustworthy person, not only a competent pilot. Roger started by telling the young man only that they were doing a sightseeing tour in the northern part of the country, with George acting as his local guide.

Roger climbed through the pilot's door and into the co-pilot's seat, followed by Romero after he had loaded George into the plane through a separate door under the high wing. The plane normally carried ten passengers and luggage, but the four rear-most seats had been removed.

"We need the room for scuba gear," Romero said. "Most of our charters are divers going out to the outer cays. Very beautiful out there."

"I know," Roger smiled. "Been out there a few times myself."

Roger watched Romero intently as the young pilot formally went through every item on his pre-flight checklist. *Thorough and methodical,* Roger thought. *I like what I see so far.* He put on a headset so he could hear the tower chatter.

Roger was happy when Romero taxied. Soon, they'd be airborne and clear of the intense heat. Roger knew Romero didn't have a lot of flying time, but he was confident and conscientious, a good combination.

He was also flying a good plane. The Islander could take off from very short and rough airstrips, especially when it was lightly loaded, and when Romero pushed the throttles forward, the powerful little twin jumped quickly into the air. Romero smoothly transitioned from takeoff to climb profile, then opened his window to clear out the air. Roger followed suit with his own window, watched Belize City and the

Caribbean stream by beneath the propeller spinning right next to his head, then turned his attention to the folded map in his lap.

En route to Indian Church, they crossed the nearly completed Northern Highway and its long runway-like features. The road-scarred land stuck out as it cut through the lush bush of the flatlands. Roger leaned back in the noisy cabin and asked George when the highway would open.

"Hard to say time-wise," George answered. "Task-wise, they only have a couple more bridges to finish before it will be passable."

"Let's fly up the highway for a while," Roger told Romero, pointing northward, "and see how the construction's going." Roger wanted to see how many places there were along the highway to put down a large plane, but he didn't want his pilot to notice, so he took some pictures with George's camera of what he called "cool images" of waterways and farms. When they reached the spot where the new route intersected with the old road, they flew over Orange Walk on up to Progresso, a small village on the western shore of Progresso Lagoon, where Roger had landed most of his past runs on a strip disguised as a cane road next to the lagoon's ghastly white water that made it so easy for the pilots to find. They did one picture pass, then turned south along the Hondo River, which marked the border between Belize and Mexico.

From their lofty vantage point, Roger easily spotted the Tres Leguas strip, and he turned to Romero.

"Mind if I set the VOR?" he asked. Romero frowned in surprise, then smiled.

"Sure," he said cheerfully, "have at it." Then he watched carefully as Roger dialed in the VOR signal at Belize International Airport and jotted down the reading.

"How long have you been flying?" he asked.

"Long time." Romero grinned at the news.

"You want to give her a try?" he asked, gesturing at the wheel.

"Yeah, that'd be nice. Thanks."

"Okay, man, you have the airplane." He watched Roger grasp the wheel like an old friend, then lifted his hands clear so Roger knew he was now running the show.

"When did you start?"

"When I was about seventeen, maybe eighteen. I—"

"I started at nineteen!" Romero interrupted. "I just love flying."

"Me too," Roger grinned. "Can't get that sensation of freedom anywhere else—or that warm feeling you get when you put her safely back on the ground."

"I feel the same way! How many hours do you have?"

"A few thousand."

"Wow! *Fantástico*! What ratings?"

"Commercial, instrument, multi-engine rated." Romero nodded in approval and appreciation, then turned serious.

"What do you think is the most important thing for a pilot to do?"

"Always stay ahead of the airplane and never ignore your gut," Roger replied without hesitation. Romero nodded.

"The same thing my instructor said every time we took off."

"You had an excellent instructor," Roger said, then smiled. "But I already knew that from the way you fly—and more importantly, the way you pre-flight."

"*Gracias, amigo*," Romero said humbly. "That means much coming from such an experienced pilot."

Roger nodded in acknowledgement and smiled inwardly. *A new friend for life*, he thought.

Roger looked back and saw George on the radio, talking to the ground crew at the farm. He leaned close to Roger's ear.

"Good thing I called," he said. "They were nervous when they saw the plane, but okay now 'cause they know it's us. Paco says he hopes you like the setup."

"I do indeed," Roger grinned, having already noted the massive size of the complex and how every foot of open ground had been cultivated. Roger was turning away from the farm when George thumped him on the shoulder. Roger looked sharply around to see George pointing to the radio, clearly distressed.

"Manu says a village girl just got hurt bad by a tractor accident and no one knows what to do!" Roger immediately turned east.

"Indian Church?" he asked. George held up a hand as he listened to the radio, then looked at Roger.

"San Felipe." Roger looked at Romero.

"We have a situation," he said. "Hold on." Then he cranked the plane around and started a rapid descent."

"What's up, man?" asked Romero, unconcerned with the sharp maneuvering but curious about what Roger was doing.

"Little girl needs a medevac," Roger said as San Felipe came into view. "We're gonna go pick her up." Romero's eyes widened in fear.

"If we land there, I'll lose my job!" he said loudly. "Company rules and national regulations!"

Roger ignored him as he spotted a tight knot of people in a cane field south of the village, and Romero did not say anything more as Roger circled the area in a tight bank and surveyed the sole dirt road. Roger pointed it out to the young pilot.

"Can you land there?"

Romero checked it out and shook his head. "No way, man. Not me."

"Well, sit tight then, 'cause I'm gonna!" Romero gasped at the notion as Roger gestured at George with his chin and George quickly handed the pilot a Grant. Romero grabbed the money and took a deep breath.

"My eyes are closed, *señor*, but please don't make me regret this."

"Thanks, man," Roger said, and patted Romero's tense shoulder comfortingly, then dropped one wing and stomped on the opposite rudder, slipping the plane rapidly from the sky. The maneuver let Roger line up on the road and all of his experience flying jumpers came together in one heart-stopping approach swoop onto a steep final approach. He settled in at 45 m.p.h. and with the stall warning horn blaring, flared close to the ground and used the ground-effect cushion to stop his descent just as the mains hit the dirt. He slowed the plane well before the end of his makeshift runway and turned to Romero.

"Keep them idling so we can get off fast," he said as he climbed out of the seat and left the plane through the under-wing door, then helped George out and kept him clear of the spinning propellers.

"Keep everyone away from the plane," he shouted over the noise. "We don't need somebody walking into a prop!"

Then he ran over to the tractor and his heart sank. The little girl lying in the cane field was Rosa, the girl who had given him an orange and helped him with his Spanish. Around him, the villagers talked in Spanish so fast he had no idea what they were saying, especially the man whose horror-stricken face marked him as Rosa's father.

Roger saw that the tractor's big wheel track intersected her tiny body, a very bad sign. *But the ground is very soft,* he thought, *so maybe there is still hope.* He knew little about medicine, but from her pain-ridden eyes and his experience with drop zone injuries, he knew there was no time to waste.

He grabbed a tarp from the tractor, laid it out next to Rosa, and rolled her carefully onto it. Then he enlisted her father and two other men and they carried her to the plane, her mother followed closely behind, hysterical with grief. George shepherded the other villagers away from the props as they laid her gently in the plane. Then Roger climbed in, George helped her parents board, and George pulled the door shut behind him.

Roger realized as he reached the cockpit that Romero had climbed into the co-pilot seat. He tapped his checklist as Roger strapped himself in.

"Ready to go," he said. Roger slapped him appreciatively on the shoulder.

"Right *on*, Romero!" Roger revved the engines slowly to warn everyone away from the plane and as he bounced the plane over part of the cane field to turn around, Romero readied the flaps and boost pumps for takeoff, then placed the trim wheel in the most ideal position. Then, with a smuggler's skill, Roger stood on the brakes and wound up the engines, creating a huge cloud of dust and a gale-force wind that blew the hats off every villager. Then he released the brakes and the plane lunged forward on the dirt road. Roger pulled the nose up quickly to reduce rolling drag, then flew the plane smoothly off the road with plenty of room to spare.

As soon as they were airborne, Romero cleaned up and re-trimmed the plane, then grabbed a map and pointed at the compass.

"Fly heading one-three-five," he said, then he keyed his radio.

"Belize Tower, Belize Air zero-six-Papa. We have a medical emergency and need an ambulance to meet us on the tarmac. ETA fifteen minutes. Over."

"Copy zero-six-Papa. Need ambulance onsite fifteen minutes, over."

"Affirmative, Belize Tower. Zero-six-Papa out."

Romero looked at Roger. Roger grinned and nodded at the young pilot like a very—very—proud papa. Romero beamed at the silent praise, then turned back and gave Rosa's parents a thumbs up and a gentle smile.

"*Una ambulancia estará allí,*" he told them. They sighed in relief as Father held his wife tightly and she in turn stroked Rosa's hair.

When they reached Belize City, Roger cranked a hard, skydiver-pilot turn to a short final, touched down halfway down the runway and kept the speed up as they rolled toward the tarmac.

"I didn't think the plane could do that!" said Romero. Roger laughed.

"Planes can usually do more than their pilots if you let them," he said.

They rolled up to the main airport building just as the ambulance arrived and the paramedics spilled out of it. Roger shut down the engines before the plane stopped and George jumped out while it was still moving to make sure the approaching paramedics didn't run into the props.

They pushed their stretcher up to the door and quickly loaded Rosa onto it, then rolled her quickly back to the ambulance. George helped the little girl's parents out of the plane and put them into the ambulance. One paramedic shut the door as the other one jumped into the driver's seat and dashed through the airport's gate, siren wailing.

Roger and Romero climbed out of the Islander as the ambulance siren faded into the distance, and saw the charter company's manager walking over to see what the commotion was all about. Romero looked scared. Roger shot him a stern glance.

"Confidence, man, *confidence*," he whispered urgently. "Just follow my lead and everything will be cool."

Roger smiled at the manager and shook his hand.

"Congratulations. Your pilot is a hero," he said earnestly, setting the tone.

"Really," said the manager, frowning at Romero, who stood stiffly.

"Yeah, really. He picked up a distress call about a badly injured young girl and told us he had to help her, then did some great flying to land close by." The manager's eye flicked over to the plane and Roger knew instantly what he was thinking. "I have been a pilot for many years, and he is one of the best I have ever seen. He took no big chances and landed softly. I am very proud of him, and you should be, too. He was very brave and kind to help like he did."

The manager eyed Romero intently, searching his young face.

"This is true?" he asked. Romero nodded but said nothing.

"He told me you might be angry that he broke the company rules," Roger went on, his eyes boring into those of the manager, "but that he was sure you would understand that even a good rule is not worth a child's life. I agree."

The manager pondered for a moment, then looked again at the plane.

"And there is no damage to the plane, nothing I have to explain to the owner?"

"No sir," Romero said.

"In my opinion," Roger interjected, "he deserves a raise. He's a very good pilot."

"Yes, he is," said the manager, "but explaining a raise is harder than explaining damage to the plane. Perhaps it's best to celebrate this good deed in our hearts instead of in the books, no?" Roger laughed out loud.

"You're a wise man, sir," he said. "I look forward to doing business with you again!"

"Thank you very much," the manager said, and finally he smiled. "I am glad you enjoyed our service. And now I must get back to the office," he said, wiping sweat from his brow. "It is too damn hot out here."

Roger and Romero watched him go, then walked back to the plane, Romero still in shock from what had just happened.

"You talk as good as you fly," he finally said, "and I thank you very much but it is you who was brave and excellent."

Roger retrieved his pack from the plane and helped Romero clean the cabin of its cane straw and dirt, then handed Romero another Grant as George looked on.

"Don't be so modest, man. You were the pilot in command of that flight. I only did what you allowed me to do, and you did many things yourself that made it possible for me to do what I did."

"Really?"

"Really, so take credit where credit is due." They all shook hands.

"Okay, Roger, I will, and I will never forget the many things I learned today from you about flying—and about life."

"Why did you do that, Roger?" George asked, as they got in the truck. "You were the real hero, not him."

"Because if there's any publicity, I don't want my name in the paper," he said simply. "I want the story to focus on Romero and his 'tourist sightseeing flight.'"

"Ah-ha," said George. "Once again, you think so far ahead. That is why I am proud to work for you."

"Besides," Roger said, "every word I said was true. He really *is* the hero. If he hadn't risked his job, and if he hadn't been a drop-dead perfect co-pilot, we may not have been able to help her or get her to help on time."

"No wonder men work so hard for you," George whispered, a hint of awe in his voice.

They arrived soon after at the hospital to see how Rosa was doing, and met her parents in the waiting room, still shaken from the mishap. They told George in Spanish what was going on.

"The doctor told them she only broke three ribs and will be fine," he told Roger, "but that one rib had punctured her lung and she had some internal bleeding, so it was very lucky that we were there to help. The doctor said she may not have made it without you, so they are forever grateful to you."

George glanced over at the parents and confirmed that he had relayed all of their words to Roger. They went to Roger and embraced him, the mother sobbing in his arms as he embraced them back.

"*Dios te bendiga, señor,*" she whispered between her sobs. "*Que dios te bendiga.*"

The next day, George and Roger returned to the hospital, along with some toiletries and a bucket of chicken for her parents, whom they knew had spent the night in the waiting room. The mother immediately disappeared into the restroom to clean up. The father munched on chicken and told George in Spanish what had happened.

"Rosa was riding next to me on the tractor and she dropped the ball you gave her," George translated for Roger. "She leaned over to catch it and fell beneath the wheel."

The father shook his head and looked toward Rosa's room, then spoke again in Spanish to George.

"The first words she spoke in the hospital, she asked for her ball," George translated. "I had to tell her that it was lost." The words hit Roger like a thunderbolt. *My God, maybe Francis is right,* he thought. *Look what has happened because I gave her a gift and she thought more of the gift than her own safety. Or am I over thinking this? Maybe it was just an accident.*

He shook the darkness from his mind and stood up.

"Back in a minute," he said to George, then went out to the truck and pulled another ball from the box in the back and put it in his pack, then stopped at the nurse's station near the waiting room.

"Is Rosa taking any visitors?" he asked, tossing the ball in the air with one hand.

The nurses smiled and one led him to her room, her parents following.

"*Buenos dias, Rosa,*" Roger said when he entered. "*Cómo está?*"

"*Cómo está usted!*" she said sassily.

"*Bueno. Y usted?*" Roger answered.

"*Bueno, señor Roger, Muchas gracias.*"

"*De nada,*" Roger said and handed Rosa the ball. She smiled and her spirits lifted as she cradled the toy and looked at her parents, eyes shining.

"It's nice to see you smile," he said, "and thank you for the Spanish lessons. Next time I see you, we will do more, okay?"

"Okay," she said. "*Vaya con Dios, señor Roger.*"

"*Vaya con Dios,*" her parents echoed, and Roger hurriedly said goodbye so he could leave the room before he burst into tears.

George saw his wet eyes as they left the hospital but didn't mention it.

"My own daughter is the same age," Roger said anyway. Then he wiped his eyes and went back into business mode. There was much to do before he left later that day on his scheduled return to the U.S.

A few hours later, he was almost done. He switched his belongings back into his original bag, counted the remaining money and left it and a task list with George, then they drove to the airport, timing it so that he spent the minimum time necessary in the airport before getting on the flight.

"Make sure they get home and everything is taken care of, okay?" Roger said to George as he got out of the truck.

"Of course, Roger. I will handle it."

"Good man," Roger said, and headed into the terminal. He saw Buddy's tooth flash near the entrance. Buddy took Roger's bag, and they reversed their arrival procedure as they went back through customs.

# CHAPTER TEN

## THE CONVENTION

The day after he returned home from Belize, Roger spent a rare day with Jeanie and the kids, and he put into effect several of the lessons he'd learned from the people in Belize. He left his notebook in the house and camped out in the back yard, watching Missy and Rook play while he snuggled and talked about little things with his wife.

"You seem different," Jeanie said after enjoying his newfound pace for a while. "What happened down there?"

Roger smiled and looked into her eyes as he gently stroked her hair.

"Nothing except some things that reminded me that true wealth lies with the people who are dear to you, not the things you have. I have some very rich people working for me in Belize who don't have a pot to piss in."

"You mean they spend a lot of time with their families?" she asked sweetly, but Roger heard the iron thrust behind it.

"Yes," he said, "that's exactly what I mean. They get to watch their kids grow up." Roger sighed and watched Missy dangling from the jungle gym, kicking her legs to avoid Rook's grasp as he stood on the ground trying to grab her. "They get to *help* their kids grow up." His mind flashed back to the emotions he felt when he saw Rosa's parents hovering over her in the field, comforting her in her time of pain and fear. "And they're there for their kids when their kids need them."

Jeanie's eyes narrowed and she sat up.

"It sounds as if you're thinking of spending more time with your own family," she said, her face brightening at the thought.

"Shhh," he whispered conspiratorially. "Don't ruin my reputation." She pouted theatrically at his evasion, but her eyes twinkled.

"I'm so happy to hear you're at least thinking of it."

"I am, honey," he admitted, as she snuggled again in his arms and his eyes followed Missy and Rook as they adventured in their back yard. "I really am. I just have a couple of more things to do, and then I promise: No more traveling."

"Except to Nationals, and Z-Hills, and the Herd Boogie, and . . ."

"Well, of course . . ."

"I can live with that."

"Thank you."

"Promises are cheap, though, especially when they're open-ended."

"But I mean it this time."

"You meant it last time, too, and the time before that and—"

Roger put his index finger across her lips to shush her, then he looked deep into her eyes, his own eyes as serious as they'd ever been.

"This. Time," he said, pausing for effect. "I. Mean. It."

Jeanie looked back at him just as seriously.

"Then. Prove. It."

"I will, my love," he said softly. "I will."

Then he went inside to get his notebook.

The next day, Roger met with Dave and Mike to brief them on his trip and hear about theirs. When he finished, they were all more psyched about the epic gig. Mickey was organizing in Florida, Roger had a great setup visit to Belize, and Dave and Mike had found many great options during their road trip from Oklahoma to Alabama and back.

Mike unfolded several maps on the farmhouse table. The first one showed Oklahoma; the second, the Dallas aviation sectional of the same area; and the third was a hand-drawn map that detailed the features of the clandestine field near Enid.

"The strip's about half a mile from this gravel road," Mike said, pointing out two lines on the map. "I'd say it runs seventy-five hundred feet before the land begins to roll."

"That's a lot longer than you thought," Roger said. "Cool."

"And more open," Mike went on, pointing to another detail, "but this row of trees along this fence blocks the view from the road. The surrounding hills should block the noise and even on takeoff, the closest house is a few miles away, and it's buried in the woods."

"Which approach direction avoids any houses or problems?" Roger asked as he nodded in approval.

"All of them! There's nothing, man! The place'll look like a black hole from the air. We sat on the strip all night and never saw a light. Then we drove around the perimeter and other than that one house, the whole area is empty. A night landing should be a piece of cake. I think the pilots'll like it."

"Well since it's gonna be your butts out there," Roger said, "how comfortable do you feel about driving out of there with a hot load?"

"Totally casual, man," Mike said. Dave nodded his agreement.

"We also found a place in Arkansas that's worth remembering," Dave said. "Not nearly as secluded, but I'd feel all right doing ground there."

"Yeah," Mike agreed, "not as good as Enid but better than most places we've used."

"Okay, then," Roger said, "from now on, Oklahoma's the Ranch and Arkansas is the Corral, and we keep both sites secret from everyone else until they need to know."

"I'll go along with that," Mike said. "Ever since I found the place, I've always thought of it as my nest egg."

Dave cracked a big smile and laid four birth certificates on the table. "Any problems?"

"Not really, but it sure wasn't as cool as the first time," Dave said. "We got paranoid and took your advice and split. We each got one. Now I'm Mike Brown and he's David Eaton. Some cover, huh? We're still Dave and Mike!" Roger thanked them as they laughed at their "new" names, then moved on to the next agenda item.

"There's gonna be some free time, at least a month or two before harvest, so if you guys wanna take a break, it's cool with me. I've got the Freak Brother Convention coming up in a few weeks so I'm gonna be jammed."

"Sounds good to me," Dave said. "I've got some things in Florida I need to do, but I'll definitely be back for the Convention to get my knees in the breeze. My Nationals burn-out is definitely over!"

I think I'll just kinda veg until then," added Mike, "but some hard-core fun jumping will be just what the doctor ordered."

"Outstanding," Roger said. "Thanks so much for your great work. Stay in touch the usual way in case something comes up. Otherwise, I'll see you at the Convention."

Later that day, Roger went to the parachute center to catch up on business and the first thing he saw was Mr. Douglas climbing to jump altitude. Roger smiled and took a deep breath. *One less thing to think about*, he thought.

He walked through the hangar, soaking up the vibes of the familiar surroundings, feeling the customary smoothness of the operation and the overall good mood and relaxed focus of his staff and customers. He walked into the main office and Kimmers gave him a back-slapping hug.

"Good to see you again, man," he said happily. "You haven't been away from the DZ so long since we started training!" He pointed toward a stack of messages stuffed into Roger's mailbox. "As you can see."

"I also see Mr. Douglas is back up," Roger said.

"First load two days ago," Kimmers said. "Nice to have Mark smiling again, that's for sure."

"Any other good news?"

"It's all good, Roger. Students are up about fifteen percent over last year to date, and we settled up with Paul and he took Sugar Alpha home, but he said he's good to go for the Convention if you want him."

"Good," Roger said as he grabbed his messages and retired to his office to sort through them. Most of them were routine DZ business that he set aside for Kimmers to deal with. One was from Tony, who said he'd be at the Freak Brother Convention. Another was from Mickey, who'd called that morning. He went out and rang Mickey from a pay phone and discovered he was 20 miles away at a Holiday Inn. A half hour later, Roger walked into Mickey's room.

"Crop's looking fine and will be ready to go in five or six weeks," Roger said as soon as they finished their hellos, "so I figure sometime in November. It'll be worth the wait though—prettiest plants I've ever seen."

"Everybody says that."

"Yeah, but this is a fact. People'll be beating our door down for this product."

"Okay, fine. How about transport?" Roger laughed.

"Old blacktop airfield a mile long nine miles from the farm. Three-foot-high grass in the cracks. No one knows why it's there, but no one's used it for years. It's just waiting for us."

"Sounds like the country hasn't been abused or even discovered with something like that sitting around," Mickey said, his face brightening.

"We're way ahead of the crowd," Roger said. "The whole scene's ripe for the picking."

Roger pulled out a map and showed Mickey the lay of the land.

"The strip here near Tres Leguas. I did an aerial recon and Helen Keller could find it. They can pick up both the Chetumal and Belize VORs, then I can talk them in after they drop down."

"Where's the heat?"

"Closest police station is ten miles by bad roads between the hills near San Felipe—and even if they got tipped that something big was going down, they'd probably head south first to Carvers Ranch, which is a huge cattle farm in the flatlands with a long grass strip next to the house. Other than the Mennonites and the ground crew, though, nobody should even know we're working."

"Great! What about fuel?"

"I'll take care of that next trip. Shouldn't be any problem, though, because several people want the business. It'll cost us five dollars a gallon so we want to make sure we bring all we can."

"How about Oklahoma?"

"Boys found a strip in Oklahoma we're calling the Ranch and one in Arkansas that's the Corral. Not sure if Ron's got a place, but we'll be ready either way."

"If they got the preliminary work done, it shouldn't take me more than a couple days to scope them out after you find out if the horses have a place of their own," Mickey said, grinning at the code. Then he grabbed his briefcase and dumped ten bundles of bills on the bed.

"Believe it or not, the Cookie Monster paid us off," he said. "The figures look good, too. Minus expenses and what we sent to Belize, we'll clear one-thirty. Not bad huh?"

He made three stacks with the bundles, one a little smaller than the other two.

"Fifty for you, fifty for me, thirty for the next gig's expenses. With all the gear we have between us, that should be plenty."

They shook hands to seal another successful venture and Roger piled his cash in a brown shopping bag, satisfied but feeling kind of empty. He liked the adventure and satisfaction of pulling it off much more than he did counting the money afterward. Mickey picked up his mood and waved a scolding finger at him.

"Don't dis the dough, man," he said, smiling. "Just consider it evidence of a job well done. Besides, it sure feels good to get something back for a change. I was starting to think we were jinxed or something."

"You're right," Roger conceded. "Better to be in the black than swimming in red."

Mickey dumped his cash and the expense money back in his briefcase and snapped it shut.

"Hey, I found out why Tony got axed from the Colombian gigs." Roger arched his eyebrows in invitation to hear more.

"Colombian Joe and him were free basing at Norman's Cay right before a run, and when they sent him back to Tampa for the plane they were using, he made love to his pipe instead of doing the pickup! The Colombians wanted to kill him, but unfortunately, he talked his way out of it." Roger nodded at the unsurprising news.

"He broke the immortal rules of old Joseph Kennedy—'If you're gonna run rum, don't drink it!' What do you wanna bet Tony gets busted within a year." Mickey laughed and shook his head.

"May as well just pay you now." Roger turned serious.

"He's such a tool. Dumped five keys on me when he visited last month and tried to pressure me to sell it by saying he couldn't take it back to Florida."

"So you sent him back with it, right?" Roger shook his head ruefully.

"Said I'd hold it until he found his own buyer." Mickey shook his head in disgust.

"Tony the Snake strikes again." Mickey picked up his briefcase. "Anyway, we've got a few weeks so I'm heading to the island. Got a barge of diesel fuel coming for the generators, and I need to be there when it arrives."

With the gig planning under control, Roger buried his head in the Freak Brother Convention, a major project in itself. It was a large gathering of skydivers and jump planes at a big airport outside a small western Illinois town that happened every year Wednesday through

Sunday during the second week of August. The Convention began as an informal gathering of the Freak Brothers skydiving fraternity, an inclusive group of skydivers dedicated to promoting fun and innovation in the sport. Success built upon success, though, and turned the informal gathering into a full-scale official "boogie" with a permissive atmosphere and multiple aircraft that drew jumpers from all over the U.S. and several other countries to jump hard and party harder with old and new friends.

The Convention had outgrown Roger's DZ, so he'd found Albertus Airport in Freeport, 100 miles away from Sandwich. It had 300 acres of open land, supportive townspeople, and no major commercial air traffic overhead. It was perfect for what had become the world's largest skydiving event. Roger oversaw the operation and brought in most of the aircraft, but Kimmers and Jeanie were his chief lieutenants and plotted out and staffed all the support operations. They needed a public announcement system that could reach every area of the airport, a radio system for staff communications, a grounds crew, Freak Police for security, and the procedures for all operations from registration to check-in to gear checks, manifesting and aircraft rotation. And of course, they needed staff for all of this and it had to run like a military operation to make sure everyone was happy and very few ended up hurt or in jail.

The Tuesday before the Convention started, a caravan of trucks and vans left the DZ and journeyed to Freeport. Within hours of their arrival, they'd staked out the barren open grounds into an outline for tents, campers, vendors, traffic lanes, a party tent, and aircraft loading areas, complete with "street" signs with names like "Flamingo Way," "Ripcord Drive," and "Propeller Street." That evening, Roger assembled the more than 50 staffers. Looking out across the group of sweaty, smiling faces, Roger spread his arms like a revival tent preacher.

"Dearly beloved, we are gathered here today to host another Freak Brother Convention!"

"Praise the Lord and all Freak Brothers!" everyone shouted in reply.

"This year promises to be the biggest non-competitive skydiving event in the history of skydiving," Roger went on after the cheering died down, "so be proud that you are a part of it!" More cheers, shouts and applause.

"I really want to thank everyone for being here," he said when the noise had once again died down. "It's a really special event and I want to make sure everything goes smoothly, and I want to give a special shout out to the one person most responsible for making it all go right, my wife Jeanie. She's the heart and soul of the Freak Brother Convention, and we couldn't do it without her. Thank you, Jeanie."

"Yeah, Jeanie!" shouted everyone, as she beamed in their appreciation, and the loudest roar of the night went up from the staffers, most of whom had worked previous Conventions and knew from their own experience how vital the sweet, unassuming but hard-as-nails Jeanie was to its success.

Roger then introduced Kimmers and the rest of the staff to each other, then broke them down into working groups, each of which went its separate way to take care of its business.

In one room, Jeanie and Kimmers met with the registration and manifest staff to discuss office operations. Roger held a separate meeting with the pilots and ramp agents responsible for fueling and loading.

When the meetings ended, Roger and Jeanie left for their hotel, Roger already a little giddy as he rode the high of the event.

"I'm glad we have such a great staff this year," he said. "It really looks like it's going to be a bigger turn out than last year."

"Yeah, that would be nice," said Jeanie distantly. Roger frowned at her obvious lack of enthusiasm.

"What's up Jeanie? Aren't you excited?"

"No, that's all great. I'm just exhausted already and I just . . . well, *I'd* like some of your undivided attention soon, where you're not thinking about your runs or skydiving."

"Jeanie," Roger sighed. "We just went over that. I told you things'll change soon, but right now we're about to start the biggest Convention ever, and I can't have you weighing me down with this now. You're the best, babe, and I really need you."

"Roger, I'm just saying you're—"

"Please, honey," Roger pleaded, "can't this wait until after the Convention? I already told you, one more run and I'm done."

"And then there will be one more," Jeanie said bitterly. "You're addicted to it, Roger. You can't stop. I know it and you know it."

"Yeah, I do know it," Roger said softly, "but I swear this time will be different. I know I can't prove it, that I have to actually do it, but for now could you please just take my promise at face value and let's just enjoy the Convention, okay?"

"Okay," Jeanie said. She smiled as they pulled up to the hotel, but she got out of the car and walked inside without another word, and without looking back. Roger thumped the steering wheel and gritted his teeth.

"You gotta quit, man," he said out loud. "You really gotta do it this time."

The next day, the Convention grounds swelled with jumpers as they turned the airport into a huge tent and motor home city named "Bagland" in honor of the infamous ghetto behind the Sandwich hangar. After they had set up their camps, the jumpers dutifully lined up at the registration tables and sifted through pages of waivers, insurance forms, event schedules and camping information handouts. Next came a gear check from a parachute rigger to make sure their equipment was airworthy. When they had passed through the administrative gauntlet, they received an event bracelet that entitled them to manifest for skydives, attend parties on-site, and guzzle all the free beer they could drink. The bracelet also alerted local business owners that their surge in business came courtesy of the Convention.

This year there were three DC-3s, a Twin Otter, a Twin Beech, and several Cessnas to haul jumpers; as Wednesday wore on, each plane made more and faster "turns" and more parachutes cracked open overhead like colorful aerial popcorn.

The event quickly blossomed into a high-energy festival of hot skydives, contagious smiles and continuous parties. Roger had rented a motor home for his office and set up a communication center for the operation with several chairs on the roof. There he mingled with his friends and was showered with compliments for hosting such a fine event.

Behind the scenes, Jeanie ran a dedicated crew of "manifest girls" who worked non-stop from sunup to sundown keeping the planes in the air as much as possible and on the ground as little as possible.

It was a tricky and demanding job, as the jumpers manifested in groups ranging from two to 20 and the girls had to find the right airplane with the right number of "slots" leaving at the right time to get every jumper and plane up with a minimum of ground time.

The PA system was constantly squawking with "calls" that ranged from five to 15 minutes, each specifying an aircraft type and load number. It was a complex carnival of people and planes in constant motion, all trying to maximize the fun and minimize the danger that came with spinning propellers, fast-moving planes and human bodies plummeting through the air at 120 miles per hour.

Roger used his abundant energy, enthusiasm, and grins to keep people happy and motivated to jump. He remained in constant motion, not just checking on the operations but doing the "customer service" of organizing and jumping with novice and intermediate groups of skydivers to help them build their RW skills, and help them have fun.

Whenever Roger was in the air, Kimmers would replace Roger atop the motor home and direct the staff, including a contingent of workers who maintained the grounds and kept order. When Roger landed, Chris would meet him with another rig and quickly repack the one Roger had just jumped.

When the traditional "sunset loads" took off, the manifest team breathed a sigh of relief and spooled down for the day. Jeanie smiled and grabbed the PA microphone.

"Green light!" she announced. "Let the party begin!"

Immediately, the hundreds of jumpers who were not on the sunset loads spooled up their partying. The beer wagons that sported multiple taps became the primary destination, followed by the various food concession tents and the campfires and barbecues of the various jumper campsites. Hundreds more flowed out of the airport and invaded the town, filling the local stores, restaurants, and hotels.

The Freak Police started canvassing the area, checking for boogie wristbands to make sure there were no freeloaders or "outsiders" at the boogie, while other grounds crew prepped the stage under the large, yellow and white circus tent for the headlining bands. Meanwhile, many jumpers rotated in and out of the shower house to wash off the dirt and sweat of the day and to get ready to party. The air was filled with campfire and BBQ grilled smoke and an exciting vibe about the day's jumps.

Dusk fell over Bagland but the canopies that cracked open above them still glowed in the golden hour light that still shone at 2,000 feet. Whoops and yells wafted down as the jumpers descended toward the landing area just as the Booze Brother Revue took the stage, surrounded by a crowd quaffing free beer from overflowing red plastic beer cups.

"Testing, testing," said the lead singer. "Is this thing on?" The skydivers gave a quick cheer and raised their cups. "How was it out there today? Did you guys have fun?"

"Woohoo!!"

"Then let's get ready to rock!"

As the jumpers mingled and danced under the circus tent, Jeanie packed up and headed back to the hotel for a relatively early evening. Roger stayed behind to put in an appearance, and to make sure the beer was flowing, the band was dialed in, the Freak Police were on patrol, and all the offices were properly secured. Then he left with a smuggler named Ted who took him out to eat at a "cook your own" steak house.

The last Roger had heard, Ted was smuggling electronics into Mexico out of McAllen, Texas, and sometimes flying for a company named Trans America Airlines that was rumored to be a CIA front operation. A former naval aviator, Ted was a wild and crazy ace pilot who, after years of putting down jets on pitching aircraft carrier decks, could land anything anywhere without breaking anything.

"You know the Mexican border's been real quiet," Ted said after they started eating. "The old timers tell me they've never seen it so open. I know of four groups punching 'em back through and everybody's making it. Just one bust that I know of, and they were snitched out before they left the ground. The only thing active against a run is all the lies about drug interdiction. Do you remember the DC-6 trip where I got stuck in Colombia behind an Aero Commander that wouldn't start? The one I had to fix just so I could get out?" Roger nodded. "Well, I was ferrying a plane to Texas from L.A. and ran into the same pilot at Southern Air. We got to talking and he offered me a job flying to Nicaragua with government stuff. Small world, huh? I did a couple of runs for him, and he wants me to do another."

"What are you hauling?" Roger asked.

"We call it the Boomer Bonanza Run," Ted smirked.

"Boomer Bonanza?"

"You know, things that go boom!" Roger chuckled.

"Are they payin'?"

"Not so much," Ted shrugged, "but it's better than the nine hundred bucks I get for T.V. runs, plus there's no heat. We have special clearance to get back in and nobody messes with us. The shame of it is I have to deadhead back."

"Who are you delivering to?"

"Guys who want to create havoc for the Sandinista government. That's supposed to be a big secret, but it's clear we're arming rebels. They call 'em contras, you know, counter-revolutionaries."

"Sounds like that could get hot in its own way."

"Already is, actually. Last run I did we took some rounds in the fuselage. Kinda like it was in the islands when the natives would try to knock you out of the sky if you were flying low just to see what you're carrying, except heavier artillery—the damn Cubans got the Sandinistas armed to the hilt, so landing's not so cool anymore. So I opened my mouth and suggested kickouts instead, and they liked it, so they gave me some specs and now I'm in a pinch and was hoping you could help me."

Roger smiled and shook his head. *When would people learn that opening your mouth almost always caused trouble?*

"Well, thanks for the thought, buddy, but no thanks," Roger said. "I want nothing to do with any government stuff. Besides, the military invented kickouts. They don't need your help or mine. I mean, what's up with that anyway? Kickouts are easy."

"More to it than that," Ted said, and his voice went serious. "I can't get into it, but it's not what you think."

"Doesn't matter. If you're coming in with special clearance and flying for the government, I'm not touching it."

"The specs I got aren't for heading down. It's for the ride back."

"Well, how are you gonna do that if—"

"Don't ask, man. Just let me know if you can help."

"I might consider it if you can make a stop in a friendly little country on the way back," Roger said, opening his own mouth when he should have kept it shut.

"No way, man. This is some weird stuff. Always somebody watching everyone and everything that goes near the plane. I'm only getting a little piece of the action. The gig's for the guys putting the run together. What's really happening I don't want to know and neither do you. I'm only telling you this because it sounds like you're considering it."

*There I go again,* Roger thought, *running my mouth about another gig when I promised I wouldn't.* Roger looked at Ted and smiled.

183

"Listen my, friend, I appreciate your faith in me, and I'd love to hear you out, but I'm getting *out*."

"Have you gone straight?"

"Yeah, pretty much. I have a family now, and a great skydiving business and that's enough on my plate. Much as I love the thrill, it's just time to be done and move on."

"Wow, never thought I'd hear that from you."

"Never hear that from anyone, really, do we?" Ted laughed and nodded. "But I'm gonna be an exception to the rule." Ted laughed and held up his glass.

"To retirement then."

"To retirement," Roger said, smiling, but his brain still resisted. *Francis is a prophet*, he thought, *and I knew the U.S. was running guns south, just didn't know anyone doing it. I wonder who's behind the return run, and how can someone always be watching when they load?*

The next three days merged together into one big continuum of jumping from sunup to sundown and partying from sundown to sunup. It had been a great boogie so far, with no broken planes and only a few broken bones among the hundreds of loads flown and the thousands of jumps made.

Now it was Saturday sunset, and Roger sat atop the motorhome half drunk on strawberry margaritas, watching a sunset load board Sugar Alpha, when saw Tony climbing up the ladder with a big grin on his face.

"Hey man, what's up?" he said as he reached the roof and shook Roger's hand.

"Great Convention is what's up, Roger said happily, as he pointed Tony to the margarita cooler just as a seriously hot young woman joined them.

"This is Tiffany Mae," Tony said proudly as they joined Roger in low-slung fabric chairs and poured themselves some margaritas. Roger noted that while Tony was smiling and Tiffany Mae was hot, both sported pale, unhealthy skin and eyes sunk deep into their faces. *Too much coke, for sure*, Roger thought, *and probably the pipe.*

They watched the jumpers and small-talked about the Convention until they finished their margaritas, then Tony sent Tiffany Mae back to their motorhome and the two men escaped into Roger's air conditioning.

184

"Hey, want to get high?" he asked, tapping a pocket as they sat down inside. Roger shook his head.

"She does it too, right?"

"Oh yeah," he said. "She was a freebase whore when I met her. Fucking fell in love and married her and here we fucking are. Have a lot of great times with her and the pipe. You really should try it. It's the best."

"Really," Roger challenged him. "You look like death warmed over and I heard you blew a run because of it."

"I don't know where they got any room to talk," he said defensively. "Did three trips for them while they sat around and got high. Loosest fucking operator I ever saw. He's into that macho shit and thinks he's bulletproof. You would've thought he'd clean up his act after they raided the place and kicked him out of the country and based police on his island. 'Course, nothing changed 'cause the cops are on the take, and he bought himself another couple years from the Prime Minister, so he says, but his days are numbered 'cause he draws too much heat, and the big guns in Colombia are rethinking the route. One of the main men has some serious connections in the Mexican government, and they're starting to move that way. And to top it off," Tony said, flashing his devilish smile, "the yahoo they got to take my place missed the runway on his first run and stuffed it in the ocean. Fucking losers."

*And you're one of them*, Roger thought.

"So have you set up the deal in New Jersey for the coke yet?" he asked. Tony snorted.

"Nah, I'm just gonna keep it for stash."

Roger laughed. *Not even the most flagrant cokehead keeps five kilos for personal use. Dude is out of control.* He glanced theatrically at his watch. "Sorry to cut this short, but I have to wrap things up before the party picnic tonight," he said and headed for the door, tired of listening to coke-speed conversation. "You kiss that girl once for me, would you," he concluded with a smile.

"Kiss her for you?" Hell, you can do her yourself if you want to. She loves to have me watch."

"Very generous of you, but no thanks," Roger said, and they went their separate ways.

*Second source this week to tell me smuggling routes are switching back to Mexico*, he thought as he walked toward the office. Certainly, the winding border provided better cover; 1,500 miles of mountains, hidden valleys and rugged terrain and border towns that planes regularly visited without crossing the border. In contrast, there was no cover through the Bahamas, and any plane there flying low at night without a flight plan could have only one purpose, and the increased pressure the U.S. was placing on the Bahamas would eventually shut down that approach, leaving the "back door" through Mexico. The changing tides would drag enforcement there, too, but he wondered how many holes there would be because of the U.S. government's covert actions. Roger hoped his final run would beat the rush west.

The final night bash before the skydivers returned to their regular lives was always the biggest party by far and Roger always paid extra attention to making it memorable. He'd adopted most of his ideas from the block parties his parents held when he was a kid, remembering how he felt sitting and eating with neighbors, and it created a family out of friends. The evening entertainment included the bands Rare Earth, Survivor, and the Booze Brothers. Registration covered the bands, beer, and meal, so no jumper was left out. During Roger's remarks to the crowd, the Freeport mayor surprised Roger with the key to the city to show his appreciation for the commerce the Convention had brought his community.

The Convention ended the following day, a great success in every respect, though as it turned out, it was only the third largest skydiving event in history in terms of participants. It had, however, flown more loads and more jumps had been made than ever before at a skydiving event and the staff was stoked by that accomplishment, though they were all exhausted.

Roger and Jeanie had both lost their voices, so Sunday night they croaked their way through the staff appreciation dinner but, once again, Roger's organizational and people skills, combined with his wife's solid if sometimes grumpy support, had resulted in another great event and set the standard for everyone else to follow.

A few weeks after the Convention, Roger was surprised when Billy Bob walked onto the drop zone and into Roger's office. After the debacle with the Cookie Monster, Roger figured that he'd never see Billy Bob again, but time and need assuaged Billy's ego, and he was back. Before

Billy could say a word, Roger reached behind him and turned on a radio to make some background noise.

"I came to apologize for what happened," Billy Bob said. "I was stupid and I know I let you down. I shouldn't have let the Cookie Monster talk me into it."

"Billy Bob, are you wearing a wire or working for the Feds?" Roger said, looking coldly into the young pilot's eyes.

"N-n-no man," Billy Bob stuttered. "I screwed up but I would never, ever betray you. I understand the risks to make this kinda money, and if I ever get busted I'm ready to sit in jail. I just want to do something. I need some work."

Roger knew Billy Bob was telling the truth because there was no way he could wear a wire and maintain his composure under Roger's pressure.

"I know you won't believe me, but there's absolutely nothing going on," Roger said, still cold.

"What about that Belize gig?"

"You of all people know that I want to get out of the business and raise a family, and your little fiasco gave me the perfect reason to do it. I just want to live a normal life."

"Man, I'll do anything, it don't have to be flyin'. I'll unload, do errands, anything."

"There's nothing here for you. You've come to the wrong place."

"Well, I'll just have to put something together on my own."

The words went through Roger like someone scratching a blackboard, but he laughed it off while calling Billy Bob's bluff.

"Listen man, don't threaten me! I've told you more than once what will happen if you start trying to think. You've proven my point already. I just wonder what would have happened if the Feds put the bright lights on."

"I could handle that, no problem."

Roger laughed. "You've lied to me once already, and you freak out under pressure, so don't insult my intelligence."

"Please keep me in mind if something comes along, okay?" Billy Bob said, eyes downcast, trying the humble route. "I've been followed once and crashed twice. Believe me, I know this business is no cakewalk. I'm here talking to you because if I can't work with you, there's nobody else who'll have me. I need another chance. You can count on me one hundred percent, even if you only need a jump pilot. Just keep me in mind, all right?"

Roger felt sorry for him and his two-edged personality trait of giving people a chance to prove themselves, even though they might not be up to it, flared up again as he heard Billy Bob's apparent sincerity. Despite everything, he liked the awkward flake, and he didn't enjoy hammering him. Plus, he didn't want to send a loose cannon like Billy Bob away in a hostile mood.

"Okay, Billy," he said in a kinder tone. "I'll see if I can get you some Cessna loads or right seat time with Mark, but don't count on anything else because there just isn't anything." Billy Bob beamed happily and pumped Roger's hand.

"Thanks, man," he said. "*Thanks*. You won't regret it, I promise."

Roger smiled and watched Billy Bob leave, then started at the ceiling.

*Smuggler promises*, he thought. *What an oxymoron.*

Roger enjoyed the rest of the parachuting season, especially jumping with low-timers and watching them get better. He especially enjoyed watching Patrick turn into a conscientious and skilled canopy pilot who was already passing on his knowledge to others. That was the part Roger liked best of all; sharing the joy of jumping with people, then watching them do the same.

Roger had also kept in touch with George because the harvest in Belize would come in just as the weather turned cold and jumping wound down in Illinois. They had recently talked by ham radio, as George had moved up to the plantation to coordinate the baling.

"Well partner," he said during one mid-October call, "things are really starting to get busy here with the cooler weather. I'll tell you what, good things are worth waiting for. You're going to love what you see."

"Hey, if you need me to help, let me know," Roger replied. "My schedule's opening up enough to give you a hand."

"I appreciate that my friend, but not necessary," George assured him. "We've got the whole family busy, everything's taken care of, so just come as scheduled. The cops are getting worse with the people, though. They've been violent with some of the locals, and they're even talking shit to the Mennonites. We keep the crews clear so we have no problems there, but it is tense just driving through the area with supplies."

"That's not good, but don't get involved. We need to lay low no matter how tough it gets in town, and please make sure the men know that. They can't react or it will be worse."

"Good advice, man. I will tell them."

"When do you think you'll be ready?"

"About two weeks."

"Good. Then I'll be there soon. If we miss our regular chat next week, I'll use a landline to get you a message."

Roger called Mickey to tell him they needed to start the active planning phase. Mickey came up the next day to finish the final details and begin implementing the plan.

"Those idiot cops worry me a little," Mickey said as they drove away from O'Hare, "but otherwise it sounds like everything's going great."

"So far," Roger said, "so I think we should call Ron and tell him to start pushing buttons."

"Yeah, time to get them spooled up."

They stopped at a convenience store and went to a pay phone hung on the outside wall. Roger dialed Ron's office. His secretary answered.

"Could I speak to Ron please?" Roger asked. There was a long pause.

"Uhhh, I'm sorry, sir. He's uhh, he's not here," she said haltingly. Roger frowned at her odd demeanor.

"I'm a personal friend. When do you expect him in?"

"We're not," she said. "Uhhh, do you—do you have his home number?"

"Yeah, I do," Roger said, now worried. He glanced at Mickey, who was also frowning at the exchange.

"Then please call there," she said. "Goodbye." She hung up abruptly.

"Damn," said Mickey, his mood turning dark. Roger quickly dialed Ron's home.

"Hello," said a weary voice. Roger recognized it as Ron's wife.

"Hi June," Roger said cautiously. "Is Ron in?" Another long silence, and then a sob.

"Ron's dead," she said. "So is Jim."

"Oh my God," Roger whispered. "I'm so sorry." He glanced at Mickey and slashed his fingers across his throat. Mickey understood the gesture and rolled his eyes in despair. "June, can I do anything to help?"

"Thanks for the offer, Roger, but everything is taken care of, and I'm surrounded by family."

"Well know you can call me if you need anything later or would just like to talk."

"Thanks, I really appreciate it. Bye." Roger hung up and stared at Mickey.

"Jesus, she just had their second kid."

"If they both bought it," Mickey surmised, "they must've been doing a run. Wonder if they left any secrets lying around."

"Let's see what happened first," Roger said, and dialed another number. A gruff voice answered, one Roger knew as a friend of Ron's that he'd worked with too.

"Hey man, what's up with Ron?"

Roger listened for a minute before he spoke.

"Okay, thanks," he said, "Appreciate it." He hung up and turned to Mickey, face grim, and nodded him into the truck and they stayed silent until they were rolling.

"Happened on the 18th," Roger said dully as he watched the road. "They were trying to kick out a ton and a half over Mississippi from a Lockheed 18 along a pipeline. No lights, no moon, hit some trees, killed all three."

"Three? Who else was on board?"

"Ron, Jim, and Sky."

"Ahhh fuck me," said Mickey and his face fell. "Sky and me been jumping buddies for years. He was good people."

They drove on in silence for a while, then Mickey glanced at Roger, his eyes moist.

"Well buddy, are we dead too, or are we gonna try and put something else together?"

"Stuff like this is why we need to retire," Roger said quietly.

"You sure that shit like this isn't what keeps you doing it?"

Roger glanced sharply at Mickey, then aimed his eyes back at the road.

"I don't know, man. I honestly don't know."

# CHAPTER ELEVEN

## SUGAR TIME

Roger and Mickey bought a bottle of Gran Patron Burdeos on the way to Mickey's hotel to drown their sorrows, but they only got one stiff drink into it before they realized that they needed to mourn their friends later. Right then, they had to figure out their next moves.

First, they needed an untraceable aircraft suitable for a heavy load and a long haul and the cash to buy it. Second, they needed experienced, trustworthy pilots.

"We still have most of the money from the Jamaican gig," Mickey said. "If we put it all on the table, it should be enough." Roger nodded without hesitation.

"Deal, partner. Ain't no turning back now. Let's figure out what we can get for it."

"Well, we do have some options. Mr. Douglas is flying, Sugar Alpha's for sale, or we could buy something else."

"Forget Mr. D," Roger said bluntly. "Too close to home, and Mark's not right for it. Good enough pilot, but he just about went to pieces when he dented it on the trees. Gotta be Sugar or something else."

"We can't really get anything but a Queen Air or Twin Beech for one-thirty and still have expense money, and it'll take at least fifty to get something decent. Anything new would hit triple digits fast."

"And then we're only talking fifteen hundred pounds max anyway," Roger said, and sat back. "Hanoi and I had this same conversation and we decided it'll take a Three to make a retirement run. We can get Sugar

Alpha for sixty, but first let's see what else is on the market." He opened his briefcase and pulled out a current copy of *Trade-A-Plane*.

Five minutes later, he shook his head and looked at Mickey.

"Looks like Sugar time."

"What the hell, man," Mickey grinned. "It all started with her so it seems proper to end it with her too. Destiny brought her right back to us."

"Maybe, but who's gonna fly it? Certainly not Billy Bob."

"Certainly not left seat, no matter how desperate we are," Mickey laughed. "No, I was thinking of Jeff."

"Blind Jeff?" Roger mused. "Yeah, he'd be perfect. He can fly the piss out of a Three and he knows Sugar."

"Let's call him and see what he thinks." They left immediately and headed for a convenience store pay phone a few blocks from the hotel. As they walked, Roger thought about Blind Jeff.

Older guy, tall and slim, very laid back. Balding, with a pointed chin accented by a straggly, leprechaun-like goatee that he constantly stroked with one hand as he squinted at you through thick lenses framed by thin wire rims that he never took off. He looked and acted more like a college professor than a pilot, let alone a smuggler, but he was an ace pilot who had, ironically, flown Sugar Alpha out of Indianapolis with his brother Jack before Paul bought her. Jeff was also a top-notch mechanic, especially with big radials. Where he got his flying chops and wrenching know-how nobody knew, but everyone agreed: he had them in spades.

"Hellooo," said a soft voice into Mickey's ear after two rings.

"Yo Jeff," it's Mickey. You got a minute?"

"Where we going?" he asked, getting right to the point. Mickey laughed.

"Want to go sightseeing in Sugar Alpha next month?"

"Love to."

"Okay, let me get back to you tomorrow."

"Looking forward to it, Mick. Thanks for thinking of me."

"You bet. See ya." He put the phone back in its cradle and gave Roger a thumbs up.

"What if we can't get Sugar?" Roger asked as they walked back to the hotel.

"Then we go smaller and make more loads," Mickey shrugged. "From what you say, that should work too, maybe even better than doing one big run."

"Agreed," said Roger. "We'll go with whatever we get and do whatever it takes."

They walked on in silence for a moment, then Mickey made a face.

"If we do go with Sugar, who's gonna fly right seat?"

Roger winced. "Hate to say this but Billy Bob may be our guy. Has a lot of Twin Beech time flying jumpers so I know he could handle right seat, especially with Blind Jeff as PIC. All he'll have to do is throw a few handles, keep Jeff's cigarettes and matches in reach, and make sure the extra tanks keep feeding into the wings."

"Yeah, he did great with that part on the Cookie Monster run."

"Yeah, but this time he'll be working for Blind Jeff, not sorting it out on his own, so hey, if you got somebody better, great, but he *is* an option."

"And he still has potential," Mickey said. "He really did save our asses on Grand Bahama, and as long as we keep his thinking window small, he should be fine."

"Plus we don't have to bring in a new man," Roger added as they walked into the hotel lobby. Mickey chuckled.

"That's right," he concluded. "Better the devil you know than the one you don't."

They continued their planning when they got back to the room.

"While you and Jeff check out Sugar, I'll see if I can get that Trans Van to help you with the load, though I still don't think that will handle it all."

"Sounds from what your boys say that we can get a rental truck back in the field as long as it don't rain," Mickey said. "I'd feel a lot more secure with an extra vehicle in case one breaks or we can't fit it all in. I like your idea of getting Mike out quickly in the first pickup just for insurance, even though it'll leave us short-handed for the rest."

"And you'll load the rest before anyone else leaves?"

"Right, plus I'll stay behind with the pickup to make sure everyone gets out and the Three gets back off. We'll have to kill the engines on this one, so if it don't start, we'll torch it, and I'll take the pilots in the pickup."

"And you'll give the trucks a head start?"

"Yeah, fifteen to thirty minutes, whatever feels right. Then they're off to Memphis and Sugar will have a new daddy by morning."

"Sounds like a plan," Roger said. "Also be nice to have a strong back to help me on my end. Any ideas?"

"What about Kong? Dude's as solid as they come."

"That's for sure, and he'll do it if I ask, but this may be a little much to lay on him for his first gig—kinda like putting a 100-jump wonder last on a serious ten-way team. I'll see what I can figure while you're dealing for Sugar but either way I'll have the boys and vehicles ready to head out and show you the strips when you get back."

"Then I think we're set for now," Mickey said. Roger nodded and Mickey reached for the Patron. "And now back to our other unfinished business."

The next day, Roger called George on the ham radio at their regular time. George answered promptly and they each took turns counting to ten as they tuned in crystal-clear reception. Then they worked out the schedule with a goal of getting Roger to the plantation within the week. When they were done, George added another bit of news.

"I ran out of money, so I sold a few hundred pounds to keep things going." Roger didn't like hearing this because the money he sent George should have lasted, but he bit his tongue and made light of it.

"Okay, good problem solving, but do me a favor and make sure you save the best for us, all right?" George laughed.

"Whose team do you think I am on? There could be no other way! I sell only what you would not take anyway and it is still the best on the square."

"Don't get too proud of it," Roger cautioned. "It's important to lie low, especially with the cops going crazy."

"Of course, my friend, always."

Roger told Mickey at their next meeting that things were set in Belize. The next order of business was figuring out how to buy Sugar Alpha in a manner that hid its true ownership from both the FAA and Paul.

"He won't do the deal if he suspects what it's for," Roger explained.

"No problem buddy," Mickey said. "Neither Jeff nor I have ever met him plus he'll never think smugglers would buy a plane painted like that. I mean, that'd be fucking nuts, right?" He grinned wolfishly at Roger, whose eyes twinkled back. "So we can take care of that. Hell, give me his number, and I'll call him right now."

When Paul picked up, Mickey winked at Roger.

"Yo, Paul, this is Matt Kempton, I'm a rancher down in Arizona and heard through the skydiving grapevine that you have a nice Three for sale. You still got it? . . . And you're asking sixty-ish? . . . okay, sounds good . . . nah, I don't care about that . . . it's just for hauling stuff around my spread . . . uh uh . . . . Yeah, I'd like to send my pilot out there tomorrow to check it out if that works for you . . . okay, good, I'll have him call and you guys work out the details. You're on eastern time, right? . . . Okay, thank you, sir. Bye."

Mickey hung up and the two men laughed at the exchange.

"Sounds like he's a little sensitive about the paint job," Roger said.

"Yeah, but he's really ready to sell his 'baby,'" Mickey said. "Told me he'll give Jeff the ol' VIP treatment."

"Be sure Blind Jeff wears cowboy boots, though, will ya?" Mickey grinned.

"Yeah, tennies don't exactly scream Arizona rancher, do they?"

As Roger drove Mickey to the airport for his flight to Indianapolis to meet up with Blind Jeff, he explained to Roger why he'd chosen Arizona for his cover story.

"Last time I was in Phoenix, I wrote down random names and addresses of several ranchers around the area. I mean, there are some big spreads out there run by people you never heard of, so that way I'd have cover for buying planes and if the Feds investigate the ownership, they find real people and real ranches—"

"And then they reach a dead end," Roger finished, smiling at Mickey's handiwork. "Definitely a nice touch to keep Paul calm, that's for sure. All we need to do is add one of the 800 numbers I have to the mix and we're set."

"I love it when a plan comes together," Mickey said.

Blind Jeff greeted Mickey warmly when they met at the Indianapolis airport, and they headed immediately for an off-airport car rental agency, where Mickey rented a car under one of his aliases. They dropped Jeff's truck off at his house and got on the highway to Ohio. As they drove, Jeff smoked one cigarette after another as Mickey filled him in on the Arizona ranch story, had him memorize some names and details about the place, and gave him the phone numbers and other information.

"I see you got yourself a cowboy hat," Mickey said, pointing into the back seat."

"Had that for years, actually," Jeff replied, then lifted one jean leg a bit to show Mickey the well-worn cowboy boots he was wearing.

"Jeez, man, how long have you had those things?" Mickey asked, incredulous that Jeff actually owned a pair.

"Got 'em yesterday at Goodwill, actually. Don't usually wear 'em because of the rudder pedals on most planes, but they're fine for Threes and I didn't want to traipse in there looking like a dude." Mickey laughed in satisfaction. That was exactly the kind of foresight and attention to detail that made Blind Jeff such a stellar pilot and mechanic.

Soon, they were talking about Sugar Alpha herself, with Jeff telling jump stories and Mickey telling smuggling stories about the old girl—and about how in 1977 he'd spliced a "T" fitting into the fuel line beneath the floor of the pilot's seats so the crew could pump additional fuel directly into the system. It had been proven on several Colombia runs and, if it was still there, would be a blessing on the run and save them the prep time of installing and testing another. Jeff added this smuggling setup to his inspection checklist.

Outside Cincinnati they arrived at a small grass strip called "Brownies." Before Jeff could even identify the airport, he saw Sugar Alpha in all of her red and white Firestone glory and sat up in his seat and took his cigarette from his mouth, laid back no longer.

"My God, Mick, that's not a DC-3, that's a neon sign! What did they do to it?!"

"Sorry, I forgot about that," he laughed as he enjoyed Jeff's reaction. "Paul used it for an amusement park contract 'til they canceled the show. That's why he's selling it."

"So I'm flying a gig in a candy cane billboard," Jeff said.

"Well, they do call it Sugar Alpha."

"Only one DC-3 in the world looks like this," Jeff said. "I mean how indiscreet can we be?"

"True, but on the other hand, who'd ever believe someone'd be crazy enough to smuggle dope in a candy cane billboard named Sugar Alpha?"

Blind Jeff shook his head, chuckling.

"You got a point there, pardner. Let's go have a look."

Mickey drove around the airport perimeter, checking out the layout while Jeff sat silently staring at the plane, then scoping the runway.

"I'd say it's only two thousand feet," he said, "and with the power lines on both ends, there's no way we can get out of there carrying extra fuel."

"Damn," Mickey said, "now we don't have a base to prep, fuel, and launch the run without somebody noticing."

Having seen enough, they drove to a motel and got a room and settled in, then Jeff called Paul and arranged to meet him at the airstrip in 20 minutes.

Paul was waiting for him near the rear door when Jeff walked up and introduced himself as "Tucson John," and the two did a walk-around while Paul gave his sales pitch. Jeff listened, smoking cigarettes and nodding politely at all the right places while at the same time running his practiced eye over every inch of the plane that he could see from the ground. When they got back to the door, he stepped on the entry ladder.

"Let's see how she sounds," he said, and climbed aboard without waiting for Paul's answer. Jeff checked the fuselage as he walked up the cabin's tilted floor, hung his hat on the headset cradle, and sat in the pilot's seat. Paul plopped down in the right seat and settled back to see how well the odd-looking Arizona cowboy knew his way around a DC-3.

Blind Jeff traced his fingers lightly over the instruments, looking over his glasses, then stepped firmly on the brakes, ran the yoke through its range and took a quick look around, above and beside him.

"Boost pump, on," he said, and flipped on the master switch. "Tickle the prime. Crank the engine," Jeff whispered as he looked out his pilot window, watched the propeller begin rotating, and nodded as the big radial belched grey smoke and rumbled into life. "Soundin' good so far."

"Looks like you've done this before," Paul said approvingly.

"A few times," chuckled Jeff as he repeated the procedure with the right engine. When both props reached full spin, he turned the magnetos on and listened to the engines as he set the mixture to warm her up. The engines soon hit full DC-3 roar.

"I'd say you've done this more than a few times," Paul said. "You know her well."

"Finest airplane ever built," Jeff said smiling as he tinkered with the plane like a long-lost toy. "I learned long ago that they treat you the way you treat them."

Paul smiled back as the masculine engines warmed up and gently vibrated their seats. The oil temperature gauges reached the green arc and with the wheels still blocked in place, Jeff stepped on the brakes and advanced the throttles to take-off power. The restrained beast roared and shimmied as it tried to fly in place, then he gently brought it back to idle.

Jeff knew the airframe was nearly indestructible, so he focused his attention on the engines, which were not. When the cylinder temperatures cooled down, he leaned out the fuel mixtures until the engine shut down and climbed out, Paul following. Together they removed the engine cowlings and Jeff checked for cracks and excessive oil leaks. He crawled slowly around the vital components and inspected the wiring and the exhaust. Jeff knew full well that his life would depend on these engines, and he left no detail unchecked. Paul was impressed by his thoroughness, then uncomfortable as the sun set and the late fall air turned bitter.

"Hey listen, John, I'm freezing my butt off here, so I'm going inside. I'll send out a couple of guys to help you re-cowl her and put her to bed. Then come to the hangar and we'll check the logs over dinner."

"Thanks, pardner," Jeff said, and as soon as Paul left, Jeff re-boarded the plane, whipped a beefy Phillips head screwdriver from his jacket pocket and quickly unscrewed the inspection plate on the cockpit floor. He smiled at what he saw: the obvious blue "T" fitting sitting there in clear view and apparently perfect condition.

"Looks like no one ever knew you were there, my little diamond in the rough," he said softly, as he quickly replaced the cover and stashed his driver.

Later on at a local restaurant, Blind Jeff chuckled when he saw his own signatures from years past in the maintenance logs, but he was also happy to see that Sugar hadn't been bent or broken or had any serious problems since he last flew her, and that for the last few years she'd been reasonably well kept up by the maintenance arm of Hogan Air.

"I like her a lot and the logs look very good," he said to Paul. "Looks like you treated her with respect." Paul beamed at the compliment.

"I did indeed," he said, "and I hate to let her go, but, well, life has a way of changing your plans some times."

"That it can," Jeff said, lighting another cigarette. When he exhaled, he tapped the logs. "I want to check a few things mentioned in the logs, then do a test flight before I report back to my boss, but I gotta tell you, pardner, so far I'm a lot happier than I thought I'd be."

"Great to hear," Paul said. "I told Matt he wouldn't be disappointed, and we can fly her over to Hamilton tomorrow. Tie-down's a little pricier so I keep her here but the facilities there are much better."

Jeff returned to the motel and told Mickey how it went, along with his opinion that he needed to do a test flight, a compression check and peek in the belly to confirm that the fuel system was still plumbed for internal tanks.

"Great!" said Mickey when Jeff finished his report. "And it was Paul who suggested going to Hamilton?" Jeff nodded and lit another cigarette.

"Paul said he'd ferry it over in the morning," he said, exhaling a cloud of smoke and wrinkling Mickey's nose. "Hogan Air has a base there, so I can quiz their guys on the maintenance and use their tools."

"Perfect," said Mickey. "I've been there before and it's a much better spot for us. Longer runway, no wires, multiple ramp gates, tower on the opposite side, enough activity to hide ours but not so much we couldn't take care of business. And it'd be natural to just leave it there after we made the deal, so we could take off from there and then just never come back. Sweet."

"All right, then," Jeff said, "I'll do some snooping tomorrow to make sure all that's still current."

Jeff calculated the round trip distance from Cincinnati to Belize and back to Oklahoma at around 2,600 miles. By traveling at a conservative 150 mph and burning 100 gallons per hour, he estimated with reserve that it would take 1,800 gallons or 11,000 pounds of fuel to fly round trip.

"And I'd rather haul gas from the States than gamble my life on Third World fuel," he said when he finished doing the math, "even at the expense of cargo; less complicated, too." Mickey nodded his agreement.

"And I know Roger'll be pleased to only have to top off the auxiliary tanks."

"Wing tanks hold eight hundred gallons," Jeff went on, "plus that two-hundred-and-fifty-gallon internal fuel bladder you got. I'll ask Paul if he knows of any extra wing tanks, and if he wants to know why, I'll just tell him I want to fly non-stop back to Phoenix."

"Sounds good," Mickey said, and rubbed his tiring eyes. "I'll look around tomorrow too and see I can find something for the last seven-fifty." Blind Jeff yawned and they turned in for the night.

Paul woke up the next morning worried that Jeff might find some fault with the plane, so he left his apartment early and flew with his pilot over to Hamilton and met up with some Hogan Air mechanics who had been working all night on their own DC-3s. Together, they removed the engine cowlings and wiped off the ever-present oil, and checked for any other maintenance issues they could find.

With the inspection well underway, Paul borrowed a car and drove to the motel to pick up "Tucson John." Unfortunately, Jeff had already left to get breakfast, and Mickey got an unnerving wake-up knock on his door. He jumped from bed wearing only his underwear and carefully peeked out the curtained window at a stranger who looked like a pilot and maybe was Paul but Mickey wasn't sure because he'd never met him. Fortunately, Jeff pulled into the parking lot as Mickey fretted. The stranger waved to Jeff, got back into his own car and drove off with Jeff following.

"Give me a fucking heart attack," Mickey muttered as he climbed back into bed.

Paul pulled into the Hogan Air ramp on the south side of the long east-west runway. Sugar Alpha sat parked in a row with two other DC-3s that had come in from their nightly cargo runs. Paul introduced Jeff to the mechanics, who were dressed in a mechanic's standard cold weather uniform: grimy, insulated coveralls. The men shared a love for the legendary bird, and they quickly established a friendly rapport. They spent the morning crawling over the plane, breaking only to eat lunch together.

That afternoon, Jeff flew a few circles around the airport and satisfied himself that everything was in order. By then, he had a better feel for the movements of aircraft on the field, so he ended the day by parking Sugar Alpha back among the other DC-3s to blend in as well as she could given her candy cane color scheme.

As he sat in the left seat, shutting the aircraft down, one of the Hogan mechanics climbed aboard and joined him in the cockpit.

"I'm Jason," he said, and showed him a mechanic's dirty hand instead of offering it for a handshake.

"Tucson John," said Jeff, eyeing the mechanic curiously, noting that something was clearly on his mind.

"Just checking to make sure you know what you're getting into," he said. "Most DC-3 sales go to long-established organizations with experience handling these birds and, well, I haven't heard of you or your rancher boss so, you know, like I said, I just want to make sure you know what you're getting into with this bird."

Jeff's skin prickled with sweat even as frost glinted on the windshield. He didn't need an overly curious mechanic watching his plane's movements. Jason noted his reaction and let him off the hook with an easy smile.

"Look," he said, "All I'm saying is if you need any extra help with her, or need to know anything about how things work around here, you know who to ask."

"Thanks, pardner," Jeff said, and fished a twenty from his pocket. "I appreciate your help today and I'll definitely come to you if I need anything."

Jason took the money with a smile, then winked as he walked out of the cockpit. Jeff grabbed his hat from the headset cradle and followed him.

A few minutes later, Jeff peeled off $1,000 from his wad and handed it to Paul along with his "company" 800 number.

"Earnest money," he said. "I'll get with you within the week to finalize it."

"Thanks, John," said Paul, thumbing through the bills. "Appreciate the cash, I hate waiting for checks to clear, and I can tell by the quality of the pilot he sent that your boss is a savvy buyer. I look forward to doing business with you and seeing Sugar go to someone who'll take care of her."

On the ride back to Indianapolis that night, Jeff told Mickey he felt comfortable with the DC-3 and the activity coming in and out of the airport. He also revealed that he lined up a 200-gallon wing tank and fuel through his new mechanic friend.

"Great," said Mickey. "With the ten fifty-five gallon drums I found today, we're set on fuel capacity."

"Okay, and who're we gonna get for the right seat?" Jeff asked.

"Guy who's done a couple of gigs for Roger," Mickey said off-handedly.

"Does the poor son of a bitch know he'll be spending most of the trip hand cranking drums?" Jeff said, laughing.

"He can count his money while he's cranking," Mickey replied.

"Okay, we got the plane, the tanks, and the fuel. Do we have a place to put her when we're done?"

"Broker in Memphis. He'll take any DC-3 I can fly in for thirty-five."

Jeff nodded. The less time they held the plane, the better. Good cover stories take a lot of effort to maintain and, in the end, if the plane was long out of their hands, anyone trying to trace Sugar Alpha's short-term owners would find themselves at a dead-end in Arizona, talking to a clueless rancher with whom they had no connection.

"Okay," Jeff continued. We want to load in daylight and unload at night, so figuring nine hours each way, we need to leave Hamilton about six in the morning, right?"

"Yeah, that'll put you into Belize around two local time. Figure an hour or so on the ground and you can be at the unload point around midnight. Will that work for you?"

"I think so," said Jeff, as he lit another cigarette.

While Jeff and Mickey were busy with Sugar, Roger had inspected a four-wheel drive Trans Van his boys had custom-built for hauling weed. The oversized vehicle had a heavy-duty suspension and a 100-gallon fuel tank. It had windows painted on the side in black that looked real from a short distance, and the hollowed-out cabin was heavily reinforced. Dave and Mike had readied the van along with their two pickup trucks for immediate use. When Roger got the late-night call from Mickey confirming their acquisition of Sugar, Roger immediately dispatched the boys to the Corral with one pickup truck and the van, then went back to sleep, knowing that would probably be his last good night's rest for at least the next week.

The next morning, Roger drove out to his DZ to recruit Kong's help, but when he pulled into the parking lot, he saw Kimmers anxiously flagging him down. Kimmers jumped onto the truck's running board before Roger even stopped.

"Kong got arrested last night for shooting his machine gun off at the end of the runway. A few squad cars dragged him away in handcuffs real serious-like."

Roger rolled his eyes and wondered how much heat this would bring. He went into the office to find out more, but no one had any details. To his surprise, Kong walked in a moment later, looking more mad than sheepish.

"Man, I had permission from the farmer!" he protested to Roger. "He was cool. The police had to trespass to arrest me."

"What tipped them off?" Roger asked sarcastically.

"Someone in the forest preserve reported gunfire, and both the local and county cops came out," Kong lamented.

"You knew you were only two miles from the police station. How cool did you think it was?"

"I *was* on private property," Kong pouted. "Anyway, my attorney friend got me out on bail, but he said they had a good case." He sighed, "I might have to do some time."

"We'll see if we can find a way around that," Roger said, thumping Kong on one massive shoulder, concerned for his wild friend and thinking at the same time that he'd have to recruit someone else for the gig. "Keep me posted, all right? You know I'll do whatever I can to help."

"You got it, buddy," Kong growled. "Thanks."

"That sucks," said Mickey when Roger picked him up at O'Hare and told him the news as they drove over to Billy's house. "But if that's the worst thing that goes wrong, we're still looking damn good."

"Still sucks for Kong," Roger said sadly. "Baddest dude and best friend you could ever have when things get gnarly, but, man, everyday life is still a puzzle he hasn't figured out."

"Unlike us, right?" Mickey said, more gently than sarcastically. Roger sighed.

"Jeanie's *not* happy we're doing this one so close to Christmas," he said, "and she still doesn't believe I'm gonna retire after this one. Told me she'll believe it when I've been—quote—clean for a year, and that I'll be a recovering smuggler the rest of my life."

Mickey snorted at her description and they both laughed out loud.

"She's got a point about Christmas, though," Mickey said after the laughing faded back into silence. "It's already the seventeenth, we're running out of cash fast, you don't have an extra hand, and we haven't even left yet." Roger flashed his famous grin.

"Only thing that'll keep me from my kids at Christmas is you slowing me down!"

"Not a chance, buddy. How's the twenty-second sound?"

"That'll do," Roger said, and they shook hands to seal the deal. "The extra holiday traffic'll help provide a cover for the trucks, too." Roger sighed. "And now to tie down our loose cannon."

They met Billy for lunch at a restaurant several miles from his house. He greeted them like a lost dog who'd just been found by his master.

"We got some work for you if you're interested," Roger said as soon as the waitress left with their orders.

"Of course I'm interested, man," he said eagerly. "Thanks for thinking of me."

"But there's one condition, Billy *Bob*."

"What's that?" Billy asked, frowning at his insulting nickname.

"That you never do something on your own again."

"Absolutely!" Billy said without hesitation. "I mean, I agree. It was too much for me alone, and you guys are the pros. Like you said, Roger, I get thinking about the money, and I don't think clearly. I really want to work for you guys. Believe me, I learned my lesson. Floating out there with sharks all—"

"If the load gets in, you get fifty grand," Roger interrupted, not wanting to hear Billy's tale of woe again, "and if all the money comes back, we'll bonus you up another twenty-five for retiring." Roger gave Billy a hard look. "Now listen, man, that'll make one-hundred-and-seventy-five grand for three gigs. *Nobody* makes that kinda money when they first start out, you understand? That's big bucks even for this biz, so do us all a favor and keep your word. We don't need any trouble!"

Billy's eyes turned into dollar signs, and Roger could see him spending the money in his head. He and Mickey waited patiently for the young pilot to finish his monetary masturbation and focus his eyes on them again.

"Sure, man," Billy said. "I get it. I totally get it. You guys are the pros, and I'll do whatever you say is best."

*That'll be the day,* Roger thought, as they shook hands over it. Then their drinks arrived, but Roger didn't even take a sip from his; he went to a pay phone and made reservations to New Orleans for himself and to Little Rock for Mickey and Billy. While Roger did that, Mickey thumbed through the OAG airline guide and found a flight for Jeff from Indianapolis, and when Roger returned to the table, he took his turn on the phone.

After lunch, they followed Billy to his house to drop off his car, then drove to O'Hare's long-term lot, went into the Hilton Hotel in the center of the airport and took the underground tunnel to the terminal. Roger and Billy went to different ticket counters while Mickey stood at a phone and briefed Jeff on their schedule and his itinerary. The three men regrouped briefly to go over their plans one more time, then shook hands and said goodbye.

"Glad it's you going down, buddy," said Mickey, "because I know I won't have to worry about that end."

"Ditto, brother." Roger replied. "Just don't forget, communication is everything. I want a daily message, all right?" Mickey nodded. Roger looked at Billy. "And you listen to Mickey, right?" Billy nodded. "He's the pro, remember?" Billy nodded. "All right," Roger grinned, giving him a thumbs up. "See you soon."

Dave picked up Mickey and Billy at the Little Rock airport early that evening and drove them to a motel. Mickey called their service and retrieved two messages: the Bushman was en route to Ohio with the fuel bladder, radios, and fuel rigging parts for the DC-3; and Jeff confirmed his arrival for the following morning.

While Mickey dealt with his messages, Dave and Billy stayed in the room and went over maps of the stateside landing fields. When Mickey returned, they made plans to inspect the landing area at dawn, and the men called it a night.

When they arrived at the Corral just after sunrise, Mickey had Billy lead the hike through the field so that Billy would focus his full attention on the task. An hour later, Billy pronounced the field good to go, and Mickey trusted his judgment—he knew that, after their almost-fatal adventure on Grand Bahama, Billy would always make sure they had plenty of margin for error and the unexpected.

They returned to Little Rock to hook up with Blind Jeff. When Dave dropped them off at the terminal, Mickey sent him back to the Corral to monitor the radio while they flew over.

Jeff was waiting inside the terminal, sitting casually next to a line of phones, wearing tennis shoes with his cowboy hat and the thin wire rim glasses with the thick lenses. He was smoking a cigarette and reading a book, and didn't see them approaching. Billy stopped and glared at Mickey.

"Seriously?" he hissed. "How can you think this fucking redneck could possibly be a better pilot than me?"

"You forget already, Billy *Bob*?" said Mickey. "This is *our* gig, not yours, and we make the decisions. Hell, you don't even know what kind of airplane we're flying."

"But look at those fucking glasses he's—"

"You haven't even flown with him and you're making *assumptions*?" Mickey snorted. "Blind Jeff's a better pilot than you'll be in ten years—if you live that fucking long—*and* he's a first-class wrench too, so he's the chief pilot and *that* is *final*."

A weird vibe hung in the air between Mickey and Billy as they walked up to Jeff, who got to his feet and shook hands with Mickey.

"Hey man, nice to see you," Mickey said, and gestured. "This is Billy. Billy, Jeff."

"Nice to meet you," Jeff said, exhaling a cloud of smoke in Billy's direction as they shook. "Heard a lot about you from Mick."

"All good, I hope," said Billy, grimacing at the smell.

"Mostly," said Jeff, then looked back to Mickey. "We ready?"

Twenty minutes later, they walked into a plane rental office and Jeff handed the agent his fat and heavily-credentialed logbook.

"Like to rent a one-seventy-two," he said.

"Quite the impressive list of ratings, sir," said the agent respectfully. "Did you need to upgrade to a twin or something bigger?"

"Nah, the one-seventy-two's fine, thanks."

"Well, sir, you're more than qualified, but it's protocol to do a check out flight."

"I understand."

"Seeing this," the agent said, sliding Jeff's logbook back to him, "it'll go real quick."

The two walked out to the small plane and Jeff pre-flighted it, cigarette dangling from his lips, as Mickey and Billy watched.

"He always smoke like that?" Billy asked.

"Nah," said Mickey. "Usually more." Billy gave Mickey a panic-stricken glance.

"You gotta be fucking kidding."

Mickey smiled.

Twenty minutes later, Jeff slicked the Cessna 172 onto the runway, the rental agent deplaned, Mickey and Billy boarded and they were airborne again. As Jeff climbed out, Mickey and Billy worked to get the navigational fixes for the Corral. The cabin filled with cigarette smoke and, combined with sitting in the back with his eyes focused on the charts, Billy started sweating and feeling queasy.

"Open your windows, wouldja?" he pleaded. "I'm about to fucking barf back here with all this fucking smoke."

Both men complied and the rush of fresh air cured Billy almost instantly. His sweat disappeared and his pale face regained its color. Jeff leaned over to Mickey.

"I see you got me a co-pilot who gets air sick." Mickey just shrugged.

Jeff spotted the open grassy pasture of the Corral long before Mickey and Billy could pick it out, then did a couple of scoping passes over the isolated field surrounded by solid blocks of trees.

"Better drop in and see how it looks up close and personal," he said to Mickey. "You checked it?" he asked Billy.

"Course I did," Billy said. "It's fine." Jeff nodded at Mickey, who keyed the radio.

"Corral cowboy, are we clear?"

"You're clear," came the immediate reply.

Jeff lined up with the runway and descended to treetop height to keep anyone from seeing his actions. They swooped down into the clearing, then bounced over the rough terrain. Jeff had slowed almost to a stop when they hit a hidden rut. The nose dipped sharply and the prop hit the dirt as they jolted to a stop. Jeff quickly killed the engine.

"Thought you said you checked it, pardner," Jeff said quietly, but there was steel in his voice. Billy looked like he wanted to scramble over Mickey and run away. Jeff climbed out and examined the spot where the prop hit the dirt, then eyeballed the prop and ran his fingers over the leading edge. Mickey joined him; Billy walked away toward Dave's approaching pickup.

"What do you think?" Mickey asked anxiously.

"Sand her a little and she'll be fine," Jeff said, petting the prop gently. Then he looked down at the nose wheel. Its shroud was splintered and the strut was noticeably bent. "Your boy better have some tools for this one, though," he said as Dave backed up the truck and stopped a few yards from the Cessna's tail. While Billy hid out in the cab, Dave hopped out and got a chain from the bed, looped one end around the trailer hitch and hooked the other end into the tie-down under the plane's tail.

"I like this guy already," Jeff said to Mickey with a smile. They walked under the wing and leaned on the horizontal stabilizer to lift its nose in the air as Dave jumped back into the truck and pulled the plane back onto level ground. When he got out again, Jeff was already inspecting the toolbox in the bed.

"Nice collection," Jeff said to Dave. "Looks like you have everything I need."

Dave beamed at Jeff's compliments, Mickey laughed.

"You got a friend for life now, Jeff. Dave's *very* proud of his tools."

"As well he should be," Jeff said, shaking hands with Dave. "Nice to meet you, pardner."

"Fuck!" they heard Billy say behind them. They turned to see him squatting near the nose wheel. "There's no way we can get off here with that kinda bend. I don't know what we're gonna do." Jeff looked at Dave, his eyes twinkling.

"A pilot who gets air sick and he's a defeatist too," he said just loud enough for Dave and Mickey to hear him. Then he grabbed some tools and joined Billy at the strut. "Guess that's *another* reason why I'm here, eh, pardner?"

Billy backed away without a word.

Jeff worked on the nose strut for a few minutes, then stood up and surveyed his work. Dave and Mickey looked too.

"Looks fine to me," said Dave.

Jeff chuckled. "Not exactly fine, but good enough to get out of here," he said. "Mick?" Mickey leaned down and checked it out more closely than Dave had. "Better than you think, not as good as Dave thinks."

Jeff nodded. "Okay, we're good to go." He looked at Dave. "If we make it, pass on our departure time to your pardner in Oklahoma."

Five minutes later, they made it off the grass with no problems other than the dripping palms Billy tried to hide by wiping them constantly on his pants. He failed.

"*And* he sweats on takeoff," Jeff said softly to Mickey as they banked away from the Corral and headed for the Ranch. Mickey glared playfully at Jeff.

Blind Jeff fell in love with the Ranch as soon as he saw it from the air but after the mishap at the Corral, he decided not risk the weakened strut on a field landing. He radioed for Mike to meet them at a nearby airfield. From there, Mike drove them back to the clandestine location, and they walked the ground together. Unlike Billy, who had led the walkaround at the Corral without saying much, Jeff knew exactly what he was looking at—and exactly what he wanted.

"I want six flares," he said, "two on each end to mark the length and width and two in the middle so I know how much runway's left. Get some five-gallon jerry cans. Cut one side open, and use the flap to shield the view from the top. I only want the flares visible from the approaching direction just in case there's any air traffic close by. I'll make my final from that way, and I want the first set right here. What are you gonna use to signal me in?"

"A one-hundred-thousand candlepower spot light that plugs into a cigarette lighter," Mickey said. "You should be able to pick it up a long ways out."

"Good. Once we establish radio comm, I'll ask for three flashes. I don't want you to overdo it. Just give me a reference. If we lose comm, I'll make a pass as close to the top as I can. When you hear me coming back, give me three sets of three flashes and light 'er up. Then make sure you're clear 'cause I don't wanna do no go around!"

"Yeah, we don't need no stinking go arounds!" Mike said in his best *Treasure of the Sierra Madre* voice. "We'll be clear, and we'll have the trucks and gear where they're supposed to be."

"And you shut off the motors as quick as possible" Mickey said. Jeff smiled.

"Pardner, I'll have the props stopped before the wheels and parked right here." Now it was Mickey's turn to smile. He much preferred Jeff's cool, calm confidence to Billy's hyper bravado.

"Final thing," he said. "We'll have a flare gun at each end of the strip. If for any reason you see one, it means we're hot, so abort the landing and put down at Muskogee."

"Okay," Jeff drawled, "but I'll tell you now; I don't want to see no flares."

They ate dinner that night at a western-style café and nailed down the fine details of their plan. Mickey noticed that Billy was not only asking Jeff flying questions, he was extending an almost idol-like respect to the older pilot. Jeff noticed too, and when he and Mickey went outside for a private talk, that was the first subject on the agenda.

"Seems like Billy lost something today," he said as he lighted a cigarette.

"You mean that chip on his shoulder?"

"I do."

"Bending the plane on a field he okayed probably helped him see the light—well, that, and watching you fix it with no drama or finger pointing." Jeff nodded slowly.

"Had my doubts about him when I met him—"

"Everybody does."

"—but I think he'll work out. Talks before he thinks but he seems to sort things out once he stops talking."

"Well, good, makes me feel a lot better," Mickey said. "Sure didn't need him pissing you off for twenty hours without a break."

"So is that how it'll go?" Jeff said, moving the conversation along.

"Should be. I got the map and the frequencies Roger'll be monitoring, and he wants to be done before Christmas. He'll have the load plus four hundred gallons of green ready and waiting. He'll have that end real tight, I can assure you."

Jeff dropped his cigarette butt and stomped it dead.

"Sounds like a plan, pardner."

"Hit a damn pothole in a taxiway," Jeff said to the rental company manager as they inspected the bent Cessna upon their return. "I'm deeply embarrassed."

"Coulda been worse," said the manager. "At least you weren't stuck out there." They walked back into the office. "I need you to fill out an incident report for our insurance, and then you can go your way." Overhearing them, Mickey jumped to his feet from the waiting area couch and leaned on the counter.

"Would you consider just letting us pay for the damage instead? No need to put this on anybody's record."

"I appreciate the thought," said the manager, his brow furrowing in thought, "but it's too late to get your check approved, and I'd have to confirm the funds."

"Yeah, that's true," said Mickey, playing out the conversation, "and we're flying out of here tonight so that wouldn't work for us either. We could pay you in cash—I mean, if it's okay with you."

The manager's eyebrows raised.

"Give me a minute." He went into his office and they could hear bits and pieces of conversation as he talked with someone on the phone. He came back smiling.

Fifteen minutes later, Mickey, Jeff and Billy stepped off an airport shuttle and walked back into the terminal to catch their flight back to Cincinnati.

"Cash sure is king," Mickey said. "Dude was delighted: no paper, no adjusters, no waiting for the check."

"No taxes," added Jeff, "and a fair deal so he didn't lose his chance."

"Another paper trail evaded—for all of us!" added Mickey.

"And my fault that it happened," Billy added humbly. "Sorry, guys. Promise I'll be more thorough next time."

"Can't ask for more than that . . . pardner," Jeff said. Mickey smiled inwardly. What a gem he had in Blind Jeff, who seemed to see everything and take exactly the right action.

After the Cessna left, Dave joined Mike at the Oklahoma campground where he'd been staying with the Trans Van and they went through their To-Do list. First, they needed another load vehicle. They looked up equipment rental agencies listed in the yellow pages and found one open. They drove out and found a perfect-sized truck. Mickey had placed Mike in charge of the ground crew, so he took care of the paperwork using his new ID and arranged to pick it up the following day. Then they headed to Tulsa, where Mike rented a motel room to serve as their communications center.

While killing time before the Bushman's late night flight, Mike and Dave charged the radios and inventoried the landing equipment. With everything in order, Mike unsheathed his Buck knife and cut up the five-gallon cans to house the flares. Dave mixed up a concoction of black pepper and gunpowder in his own special blend to destroy the tracking ability of police dogs. He poured the grainy black mixture into a plastic bag and packed it into his butt pack along with a compass, some beef jerky, and similar survival items in the event things went sour and they had to "beat feet."

After Mike finished with the cans, they drove to the country to test the runway markers and the spotlights in the dark. The demonstration went well. The two returned to Tulsa, picked up the Bushman from the airport, and updated Mickey. Now the men only needed to wait as the countdown continued to close in on zero.

Back in Ohio, Jeff, Mickey and Billy drove to a motel in Jeff's truck, the passenger window rolled partly down so Billy could have some fresh air. Unfortunately for him, the draft sucked all of Jeff's smoke right past his nose before it went out the door. Jeff noted with satisfaction that Billy held both his tongue and his facial expressions all the way to the motel.

After the men paid cash for two rooms, Jeff gave Paul a late call and told him that they were ready to conclude the deal the next morning.

"Why not tonight?" Paul asked. Jeff glanced at Mickey, who gave him a thumbs up.

"That'll be fine, pardner. See you in thirty minutes." Jeff hung up and surveyed his companions: Billy, the hyper and obnoxious kid pilot, and Mickey, with his gold chains and drug dealer demeanor. As he kicked off his tennis shoes and put his cowboy boots back on, he wondered why they couldn't blend in more like he did. "You guys take your stuff and go to the other room. Better that I do this solo." Billy started to say something, then thought the better of it and just grabbed his bag instead.

"Good idea," laughed Mickey, diddling his gold chain. I don't exactly scream Arizona, do I?" He picked up one bag and left another with Jeff.

"Try to save some of it," he said. "We're getting a little tight."

After they left, Jeff straightened the room a little, then stacked $55,000 on the table, put the rest back in the bag and put it under the bed, then threw his jacket over the cash pile and kicked back on one bed to watch TV until Paul came.

Paul's knock came soon after and Jeff went casually to the door, looked through the peephole to confirm, then opened the door with a smile.

"Howdy pardner," he said. "Get your butt inside so I can close the door. Can't believe how damn cold it is up here."

"Cold?" he laughed. "This is just brisk in Ohio."

"Then God save me from real cold," Jeff said. "Glad to live where it's warm."

"Thanks for doing this tonight, man," Paul said. "I hate long goodbyes."

Jeff smiled sympathetically.

"Yeah, she's a sweet old girl. Sorry you're losing her, but happier to get her." He flipped the jacket off the cash. "My boss too. He says fifty-five's fair so that's what's on the table."

"Fair enough," Paul said, his eyes glittering as he stared at the money, his lips curling into a satisfied smile. He sat down at the table and thumbed through one bound stack.

"Mind if I count it?" he asked.

"I insist that you do," Jeff said graciously, and produced a motel notepad and pencil. Paul counted each stack, then put it into a small canvas bag he'd brought along and made a notation on the notepad. When he finished, he grinned at Jeff.

"All present and accounted for," he said, "and now for the rest of the paperwork."

He wrote out a receipt, then pulled some official Federal Aviation Administration bill of sale and registration forms with "Tucson John's" company information already filled in. He signed his name to both documents, then handed them to Jeff.

"Hope you don't mind me being formal," he said, "but I have to protect myself. Too many horror stories about new owners using planes under the former owner's name for illegal shit."

"No problem, pardner," Jeff said as Paul handed him the receipt and he added his "name" to the documents. "I suspect you'll also want to mail those yourself in the morning to make sure it gets done."

Paul grinned. "Thanks, man," he said, relieved. "I appreciate it."

Paul stood and they shook hands again.

"How soon before you fly her out of here?" he asked.

"Day or two at the most," Jeff said. "I'm already sick of this weather."

"Sure am gonna miss the old bird," Paul said wistfully. "Have a lot of good memories. If you ever need a mechanic, I know her well and could use the work."

"Yes sir," Jeff said, feeling Paul's sadness. "We'll keep you in mind and give you a holler if anything comes along. Merry Christmas."

"Merry Christmas to you too," Paul said as he left. Jeff shut the door behind him and immediately pulled off his cowboy boots, then rang Mickey's room.

"Hey man, I understand that I'm a glorified stewardess on this flight," Billy said to Mickey the next morning in their motel room, "and I don't have a problem with that. Like you said, Jeff's a hell of a pilot, but his smoking is really getting to me. Hell, even you had to bail on rooming with him and come to this room. It also doesn't take a rocket scientist to figure out we're going to be sitting inside a flying fuel tank on this mission, so with Jeff always flickin' his Bic, all I can picture is turning into another Hindenburg!"

Mickey laughed out loud at the imagery and the expression on Billy's face.

"No man, I'm serious," Billy went on. "You want your gig ending in flames fallin' to earth? The whole cabin's gonna be fumes!"

"Listen, buddy," Mickey said sternly, "if you want back out, let me know now and I'll hop in your place. We can do this without you. Like you said, you're his hostess, so I guess it's your job to make sure that doesn't happen."

"You know I don't back out," Billy said, pouting. "If anything, my problem's getting into things I shouldn't, but c'mon, man, you gotta admit the dude's a walking, flying fire hazard."

"Might seem that way," Mickey said more gently, "but unless Jeff's kept it from me, none of his trips have ever gone up or down in flames—and he's done a *lot* of trips, blowing smoke like a Three with a busted oil line on every one of them. So just relax, you'll get it through."

Billy pondered his defeat for a moment, then rubbed his hair with his hands and sniffed them and made a face.

"I'm gonna take a shower, man, see if I can get some of the smell off me."

When Billy shut the bathroom door, Mickey grabbed his briefcase and went to Jeff's room, where he found the pilot smoking a cigarette as he studied several maps spread across every flat surface.

"Just lookin' at these," Jeff said, "it should be easy enough to find. Let's see the one Roger made for us."

Mickey opened his briefcase and took out a hand-drawn page and laid it over one of the other maps. Jeff leaned close over it, nodding approval.

"Roger wants you to swing over the water around Chetumal," Mickey said, "then turn south-west just south of the city. He said you can use the VOR but to remember they have radar. When you enter Belize, you'll see two rivers north of several lagoons that dump into the bay. Just stay between them. The bigger one to the north is on the Mexican border, and it'll almost lead you right to the place. With Roger down there, we won't be using the ham radio, so you'll need to get close."

"What kind of approach does he want?"

"Land to the west, take off to the east. That's the fastest, but if the winds change you can take off west. East is more likely, though." Jeff gave a confirming nod and put Roger's map in his flight case. "You already know the way home,' Mickey continued. "Without a radio, we'll have to do a tail check in Ohio. We'll let them know your departure time via the message service, and they can do the same for the boys at the Ranch."

There was a coded knock on the door and Mickey opened it to let in Billy. He saw the maps and smiled.

"Looks like we're getting closer to the fun part," he said.

"Then the work," Mickey said. "Roger wants you to refuel the wings while they're loading. You'll have one man to help and you need to do it fast, before you do anything else."

"And when you finish that, dump ten gallons of oil in each engine."

"How can I check the level when the engines are running?" Billy asked.

"Never did a radial gig before, have you?" Jeff asked kindly.

"Just jumpers in a Twin Beech, and other people did the wrenching then."

"With radials, it's always better we have too much than not enough," Jeff explained. "Them puppies'll be working hard when we leave here, and coming off that strip, if she doesn't have enough, ooh doggies, gonna be a short trip, but if she has too much, she'll just spit it out the overflow. A little messy but it won't hurt anything." Billy nodded and smiled at the lesson.

"Thanks, man," he said. "That's something I'll never forget."

"My pleasure, pardner," Jeff said, and pointed to a box full of rubber hoses and clamps.

"And now for the next lesson," he said. "Turning those parts into fuel lines."

After they built the fuel line, they went shopping. Mickey bought two large coolers at a liquor store while Jeff and Billy went to a grocery store to buy food. Jeff grabbed coffee, water, pre-made sandwiches, beef jerky and other snacks. Billy loaded up on chocolate cakes and cream pies.

"We're not going on a picnic, pardner," Jeff said. Billy frowned, then put the sugary stuff back and picked up trail mix, crackers, sliced cheese and a few apples instead. Jeff added two cartons of cigarettes at the checkout counter, prompting Billy to smirk.

"You think that'll get you through the trip?" he asked.

"On top of what I already got, probably," Jeff replied seriously. Billy rolled his eyes in wonderment at the news.

The men went outside and found Mickey dropping a $20 bill into the Salvation Army pot for luck. Jeff nodded approvingly.

"Always good to make a deposit in the karma bank," he said.

Back at the motel, the pilots packed their coolers with ice, drinks, and food, and lounged around watching the Weather Channel, waiting for Mickey to finish his final calls at a nearby pay phone.

When he walked in the door a while later, he watched with them for a few moments, then took a deep breath.

"This is it, guys," he said, "Sugar Time. Let's make a final call to Flight Service and get going."

As Billy and Jeff climbed off the beds, Jeff cocked an eyebrow at Mickey.

"One thing, Santa," he said. "Lose those chains before we get to the airport, and be sure to smear some grease on your jeans or something, okay, pardner?"

"Good idea," Mickey said, lifting the gold from around his neck, chastened. "Sorry about that." Nearby, Billy smiled when he saw that he wasn't the only one getting instructed by Blind Jeff who seemed to see everything.

It was sunset when they drove in the back gate at the airport in the truck with Mickey's 55-gallon drums covered by a tarp. Jason was waiting as they rolled up to Sugar Alpha in its spot between two other DC-3s.

Mickey and Jason started loading the drums into the plane, wincing at the occasional metallic "boing" when they bumped an empty barrel against the door frame. At this end of the airport, they risked discovery only by airport workers, but any airport worker would instantly know what they were up to, so they worked as fast as they could without making too much noise.

Meanwhile, Jeff and Billy inspected Sugar one more time before the light faded to make sure they hadn't missed anything. Jeff checked the oil levels and, as he expected, found each side about ten gallons low.

"Want me to fill them now?' Billy asked from the ground. Jeff shook his head.

"Not yet, pardner," he said, his breath puffing blue in the frigid air. "Oil's still in the room, staying warm. We'll pour it in when we're ready to crank."

"And make the start easier on the engines," Billy finished, nodding in admiration at Jeff's savvy procedures. "Dude, you think of everything."

"Try to," Jeff said, and winked at Billy.

Next, the four of them worked together to move the external wing tank from Jason's truck through the cargo door, then Jason drove and Jeff pulled the aircraft door shut.

"So far, so good," Mickey said, puffing a blue breath of relief into the cold cabin.

"Okay," Jeff said as he surveyed the tank, barrels and fuel lines. "We use the wing tank as the primary container, and as it drains, Billy will pump the drum fuel into it."

Billy frowned at the stewardess station built against the cockpit bulkhead.

"You said you wanted it right behind the seats," he said to Jeff, "but this stuff's blocking it. What are we gonna do about that?"

"Nothing," said Mickey. "Just butt it up against there. It's not that much farther. It'll be fine."

"Says the guy who'll be sitting on the ground," said Jeff with a smile. "Nah, it needs to be as close as possible to the fuel splice because the fuck-up factor increases exponentially every inch farther away it is, right, pardner?" he said, shooting a knowing glance at Billy, who had direct experience with the concept.

"Fuckin' A," he said. "If that's what Jeff wants, that's what we're going to do." Mickey laughed and slapped Billy on the shoulder.

"Spoken like a true co-pilot," he said. "We're going to make a fucking team player out of you yet."

"Hey, fuck you," Billy said, but he smiled proudly at the praise.

Jeff inspected the cabin side of the wall, then abruptly tore the thin paneling off to expose the aluminum framing. He sized up the tank and marked out a section of the wall three feet from the floor, his cigarette tip casting an orange glow on his face every time he took a drag. He pointed his flashlight beam at the marks.

"Cut it on those marks," he said to Billy. Billy stared at him blankly.

"With what?" Jeff handed Billy a hatchet.

"Here ya go, pardner. Get a little practice with the ol' can opener in case we stuff 'er in the trees and gotta use it."

"You got to be kidding."

"Thought you told me you knew about fire. Unless you'd like to be toasted, you better be able to use one of these things. In most crashes, you're too messed up to pull yourself through the roof hatch, the access door behind the seats is next to the props, and this here tank'll be blocking the back door."

"Damn," said Billy, holding the hatchet limply in his hand. "That's a fucked up thought."

Jeff took back the hatchet, touched it to the top right corner of the mark and sliced through it with a short quick chop, then used a hacksaw

218

to cut through the rest of the wall, sending sparks flying in all directions. Soon he made a crude but substantial opening, and they slid the tank through. Jeff then went to work building a cradle for the tank from 2x4s and secured the rig using cargo straps.

Mickey and Billy went back and moved the empty drums forward against Jeff's customized bulkhead and fastened them together with steel bands. They anchored the system to structural attachment points on the wall and floor while Jeff rigged up the fuel lines. Then they tidied up the plane, Jeff re-locked the aircraft door, and they left to have the customary "last supper."

After they finished eating, Mickey dropped the pilots off at the motel, then drove to a pay phone and left a "waiting for your invite" message on Roger's service. Now everything was done, so he returned the truck to the rental place, then took a taxi back to the motel, wound up like a tight spring. Billy was already asleep. Mickey hoped he could get a few winks too.

At 4 a.m. on December 22, the three smugglers arrived at Hogan Air, the rental car packed with the pilot coolers and bags, and 20 gallons of warm oil. Jason greeted them as he unlocked the company gate, then went back into the hangar. They proceeded to Sugar Alpha and Jeff began his preflight routine while Mickey and Billy put the gear in the plane, then removed the wheel chocks, added the warm oil to each engine, and rotated the propellers to coat the oil on the frozen cylinders. Jeff did a final walkaround, then signaled Jason with his flashlight as Mickey climbed up on the right wing.

Moments later the fuel truck slowly rolled towards Sugar Alpha and stopped behind the right wing. Jeff handed the hose up to Mickey, who quickly topped off the tank, handed the hose back to Jeff, surveyed the airport and hopped down.

At the same time, Jason moved the truck around behind the left wing, near the cargo door, and Jeff handed the hose to Billy. At Jeff's signal, Jason increased the tanker's idle speed so Billy could more quickly fill the wing tank and 55-gallon drums. As Billy closed the last fuel cap, Mickey climbed onto the left wing. Jeff took the hose from Billy and handed it to Mickey, who quickly topped off the left wing too. He handed the hose back to Jeff, surveyed the airport again—and gritted his teeth.

"Fuck!" he muttered, staring at the airport security car that was driving their way. "We got company."

Mickey hopped down from the wing and helped Jeff quietly pull the cargo door shut, then waited tensely as Jason reeled the fuel hose back onto its spool. One glance inside by the security officer would expose them and the whole operation just moments before takeoff. Mickey waited tensely, but somewhat confidently, glad that Jeff had told him to remove his telltale drug dealer gold.

Jason saw Mickey's tension and laughed.

"Chill, dude," he said. Mickey laughed.

"Chill? I'm fucking freezing."

"Exactly, man," Jason said. "It's too fucking cold for him to go snooping around. Betcha twenty he doesn't even get out of the fucking car."

"You're on," Mickey said.

Sure enough, the security officer stopped next to Jason and Mickey at the side of the fuel truck and rolled down his window.

"Hello Jason," greeted the officer. "Good thing you fixed the heater."

"No shit, Harry," Jason said. "Hate these early fuelings but hey, that's why they pay me the big bucks."

"Yeah, right," laughed Harry. He glanced at Mickey. "You got a heater in that thing?"

"Sure do. We'd be ice cubes in an hour if we didn't."

"Good thing. Well, stay warm and have a good flight, sir," he said as he rolled up his window and drove away.

"Fuck me," said Mickey as he handed Jason a twenty and rapped on Sugar's cargo door. "All clear." The door opened and Jeff peered out, eyes alert.

"No worries, man," he said. "Totally casual. Dude even called me 'sir.' Grab my briefcase, will ya?"

Jeff handed the briefcase over as he and Billy climbed out and all of them joined Jason in the warmth of the fuel truck's heated cab, and drove back to the hangar.

"How do you want this billed?" Jason asked after they'd piled out of the truck and walked into the hangar office.

"Make it out to cash," Mickey said.

"That'll be one thousand, nine hundred seventy nine, and we can forget the cents."

"Here you go," said Mickey as he laid four $1,000 dollar stacks of twenties on the counter.

Jason's eyes bulged as he picked up one stack and thumbed quickly through it, then glanced sharply at Mickey.

"This is a lot more than two grand," he said quietly.

"Wish it could be more, pardner," said Jeff, as Mickey walked over to a pay phone in the hangar waiting area. "You've been a big help."

"Wow," said Jason, still in shock at the size of his payday. "Thanks, man."

"Just remember one thing, pardner," Jeff said, then took a drag on his cigarette. "Don't flash the cash." Jason nodded vigorously.

"No problem, man. I'll be cool."

Over at the pay phone, Mickey dialed their message service and picked up a positive message from Mike and the final confirmation from Roger, and hung up with a smile.

"Wendy's expecting you for lunch," he said to Jeff as he rejoined the pilots.

"Okay," Jeff said, turning to Billy, "take a final pee and let's go."

"Thanks again," Mickey said to Jason as they shook hands. "Maybe we'll see you again some time."

"Hope so," said the mechanic. "You guys are real gentlemen." Mickey grinned.

"Well, I don't know about that. We just try to be fair."

When they got back to Sugar, Mickey watched from behind the pilot seats as Billy held a flashlight so Jeff could see while he purged the air from the lines. In a series of spurts, the aviation fuel bubbled out and then flowed in a steady stream. Jeff accidentally splashed some on his arms when he replaced the connection.

"Want me to light you a smoke?" Billy asked, smirking.

"I'll take a rain check until this evaporates," Jeff said, smirking right back. "But thanks for asking, pardner."

Satisfied that everything was ready, Jeff moved forward and arranged the pilot's station with maps and a blanket for his legs, then poured himself a cup of steaming coffee from their large thermos. Billy followed Jeff's cue, placing his sleeping bag so he could lean on it, and pouring himself a cup of coffee too.

Mickey watched Jeff start his pre-start checklist and knew it was time to go. He stuck his hand between the two pilots.

"All right, gentlemen," he said, recalling Jason's words, "it's Sugar Time!"

Jeff and Billy both clasped their inboard hands over Mickey's and grinned at him.

"It's Sugar Time!"

And with that, Mickey walked through the sloping cabin and out the cargo door. He latched it securely, then looked at his watch. It was five minutes after five.

# CHAPTER TWELVE

## BURNED OUT

As Roger flew to Belize on the afternoon of the 18th, he calculated that he didn't have a minute to spare in order to make the deadline. He also felt unsettled, a feeling he'd never had on his previous trips. He watched the stewardesses scuttle about the cabin, executing their duties with plastic smiles and practiced movements. Leaning into the aisle, he scanned the other passengers, looking for others bearing some outward sign of concern. He looked at the right engine, and he listened for unusual sounds that might signify a mechanical problem. He saw the Mexican shoreline in its proper place. Everything appeared in order, so he shrugged off his concern as retirement run jitters and tried to read a magazine.

When the plane started its descent and crossed the Belizean border, Roger heard the "ding dong" of the intercom and knew without hearing the announcement that his sixth sense was spot on.

"Ladies and gentlemen," said the stewardess in both English and Spanish, "the captain has been alerted that there may be a bomb on board. We are presently on course for Belize International Airport and should be on the ground in a matter of minutes. Please remain seated and await instructions after the aircraft has come to a complete stop. Then we ask for your complete cooperation for an orderly evacuation."

As passengers shifted nervously in their seats around him, Roger wondered why they hadn't landed sooner in Mexico. He grabbed his bag and envisioned leaping down the rubber chute pictured on the emergency card in back of the seat.

A short time later, the pilot roughly set the Boeing 727 on the runway. Roger braced for an abrupt stop, but the plane continued to the tarmac in front of the terminal. Fear and anticipation grew among the Central American passengers, who tightly clutched their children. Finally, the plane came to a halt, and the stewardess opened the door and lowered the hydraulic stairs for a normal exit. Uncertain about the situation's seriousness, Roger followed the flow down the stairs, and the police hurriedly ushered them over to a gazebo-style building.

Under the shelter, Roger saw a man of 50 wearing street clothes who surveyed each passenger suspiciously. His gray curly hair and sharp Creole features enhanced his authority as he issued orders to the uniformed officers. Approaching the man, Roger noticed a .45 caliber pistol protruding from a pancake holster on his belt.

"What's going on?" Roger asked as he passed him.

"Oh, these flights heading deeper into Central America pass through a lot of political trouble spots, and they sometimes bring an extra bit of excitement," the man said as he kept his eyes on the line. He waved Roger on dismissively.

Roger noticed a furtive movement by the terminal and spotted Buddy trying to get his attention. Buddy held up his palms in silent question. Roger knew he was asking if he had any special luggage that had to avoid detection. Roger gestured subtly back that he had none. Buddy disappeared without acknowledgement.

After some delay, a tall black airport official entered the scene and raised his hands to quiet the chatter. He spoke privately to the Creole man in charge, handed him the flight's manifest, and left. The Creole started calling out the names of all the people who were terminating their trip in Belize. One by one, he asked each passenger a few brief questions. While he waited anxiously, Roger rehearsed the personal details belonging to the bogus alias on his passport.

Before Roger's turn came up, another official entered and announced that no bomb had been found. Things went immediately back to normal, as if nothing happened, and the transit passengers going farther south re-boarded the aircraft. Roger hoped to discover how the police determined that the flight was "safe," so he mingled closely with the pack forming a line at immigration, hoping to overhear a useful word.

He heard nothing useful as he worked himself through the checkpoints and out the double swinging doors, and saw Buddy's tooth flashing in the sun.

"Hey monn," he said, "every ting cool?"

"Yeah, no problem," he replied, "and they decided there was no bomb."

"Was a little worried, monn," Buddy said as they walked briskly toward George's waiting red Ford pickup. "The searchers are elite special police and they are the best in the country, so if your luggage was hot . . ." Roger slapped him on the shoulder.

"But it wasn't and they blew it off anyway, so thanks for worrying but forget about it, okay, my friend?"

He handed Buddy a twenty when he got to George's truck, then climbed into the passenger seat, and the two drove off, talking business before they got off the airport grounds.

"Everything is going smoothly," George said, "but we are not so relaxed as when you were here before. The helicopters have been spraying around Orange Walk again. They pretty much knocked out the local crop, and the wind was blowing towards town when they came, so lots of people got sick. But worse, the farmers harvested what dope they could and sold it cheaply to the greedy gringos."

"Poisoned weed going to America," Roger said bitterly. "I sure hope the buyers hear through the grapevine that something's wrong."

"And I wonder," added George, "how Americans will react when they learn their own government is poisoning them."

"I'm more worried about my government poisoning you. How's your family?"

"Praise God, the wind did not blow our way. Everybody is fine."

"Really sucks that you have no say in the matter," Roger said sadly. "Makes me wonder about what causes you more harm—me and my drugs, my government's efforts to get rid of them, or busting your ass your whole life to scratch out a living?" George looked at Roger with kindly eyes.

"Harm comes from the helicopters, yes," George said, "and they are here because of you and those like you, but don't be troubled by it; it is a small price to pay for all the benefits that come to us from your business."

"Thanks, George," Roger said, "I appreciate that, and I'm even happier that your family is safe. How about our green family though?"

"They are fine, Roger. They only worked around Orange Walk as a show of force, like you said when you explained why we set up so far back in the bush."

"What else needs to be done before we're ready?"

"Get the gas. I even have expense money left over from what I've sold."

"How much did you have to sell?"

"I don't know for sure," George said, "but I wrote it down. I can tell you it was more than a thousand pounds. I met a short-haired American through Pete Smith who bought most of it. There was something very unusual about him, though. He wasn't like you at all. He always spoke of having to check with someone before he did anything—and he was very curious about the American in charge. I couldn't tell if he was fishing or if Pete mentioned something about you to him. He said the weed was the best he'd seen in Belize, so he knew a professional put it together."

"What all does he know?" Roger asked, and he could feel the hairs prickling on the back of his neck.

"Only what Pete could have told him, but he doesn't know where the farm is. I'd say he was only guessing, but he did say he wanted to meet you."

"*Me!*"

"Well, not *you*, but the guy in charge. He was really interested in airstrips and flashed plenty of money, saying he could work things out."

"Then let's not go see him or Pete until we get this done, all right?"

"Don't worry Roger," George laughed, nodding in agreement. "I've heard too many gringos talk to believe there's anyone else like you out there. You're the only American I know who hasn't ripped someone off. Besides, I have a weird feeling about him too."

A few minutes later, they reached the Sand Hill junction and George drove through a ditch to avoid a cement pillar blocking the entrance to the new Northern Highway. As he lumbered back onto the smooth surface, Roger marveled as they drove at high speed that such a modern thoroughfare existed here.

"There are a lot of places to land on this road," Roger said, "and absolutely nobody around to see us."

"I think we're too late for that," George said, sighing. "Tomorrow they officially open the highway."

"Yeah, well let's do some odometer readings anyway," Roger said, undeterred as he looked at the well-constructed highway. "You never know how things might work out."

It took little time on the new route before they reached the end where it merged back into the old road, and soon after that they stopped at a toll booth. Roger noticed several smashed and burned cars rusting in the humidity just off the road as George paid their toll and they continued on their way.

A few miles later, they passed a sugar cane processing factory just outside of Orange Walk and pulled into a gas station with a strange ornament on one side: a single-engine Mooney 4-seater with a bent prop. George noted Roger's stare.

"Someone tried to fly three hundred pounds off a nearby dirt strip," he said, "but they didn't make it."

"Interesting," Roger said, and walked over to inspect the wounded bird while George gassed up the truck. He bought a bottle of soda on the way and drank it as he looked into the cockpit. He found the instrument panel completely stripped. The seats were gone too. Then he saw George talking to Jose, the station owner, and not wanting to appear too curious about something smuggling-related, he sauntered back to the soda machine, returned the empty bottle to the wooden empties crate next to the machine and got back in the truck.

"The green is on the way from Mexico," he said with a grin. "Be here in the morning." Roger nodded, and sighed in relief.

They went to a local restaurant for dinner when they got to town and worked out a new schedule while they killed time waiting for the gas.

"How are the Blue Creek police behaving?" he asked as they started eating.

"It's not good," he said, suddenly nervous, his smile gone. "All the trips I've made past there alerted them I'm up to something in the hills. I've been told they're waiting for me to move a load to sell in town. I hate to go by there anymore, especially with this truck."

"Can we find a different vehicle for a few days?"

"We should. We can't afford any trouble this close to the deadline. We've come too far to blow it here. And yes, Manu will know of something."

They soon found themselves bouncing down a back road, dimly illuminated by a thick crescent moon. They arrived at Manu's humble one-room home perched on stilts five feet in the air. George beeped and he came out, jumped into the cab and they went to town to get a different vehicle.

Down in the ragged part of town, they stopped outside a house with a dilapidated white Ford van parked in front of it. Even in the dim light, Roger could see large dents and lots of rust.

"Does it run?" he asked dubiously.

"It has many rough miles on it," George said, "but I put them on her, so I know what she can still do. We've used it many times and spent hundreds of dollars fixing it up."

"I do the maintenance," Manu added, "and she looks very bad, but she still runs very good. No problem for sure."

Roger nodded, confident that Manu knew his stuff, so George went inside to make the deal. When he came back out with the keys, Manu drove it back to his house, with George and Roger following, to pick up the fuel transfer pumps they needed for the night's mission, and to hang out until it was time to get the gas.

They drove into Jose's home driveway at precisely one a.m. The large fuel storage tank alongside the home attested to its ownership and the region's general lack of security. George met Jose at the door and learned that only three drums had arrived. He expected the rest the following day. George confirmed the reliability of the connection, and they loaded the van under the cover of darkness.

Before leaving for the bush, George took Roger to a home with a communal phone so he could check his messages and update Mickey. He woke up the owners, who were unhappy until Roger gave them a twenty.

After he called his service, Roger received a coded number and instructions to call Mickey at six a.m. George didn't want the van sitting in public reeking of aviation fuel, so he dispatched Manu to the farm with it. Roger and George attempted to grab some sleep in the truck while waiting for the appointed call time.

Roger dialed the number through the operator just before six and spoke directly to Mickey.

"Well, buddy, it's certainly good to be here soaking up the sun," Roger said in code. "Everybody's doing great, and we'll all be at the Ambergris Caye dive party like we wanted."

"Glad you're enjoying yourself," Mickey said. "It's colder'n a witch's tit up here. Don't forget mom and dad are expecting you for Christmas, and you can bet Sally will be pissed if you stay down there over the holidays."

"I won't let the folks down, but listen, I'll be out on the boat for a few days and won't be able to get to the phone. I'll give you a call at Trudy's."

"Okay, talk to you later."

Roger hung up, confident his message was understood and comfortable that anyone listening wouldn't have been alerted by the conversation. He woke up George and they headed for the farm as the eastern stars began fading in the pre-dawn light.

"Everything's still on schedule," Roger said, "so we definitely need those other five barrels tomorrow." George nodded.

"Like I say, no problem. Very reliable connection."

George rapidly navigated the desolate roads past San Felipe, leaving a trail of dust and barking dogs. Roger felt George's concern as they approached the Blue Creek police station. The two-story station sat only feet from the road, but they passed without seeing a soul. Roger probed more about George's concerns.

"They are really bad," George said intensely. "They use their power to loot from the people like they do in Mexico and Guatemala. One of the locals told me they stopped him and demanded money. When he refused, the police took everything he had and made him walk. The villagers have been waiting for you to return, saying you'd take care of them."

"Who do the villagers think I am, Superman or something?" Roger said sharply, and looked over his shoulder at the receding station with a new apprehension.

"The men in the village call you '*Señor Huevos Grandes*'."

"Big eggs?"

George laughed. "In English, you would say 'the one with big balls'."

"That's not a good way to keep a low profile."

"What do you expect, Roger? The thing you did with the plane to save Rosa. No one here ever see anything like that. And every time the story gets told the plane is bigger and the strip is shorter and the weather is worse."

"I see," said Roger. "And how is Rosa?"

"Completely recovered," George said, "and now she draws pictures of airplanes."

Roger smiled and looked out the window at the lush scenery as they traveled through the hills to the Mennonite area and saw the white van parked outside Jacob's house. George parked alongside it, and Jacob and Manu suddenly appeared from behind an old stake bed truck.

"That sure was good timing," George said.

"We had our guard up," Manu replied. "You didn't see us, did you?"

"Told you this place will be fine," Jacob said with a grin.

The group exchanged greetings, and Manu explained that Jacob had showed him a site where they could stash the load when it came out from the farm—and how they'd watched the truck approach from a long ways out. Then he pointed to a grove of trees across the road.

"That's the place," Manu said to Roger.

"And I can watch it from my house," Jacob added.

"Let's go check it out," Roger said, so they all crowded into the van and drove over to inspect the spot, a secluded little glen at the back side of the grove.

"This'll do," Roger said, a small smile of satisfaction creasing his face. "Let's park the drums here now." George and Manu started rolling the heavy fuel containers out of the van. Roger turned to Jacob. "How about the strip?"

"Mowed it, even filled in a few little holes," the Mennonite said. "And George already took care of me."

"Great, thanks" Roger said. "I still want to look at it, but that'll have to wait until we get back from the bush."

They dropped Jacob off at his home and drove the road further until it petered out near the watchmen. Roger's eyebrows went up when he saw that the previously hidden trails were now obvious paths heading into the jungle.

"We tried to be careful," he explained, as they put on their knapsacks and prepared to hike, "but with the extra traffic during harvest, there's little we can do about it."

Roger better understood what George meant about all the activity after they got to camp. A flurry of workers moved about a shanty town of shelters to the rhythm of pulsating generators. The 100-foot long row of stations erected on the dark ground and shaded by a canopy of trees resembled booths at a carnival. Some of the men called his name, and Roger returned their waves. He smelled the sweet pine aroma of fresh colas.

"Well Roger, what do you think?" George asked, beaming proudly.

"Looks like you got it together, my friend."

"I had a good teacher."

They walked over to the well and looked out over the stubbly field. Roger saw Paco, the chief grower, and George's brother Hector leading in heavily loaded horses. Stopping at the first station, they passed their reins to a younger boy, and Hector quickly unloaded the freshly cut plants. Hector welcomed them warmly and took them on a tour.

He started at a large mound covered with thick black plastic. He held up a corner and asked Roger to pull out a bale. Roger grabbed one of the neatly shaped cubes at random and placed it in a ray of light. He carefully slipped his knife through the folds and exposed the contents. Inside, a beautiful array of colors glistened in the sun like jewels. Hector sliced the heavy brown paper completely down the side to reveal a perfect consistency throughout. George smiled at Roger's reactions to the resin-covered wonder.

"Can you see now why the other gringo wanted to make the business with us?"

"I think we're about to spoil the Americans and change their taste from Colombian," Roger replied, nodding. "This stuff will *fly* in the States." He stepped back, estimating the amount in the pile. "Looks like about ten thousand pounds."

"No, the weed is very fluffy. This is about the five thousand you requested."

Roger paled. He'd forgotten to tell George to increase the amount for the DC-3!

"I'm sorry, George," he said sheepishly, "I forgot to tell you I'm bringing a bigger plane. We're gonna need three thousand more. Can you do it in time for the run?"

George looked at Hector, who nodded.

"We have worked hard to finish baling but we have much more ready to package," George said.

"We are now in the back field and have found the prize colas," Hector added. "Let me show you."

Roger watched the dirty, resin-covered men strip branches off stalks and place them in the sun across drying racks made of parallel poles lashed between trees. The simple system kept the plants off the ground and allowed air to fully circulate. With the boss watching, the crew picked up their pace, snipping buds onto a sheet of plastic. A familiar smell dominated the station. Other men gathered small sections of plant and stuffed them into a nylon bag.

The sweet fragrance beckoned Roger to grab a ten-inch cola, and he squeezed its juices and held it to his nose. The workers smiled at his reaction. They carried the bag over to the next station and poured it on a stretcher made of chicken wire. There, they bounced the flowers rhythmically to separate excess leaves and a few seeds. After they finished, they dumped it onto another sheet.

"We'll do this again tomorrow," Hector explained. "Shaking it twice creates an impressive uniformity."

Roger smiled and tapped his fingers together, feeling the sticky bud.

"This is the best product I've ever seen," he said softly, nodding appreciatively at Hector and George. "Excellent, excellent work." The brothers grinned proudly.

They moved down the line to the baling machines, where they saw Rubin, another of George's brothers, pulling a block from a trash compactor. He spotted Roger and quickly stepped forward to acknowledge him with a handshake. His assistant took over, inserting a fresh wrapper into the compactor, and feeding dried buds to the unit. When he was done, Hector placed the finished cube on a spring scale. Roger was delighted; from plant to packaging, they had a fully functional jungle factory.

"You really think you can do three thousand pounds in two days?" Roger asked George after the production tour was done, and they sat near the food tent.

"These men, they are good workers," George said confidently. "This is much work, but I know they can do it."

Roger turned and looked at his crew. These men looked like the descendents of many generations of farmers, men accustomed to hard, dirty work at harvest time, men used to low wages and long hours laboring for far-away landlords. He paid a little better than the ones in the old days—no, make that a lot better—but still, he was slightly uncomfortable thinking how easily he had slipped into that role. He looked back at George.

"We'll make money with only five or six thousand pounds," he said, "but this plane can hold much more, and I've always figured, if you're going to do it at all, there's no sense in not filling it up."

"Yes," said George, "and because you have the expenses either way, whatever else we put into it will be pure profit, no?"

"That is correct, my friend," Roger said, smiling at his companion's business acumen, "so we have no margin for error. You and I should roll up our sleeves and join in with them. They are working their hearts out. We should, too. What do you say?"

"You're serious?" George asked. "You always surprise me, Roger. No other Yankee ever gets down in the dirt with us." Roger grinned and flexed one bicep.

"I'm young, I'm fit, and you bet I'm serious. I meant exactly what I said."

"As you wish, my friend," George shrugged.

"Great! Now, have the men take a break over here in the shade. I want to make them an offer."

George called out for the men to take a break and gather around. Some men took the opportunity to grab a drink from the well; others stepped away from their work area to relieve themselves. Soon, all but those cutting in the far fields sat in a semi-circle around Roger and George. Roger trusted that word would filter out to the rest of them soon enough.

"My friends, you should be proud of the work you have done. This . . ." Roger said looking around at the operation, ". . . is the most impressive organization I have ever worked with. You have accomplished a great deal. With work like this, you will put the Jamaicans and the Colombians out of business."

The men listened quietly as George translated, then they smiled and laughed and some made obscene comments about their competition. Roger was glad his words had lifted their spirits before he delivered the more difficult news—even if it was good news in a way, too.

"However, I have made a mistake. I've sent for a much bigger airplane, and I forgot to tell George. I am very sorry, but for this run to work, we need to prepare another three thousand pounds in the next two days. Now, there's no doubt you're all very tired and this is far beyond your duties, but I'll make you a deal: if you can have eight thousand pounds ready by the day after tomorrow, I will double the wage you've been promised."

Roger looked closely at the faces in his audience to take their measure as George translated. When he finished, all the workers stuck out their chests and nodded fiercely at Roger and started talking to him in Spanish and two or three Indian languages. He gestured for them to quiet down so George could translate.

"They say they will work non-stop until they have your eight thousand pounds," George said, grinning. "They will stop only to sleep for a few hours and to eat and drink only enough to keep going until it is done."

To prove their point, they jogged back to their stations and resumed working even before George had finished translating. George grinned slyly at Roger.

"Does that go for me too?"

"How could it not?" Roger said, returning the grin and slapping him on the back.

The surge in excitement gave the forest encampment the ambiance of a tropical Santa's workshop during the week before Christmas—and of course, it *was* the week before Christmas, and Roger's thoughts turned to home.

With the skydiving season over, Jeanie had the time to add those special touches that made the holiday so magical for little children. A home, a wife, and two healthy children made Roger feel fortunate. Not everyone had such luck. The holiday season also created the strongest market for quality buds in the States . . .

"You know we'll need an accurate weight for loading," Roger mused while looking over the pile.

"That's a lot to fit into just one airplane," George said, shaking his head doubtfully. "Maybe we should compact them again."

"The Three has room for more," Roger said, balancing in his mind reworking the pile against losing more time and cargo, "so let's see exactly how many more pounds we need."

George, Manu, and Roger started up the weighing operation and attacked the pile stacked under the plastic. The new incentive had the entire crew bustling with energy, and they labored into the night under the glow of drop lights.

They finished weighing the pile just after two in the morning, and Roger decided to get some sleep before the last big push. Content with their momentum and progress, he curled up next to a tree and fell asleep to the sound of the compactors making a new pile for him to weigh.

Roger awoke as the sun warmed another day and found George and Manu still hard at it. He filled a pan at the spring and washed off a layer of crud, laughing as he found buds stuck in his hair and clothing. Roger finished the ritual feeling somewhat better and strolled over to speak with George.

"Did you get any sleep?" he asked, frowning as George shook his head glumly.

"Last night we burned up one of the compactors, so I sent the other men to bed and decided to keep going. When they wake, we'll get the spare machines and finish tomorrow."

Roger sat on a log, adding figures from the night before as the camp woke up. He paused for a moment to watch a crew replenish the pile of colas to compact. As the men stumbled to the spring or the latrine, Manu unbolted the broken compactor and mounted a new one in its place. Minutes later, they were again running at full capacity.

Before long, the group's enthusiasm pushed the limits of another machine, and it died with a puff of smoldering wires. Now the crew worked without reserves, so George instructed them to give the units periodic cooling breaks, hoping they would hold out.

The exhausted team worked long past nightfall and called it quits *en masse* to rest up for the final day. Roger dismissed the younger men and held a meeting with the leaders to discuss the strategy for the final morning.

"I'm comfortable with being done on time, but it's still going to be close. We've baled just over seven thousand pounds, so what would you estimate it will take from here?"

"With an early start, we can be packing out before noon," Hector answered. "With both horses and all the men, I'd guess it would take four trips."

"Good. I need a couple hours to check out the strip and finalize things there. We also have to set up a camp at the staging point before we relocate."

"Let's take Hector and Rubin with the first batch," George suggested. "They can organize the staging camp while we drive to the airfield, and we still have to get the fuel in Orange Walk. I should also go to San Felipe and pick up the hand pumps just in case. That way, we can limit our trips past the police station to only once in each direction."

With the plan dialed in, Manu rolled a joint fresh from the crop and asked Roger if he was interested in "testing the water." Roger smiled.

"Yeah. Light 'er up."

Manu lit up a hand-made cigar the diameter of a dime and handed it to him. Roger took a deep drag for the first time in six months and handed it back. He'd quit smoking in July to focus for Nationals, so he justified this dalliance to himself as "quality control."

The potent weed expanded in his lungs past his out-of-practice ability to hold it in and he erupted in a coughing attack.

"Is very smooth, yes?" Hector said, grinning broadly.

"Actually, it is," Roger said as he got his breath under control again. "Outstanding flavor and I can feel it already."

"You keep that one," Hector said. "I'll roll another."

Roger slid off the log and leaned up against a tree, and slowly nursed the billowing torch. He greatly enjoyed the break and struggled with the temptation to get totally wasted. But he didn't; he needed to maintain control in case his leadership was quickly needed, so he took one last draw and rested his hand on the ground. He maintained the smoke in his lungs until his brain told him he needed to breathe and exhaled. Letting the stress of the past week all unwind, he closed his eyes and experienced the high quality fruit of his labors. The buzz overcame his fatigue with gentle hallucinations, and he drifted into sleep.

He awoke at sunrise still slumped at the base of the tree. Most of his joint lay beside him. Manu's tolerance was much higher, and as he saw Roger regaining consciousness he smiled gently.

"Well, look who's up. Got some kick, huh."

"Too much," Roger nodded and smiled back. "That's enough of that while I'm working."

He got up and walked over to the hole a few hundred feet away and poured a bag of lime in the pit to kill the stench, then took care of business and quickly got back into his work rhythm. With his trusty calculator in hand, he met the crew by the new pile and added in the morning's progress. The men had indeed been working almost non-stop and, to his amazement and great pleasure they were only 300 pounds short of his goal. Better yet, two men kept the last few functioning compactors whining away. Roger grinned. By the time they hit the trail, those last 300 pounds would be ready, too.

With time nearly up, Paco directed the men who weren't busy compacting buds or breaking down camp to start packing the finished cubes into nylon and burlap grain bags. They stuffed the sacks with four or five bales in each. Even before they finished packing, the compactors fell silent. Roger held his arms up in triumph, then gave his crew an overhead round of applause. Some of them smiled, but mostly they were too tired to do anything except pack up the cubes for transport.

When they finished, they took a much-needed break, eating and drinking to recharge their bodies for the hike through the jungle.

Then they loaded the horses, and each man took a sack and they started out. George sent Juan to run ahead and alert the trucks to the group's imminent arrival so that they would be exposed at the trailhead as briefly as possible.

The ease with which the natives carried the parcels amazed Roger. He worked hard just to keep the pace. His ego refused to allow him to fall behind or lighten his load, so he fought the rugged trail. While straining to keep up, Roger saw the group chewing something and asked George if they chewed coca leaves like the coca farmers in Peru did to maintain their stamina at high altitude.

"No, it's just cane," George said, laughing.

"Cane?"

"Yes. Sugar cane. In the bush, it's the same as candy. Want some?"

"Can't hurt," Roger said, thinking he could use a sugar buzz.

George pulled out a length of sugar cane the thickness and color of a fresh corn stalk. Using his sharp knife, George easily cut the dirty end off the bottom on an angle. He then bit into the fibrous outer layer at the cut and pulled it away in strips with his teeth. This left only the clean, yellow, juicy pulp in the center which he bit off and chomped down on with his back teeth to enjoy the flow of the sticky, sweet liquid. He crushed and sucked the pulp a few more times and then spit out the soft, spent, fibrous wad.

George cut a section of pulp off and handed it to Roger on the edge of his knife. Roger inserted it in his cheek and bit down trying to imitate

George. Roger's instant dislike for the raw green taste had him rapidly spit it out, and he decided to make it out using his own energy reserves.

Tension grew as they neared the trailhead. Watchmen scouting ahead defensively positioned themselves. The men used native animal sounds to communicate remarkably well. When the caravan approached the road with a ton of weed, they quickly deposited it in the waiting vehicles. The men then reversed their route to retrieve the next batch.

The bulky load completely filled the van and forced them to fill the pickup to capacity. To keep the contents from falling overboard, they jammed thick branches in the bed wall holes and tied them together to make a rope fence. Then, with George's brothers standing on the rear bumper, they slowly rolled down the trail. The rutted path stopped them completely at times as the driver carefully lowered each wheel into washed-out sections. At the main road, they progressed at a better rate. However, the Mennonites they passed had full view of their cargo.

Finally, the vehicles reached the staging area and penetrated as far back into the bush as possible. Right before stopping, George removed the rope and the driver swerved the truck to jar off some of the load, then they rapidly tossed out the remainder and walked it a short distance into the trees. While they worked, Jacob and his partner Pedro drove up, and in no time at all the seven men secured the stash and departed. George's brothers remained behind as guards.

The men needed time to make the round trip from the trailhead to camp and back with their next load, and Roger needed to review the landing strip Jacob had prepared, so George drove the truck between the hills to the hidden site and stopped when the runway came into view. Jacob showed them the freshly cut runway and pointed out the easily movable farm implements blocking it to make it appear inactive. Roger liked this touch, and they drove the length several times until satisfied. The men disembarked near the entrance and climbed a hill Roger had chosen for the lookout.

Roger visualized the entire operation and identified the likely route police would take. He then surveyed the surrounding land and sketched each lookout position.

"Man, this is beautiful," he said to George. "So far back in the hills with a view like this gives me a peaceful feeling. All we have to do is run through a few rehearsals with the boys so they all know their jobs and don't walk into the props. There's gonna be plenty of time, and we don't need any extra pressure, so I don't want any guns around, all right?"

George wrinkled his face, knowing Roger was aware he always carried a cut-down .30 caliber carbine he called the "Enforcer."

"Okay, man, whatever you say," he said reluctantly. Roger's eyes narrowed.

"George, we're not cocaine cowboys," Roger said sternly. "We don't need those vibes around this run, all right?"

"All right," George said. "No problem. I know you know what you're doing."

Roger held George's eye for a moment until he was satisfied, then they went back to the truck and drove back to the staging area, retrieved the van and went to get another load at the trailhead.

While moving the second ton to the staging area, George recruited Jacob and his large truck to ferry the remaining bales so he could head into town to refuel and retrieve the hand pumps.

They drove the two vehicles past the Blue Creek police station without incident and made a slight detour into San Felipe to pick up the hand pumps. Word of their presence in the village quickly spread and soon, one of Rosa's brothers ran up to Roger.

"Grandmother would like you to join us for dinner," he announced. George and Roger traded consultative glances.

"We have time," George said. "If you want, I can send Manu ahead with the pumps. Besides, it would be an insult to refuse, and we should wait until later in the night to move past the cops again anyway."

"I agree," Roger said, nodding, "thanks." He walked over to Rosa's house with the boy while George finished his business, thinking how appealing a home cooked meal would be. When they got to the house, the boy proudly led him in and ran to get his grandmother.

Roger crossed the threshold and walked into a cloud of smoke that dropped him to his knees, coughing and gagging, eyes stinging. He pulled his head inside his T-shirt and crawled outside to clear his eyes and suck clean air into his tortured lungs. Blinded by his improvised smoke mask, he stumbled over a chicken and fell down. Clearly something was horribly wrong.

Roger realized the youngster was still inside, so he jumped to his feet, gulped one more breath of clean air, and charged back in. Eyes stinging again, he stayed low and quickly made his way through the living area through the far door into the kitchen—where he found the boy sitting at a table talking with his grandmother as she stirred something in a smoking iron kettle.

She hooked the ladle on the edge of the pot and gave Roger a big hug, then held him at arm's length to "have a look at him"—and realized from his tear-stained face how uncomfortable he was. She smiled and patted his face, then said something in an Indian language to the boy, who took Roger's hand and led him back to the fresh air out front.

"Jeez," said Roger, coughing and wiping his eyes. When he could see again, he noticed George standing nearby talking with Rosa's father. The man bear-hugged Roger and slapped him on the back.

"Thank you for coming, *Señor Huevos Grandes*," he said. "Welcome to our home."

"Thank you for the invitation," Roger said, smiling at his adventure.

"We are glad to have you," said Rosa's father. "I hope you brought your appetite!"

"What's she cooking?" Roger asked cautiously.

"Mama's making her special sauce. She cooks the best chili pepper in the village. You will soon see!" Roger kept smiling but George could see past the smile and laughed as Roger wiped the remaining tears from his burning face.

"That was worse than the *habanero* your cook fed me," he said to George, "and I didn't even eat any yet. I mean, it's a condiment, right? It's not a dish, right?"

"Now you know why we leave the cooking to the women," George chuckled. "Even I have trouble smelling too much of those spices."

George's admission made Roger feel less like an idiot American who couldn't stomach—or even be around—the native foods. Then he saw Rosa and forgot his momentary discomfort as she ran over and jumped into his arms.

"*Hola Señor* Roger," she said and kissed him on the cheek. "Thank you for the airplane ride."

"Thank you for getting well!" he said and kissed her back. "Are you okay now?" She nodded. "Do you remember anything other than the airplane ride?"

"Not really," she said, "except that it was hard to breathe." She grinned mischievously at him. "And I remember that you needed Spanish lessons." She giggled and ran into the house.

George and Roger talked outside for a while, then went inside and sat down at a small table. The house air was miraculously clear of smoke and with just a hint left of Grandmother's chili peppers. As she and the boy filled the table with chicken, beans, rice and tortillas, Roger absorbed the scene: men drinking, children playing, women watching over all, everyone smiling and glowing with pleasure. It reminded him how good his own life was, not just with material things, but with his own family, his good health, and his loyal friends.

As they ate, he realized how much he also enjoyed the peaceful life and the simple but genuine pleasures of the Third World, and he hated to go when George said it was time to start working again.

When they got back to Orange Walk, Roger sent a message to Mickey to confirm their schedule. He received a coded seven digit number in reply, so he guessed the area code and gave it a try, wondering as he waited for Mickey to pick up if anything had gone amiss on Mickey's end.

"Hey buddy, how was the dive?" said a cheery voice on the other end of the call.

"So beautiful you won't believe me," Roger said, relieved to know from his partner's tone of voice that everything was fine. "It was all virgin and still fresh in my mind. Weather cold up there?"

"You betcha, but that can't damper our holiday spirits, that is, if you're here."

"Count on it, my friend. I'm already getting primed to leave. I've got three six packs waiting and on my way to get five more right now. You know how I hate flying, I'm gonna be totally tanked for the trip back."

They finished their coded conversation confirming their readiness, then Roger and George went to Jose's home first, where they, Manu and the van were waiting in the driveway.

"The fuel's not here," Manu said before they got out, "but it's expected at any time."

"It was supposed to be here yesterday," Roger said sharply. "If that's all you know, then go get that guy right now. The trip is going down in the morning."

"Okay, boss," said Manu in a subdued voice. "I go get him."

Roger gritted his teeth in frustration as he watched Manu walk inside the house. He knew the DC-3 could fly the whole run with what it had on board—if nothing unexpected happened. But that's where his Rule of Three came in; that extra fuel was crucial in case there *were* hiccups in the plan. Manu reappeared, Jose at his side.

"The gas is coming from the airport in Chetumal," Jose explained through the truck window. "My brother's friend on the border couldn't get it through on the main road, so they're crossing the river by boat. He should have been back long ago. Right now all I can do is wait."

"Okay, *gracias*," Roger said calmly, though he didn't feel that way as Jose walked past the bent Mooney and went back in the house. Roger stared at the Mooney for a long moment, hoping it wasn't an omen for his own run.

"Hey, at least he had a story," George said, as he got out of the truck, grabbed the cooler from the back, and set up on the porch to wait it out.

They waited a long time. When the clock hit midnight, Roger hit the end of his patience rope. He glared at George.

"The plane will be here in twelve hours. I can't just sit around wasting time."

George jumped to his feet without a word and went inside the house. Roger heard voices speaking Spanish, then a ringing phone. A moment later, George came outside.

"The gas is across the river, but his brother's truck is stuck in the mud."

"Does he know where?" asked Roger, relieved that at least things were moving the right way, even if they were temporarily stalled again. Jose walked outside before George could answer.

"He say a long rope and a pull will break him free," Jose said, and gestured to George's truck. "That will be enough truck, and we can be there in an hour."

"*Gracias, mi amigo*," Roger said and without another word they piled into truck and van and headed northward towards Corozal Town. They bounced off the main road with Jose in the truck guiding George through some nearly impassable stretches as they paralleled the banks of the Hondo River. Then Jose signaled him to stop and flashed his flashlight several times into the jungle. A moment later, there was an answering flash a few yards away and his very muddy brother Hernan appeared.

He led them a short distance to a pickup truck buried up to its axles in mud, and pointed to a log on the edge of the road.

"I tried to drive around it and the weight shifted," he said, "and I slid off the path, then got more stuck when I tried to get out."

George snapped into action, jumping into his truck and backing it into place. Manu tied the vehicles together. When George hit the gas, though, Hernan's truck didn't budge, and George's wheels started to dig into the mud too.

"Stop!" yelled Roger. He pondered the situation for a moment, his hands on his hips, then he reached down and unhooked the rope as Manu and George joined him.

"We need the barrels, not the truck," he said. "Put them in the van and let's go."

George and Manu jumped into action and as soon as they rolled the first barrel off the truck, Jose frowned and waved his arms.

"But what about my brother's truck?" Jose said.

"First things first," Roger said sternly, and put two twenties in the man's hand. "We'll take you guys home, then you can have a tow truck yank him out of there in the morning. Without the fuel drums, he won't have to answer any questions, *sí*?" Jose calmed down instantly as he saw that Roger's idea solved everybody's problems.

"*Sí, Señor Huevos Grandes*," he grinned. "You are a good thinker."

Roger smiled and patted Jose on the shoulder, then turned his attention to helping George and Manu finish transferring the barrels to the van.

"All right, here's the new plan," Roger said to George and Manu when they were done. "You guys take the van and go straight through. That way nobody'll see the van in town during daylight. I'll take these guys home in the truck, then make my final confirmation call and I'll hook up with you at the camp."

An hour later, Roger pulled up to a pay phone after dropping off Jose and Hernan.

"I'll see Sally at the party," he said wearily to Mickey's message service. He returned to George's truck and drove out to the Chula Vista Hotel. He had just enough energy left to smile at the desk clerk and walk upstairs to his room without staggering.

As soon as he shut the door behind him, though, the emotional and physical pace of the last few days finally caught up with him. Laden with fatigue but content that everything was on track, he collapsed onto the bed without undressing and was asleep the moment his head hit the pillow.

While Roger slept, two men from his loading crew patrolled the camp perimeter. The rest of the crew was sleeping, also exhausted by the frenzy of the past week but their work also done. The load was hidden and ready to go, Jacob's truck was stashed in the bush, their perimeter was secure, and everything was in order except for the remaining five fuel barrels.

Manu and George made their way around Orange Walk without incident and approached the only place where there might be a checkpoint between them and the hills of safety.

"Please, just let us get by one more time," Manu prayed. His prayer rattled George, so he pulled his Enforcer from under the driver's seat—which rattled Manu.

"Roger said no guns, man," he said nervously, eyes frozen on the carbine.

"Roger's not here, man," George said quietly, setting the gun between his legs as they rolled down the final straightaway. They saw a brief reflection in the middle of the road.

"That's the police jeep!" Manu exclaimed.

"It's a roadblock, all right. This is not good." George slapped the bottom of the magazine to confirm it was seated and scanned the dark to see more clearly the size of the opposing force. Manu did the same, running his fingers nervously through his hair.

"Only two I think," George said, and eased off the accelerator as if he was cooperating.

"Don't hit them," Manu hissed.

"They'll step aside," George said, "and come to either window."

The two police officers did exactly that, moving out of the headlight beams as the van rolled up to them. George waited another second, then gunned the engine.

"Hang on, Manu! We're gonna bust it!"

The revving engine alerted the officers, and they jumped clear as the heavily weighted van roared past the checkpoint, drums bouncing around in the back as the police fired their pistols at them. One round broke the rear window, whizzed by George's ear, and shattered the windshield. The rest sounded like hail stones slamming into the vehicle's rear doors.

"Bastards are trying to kill us!" George screamed. "Why would they just shoot without a chase? Don't they know the fucking *rules?*"

In blind rage, George chambered a round, spun around in his seat, stuck his head and shoulders out of his window and emptied his magazine. Manu grabbed the steering wheel and kept the van on the road. Unaccustomed to receiving fire, the police took cover behind their jeep and reloaded. George slid back behind the wheel, handled the Enforcer to Manu and, cursing loudly, sped towards the safety of the Blue Mountains.

At the roadblock, the shaken officers radioed their commander. In their excitement, they greatly exaggerated the intensity and duration of the firefight. Their commander knew the local growers were due to move their product soon and had hoped the nightly roadblocks might force them into making a mistake. Hoping this was it, he immediately dispatched a 30-man rapid response team in hopes of tracking down the offenders. He wanted these guys bad, too. They had tried to shoot his men.

George and Manu relaxed a little when they entered the hills, but they were still in shock from the violent altercation when they got to Jacob's and banged on his door. Before Jacob could answer, a whoosh of flame cast their shadows against the house and a moment later the fuel barrels started exploding, sending a 100-foot-high mushroom of fire curling into the night sky. The heat was so intense they scrambled away from Jacob's door, shielding their faces from the flames and smoke.

Jacob opened the door and stared in shock at the hell that used to be his front yard, then shut the door and ran over to where George and Manu cowered behind a shed.

"What is going on here!?"

"We had to blow a road block!"

"Damn it!" Manu said, looking around the area that was lighted as bright as day. "We ought to put that fire out with something."

"Indeed," Jacob said, stunned at the devastation. He grabbed a few shovels from the shed and the men went to work shoveling dirt on the van to smother the fire.

By dawn, a small army had reached the hills, hoping to scare enough information out of the inhabitants to find the roadblock runners who'd dared to shoot at them. They didn't need to; the pillar of smoke rising from the still-smoldering van in Jacob's front yard told them all they needed to know. The police surrounded the area, and two men broke down the front door. Other men quickly followed through the door with their guns drawn. They dragged Jacob out of the house, and when his wife and children ran to the front door, demanding answers, one officer buttstroked Jacob with his rifle, knocking him to the ground. His wife fell silent in horror, then ushered the children back into the house.

The commander walked up and looked sternly at Jacob.

"Tell me why you blew the checkpoint."

"I don't know what you mean, sir!" he said, pleadingly. "I woke up to the explosions and this burning van in my yard. I was afraid for my family so I stayed inside. I saw nothing and it is not my van."

Jacob tried to stay loyal to his business partners, but the police officer who buttstroked him now kicked him in the ribs. Jacob groaned and doubled over.

"Someone else parked that van here," he gasped. "I swear! It *wasn't* me."

"You are a strong man," said the commander calmly. "I wonder if your wife is as strong as you are."

Jacob's head snapped up. The other officer grinned sadistically and started back toward the house.

"Wait, wait! I remember something," Jacob said. The commander smiled and held up his hand. The other officer stopped.

"I see you are a wise man, too. Please go on."

"I remember hearing the explosion and seeing two men running that way," Jacob said, pointing to the tree grove across the street "I followed them for a while to make sure my family was safe."

The commander gestured for the other officer to help Jacob to his feet.

"Let's go for a walk?" he asked gently, but there was menace in his voice. Jacob nodded numbly and started off toward the tree grove, holding his ribs.

The sentries at the staging area watched the authorities fan out, rifles at the ready, as they approached the camp in a well-ordered line

200 yards across. The sentries ran back to camp and alerted the growers, who abandoned their stash and ran for the jungle. George and Manu tried to carry off some bales but they struggled to keep up with their companions, so they dumped their loads and disappeared into the jungle with the others.

With Jacob's help, the police reached the staging area quickly, and were astonished at its scale. Their commander laughed and looked at Jacob.

"Congratulations," he said mockingly. "You are now part of this country's biggest-ever marijuana bust." Jacob's shoulders sagged for a moment, then he straightened up and looked intently into the commander's eyes.

"And I led you to it," he said evenly. "I pray you will remember that when the time comes." The commander measured the man in front of him, then smiled gently.

"Somehow I do not think you will be long away from your loved ones." Jacob's strong face dissolved into tears at the words, and he sat down on the ground and sobbed.

"Thank you, sir," he blubbered. "May God bless you and your family."

The commander patted Jacob's big shoulder and at the same moment he ordered his sergeants to break his team into three groups; one to secure the camp, the others to hunt down the smugglers. Then he turned back to Jacob.

"But first, you must tell me more," he said more firmly.

"What do you want to know?" asked Jacob, hope growing in his eyes.

"To start with," the commander said, "how many there are, how many weapons, when and how they planned to move this load."

While Jacob spilled everything, and seized the opportunity to play up the sophistication and might of "Mr. Roger," part of the perimeter team watched for a counterattack while other stacked the bales on the grove road or retrieved their vehicles so they could take the load back to their base.

It was just after 5 a.m. in Ohio when Jeff and Billy fired up Sugar Alpha in the icy winter air. As the engines warmed up, Jeff sipped coffee to warm up his body before the frigid temperatures after takeoff pierced the plane. Billy drank coffee too and kept an eye on the temperature gauges. When the needled hit the green, Billy keyed his mic.

"Tower, this is Sierra Alpha. Request permission to taxi. Over."

"Cleared to taxi, Sierra Alpha, Cleared for takeoff when ready. Over."

"Roger, Tower. Sierra Alpha cleared for takeoff."

Jeff looked outside and gave a thumbs up to a very cold Mickey standing outside the wing arc next to his rental car. He acknowledged the signal with a thumbs up of his own, then jumped into his car and started the engine.

Jeff throttled up and taxied to the runway, set the brake and carefully went through the checklist. He knew the two takeoffs were the riskiest parts of the trip because they'd strain the engines the most. He ran up the engines, and Sugar growled like a contented lion, so he rolled onto the runway, taxied to the downwind end, and turned around. The tail wheel stopped just two feet from the end of the asphalt, giving Jeff every inch of the 5,000-foot strip available for the heavy departure. Then he lit a cigarette and nodded to Billy. Billy pushed the throttles to takeoff power and held them in place with both hands.

Sugar Alpha picked up speed slowly and when they were going fast enough to fly the tail, Jeff pushed the wheel forward to raise the fuselage and reduce their drag.

Sugar immediately accelerated faster but the far end of the runway was coming fast and they were still stuck hard to the ground. Billy started sweating. Jeff grinned.

"Good thing it's cold, eh, pardner?" Billy chewed his lip as they reached takeoff speed, and Jeff retracted the landing gear the moment he felt liftoff, then kept her flying low until they reached 130 mph, then started a slow climbout. When they hit 150 mph and 1,000 feet, he turned south. "You can quit sweating now," he said to Billy. His co-pilot smiled weakly and wiped his forehead with his forearm.

"Thought we'd never get off the fucking ground," he said, reaching for the thermos.

Five minutes later, the right engine started missing. Jeff's eyes darted to the instrument panel and saw the oil pressure dropping. He leveled off to maintain airspeed, and lit another cigarette. Billy stared hard at him.

"Well pardner, looks like we're about to lose the right horses. Close the cowl flap on her and trail the cowl on number one."

Billy adjusted the engine cowls while Jeff turned back towards Hamilton. Given the extra fuel load, he wondered if she would fly that far on one engine. Without warning, the engine coughed violently, so he quickly feathered the engine, which turned the prop blades sideways to the airflow so they wouldn't drag as much as the engine stopped.

Billy watched the blades spin to a stop, and the erratic rumbling ceased.

"We're sinking," he said as he watched the vertical speed indicator.

"Naw," Jeff said, "we're making a controlled descent to the airport, pardner." He pointed the nose towards the airport's rotating beacon and zeroed in on the field.

"Hamilton Tower, this is Douglas, Eight, Five, Sierra Alpha," Jeff called on his radio. "I'm declaring an emergency. We'll be there in about zero-two minutes. Over."

"Roger, Sierra Alpha. Do you need crash equipment?"

"Negative, Tower, negative on crash equipment. We got her under control."

"We *do*?" Billy stammered, sweat breaking out on his forehead again. "With *this* fuel load?" Jeff chuckled.

"Give me ten degrees of flaps, wouldja?" Jeff said, ignoring the question. Billy complied, then Jeff adjusted the mixture on his remaining engine. "Yeah, pardner, we *do*—and if it turns out we *don't*, well, no sense inviting anyone else to the fireball."

"Fucking great," muttered Billy, "just fucking great."

"Give me ten more degrees of flaps, wouldja?" Jeff said. Billy complied and calmed down a little as he watched Jeff puff away and line up Sugar Alpha on the runway like he didn't have a care in the world.

"Dude, you're fucking awesome," he said admiringly.

Jeff chuckled. "We'll know in a couple of minutes, won't we?"

Billy laughed at the old pilot. "I already do, brother. Thanks."

"Give me ten more degrees flaps, wouldja?"

Mickey was in the hangar chatting with Jason when they heard the sound of one big radial engine.

"That doesn't sound good," said Jason and they ran outside as Sugar Alpha settled in on short final. "And with all that fuel aboard. Hope your guy's good."

"Better than good," Mickey said.

"Good thing," Jason said. "Hope he's lucky too."

"Co-pilot's got that covered."

"Cool."

"Cool? It's fucking freezing out here."

Sugar Alpha crossed the threshold and Jeff slicked her onto the runway like she was empty and with one last burst of power brought her to a stop sideways on the ramp.

"Now *that* was good," Jason said.

"Lucky for us," Mickey riposted. They high fived each other, then looked more closely at the plane and saw the feathered right prop.

"Damn," Mickey said. "Hope it's not serious."

"Whether it is or not," Jason said, "I'll get the truck. We gotta tow it off the taxiway and then pull the fuel out before anybody sees it."

While Jason went for the truck, Mickey climbed aboard.

"Where's the truck?" Jeff asked.

"On the way," Mickey said.

"We blew one, man," Billy blurted out.

"Later," Jeff said as he climbed from his seat over the wing tank and started unhooking the fuel lines. "Go help Jason hook up the tow bar."

It was still dark when crowing roosters roused Roger and he got up feeling much better. A shower further revived him and as he soaked under the weak but welcome spray, he finalized the loading plans in his mind. When he went downstairs, he used a hose on the building to wash off the worst of the mud and dirt on the truck, made a quick gas and breakfast stop and headed for San Felipe.

The closer he got to the village, though, the more he felt the same unsettled feeling he'd had before the bomb scare on the plane ride down. He hoped nothing was going to blow up on him now, but when he saw a truck racing down the road from San Felipe—and recognized it as belonging to Jacob's partner Pedro, he knew he was out of luck.

He pulled over and stopped and got out of the truck. Pedro slid to a halt alongside him in a cloud of dust.

"The police are right behind me with your load," Pedro panted. "Get rid of that truck and come with me. They got Jacob, and he's talking and there's a bunch of them with automatic weapons at the airstrip waiting for your plane. Come on, let's go!"

Roger's pulse pounded, his face reddened, and he decided to take Pedro's advice.

"Follow me!" he shouted and jumped back in the truck. He turned around and raced back toward Orange Walk as the eastern sky lightened. He turned onto a side road and parked the truck in a thicket of trees and left the keys under the passenger floor mat as Pedro stopped behind him and he jumped in.

"What happened?" Roger said as Pedro returned to the main road.

"Don't know for sure," Pedro said, looking compulsively in his rear view mirrors as they drove through town. "All I can tell you is Jacob's son, Esau, came running to my house and told me the police beat up his dad and took him away. When I drove past their house, I saw a burnt-out van in the front yard that looked like it had been bombed. There were police everywhere, so I dropped Esau off around the bend. Then a convoy of Jeeps passed with Jacob's truck full of bales in the middle of it. You're in big trouble, and I can't afford to be seen with you. I'm going to the police station to see what I can do for Jacob, so tell me where to take you."

"The Chula Vista Hotel," he said quietly, trying to think but despairing that he could work his way out of this one.

"Not exactly the retirement run I had in mind," he muttered.

"What's that?" Pedro asked.

"Nothing," said Roger, thinking as they drove that *nothing* was exactly what he had left in his bag of tricks.

Roger jumped out of Pedro's truck at the hotel before it stopped rolling, and as Pedro sped away, he stood in the hotel's dirt drive with his backpack slung over one shoulder, feeling very alone. He walked inside the gas station and gave his host a twenty and asked him to tell no one that he was there except for George or Manu. Then he went up to his room and locked the door.

His mind raced as he dug through his belongings, looking for incriminating papers to tear up and flush down the toilet. He checked his return ticket for the following day and decided it would be foolish to try to leave that way. The sudden and serious change in circumstances threatened to overwhelm his renowned problem-solving prowess. On the verge of tearing up his ticket and current identity documents, Roger suddenly realized that all his panic stemmed from mere talk.

251

He paced the room and looked in the mirror. He saw a tired man filled with anguish. He grabbed the sink with both hands, lowered his head under the faucet, and shuddered. He closed his eyes and took several deep breaths, then splashed water in his face to wash off the gloom he felt. He looked at himself in the mirror again and steeled the man he saw there to fight the pain.

"Figure it out, man," he told the face. "That's what you do, so do it and quit sniveling." Then he wetted a towel, flopped on the bed, put the towel on his forehead, and started thinking.

First off, if he could believe the reports, he'd lost his load, the police were hunting his men, and his pilots were flying into a trap. With that as a starting point, he worked through the ways he might save the plane and pilots, his men, himself and his load, in that order.

A few minutes into his meditation, he heard someone urgently honking a car horn just outside. He peeked out the window at the parking lot and saw an old green station wagon with a man looking right at him. The driver gestured for him to wait and quickly ran inside. A knock came on Roger's door a few moments later, and when he cautiously opened it, he found an Asian-looking Indian trying to enter the room. Roger's foot prevented him from pushing through. The man nodded deferentially.

"I'm sorry, Mr. Roger, my name is Rudy," he said quietly but firmly. "I know you don't know who I am, but I know of you. Please let me in to explain. I want to help."

Wary but definitely in need of a friend with a car, Roger let him in and locked the door behind him.

"Ooooh, Mr. Roger, your trouble comes from those you work with," Rudy said immediately. "George has been selling much weed in the square, and the police were out to get him. Jacob and his truck are at the police station with your load now, and he's telling all. George will do the same when they get him."

"I just took a big loss for me and my people," Roger blurted out in frustration. "I know I'm a sitting duck here, but I can't leave until I know exactly what happened. You say the load's at the police station?"

"Yes."

"Then take me there. I need to see for myself."

"It would be foolish to go to the police station."

"I know, but I'm responsible for this end of the deal, so I can't go back without knowing for sure."

"Okay then," Rudy sighed. "Get your stuff because you can't come back here. They'll be here as soon as they catch George—and other people know you stay here too. That's how I found you." Roger shook his head at this obvious revelation. Things were getting worse by the minute.

They drove to the police station in Rudy's old car and, just as he said, there sat Jacob's truck stacked to the hilt with Roger's weed and surrounded by heavily-armed guards. A parade of local growers circled the display on the outer streets.

"Probably thinking of ways to steal it," Rudy said as they passed. Roger slammed his hand into the dashboard, upset at the sight of his "babies" in police custody and being circled by vultures. He sighed and looked at Rudy.

"Thanks, man. At least now I know that what I heard is fact. What's next?"

"Let me take you to Mexico right now," Rudy said, driving away from the police station. "If you're still in Belize when they catch the plane, your troubles will get worse."

Roger sat back, completely disheartened. Even as the mission's failure hit him like a kick in his *huevos grandes*, he couldn't leave yet. His pilots would be screwed without him—and maybe even with him. He knew the DC-3 was somewhere over the Gulf and unreachable, even if he could contact Mickey. But he had to figure out something; too many people were counting on him for him to fall apart or cut and run.

Thinking of others instead of feeling sorry for himself helped Roger refocus, and he reached in his bag to pull out the last incriminating piece of evidence, his radio. He looked at Rudy.

"Then we have to make sure they don't catch the plane," he said, showing Rudy the radio. "If we can get close to the plane's path, I can warn the pilots to abort."

"It's too dangerous to stay," Rudy pleaded.

"It's more dangerous not to," Roger said, smiling grimly, "and taking care of them is part of the job description, you know?" Rudy nodded and smiled back just as grimly.

"No wonder the people speak so highly of you," he said, "and why they call you *Señor Huevos Grandes*." Roger held out his hand and the two men shook.

"Thanks, Rudy," he said, "and I can't tell you how much your help means to me. You know the trouble I'm in, and if you're caught with me you're in the same boat, and you're helping anyway, so you are *Señor Huevos Grandes* too!"

Rudy smiled at the compliment, then turned serious again.

"So what's next?"

"I want to take good care of you for helping, but I don't have any money to spare, so all I can give you is my word that I'll take care of you. Good enough?"

"Good enough," Rudy said, "and here is some more help right now. You need not worry about me if something happens. I know the police commissioner in Belize City, and I've worked with him many times. And for your plane, if you can talk to them I can help, but I will need to get to a phone. I'm also a friend with Carlos Weatherton, the manager at the big airport. It will cost, but he'll see to their safety."

Roger's eyebrows arched at this news and he sighed in relief.

"That's the first good news I've heard since I got to San Felipe," he said. "Now let's get to a phone."

Rudy turned at the next intersection and Roger started to relax as he saw for the first time that he and his team might get out of this mess with their freedom intact.

"So how do you know these guys?" he asked.

"For many years, the Colombians have been stopping to refuel at the international airport on the way to the U.S."

"Why would they stop there and risk the exposure?"

"The planes are big, four engines big, and can land nowhere else. Through the Colombians, I have been at the meetings between Carlos, Martin and the Americans."

"The *Americans*? I thought you just said Colombians—and who's Martin?"

"Martin is the police commissioner. He's in charge of the anti-narcotics division. The Americans, from what I've been told, work for your government. They're raising money for their military operations in Latin America, especially Nicaragua."

"That's quite a story," Roger said to hide his shock and disbelief.

"A true story," Rudy said, smiling. "I was surprised when I heard it too," he added, and Roger knew then that his disbelief had showed on his face.

"Sorry," he said, "I don't mean to doubt you, but that's the wildest story I've heard in a while."

"What will people say when they hear the story we're making now?" Rudy asked gently, smiling. Roger chuckled.

"You got a point there," he said, and felt himself relax even more. He was finding his feet again, getting his mojo back, climbing back on the horse.

When they got to the pay phone, he called his service and found no messages, so he called Mickey's service and said, "I've had to play hockey and *get the puck out of here.*" He hung up the phone and climbed back into the car.

"Where to?" Rudy asked.

"North," said Roger.

Jason and Billy worked quickly in the freezing temperatures to hook up Sugar to the truck, then towed her to her parking space and started offloading the full barrels into the truck bed while Jeff checked the engine. He'd seen oil everywhere and lit a cigarette as Mickey joined him.

"What's the verdict?"

"She's shot, pardner. Fastest way to get her back in the air is hang a new one."

Mickey shook his head in disbelief and stared at the ruined engine.

"Roger's gonna be sitting on the strip with the load and won't be able to check in," Mickey said, a hint of panic in his voice. "Man, this is the absolute worst time this could have happened!"

"Nothing I can do about that, but unless you tell me it's over, I'm gonna find another motor. We'll check with Hogan first and if they got nothing, then I'll start calling engine shops as soon as they open."

"Cool, man, thanks," Mickey said, "but even if you find one, I may not have the bucks to buy it. What a fucking dilemma." He looked at Blind Jeff, leisurely smoking his cigarette, waiting calmly for instructions. His attitude lifted Mickey.

"You start shopping," he said. "I'll figure something out, and in the meantime, I'll let Roger know what's happening." Jeff nodded and went to help Jason and Billy finish moving the fuel out of the plane.

Mickey walked to the pay phone in the hangar, wondering how much trouble Roger might find being stuck in the open for so long with such a big pile of weed and no plane to put it in. Well, he'd do his best to keep Roger waiting as short a time as possible. He picked up the phone and dialed a number.

"Sally's sick and can't come to the party. Call me tomorrow at eight a.m. Sorry."

# CHAPTER THIRTEEN

## DESPERADOS

After waiting near a lagoon under Sugar Alpha's planned flight path the rest of the afternoon and all night, Roger and Rudy gave up their effort to warn the pilots. Roger hoped for the best—that the flight had been delayed enough for Mickey to get his wave-off message—and pushed out of his mind the many worst-case alternatives for the plane's failure to show. With pressure to flee increasing by the hour, they drove to Corozal Town for messages and news. He was elated to hear Mickey's message but the feeling evaporated as they refocused on their own situation.

"How much do you think they know?" Roger asked Rudy. He knew the answer would be pure speculation, but it would give also him a little glimpse of the judgment, thinking and integrity of this new friend he didn't really know.

"Can't say for sure, of course," Rudy said, eyes focused in the distance as he ran over things in his mind. "A lot depends on if they caught George or Manu or some of your crew bosses. But even if they only have Jacob, I'm sure they know what you look like, and that's too much for you to be safe here."

"Agreed," Roger said. "We best get to the border. It'll be easy for me to cross and safer to figure it out from there."

Later on that morning, December 23rd, Rudy dropped Roger off in Santa Elena, a town that straddled the Belize-Mexico border. Roger gave Rudy his radio. Rudy gave Roger his phone number.

Roger was tired and apprehensive when he approached the bridge over the Rio Hondo, wondering if the authorities were looking for him. He mingled with a group of peasants as he passed through the customs checkpoint, hoping that he looked like an American college student hitchhiking around Latin America on winter break, crossing his fingers that there would be no unwelcome questions.

He discreetly checked the customs officers for stares and signs of tension or extra alertness and saw none; he just paid the $5 departure tax like everyone else and, staying close to the other pedestrians, walked into Mexico past their customs point without stopping. He was amazed and more relieved than he'd ever felt before. For a moment, he felt as if he'd collapse after all the strain of his escape, but then he felt a second wind of energy fill his body and soul and he walked with a renewed spring in his step toward his next destination: Chetumal Airport.

He soon faced another problem; his limited Spanish was a distinct handicap. Unlike Belize, where English remained the language of government and almost everyone spoke and understood English at some level, almost no one in this part of Mexico knew even the most basic English words or phrases. He became rapidly flustered by repeated failures to communicate and only found the bus stop because it was marked with an international sign. The schedule only indicated route numbers, so he didn't know where the bus went, but he knew the airport was northeast of Santa Elena so if the bus went that general direction, he knew he'd end up there. Still, he'd rather be sure, so he eyed his fellow travelers while pointing to the sign and asking "Chetumal? Chetumal?"

"*Sí*," said an old woman with a cage holding two chickens. She led him onto an old bus and he dug in his pocket to pay the driver. He had nothing smaller than an American ten so he handed that to him and nervously signaled that he had no change. The bus driver looked at him curiously but otherwise made no move, so with one eye on the driver, Roger walked to the rear. He saw the driver stuff the money in his pocket.

Roger plopped down in a seat and the bus headed to Chetumal. They entered the bustling town a few minutes later and the driver stopped at a fancy tourist hotel in the center of the business district and waved him forward. Roger shook his head and made jet sounds while holding his arms out, but the driver and the other passengers looked at him like he was crazy so he gave up and got off.

Feeling like an alien on an unknown planet, Roger went inside the impressive building. The beautiful lobby gave him a sense of security, and he took a seat near a huge supporting column by a fountain. He sat quietly for a long while, gathering his composure as he listened to the tinkling fountains, its sound reflecting off the blue mosaic tiles that covered every wall. Then he opened his gray Cordura bag and inspected his last few resources. The first thing he found was the second half of a round-trip ticket he'd so confidently bought in New Orleans that was to take him home on Christmas Eve. He stared at the ticket, wondering if he could exchange it, when he spotted a young couple who looked American. Roger approached them and they smiled at him.

"Excuse me, do you know what city this is?" he asked indirectly. "I got a little confused on the bus."

They frowned at him and looked at each other, then the man looked at him with disappointment in his eyes.

"No English," he said haltingly. "*Dispiace signore, non possiamo aiutarti.*"

Roger's enthusiasm faded quickly, and he held up his hands and smiled in thanks. Without a translator or contacts, Roger started thinking his chances might be better if he went back to Belize—especially since he was also a wanted man in Mexico from previous affairs. Surrounded by uncertainty, he knew for sure that he didn't want to become another lost gringo rotting in a Mexican prison.

He lounged around the hotel until near sunset, then took a bus back to the border. From the shadows, he watched the customs officers search a large truck, then sneaked around them without checking in. After he made it back across the river, he handed the Belizean immigration officer his fake birth certificate and was quickly processed.

Once again on familiar ground, Roger felt much better as he walked through town to the Northern Highway. A cool sea breeze slowly dropped the temperature while he thumbed for a ride. His efforts were rewarded when a truck stopped and a smiling Belizean Indian picked him up.

"Thank you," he said as he climbed aboard. "How far are you going?"

"Orange Walk," said the driver, "to deliver some miniature bananas." He pointed to a bag between the seats. "Have some."

"That's great! I'm going to Orange Walk, too," Roger said, unable to suppress the smile that spread across his face as he grabbed one bunch. "Do you happen to know an Indian named Rudy?"

"This is your lucky day, *amigo*. I can take you to his house. I'm Emilio."

"Wow, thanks," he said. "I'm Freddy," he added, using the name on his fake birth certificate. Then he tried not to look as hungry as he was while he ate the bananas. When he finished eating, they exchanged small talk as they cruised down the smooth highway until Emilio turned onto a small street with Rudy's station wagon parked alongside a small house.

"Thank you so much for the ride, my friend," Roger said as he climbed out, and laid a twenty on the seat. "And for the bananas."

"You don't need to give me any money," said Emilio, waving him off. "You keep it." Then he smiled and handed the exhausted American another bunch of bananas.

"I can tell you're a little hungry, no?'

"Yes, a little," Roger said. "Thank you," laughing inwardly at his failure to hide it from the Belizean. He waved goodbye and knocked on Rudy's door, thinking to himself how ironic it was that the poor were often so much more charitable than the rich. The small-framed, dark skinned Indian's eyes widened when he saw Roger, dirty, tired, and unshaven. He looked around to see if anyone was watching.

"Go wait in the car," he said quietly, then shut the door. Roger collapsed into the passenger seat and closed his eyes. Rudy seemed to appear in the same instant, and drove away quickly from his house.

"Why did you come back?" he hissed. "It's too dangerous here for you."

"It was worse in Mexico," Roger replied wearily. "Better to be here where I have friends and people speak English." Rudy smiled grimly.

"I'm sorry, my friend. I'd forgotten it's all Spanish on the other side of the river."

"No problem, it was probably good to get away for a day or so. Maybe things have cooled off just a bit around here."

"A little, that is true," said Rudy, "but they were hotter than we thought when you left. What started it all was George and Manu getting into a gunfight at a roadblock."

"You're kidding," Roger said, incredulous that George would so blatantly disobey his "no guns" order. "How do you know this?"

"I saw bullet holes in the police Jeeps, and other growers confirmed it. That was why the van blew up; the police shot at them as they ran the checkpoint, and they hit the fuel tanks."

"And they didn't know it," said Roger, talking mostly to himself. "Then they stopped at Jacob's and the fuel leaked onto the hot exhaust and that was it."

"Some people in San Felipe said they could see the fireball even from there, so the cops went to Jacob's house and beat him."

"And he talked," Roger said flatly.

"Not until they threatened to hurt his wife." Roger gritted his teeth in anger.

"Cowards."

"But effective. He took them to the camp and they took the weed and blew a big hole in the middle of the runway. You cannot land there now."

"Did you check it out?"

"Not me! I wouldn't go anywhere near that place now. No, the growers trying to steal your load from the police, they talk to the cops and the cops are talking a lot. They are very proud of this bust, and they are now hunting the man they now call *Señor Heuvos Grandes*."

"Great," Roger muttered. "What about George and Manu?"

"Both are still loose and they may not know about Manu, but they are hunting George because he talks too much and sells too much. It was because of him that they put up the checkpoints in the first place."

"Well, at least they don't have them yet," Roger said, wondering how much weight to give Rudy's account, given how he wanted to replace George as Roger's Belizean connection. As if on cue, Rudy continued.

"Mr. Roger, I speak Spanish, English, and Mayan, I have many contacts, and we can use the international airport for landing and fuel. Let me help you." Rudy's persistence grated on Roger, and American government-tainted connections made him more than a little paranoid.

"Listen, after what's happened, I can't tell you what I can do. Right now, my priority is to get back to the States and re-group. And I gotta tell you, man, I don't like the idea of working with any government. It gets real crazy when you do that."

"Okay, then," Rudy said, nodding, "I understand, get you out of here first, then figure out how we can work together later, yes?" Roger nodded. "Then we must hide you until morning when your flight leaves." Roger held out his hand to Rudy. They shook and then Roger settled back into his seat, more tired than he had ever been.

Rudy pulled into a narrow alley in the center of town between rows of old, two-story wooden buildings. They climbed a rickety staircase and entered a small apartment that doubled as an office. Rudy gave the owner $2 for the night, then carefully led Roger over planks in the middle of a rotten hallway floor to his room. Roger walked inside and turned on the light. Roaches scattered in all directions and the stench of sweat and urine assailed his nostrils. Flies buzzed around him and the sounds from the street and other rooms drifted in unimpeded. A flattened mattress slumped across rough boards unevenly spaced on a rusted metal frame. A sink with no faucet drained into a rusty can. The room had no water except probably for probably the sink, and there was no toilet. There was no lock on the door, either.

"They won't look for you here," Rudy said proudly. "This place is very safe."

"From the cops maybe," Roger said wearily of the surroundings that weren't fit for a stray dog—but he was a stray human and Rudy thought this was the best solution, so he didn't argue. "Thanks for the help," he said instead. "Much appreciated."

"You're welcome," Rudy said. "I come get you tomorrow morning at six."

Roger sat on the edge of his bed after Rudy left, soaking up his surroundings, getting a feel for the place. He could easily hear his neighbors, not just in his building but throughout the neighborhood. He heard no excited talk, no engines racing or tires squealing. No police knocked on doors, barking orders or demanding answers. Despite the grinding poverty in which he was immersed, the place felt peaceful, serene even.

Finally, he had the strength to chew on a crushed granola bar and washed it down with the bit of water left in his bottle. He considered going out for a street vendor meal, but as he pondered the notion, he fell asleep in a sitting position and fell back onto the bare mattress, oblivious to the flies and bedbugs.

Christmas Eve dawned sunny and hot, and Roger woke at first light, feeling like newspaper at the bottom of a bird cage. He cleaned up the best he could at the pathetic sink, reminding himself that at least there was running water, then he relieved himself in the corner that stank most of urine. When Rudy showed up, he felt half-way human and more or less presentable, and he didn't feel nervous when they bought bottled water and enough food to calm his stomach before they left. After they started down the Northern Highway to Belize City, he felt better with each added mile they put between them and the debacle in San Felipe.

"Sure hope they haven't figured out my traveling identity," he said to Rudy after they went through the toll station. "It was easy to pass the border, so it shouldn't be a problem at the airport security."

"Maybe they just didn't get the word up there," Rudy teased. "Not a very active crossing."

"Gee, thanks," Roger said. "I'm trying to be optimistic here." Rudy winked.

"But you still look so intense. Try to relax a little, my friend. It is the best thing to do, even in the face of death."

Roger laughed out loud, remembering how many times he had told young skydivers the exact same thing. So he took Rudy's advice—and his own—and kicked back in his seat to clear his mind of everything else and enjoy the view for a while. It was a beautiful country after all.

His plan worked for a while. Then he started surveying straight sections to be used as runways and when they rounded one huge curve, Roger recognized the long straightaway as the one he'd picked out from the air during his Islander tour. Roger looked over his shoulder to see how the landmarks looked from that angle when Rudy swerved off the road and thumped something with one wheel. He braked to a quick stop and jumped from the car.

"What are you *doing*?" Roger barked, startled at the sudden twist in their trip.

"*Armadilly*, Roger, *armadilly!*" Rudy shouted joyfully, as he ran behind the car and picked up a now-dead armadillo from the side of the road. Roger shook his head in wonder at Rudy's antics, then took advantage of the brief halt to get out of the car and feel the place around him. He could see no dwellings, animals or even fences in any direction. No cars passed while they sat on the side of the road.

He paced off the width of the pavement as Rudy flipped the armadillo through the rear window onto the station wagon's spare tire.

"Now isn't this sweet," Roger said to himself as much to Rudy. "Just wide enough for the landing gear of a Three. We could block the road on the blind side of both curves and nobody would see anything." Rudy looked dubious.

"It's really wide enough?" he asked, looking at the soft shoulders and trees that grew not too far from the road. Roger nodded.

"The pilot I have can handle it. Shoulders won't support much weight, but the trees are so close he has to dead center the landing anyway." He pointed to a dirt road that led off the main road through a cleft in a rock face. "Where does that go?"

"Gravel quarry. They made it to build the road."

"They still use it?"

"No. Only for the road. Just sits there now." Roger smiled.

"We could hide the load in the quarry and have the plane stop right at the road." He studied it for another moment, then headed back to the car. "Yeah, that would work. Let's get an odometer reading on this stretch."

They measured three miles from curve to curve, then continued on their way.

"The road is a better runway than the international airport," Rudy said, "and if that spot doesn't work out, I know there are several more."

During the rest of their trip to Belize City, Rudy kept pointing out other suitable sites and hitting on Roger for a commitment to work. When the new Northern Highway rejoined the old one at Sand Hill junction, Roger decided to give him a try.

"All right, Rudy, let's see what you can do. I want you to line up as much weight as you can from your contacts. Put together a team of about ten good men who can load a plane in case I get back to do something. Right now, everything's up in the air, but just in case. All right?"

"You'll be pleased with what I can do, Mr. Roger," he said with a smile. "Even more, I will bring you together with Martin Gillette, the head of the anti-narcotics squad. That is insurance worth having."

"Take care of the other stuff first, and then we'll see about speaking to him."

"You need not be concerned," Rudy said. "He's trustworthy. I will speak to him while you're away and see how he feels."

They stopped a few miles down the road at Sand Hill's new telecommunication facility, and Roger called Mickey.

"Sorry Sally was sick," Roger said, "but you didn't miss anything. Pretty boring party all around," knowing that Mickey would take that to mean the exact opposite.

"Oh well, more fun next time," Mickey said. "Pick you up tomorrow morning as planned?"

"You got it. Thanks." Roger hung, smiling at their pickup protocol. Morning meant afternoon, tomorrow meant today. He dialed his message service.

"I can't believe you're still gone so close to Christmas," said Jeanie's testy voice. "The kids keep asking where you are, so you better be here before Santa comes." Roger hung up and sighed, then flashed his devil-may-care smile at Rudy.

"Now for the last hurdle."

Rudy dropped him off at a hotel shuttle stop near the airport and promised to fulfill his mission by the time Roger returned. Roger rode to the terminal on the hotel shuttle surrounded by Americans and Europeans, and mingled with them as they disembarked and went to their respective airline counters.

Roger ducked into a restroom, soaped and wetted several paper towels, then took those and several dry ones into the stall farthest from the door and did as thorough a cleanup as he could, starting with his face and skin, then scrubbing as many smudges as he could from his shirt, then wiping down his pants and backpack, then using what was left of the towels to clean up his shoes. He checked the mirror when he left the stall and smiled at what he saw: a clean-cut young American who looked tired from a great Belizean vacation. He was good to go and the Roger who walked out of the restroom was much more confident of his chances of getting home for Christmas than the Roger who had walked into the restroom a few minutes before.

His confidence was justified. The customs officials were neither tense nor alert and clearly not looking for anyone in particular. As he passed through the gauntlet with routine ease, he wondered if the cops up north were keeping the whole bust secret so they could cash in on it themselves. *That would be par for the course*, Roger thought. *Governments are almost always more corrupt than the criminals they chase.*

He settled wearily into his window seat near the rear of the plane where few people would pass by him, stashed his backpack between his feet and went to sleep.

"Merry Christmas, buddy," a tired and depressed Mickey said to Roger when they met in the New Orleans airport.

"Sugar's fixable, right?"

"Blew a motor," Mickey said, nodding glumly. Roger smiled and slapped his partner on the back as they headed for an airport lounge.

"Then it is a Merry Christmas. I dodged the Man, Sugar dodged the Man and the Reaper, and I'll be home in time to see my kids open their presents."

"Yeah, I guess it coulda been a lot less merry. At least she broke at the right time and place."

"Never been happier to hear an abort message," Roger said as they entered the lounge and sat down in the most secluded corner they could find.

"So where do we go from here, man? I got less than thirty grand left, we have people strung across the country, and Christmas is tomorrow."

"Plus we lost the load, drew incredible heat, and our plane is missing a motor."

"Like I said," Mickey responded with a gallows smile, "Merry Christmas. Jeff found one in Florida for twenty-two large that's set up for a quick engine change. He's there now waiting for our decision—and let me tell you, Blind Jeff's a real warrior. Never lost his cool, never lost his heart, kept Billy cool and kept me hot to trot, so I sure don't want to give up now. How about your end?"

"Let's finish your end first. How long before Sugar's ready to go?"

"The crew in Hamilton says they can have her back in the air twenty-four hours after they get the engine."

"Yeah, right. Mark couldn't do it that fast even if a skydiving meet depended on it."

"These guys can do it. They have the tools and equipment through Hogan, and said they'll work on Christmas if you give the word." Roger sat back and pondered.

"Gotta admit, man," he said after a long moment, "things are more together than I thought they'd be. I can see this gig isn't as close to death as I'd thought it was, but before I get too excited, who's 'they'?"

"Jeff, Jason the mechanic, Paul, and his helpers."

"*Paul?*"

"Yeah, man, he heard we were down, and felt kinda guilty that she blew on our way 'home,' and he needed the money, so he not only volunteered to help, he steered us to this motor when we were having no luck. It fell in our lap, and I have enough money left to make it happen so I couldn't pass it up."

"All right," Roger said, and he felt hope building in his bones again, "that sounds pretty solid. Great work, man. Great work."

"Thanks," Mickey replied, so do I pull the trigger with Jeff?"

"Let's say we can hang the motor in two days. Add one more for test flying and tweaking. Are the boys still set at the Ranch?" Mickey nodded. "All right, then, that leaves Belize. We lost our load, the cops blew up our runway, and it's way too hot up there now anyway—but the crops are coming in, and there aren't many buyers, so we can pick up all we need for about fifteen a pound U.S."

"What do we do for expense money?" Mickey asked.

Roger grabbed a calculator from his bag and punched in the numbers.

"Eight thousand will cost one-twenty and I need at least thirty-five to work with, and throw in fifteen for you. That's one-seventy, so let's just say we need two hundred grand."

"Okay, that's what we need—where does it come from?"

Roger grinned wolfishly. "Tony."

"No fucking way!" Mickey snarled. "No way I'll work with him, no way he'll work with me."

"Who said you gotta work with him? All we need is cash, right?" Mickey nodded reluctantly. "All right, then. He's been hounding me to get involved, so I work out a deal using his money. He doesn't even have to know you're involved." Mickey pondered Roger's plan for a long moment, then shrugged.

"I'll take his money as long as I don't have to look at the fucker," he said. Roger smiled and held out his hand for a seal-the-deal shake. Mickey held back.

One more thing," he said. "Where's Sugar gonna land?"

Roger left his hand out as he eyed Mickey steadily.

"Let's see if Tony's in first or we got nothing anyway. If he is, then I'll tell you about the new runway." Mollified, Mickey grabbed Roger's hand and they sealed the deal, then went to a phone bank across from a boarding gate. Tony picked up after two rings.

"Hey man, how ya doing?" Roger said. "Ahh, you got time to give me a call?"

"Give me fifteen."

Roger hung up and smiled at Mickey. "So far, so good," he said. "He's interested."

"Okay then," riposted Mickey, "where do you put her down?" Roger looked around to make sure no one was close enough to overhear them, then spoke softly.

"Remember the aerial photos I showed you of the new road?"

"You want to land on the fucking *highway?*" Roger nodded. "That's a big risk, isn't? Dude, we can't afford to lose another load, not to mention another plane and two more pilots—and you want to land on the only north-south road in the whole fucking country. Are you fucking *nuts?*" Roger flashed his devil-may-care smile and paused for effect before answering.

"We've already decided this is for all the marbles," he said patiently, "and we've put too much into it to quit here, so yes, we're gonna land on the highway, and sure, there'll be some risk multipliers doing it there, but there are some minimizers too. I haven't worked it all out yet because I didn't know Sugar's status, but yeah, it's very doable."

"Fucking A," Mickey exclaimed, savoring Roger's confidence. "One thing I love about you, man, is when you set your mind on something, there's no stopping you."

"All right, then, call Jeff and let's get on with it."

Mickey nodded and stepped over to a pay phone. Roger sat down in a nearby chair and closed his eyes.

"Okay, we're rolling," Mickey said what seemed to Roger to be an instant later. "Took a while to get him on the horn 'cause he was in a hangar getting ready to load it up." Roger snorted and rubbed his eyes.

"The blind man who sees everything." He looked at his watch. "If we can forgo the fuel, I can be ready in three days. Since I'll be working with a different group, let's figure in one extra. If Tony comes through and I can get there by the day after tomorrow, we can do it on the thirtieth."

"That should work," Mickey said. "We already planned to haul round-trip fuel, but that doesn't cover rule-of-three contingencies, so if you can fit in a couple of drums to top off the mains, that'd sure be cool. You may also want to swing by Ohio before you go for a little moral support. Like I said, Jeff's been holding down the fort, but even he must be feeling a little low."

"I'll try," Roger said, "but I gotta make sure I do enough family time." Mickey nodded his understanding. "Anyway, we missed knocking it off before Christmas, but if we get her done on the thirtieth, I'll be back in time to tip a glass of champagne with you for New Year's."

"Looking forward to it, but how about Jeanie? How's she holding up?"

"Not so good. Really frustrated about me being gone during the holidays and the kids aren't happy either, so that's stressing me out too and it gets worse by the minute because I sure can't call her and tell her what happened. Gotta do that in person—and even then I gotta be vague."

Mickey grimaced sympathetically as Roger got up and went to the phone to get Tony's number from his message service.

"So what's happening?" Tony asked after picking up on the first ring, Roger felt his interest and gave Mickey a thumbs up.

"If you're interested, something may be happening. Good numbers, but if you want in, you have to move quick."

"What are we talking, a phone number?"

"Nah, this action's too sweet to go there," Roger said, understanding "phone number" to mean seven digits—$1 million or more. "We're talking Johnny Walker," he added, meaning a fifth of that.

"Are you riding on this too?"

"You betcha! Listen, man, it's no big deal either way. There was a little room, so I thought of you."

Mickey laughed into his sleeve at the way Roger worked Tony.

"Okay, then," Tony replied, taking the bait, "if you think it's that good, I can be ready tomorrow."

"Tomorrow's Christmas."

"Oh, yeah, yeah. Then the day after."

Roger held up two fingers to Mickey, who slumped into a nearby chair and flipped him a thumbs up.

"All right, but that's the deadline 'cause I'm leaving that day, too, so can you meet me somewhere?"

"I doubt it, man, I forgot about Christmas. You'll have to come here."

"All right," Roger agreed. "I'll call later with the flight number."

"Okay, see you then."

"Merry Christmas," Roger said, and hung up and sat down next to Mickey.

"So now all we gotta do is work out a fair repayment schedule with that fucker," Mickey said. "You know of course he'll try to burn you on it."

"You leave Tony the Snake to me."

"Gladly, but listen, you're gonna be home for Christmas, then to Ohio and Tampa the twenty-sixth *and* fly to Belize the same day. Sure you'll be ready to pitch the thirtieth?"

Roger arched his eyebrows at him. Mickey chuckled.

"Okay, never mind. I guess by now I should know better than to doubt you."

They stood and slapped together their traditional scammer handshake.

"Merry Christmas, man," Mickey said warmly.

"Merry Christmas to you too," Roger replied in kind.

Christmas lights blinked from the eaves and picture window of Roger's house when he returned late in the evening to the frozen farmlands of middle America. The combination of ice, snow, cold and Yuletide ambiance made him again feel like an alien on another planet after his grueling adventure in the tropical jungle of Central America.

He walked inside to the warm glow of Christmas tree lights washing over the living room, presents already stacked under the tree. Unlike Santa, he thought, his sack contained mostly dirty laundry, though, fortunately he'd had time to buy Jeanie some very chic perfume at the airport duty-free store while he waited for his connecting flight. He went upstairs to look in on his family.

The children were nestled all snug in their beds, and Jeanie was slumbering too. He retreated quietly and took a long shower in the downstairs bathroom, watching the water turn brown as it rolled over him, then clear again as the last of the Belizean dirt swirled down the drain. He hand-washed his clothes and pack too, to get the worst of the filth and smell out of them, then hung them on the faucets to drain after he got out.

He luxuriated in the feel of the soft fluffy clean towel as he dried himself off, stopped in the kitchen for a long drink of orange juice he found in the fridge, then, towel-wrapped, went into the living room with

Jeanie's perfume in hand. He had no idea where the wrapping paper was, so he stole the bow from a small, elegantly wrapped present with his name on it and stuck it on the top of the box, then snuggled it in with the rest of the gifts.

He went upstairs quietly, put on his pajamas and tried to climb into bed without waking Jeanie, but she stirred and looked at him with sleepy eyes.

"Merry Christmas, honey," he said softly, but when he tried to kiss her, she turned a cold shoulder to him. He sighed and pulled the covers around him. He wished he could tell her how his week had gone, how hard he'd fought to get home for Christmas, but he knew he never could. To protect her and his family, he could never say more than the most general things about his "work." He sighed and started thinking about what it would be like to sleep every night in his own bed, to see his children every morning, to . . . he fell asleep before he thought any farther.

Roger slept late on Christmas morning, glad to be back in his own bed, glad to be clean, glad to be free of roaches and bedbugs and the threat of arrest and a long stay in a hellhole foreign prison. He looked out the window at the bright, bitterly cold day. Frost wrapped everything in icy beauty and a cutting wind had dragged the thermometer outside the window well below zero.

Roger's first thought was not of Christmas, or his wife, or his children, but of his crew working in the same weather to hang a motor on a DC-3, giving up their Christmas in hopes of a big payoff. The responsibility of making that dream come true for them weighed heavily on him.

The dark moment evaporated as the sound of children laughing wafted up the stairs. He smiled and got up, went into the bathroom and grabbed his electric razor.

When he got downstairs, he saw Missy and Rook surrounded by toys and new clothes and shredded wrapping paper scattered everywhere.

"Daddy, Daddy!" shouted Missy, her eyes shining as she held up a Barbie doll. "Look what Santa brought me!" Rook paid his father no attention; he was engrossed with a shiny toy airplane.

"Well, look at that," Roger said, smiling brightly. "You must have been a good little girl."

She ran into his arms and he gave her a big hug and a smooth-faced kiss. Jeanie smiled for Missy's sake but her crossed arms and legs told the real story of her still-frosty feelings. Roger gave her space for the moment, tousling Missy's hair instead.

"Mama and I didn't think you'd be home for Christmas. You must have a lot of work, huh?"

"Yes, honey. It's been really crazy for daddy."

Roger looked into his daughter's blue eyes and brushed her blonde curls from her face. He felt so distant from his loving family, felt more connected to Rosa and her family than he did with his own. That was the main reason why he wanted to quit; he was tired of feeling like a stranger in his own home. Still, he worried that deep down, a normal family life wouldn't be exciting enough to keep him happy, that the restrictions and routines of being a "family man" might make him resent them. But he'd worry about that later. Today he'd try to be that guy he hoped he could be every day; a father and husband who was there for his family.

"Roger," Jeanie said gently, though her arms and legs were still crossed. "Santa brought something for you, too."

"I'll get it!" Missy said, bounding from his arms over to the tree, where she found the elegantly wrapped little present and handed it to him, looking slightly puzzled.

"Gee, I wonder why it doesn't have a bow?"

"Looks like Santa put it on Mommy's present." Missy's eyes widened.

"*Mommy's* present? Where?" She scampered over to the tree again, where she quickly found it and gave it to Jeanie, giggling at getting to be a gift giver twice.

Jeanie finally thawed out as she cradled his present, her face cracking into a smile like pond ice breaking up in springtime, arms and legs easing into a more welcoming posture.

Roger opened his own present; it was a gold watch, engraved on the back with the words: "Congratulations on your retirement. Love, Jeanie." He looked up to see his wife eyeing him slyly. He eyed her back just as slyly, then went over and kissed her. This time, there was no cold shoulder, she embraced him warmly and their kiss lingered.

It ended only when Missy tugged on their arms.

"Come *on*, you guys," she said impatiently. "Can't you see we still have *presents* to open?" Roger looked at her and laughed, then sat down between his children and immersed himself in Christmas. He saw Jeanie smiling at him and suddenly realized that he couldn't tell her he was leaving again tomorrow. No sense ruining what little holiday time they had together. No, he'd just bail in the morning and leave her a note.

Mickey picked up Roger at the Cincinnati airport at 9 a.m. on the 26th. When they got to the south side of Hamilton Field 45 minutes later, they could see Sugar Alpha's front quarter draped in plastic sheeting that fluttered lazily in an icy breeze.

"Park here," said Roger, indicating a spot by the fence behind a hangar. "This end of the deal'll fall apart if Paul knows I'm involved."

"Good thinking," Mickey said.

When he returned several minutes later, he started up the car as soon as he got in.

"Paul's in town chasing down some parts," he told Roger. "We got time for you to see what the boys are doing—and for them to see you're on the case."

Mickey drove in and parked by the plane. Roger got out and went through the protective plastic walls wrapped around the wing and scaffolding. He smelled cigarette smoke and felt the slight warmth from the salamander heaters when he got inside. He looked up and was amazed to see the new motor already mounted and Billy and Jeff camped out on the scaffold, Jeff with his ever-present cigarette, hooking up the remaining connections. He raised a thumb to them and grinned.

"Amazing job, guys," he said, grinning appreciatively. "Especially in these conditions." They raised wrenches in acknowledgement and salute as Mickey joined Roger.

"Determined motherfuckers, aren't they?" Mickey said proudly. Roger nodded in hearty agreement. "Okay, guys, he shouted up to them. "Take a break."

They came off the scaffold and everybody shook hands. Roger and Jeff looked at each other with a happy gleam in their eyes that spoke of tales best left untold until they were in a more secure place. Roger also noticed that Jeff was tired and stressed—but he seemed to noticeably relax as soon as he saw Roger.

"Really appreciate the way you've been hauling the freight since you came aboard, Jeff," Roger said quietly. "We'd be nowhere if you weren't along, so more thanks than I can say."

"You're welcome, pardner," Jeff said, "my pleasure." He lit another cigarette.

They piled into Mickey's car and went to the hotel and parked themselves in Jeff's room. They sat down and decompressed for a few minutes and Jeff started some coffee. Then Roger turned to Billy and handed him two twenties.

"Would you please go pick up some breakfast?"

"Sure thing, Roger," Billy said with a smile. He hopped to his feet and out the door.

"What's up with that?" Roger asked, surprised at Billy's behavior. Mickey grinned and nodded in Jeff's direction.

"He sees how a real professional operates and some of it seems to be rubbing off on him. He's pretty tolerable now, believe it or not."

"Heck, sometimes it's almost a pleasure to have him around," Jeff said, then he settled back in his chair. "But I must say, it sure feels good to be with two real smugglers at the same time for a change. This new generation isn't cut out of the same mold."

"No, they're not," Roger agreed, "but then again, we may not even remember some of the things we did when we were just starting." They all laughed like old soldiers.

"And probably best left that way, pardner," Jeff added.

"Like our little episode in Texas, eh?" Roger said, grinning.

"Texas?" Jeff deadpanned. "Never been in Texas."

"Yeah, that's right," said Roger, "what was I thinking? But if I don't remember correctly, that time I didn't see you in Texas was the last time I saw you."

Jeff chuckled. "Indeed," he said, "I hadn't heard a word about you until you hooked up with Mickey. I thought you were mad at me or something."

"At you?" Roger asked incredulously. "If I ever get mad at you, that'll be the day when I know I'm wrong about something."

"Well, thank you, pardner," said Jeff, genuinely touched at such praise from Roger. "Means a lot coming from a feller like you—and quite the subtle motivator, too."

"If you noticed, then I guess it wasn't so subtle," Roger laughed.

"Yeah it was," said Mickey. "The problem is, Blind Jeff sees everything."

"Didn't see that bad jug," Jeff corrected. "Good thing it didn't bite us too bad." He looked at Roger. "So I hear the dogs of war have been nipping at your heels and you've had to change the itinerary a little." Roger smiled at Jeff's imagery.

"More than I have time to tell you about right now, but the bottom line is, we lost our beautiful little Shangri-la in the hills, so my question is: How comfortable do you feel in Sugar? How straight a line can you drive with her?"

"I can slip her through the eye of a needle drunk and in the dark."

"That's what I had to hear, 'cause you're gonna slick her onto and back off of a three-mile stretch on the new highway they just completed. Five feet of leeway on either side of the mains and nowhere to turn around." Jeff and Roger held each other's gaze for a long moment, then Jeff lit another cigarette and looked back at him through his fragile wire rims with the thick lenses.

"So what're you asking me that for, pardner? Is there a curve in the middle of it or something?"

"No, it's an arrow, but the shoulders are unsettled gravel that'll suck you in the ditch if you get a wheel on them." Calmly, Jeff took another drag.

"And you're telling me this because . . ."

"It's a subtle motivator," Roger said, cracking a big grin, "for both of us."

"Okay, then, pardner, let's see what you got."

Roger dug some maps from his bag and handed them over.

"Oh yeah, I almost forgot. There are trees on both sides a few feet off your wingtips."

"Billy's gonna love that," Mickey chuckled.

"How big?" Jeff asked.

"Those young shrub types that grow in the swamps. If you clip a few it might leave a little wing rash, that's all."

Jeff nodded. "Should be pretty easy to find," he said as he spread the maps on the bed.

"Easier than the other one, yes," Roger said, pointing out a spot on one map. "Ten miles south of Orange Walk give or take. This red line here that I drew shows where the new highway goes. It starts right here by this little river. Fly one-eight-five from town and you can't miss it. Helen Keller could find it."

"Hey, now," said Jeff, adjusting his glasses.

"We'll be right about here a third of the way down the longest straight away," Roger continued. "Start calling when you cross the coast and set up for landing over Orange Walk. I want you to come straight in, no passes. There's an active military base at the airport, so we have to go fast. We'll block off the road at each of the curves, so nobody will be able to see you land. I'll paint a big white spot in the center of the pavement about a half a mile from the first bend. That's your pre—touchdown point. The actual threshold will be a three-foot-wide white stripe across the road. Set down anywhere near there and we're good to go. We'll be about four thousand feet from the stripe here on the left, on a trail that leads to a quarry. I'll stand in the middle of the road and tell you where to stop. We need to line up the door so we can back right up to it from the dirt road. The big thing is, if you go past the stopping point, we won't be able to get the truck around the tail."

"Thereby doubling or tripling our ground time," Jeff said, blowing smoke through his nose. "Everything else the same?"

Roger nodded.

"Well, then, I'd say we're about ready for breakfast."

Almost on cue, Billy walked through the door carrying a bag of Egg McMuffins. Jeff tossed the maps on one bed and Billy set the food on the table.

"Ho ho ho," he added, and handed Roger his change. "Santa bring you everything you wanted for Christmas?"

"Not yet," Roger said, "but it looks like one of his little helpers is growing up right before our eyes."

"Well, I don't know if I'd go that far," Mickey chuckled.

"Fuck you," Billy said lightheartedly and grabbed an Egg McMuffin. "What'd I miss?"

Roger repeated the operational outline in more general terms for Billy and didn't mention the trees. Billy sweated the small stuff too much as it was.

"Here's another thing you guys'll be happy to know in case you didn't guess it yourself—"

"You got the Belize government in your pocket!" Billy blurted out, only half kiddingly. They all laughed, knowing it wasn't totally out of the question that Roger could indeed pull off such a thing.

"Better," Roger grinned. "I found out that the Feds take New Year's Eve really seriously."

"For patrolling?" asked Billy, alarmed.

"For partying," Roger answered, laughing. Billy blushed. "So we break in on New Year's Eve when they're waiting for their shift to end. They sure won't want to do *any* work, let alone kick off a major interdiction that eats their party time."

"Bunch of fucking alkies," Mickey snorted. "All they'll be thinking about is getting hammered somewhere."

Billy glanced at Jeff, who nodded and smiled at him, then at Roger.

"Sounds like the perfect New Year's Eve, pardner. Quiet and no guests." He finished his breakfast and stood up. "Now if you wouldn't mind, we need to get back to Sugar so I have something to land on that new runway the Belizean government built for you."

Roger and Mickey fine-tuned their plan on the way to the airport after dropping Billy and Jeff back at Sugar Alpha.

"I'm telling you," Roger said, "I'm really starting to like all these flights. Lets me catch up on my sleep. Last night was good but I'm still way behind."

"You can sleep for a week when this is over," Mickey replied without sympathy, "but first," he added more earnestly, "you gotta take care of yourself down there. The shit you stirred up will still be hanging over your head when you get back, and your eyes tell me we're really pushing it landing on the road. So I know this is really out there, even for you, but inside I can feel it—this is gonna be the one!"

"Appreciate your confidence, man," Roger said quietly. "I'm just marching *onward*. No time for looking back and trust me, there are places I won't be going. Our biggest advantage will be the element of surprise. That's why the ground time's gonna be so critical. Sugar's gotta be down and out fast and after she flies, it'll still take me twenty minutes to get clear, to get around whatever traffic built up at the roadblock and onto a spur road that goes somewhere. But I feel it too; this one's getting in!"

They laughed at the wildness of it all, then Mickey turned morose.

"I just hope we're not getting ahead of ourselves counting on that mother fucking *snake* to come through. A lot riding on his word."

"Yeah, but he's got a pile of money and not much to do and he knows I've been doing good weed work—and that I'll cut him away in a heartbeat if he strings me along or burns me on this."

"Just don't let him get the better of you in the negotiations," Mickey said wearily. "If he plays *any* games, I'd rather delay the gig until we can work something else out."

"He is a snake," Roger agreed. "He was all right at first, but you're right; he's gotten pretty evil, so I'll be sure to be on my toes every second I'm with him. Fair enough?"

"Fair enough."

Mickey stopped in front of the terminal.

"Charles will be waiting in Tampa to pick up that fifteen," he said as Roger got out of the car, "and I'll see you New Year's Eve for that drink!"

"It's a date," Roger said and headed to his gate, thinking as he walked about how crazy his life had been during the past half-week: like a high-flying businessman, he'd held meetings in Belize, New Orleans, Chicago, Cincinnati, and now was on his way to Tampa—all within three days. On top of all that, he'd squeezed in Christmas Day with his family. The stress and fatigue was beginning to take its toll. The pace of the regroup had allowed no relief, and Roger was reaching the limits of his endurance. Only his determination to come through for his team kept him from collapsing in exhaustion—that and the frequent flying. He dragged himself aboard his flight, stowed his bag and settled into his seat. He was asleep before they closed the door.

Roger woke up two hours later when the pilot stuck the jetliner to the runway. He met Tony outside the terminal, driving a brand new Ferrari and wearing a big grin.

"Hey man, welcome to Tampa!" he said warmly as Roger got in.

"Nice to see you again, Tony," Roger said as they shook hands. Tony concentrated on weaving through the airport traffic, then sprinted onto the freeway and rocketed into the fast lane. He grinned at Roger.

"You want to see my new toy?"

"You mean this isn't it?"

"Nah, I've had this for a month."

"All right, if it doesn't take too long."

As they drove, Tony detailed his latest adventures. Roger listened actively, and filed away several useful bits of information about the feds and their operations before they passed through a gate at the south end of the Tampa Executive Airport. Tony parked in front of a beautiful Super King Air 200.

"Got her last week," he said as they got out of the car. Roger circled the craft, admiring the new 13-passenger turbine twin.

"Hey buddy, check this shit out!" Tony said as he opened the door and showed Roger the luxurious interior.

"Wow, this is real nice."

"Yeah, she's a beauty. C'mon, check out the cockpit."

Roger already knew what a King Air 200 cockpit looked like, but he wanted to appease the guy who was about to lay two hundred grand on him, so he sat down in the pilot seat and studied the well-appointed instrument panel.

"Good stuff, man, but we gotta get down to business."

"Yeah, yeah, sure. Let's go."

Tony kept talking as they left the airport for his house.

"Guy at Sunny South lined it up for me. Only paid one point two."

"How'd you cover that?" Roger said, startled by the figure.

"He takes cash," Tony said, laughing devilishly.

"You didn't."

"Sure did! Four grocery bags full of twenties."

"Cool," said Roger, humoring his reckless companion. Inside, though, he wondered how long Tony could go before he got himself caught doing something stupid.

"Dumped another plane off for him to sell after my last trip and told him to find me a 402C. I started an aircraft sales company to cover my ass, specializing in mid-size twins. Having them around'll come in handy for toot runs from the islands, and with all the scammers I can sell to, I'll make a fortune."

"Smart," said Roger, schmoozing the snake next to him. "A good business front makes sense, but a 404's the only way to go."

"No way man, a 402C is where it's at."

Roger knew Tony had more ratings than he did, but not as many facts. He couldn't help himself. "A 404'll go fifteen hundred miles with factory tanks, costs one-fifty to two hundred, lifts two thousand pounds, and operates from the same strip 402s do."

"I know that," Tony said, trying to save face. "That's why I have two of them on the ramp. A 402 has its own niche, though, and nobody else is filling it."

"Glad to see you're thinking it all through," Roger said, smoothing things over. "A 404'll gross between three quarters and a million with what we're yanking out of Belize."

"Okay, then, man, tell me about what you got going."

"Big load coming out of Belize that I've been working for a while. Hottest scam I've ever found—better product than Colombian and it's five hundred miles closer and it turns as soon as it's unloaded. There's some room, so I wanted to see if you wanted in."

"How much can I invest?"

"Two hundred max, and if you go there, I'll have to cut another dude out."

"What's the return on two hundred?"

Roger smiled inwardly. He could tell already that this would end well, but he could still blow it if he didn't play the game well and he knew Tony was a good gamer himself, even when he played straight. Roger reminded himself to hold tight to negotiation rule number one: Never be first to commit a figure.

"If we lose the load, we both lose. If it gets in, I double your money in thirty days or less."

Tony laughed dismissively. "Forget it man. Three-to-one, and if there's any problems a guarantee on half."

Roger flashed his famous grin and looked him right in the eye.

"I didn't come to ask you for a job, buddy. I'm doing you a favor so you can make some money."

"I can do better on a toot gig."

"No doubt, but this isn't a toot gig, and all you're doing is putting up some cash. Anyone else offering to double your money without you having to raise a finger?"

Tony made a face and concentrated on the road for a while. He weaved through traffic to an open space in the flow and looked at Roger again.

"You already told me you'll make a killing. Don't be so greedy."

"You'd offer the same to me if it was your scam, buddy," Roger said, hoping he hadn't oversold it, "so don't even try the greed rap. I'm telling you straight up what I can do. I'm not going to bullshit you and then have problems later. You know I don't work like that. Besides, I don't need you or your money."

"Then I'll send a plane. Let's talk about those numbers."

"Sorry, no, but if we can settle this now, I'll load you up one time after this one's in, so make up your mind."

Tony nodded at Roger's pot sweetener. "That plus half a mil and we got a deal," he said as he turned off the main route into a middle class sub-division.

"Four hundred, and on your run, you provide the plane and pilot, I'll unload it in the States and give you four hundred a pound."

"Give me a second to think about that," Tony said as he pulled into a driveway bordered by street-parked Mercedes, Porsches, and other expensive vehicles. He stopped in front of the garage of his one-story house as his wife Tiffany Mae walked out the front door with her mother. She kissed Tony as he and Roger got out of the car, then drove off in a red 450 SL. The men went inside and Tony flipped on the stereo.

"Come on, man, I need to get a half out of this," he said, and Roger could tell The Snake felt stronger in his own den. "Give me a half and I'll give you the Titan after I do mine." Roger arched his eyebrows at the notion. The 404 was a highly marketable item.

"I'd have to clear that with my partners first."

"Your partners don't need to know."

"No thanks," Roger said coldly, reminded again why he disliked this man and was always on his guard around him. "You know I work straight with my partners and only work with others who do the same."

"Hey, don't get so excited, man. I was only kidding. Make it four fifty and I'll do it." Roger paused, seemingly pondering, but doing it just for effect because that was exactly the number he was ready to pay.

"Deal," he said and stuck out his hand. They shook emphatically and Tony smiled.

"Fair deal, and I want you to know you can count on me. Any time you need wings for a scam, I'll get it for cost, and you don't have to pay me until you get one in."

"I appreciate that, let's keep that separate, all right?"

"Right, separate deal. Just saying, man, I'll be turning planes, and that will move another, so keep it in the back of your head. Now let's check out the kitchen."

Tony's mood turned positively cheery as he walked into the first class kitchen and stood next to a steaming double boiler.

"Wanna get high?"

"What are you doing?" Roger asked, mystified at the change of course.

"Cookin' rocks!" Tony said gleefully. He pulled off the top pan and spooned a clump of the mixture into a glass pipe.

"Converting toot to freebase. It's the only way to fly, man."

"Didn't anyone ever tell you not to get high on your own supply?"

"Yeah, but so what? Want some?"

"No thank you, and I don't expect you to party while we're doing business, so make a decision: blow your brains or deal. This ain't no street gig, and I don't work with punks!"

Tony frowned, but he got the message. He set aside the pipe and led Roger to his bedroom, where he dug through his cluttered closet and tossed a large lizard-skinned briefcase on the bed. He popped the latches and exposed rows of cash.

"I got a hundred ten here." Roger groaned. He could tell by the bulk and tattered fluffiness that it was all small bills.

"Don't you have any large? I have to pack this on my body to get it down. How about the rest?"

"I forgot about Christmas, so I have to get my broker to cash me outta some securities. I'll make sure that's in hundreds."

"You gotta be kidding. I tell you I'm leaving tonight, and you waste my time cutting a deal you aren't ready to make?"

"Don't worry, man, I can get it. My brother Tim's got some, and I'll see what my assistant Eddie can come up with." He picked up a phone and dialed a number. Roger went back in the living room to hide his displeasure and paged through his airline guide. He saw that he'd miss his scheduled flight, but saw also that there were plenty of Tampa-Miami flights, so he was good to go on that and his anger eased. He even scolded himself for getting upset at Tony's antics. *Did you really expect to play with a snake and not get bitten at least a little bit?*

Tony walked into the room smiling.

"Told you not to worry. It'll all be here shortly."

"I still don't know how I'll get all these small bills down. You got any ideas?"

"How about you take Eddie along to mule in what you can't fit?"

"Now that's an idea," Roger said more to himself than to Tony. He knew Eddie as one of Tony's only good people.

"And if I slowed you down and he wants to, you can keep him there to help." Roger nodded and struggled to keep from smiling. He still needed American loading assistance, so bringing Eddie along would solve that problem too. That was something Tony definitely didn't need to know.

"Let me talk to him when he gets here, and we'll go from there."

Eddie showed up ten minutes later with some of the cash. Roger had previously met the tall, lanky, sandy-haired smuggler, but he'd forgotten that he could pass for Mickey's younger brother.

"Want to take a trip?" Roger asked as Eddie dumped the cash on the coffee table. Eddie looked at Tony, who nodded his approval, and he smiled at Roger.

"When do we leave?" said Eddie.

"In an hour," Roger replied, noticing that Eddie didn't even ask how much he'd make. Good man for sure.

"Then I better get packed. How long?"

"Five days."

"Okay, back in a flash."

Roger checked out the cash after Eddie left.

"The two of us ought to be able to get this through," he said after he counted it, "but we're still short. What do you propose on that?"

"You're not going to spend it all the first day are you?"

"I doubt it."

"Then I can be there the next day with the rest, and anything else you need me for."

Roger sat back and thought about that for a few moments. The largest part of the case was for purchasing product and paying the Belizeans, and would almost certainly take more than a day.

"All right, he said, "that'll work, and I could use a few hand-helds."

"You got it," Tony said happily, and led him to a box of radios sitting next to an aircraft ham radio powered by two car batteries. He placed four hand-held radios into a separate box for Roger, and they cracked open a beer and waited for Tony's brother to get there. When he showed up 15 minutes later, he brought $20,000, a big mouth, and a small brain.

"Hey brother! What's happenin'? I got the goods, what's the story?"

"Hey Tim, this is Roger."

"Nice to meet you, man," he said nodding to Roger but not really registering him as he dropped his bag on the coffee table next to Eddie's cash and turned back to Tony. "Oh man! You shoulda seen this gig I just pulled off from South America. *Premier* fucking toot, man! When I got home I bought myself a few ladies to celebrate!"

Roger despised him immediately. He picked up the bag.

"I'll count it while you finish your war story."

"What, you don't trust me?" he blurted. "So hey, Roger Dodger, what's the gig here?" Roger stared at him, then at Tony, astonished at Tim's bad style, but before Tony could shut him up, he plunged on. "Where're we pulling this out of? What kind of plane? What kind of product? What are the details? Let's get to the goods, man!" When Roger ignored him and started sifting through the bills, he turned to Tony. "Got any rocks, man?"

Roger glared at Tony, then Eddie walked in.

Tony smiled at the diversion. "Other than dropping you off at the airport," he said, "my job's done for now. A few tokes won't interfere with that. You won't even be able to tell."

"Fine," Roger said, rolling with it and realizing at the same moment that it would be a good test to see if Eddie joined them. The two brothers took a seat on the floor and made love to the pipe like two kids with their heads together intently playing marbles. After they both recovered from the first blast, Tony offered the pipe to Roger and Eddie. Roger waved him off.

"No thanks," said Eddie firmly.

"You don't smoke?" he asked evenly.

"Time and a place for everything and this ain't it. I appreciate your offer and *that* is what I'm here to do."

"Welcome aboard," Roger said, extending his hand, and smiling at this young man he liked more every minute. He knew he was shaking hands with a guy he could count on, and who would be watching his back, when the action started.

"How about you, man?" Eddie asked, and Roger saw instantly that the test was going both ways.

"Never have, never will," he said simply. "I snorted some back in the day, but I quit a long time ago. Hard to believe people are dumb enough

284

to pay fifty grand a key to be like them jelly heads," he added, nodding toward their two semi-conscious companions.

"Yeah, I join these jellyheads sometimes when all the work is done, but I'd never spend a dime on it myself. Better to buy gold or real estate."

"Hear, hear," said Roger, as they walked into Tony's room and started packing layers of money in their boots, taping it on their legs and putting the rest along their waistbands. Eddie had most of it and he laughed when he looked at himself in the mirror.

"I look like the Pillsbury Doughboy," he said, "and my feet are killing me already.

"Fortunately, it'll only be a few hours, but let's see if we can make you look a little more normal."

They rearranged the notes until they were satisfied that Eddie could escape casual scrutiny, then grabbed their bags and went into the living room. Tim was drooling on the floor near Tony, who upright and listening to music.

"You ready to go?" Tony asked, and it was indeed hard for Roger to tell that Tony had also been a puddle on the floor just a few minutes before.

When they entered the terminal, Roger sent Eddie ahead to buy the tickets and stopped at a phone. He was two hours late to meet Charles with Mickey's $15,000. He checked his messages and learned Charles was faithfully waiting on the top floor in the CQ's rotating restaurant. Roger called the restaurant and had him paged.

"Sorry I'm late," Roger said, "and I have company, so I gotta have an excuse to peel off for a few minutes."

"No worries, my man," Charles said in a low-key voice, "how about that ice cream parlor in the departure corridor?"

"All right, see you fifteen?"

"Works for me. Bye."

A few minutes later, Roger and Eddie strolled down the departure corridor toward their gate. Roger saw Charles in the ice cream parlor as they passed. Several steps later, he stopped.

"You go ahead to the waiting area and score some seats," he said to Eddie. "I'm gonna grab us some ice cream. I haven't had a treat in weeks."

"Sure thing, man," Eddie grinned. "I know you been burning it at both ends for a while."

He watched Eddie disappear into the thin crowd, then went into the ice cream parlor.

"Thanks for waiting," he said to Charles as he laid a thick folded newspaper on the table where Mickey's contact was sitting, eating a sundae.

"Hey, no problem, man. It's a nice airport. Good ice cream, too."

"So I hear," Roger said and bought two cones. He nodded goodbye to Charles as he left, and merged with the traffic flow in the corridor. With the last of his business in Tampa dialed in and done, he headed for the waiting area to enjoy his ice cream.

# CHAPTER FOURTEEN

———— ∞ ————

## The Razor

"I sure hope I get to see some Mayan temples," Eddie said while looking out the window at the lush jungle as the Tan-Sasha 737 approached Belize International Airport. "Sure beats the hell out of hitting bars and whorehouses with Tony."

Roger grinned at his companion, whom he liked more with each passing hour. They had gotten to know each other better as they'd hung out in their hotel room, discussing the plan and the places where it would happen. Eddie's sharp questioning and quick grasp not just of the tactics but the strategies involved earned Roger's respect and added to his strengthening assessment that he could trust Eddie as much as he distrusted Tony. He also liked Eddie's interest in the country and its history, not just the money he could make smuggling weed.

"Yeah," Roger said, "a lot of them are in the wetlands and only become accessible by car in December. Our little tour will loop us through these regions, so we'll probably get to visit some places very few non-Belizeans get to see."

Eddie's eyes widened as the jet touched down and rolled out past anti-aircraft gun emplacements and a heavy military presence, including a gaggle of British-marked Harrier combat jets.

"Jeez," he said to Roger, "is there a war going on or something?"

"Or something," Roger said casually. "Guatemala thinks Belize is theirs, so the Brits are sticking around for a while to keep them from doing something stupid."

"Sort of a mind war to prevent a shooting war," Eddie concluded.

Roger nodded. "Exactly."

They split up before they got off the plane and, after passing through customs, Roger stepped outside and scanned the small circle drive for Rudy's car. It wasn't there. Discouraged, he went back into the terminal, and sighed in relief as he saw Rudy inside by the stairs leading to the administrative offices, speaking to a large black man neatly dressed in starched khaki slacks and a partly unbuttoned floral-print shirt that revealed a thick gold chain weighted by a huge pendant. Roger recognized the man's face and paused to remember his identity. The two made accidental eye contact, then Rudy saw Roger and nodded a quick good-bye. The man went up the stairs as Rudy joined Roger. They met Eddie outside and within minutes were headed out of the airport in Rudy's station wagon.

"You have rewarded my faith," Rudy said happily as he turned from the airport road onto the Northern Highway toward Orange Walk, driving even more slowly than the general traffic. "Everyone who knew what happened said you'd never return, but I had no doubt. I had your word and knew you would keep it."

"What's the word on the street about the bust?" Roger asked.

"That what they seized in the hills was the largest capture ever," he replied. "It's also created much talk about its owner, *Señor Huevos Grandes*.'"

Roger and Eddie exchanged concerned glances, then Roger nodded down the road.

"Could you speed it up a little?" he asked. "We have a lot to do and not much time to do it."

"Sure, Mr. Roger," said Rudy, and increased his speed by five miles per hour. Eddie chuckled in the back seat as Roger shook his head but didn't urge Rudy on even more. "I set up an appointment with Carlos Weatherton, the man I was speaking to in the terminal," Rudy continued, oblivious to the discomfort he was causing the Americans with his slow driving. "I wanted him to meet you, but he's the airport manager, so we can't talk there. We'll pick him up tonight and he'll introduce you to Martin Gillette, the man in charge of the strike force who captured your load."

Roger nodded, poker-faced, but inside he smiled. Clearly, Rudy did know the people he claimed to know, and there might be a chance to join the club and work directly with Belize's officials. The old adage of *"it's not what you know, but who you know"* was certainly true in every country, including the U.S., and Roger looked forward to the opportunity.

"Man, Tony never had anything like this organized," Eddie said quietly, admiration coloring his voice.

"We do a lot of things differently," Roger said. "Now listen, I'm not sold yet on this cop thing, but after the beating I took a couple of weeks ago, it might not be a bad idea. Rudy, do your friends know it was my load they grabbed at Tres Legos?"

"Oh yes!" Rudy nodded enthusiastically. "They were very impressed, so I got a feeling we can get some mileage out of that. We may as well take advantage of your reputation, yes?"

"Can they be bought?" Roger asked.

"We shall know tonight how it goes," Rudy answered.

"And our growers?" asked Roger.

"There is much more than you need," Rudy said confidently, "thousands more. We start in Corozal district and go all the way to Cayo if we need. The weed is coming in, and there are few buyers. They all want to make the business with you."

"Well, we'll see," Roger said. He knew how much these regions produced, so he knew Rudy was exaggerating—but his apparent government contacts seemed to be exactly what he's said, so maybe there would be enough. "We need a lot and we only take the best quality."

"Of course, Mr. Roger," Rudy said. "only the best. As soon as you are rested, we will begin."

"Rested?" Roger snorted. "We got three days, and I expect to be buying before we meet Carlos and Gillette!"

"Okay," Rudy said. "We can start as soon as we get to Orange Walk."

"What have you heard about George and Manu?"

Rudy cringed. "Those two are very lucky they have escaped trouble," Rudy said. "You must stay away from them. Jacob told the police they were responsible for the checkpoint shootout. Then George found out I am now helping you to find the large amount you need and said he had a message—that he needed to speak with you. But that would be a mistake! Believe me, I have everything arranged."

"Don't worry my friend, this run is all yours," Roger said. Rudy visibly relaxed, then Roger smiled his famous grin. "That is, if you drive fast enough so we can get this done on time."

"But that would be hard on this old car and waste gas."

"Listen buddy, you'll be able to buy a new car with what you're making on this gig."

"This one cost me twenty-five hundred."

"Twenty five hundred B.H? Will you take twenty-five hundred U.S. right now?"

"Yes!"

"Then it's a deal. Now, since this is my car step on it, and when we're done you can have it back."

Rudy punched the accelerator and established an acceptable pace. Roger and Eddie exchanged grins. Shortly thereafter, they reached the southern curve of their future runway and Roger pointed it out to Eddie.

"This is where we'll block the road on this end so we can put her down on the straight section without anyone seeing us."

"Nice," he said, nodding his approval as the road straightened and he saw the straightaway. "Way better than some of the shitholes Tony sets up for us." Rudy was astonished at what he heard.

"You will land *here*, Mr. Roger?" he blurted out.

"Yep. We're on the runway now." Rudy shook his head in amazement.

"You know best, Mr. Roger," he said, "but *hay caramba, tiene huevos grandes!*"

"Man, this thing just seems like it goes on forever," Eddie said.

"This is only the overrun," Roger laughed. "The working area's up ahead. No houses along this whole stretch and another curve blocks the view on the north end." He gestured for Rudy to turn onto the gravel quarry road.

"How long do you think we can hold up traffic before it'll be a problem?" Eddie asked as Rudy parked out of sight of the road. "Not many cars, but it's the main road, right?"

"There is *no* traffic at night," Rudy said proudly. "It will be perfect." Eddie darted a glance at Roger, who gestured for him to let Rudy's comment pass.

"We'll be back in a minute, man," Roger said to his driver. "I want to show him a couple of things he'll have to do."

"Guy's never done an aircraft load, has he?" Eddie said as soon as they walked out of earshot.

Roger shrugged. "I'm sure he helped the Colombians refuel their seaside connection," he said, "and his boat-packing stories sounded realistic, but no, he clearly hasn't done any air ops or he'd know better than to talk about doing them at night."

"Well, you gotta work with the tools you have," Eddie said.

"That's right," Roger said, "and having you along more than makes up for Rudy's shortcomings. We'll just need to keep a tight rein on him around the plane."

They returned to the car and continued on their way. A couple of minutes later, they reached the northern curve and Roger pointed to a small creek that passed under the road through a large culvert.

"Perfect roadblock spot," he said. "All we need is two vehicles and no one can get around them."

"I don't suppose there's time to build a culvert on the other end," Eddie said, grinning.

Several minutes later, Rudy pointed out another small gravel road. "That's where we will stash the load," he said. "That way we won't have to pass any checkpoints before we move it to the quarry."

Roger nodded, recognizing it as the spot George had showed him a few weeks earlier, after the helicopters had sprayed it with paraquat. Soon after, they passed the small cement toll station that marked the end of the Northern Highway's new section and rejoined the old, narrow, pot-holed route. The pace slowed to "Rudy speed" until they reached Orange Walk 15 minutes later, where Rudy navigated several dirt side streets and parked in front of his ramshackle home. At the end of his road, two men were jacking up a large truck box.

"My cousin Francisco will mount it on his flat bed truck today," Rudy explained. "We will use it to store and transport our load."

"Good enough," Roger said. "That will work." Rudy pointed across the street to a 1959 Chevy pickup that looked to be in pretty solid condition.

"That's how we'll shuttle our buys," he said as he got out of the car. "Wait here." Then he disappeared into the house.

"Guy seems a little sketchy," Eddie said.

"A little," Roger agreed, "but he's honest and he figures out ways to get things done. He sure saved my bacon before Christmas, that's for sure."

"Seems like a fast learner, too."

"Yeah, and that's the thing," Roger continued. "These folks haven't been at it that long. Most people aren't hip to Belize as a source yet because they haven't cultivated enough to get the word out, but that day's coming. So for now, we have to teach them how to do it right. I'm telling you, if George hadn't stirred things up with the police, we'd be coasting."

"Only time I heard of this place is a story about some guys stopping for gas on the way back from Jamaica."

"I know the story," Roger laughed. "In fact, I know those guys. If only they knew they were bypassing a gold mine. You know, I'd like to come here and get into politics and legalize the stuff. It really wouldn't matter even if the U.S. cut off the aid because legalization would put Belize in the black and produce a surplus. The problem would be getting the wealth to work for the people and not the politicians."

"Yeah, how would you solve that?" Eddie asked. Roger pondered, then sighed.

"Good question," he said. "So much for that idea. Wouldn't work."

Rudy returned with a teenage boy, some large flashlights, and a hanging spring scale.

"This is my son, Rudy Junior," Rudy said proudly, but Roger saw instantly that the kid was hyper, unfocused and overwhelmed with what was happening.

"You are the famous *ganjanero, Señor Huevos Grandes, sí*?" he blurted out. "How many cars and houses and women do you have? Do you have a Ferrari?" Roger looked at him so coldly the boy clammed up and recoiled as if he'd been slapped. Roger stared at Rudy.

"I think it's time he learns to listen more and talk less."

The words cut Junior like a knife. He backed away, then turned and ran into the house.

"I'm sorry, Mr. Roger," said Rudy, embarrassed. "He's a good boy. He's just excited to meet you. He will be a good helper. You will see. He will drive the pickup for us and he will stay quiet. You gave him a good lesson and I thank you." Roger held Rudy's gaze for a long moment and saw the sincerity in his eyes, but he knew he had to hard-wire the moment into both of their souls.

"You make sure you reinforce it," he said harshly, pointing a finger at Rudy that he knew was very disrespectful in Belizean culture. "If you don't . . ." then he stopped, as he saw pain flare in Rudy's eyes and knew he needed to say no more.

"I promise you he will—" Rudy pleaded, but Roger held up his hand for silence. Rudy shut up instantly.

"Enough," Roger said, and smiled to put a calm edge on the end of the moment, "let's go shopping."

They walked a few doors down to a porch-front store, where Roger bought non-perishable food and lots of batteries. Rudy filled up two gas cans and packed their knapsacks with Roger's rations. Roger also added his calculator, paper pad, several pen flashlights, and $20,000 to an inside pouch.

They began buying southeast of a small village named Copper Bank.

"If the boonies had boonies, it would be here," Eddie said, as they bounced along a narrow, rutted jungle road on the way to inspect a 2,000-pound lot Rudy knew about. As they rounded a corner, an old peasant emerged from the bush with a boy in tow who wore a faded Chicago Cubs t-shirt. Rudy stopped and spoke with him in Mayan. Then Rudy turned to Roger.

"He says he's been waiting for days and had something to show. He needs a buyer so he can afford to buy some late Christmas presents for his boys."

"Dude's a mess," Eddie whispered to Roger.

"Lot of them are," Roger whispered back. "Let's see what he has."

They climbed out of the car. Rudy gestured for Junior to stay in his truck. Then the man led them a few rows into some sugar cane to his small stash and invited Roger to inspect it.

Roger smelled an unpleasant acidic odor as he untied the top of the sack and, without even digging in, he knew it was contaminated with paraquat. He looked closely at the boy's eyes and saw signs of irritation. Roger tied the sack closed.

"Put it in the car," he said to Rudy, then fished a package of cookies from his backpack and handed them to the boy, whose dirt-streaked cheeks grew a smile. Rudy returned as the boy peeled open the package and the old man smiled his thanks.

"Ask him how much he wants," Roger said to Rudy when he returned for the car.

"Two hundred dollars U.S." Rudy said after a brief conversation in Mayan.

"Tell him two-hundred-fifty B.H." Roger replied. The old man nodded and they shook hands. Roger pulled some Belizean money from his pack and handed them to the man.

"Tell him that neither he nor his family nor any of their animals should go into the field until it has rained several times," he said to Rudy while keeping his eyes on the man. The man realized instantly that Roger knew his stash was contaminated—and had bought it anyway. He clasped his hands in thanks and the two peasants disappeared back into the bush.

"Why did you buy that crap?" Eddie asked sharply as they drove away. "Something's wrong with it."

"American paraquat," Roger said. "Just cleaning up the mess." He pointed to a clearing. "Pull over here and tell Junior to bring me one of the gas cans." They got out and Roger threw the bale on the ground, slashed the wrappings with his knife, and kicked it apart. Junior walked up with the gas can and Roger poured some of it on the broken bale, then sent Junior and the can back to the truck. Then he threw a match on the bad weed and they watched it burn.

"No wonder these people work so hard for you, man," Eddie smiled.

They continued on down the rough road until they approached a Mayan ruin.

"Oh my God," he whispered. "There's one." To his delight, Rudy turned toward it on a cut made through the swampy jungle by a bulldozer. They reached the end of the freshly carved path after just a few hundred yards and parked. As they got out, he pointed to several mounds that looked like little hills entangled with trees, vines, and roots.

"They had to stop bulldozing because that's a cluster of ruins," he said as they grabbed their bags and walked into the jungle along the path the bulldozer had followed until an odd animal sound interrupted their journey. Rudy returned the call and a small, round-faced man appeared on the path. He eyed the Americans with caution until Rudy smiled and gestured toward Roger.

"*Señor Huevos Grandes*," he said simply. The small man smiled in recognition and motioned for them to follow him deeper into the swampy bush.

They reached a temporary camp after several minutes of hiking and inspected nine 50-pound bales watched over by a second man who looked much like the first. Roger showed Eddie how to check for consistency by squeezing inwards on the bags and sliding his hands inside to see if it layered as he picked up on different sections. Eddie easily learned how to detect poor quality because Roger rejected the first few bales for "shake."

"Only four are worth taking," Roger said to Rudy. "Tell him in the future not to bale the dust and leaves."

This angered the peasants, but Roger eased their ire when he counted out a fair price in American dollars. The farmers then told Rudy about a shortcut to the tiny village of New Hope, where they could merge with the old Northern Highway and they walked back to their vehicles lugging the bales.

"I don't need to see any more five-hundred pound batches," Roger told Rudy as they bounced down the rutted trail. "If we don't start scoring bigger and much better buys, we're going to have a problem."

"Okay," Rudy said, nodding. "We're going to Altun Ha next. My—"

"Altun Ha?" Eddie interrupted. "That's a famous ruin, right?"

"Yes, it is," Rudy nodded, "and my brother-in-law is the caretaker there." Roger flashed his famous grin at Eddie. "Do I take care of my staff or what?"

"That you do," said Eddie, and settled back into his seat, content.

They made good time when they headed south on the Old Northern Highway and turned off at the entrance to Altun Ha while the sun was still above the treetops. They followed a dirt road through the thick vegetation for a mile and a half, past many shacks and small houses, until they reached a large grass parking lot. Roger slung his knapsack over one shoulder for the short hike to the site and grinned at Eddie, whose face was lit up like a kid on Christmas morning.

"This is so *cool*," he almost whispered as the sun touched the treetops in the distance and they started walking with their haul bags toward the ruins, some of which he could see through the foliage.

A huge weathered pyramid stood boldly at the edge of the site, a large, bare field with a primal jungle backdrop. Watchmen guarded the site to keep grave robbers from stealing the precious artifacts.

"There are over two hundred structures here," Rudy told Eddie, "But many of them are still covered by the jungle like the ones we saw before."

Eddie stared around him in awe. "I can still feel them," he said as the sunset intensified its eerie aura, "even though they've been gone a thousand years."

"Course you can," Rudy chuckled. "I'll introduce you to some of them now."

"Living fossils," Roger said as a smiling Mayan walked up to them with his hand out.

"Hello," he said. "I'm Hernan. Would you like me to show you around a little before we get down to business?" Eddie shot a "Can we? Can we?" glance at Roger, who smiled at Hernan.

"Thank you," he said. "That would be great."

Hernan pointed out the details of several structures as he led them to a funeral chamber near the pyramid.

"I've even found human remains while digging for things to sell," he said as he showed them a small excavation in one corner.

"They don't care if you take stuff?" Eddie asked incredulously. Hernan shook his head.

"They pay us very little," he said without resentment, "so as long as we keep the important things safe, we are free to dig a bit on our own as long as we don't get greedy."

Hernan pulled a painted clay pot from the dirt next to his outlaw excavation. It had been crudely pieced together with epoxy. He also uncovered a jade carving of a man with an aquiline nose, large square eyes that were cross-eyed, and a filed incisor in the upper row of teeth.

"Kinich Ahau, the face of the sun," Eddie whispered.

Hernan looked at him in surprise. "Legend says that whoever finds it must give it to someone who will appreciate it," he said to Eddie solemnly. He rubbed the head, then took a thin vine and made it into a necklace onto which he fastened the talisman. "So I give it to you," he said as he draped it over Eddie's neck. "It will keep you safe from the creatures of the jungle. The god of the sun will protect you."

"Thank you," Eddie said earnestly. "May your sleep be peaceful."

Hernan glanced at Rudy. "Who is this fine man who knows even our proverbs?" he asked.

Rudy grinned. "This is Eddie," Rudy said. "He is a friend of *Señor Huevos Grandes.*" Hernan nodded approvingly. "Kinich Ahau has guided my hand well," he said to the American. "Please come again when I can show you everything I know about Altun Ha."

"Deal!" said Eddie and they shook hands. Then Hernan led them out of the funeral chamber onto a dark, winding path that led to another uncovered temple. A campfire illuminated a wealthier, more sophisticated group of growers who had assembled more than 1,000 pounds of weed that filled their camp with its unmistakably potent smell. Each grower sat with his own bags while Roger and Eddie moved among them with their flashlights, checking the quality.

"*This* is what you're looking for, right?" Eddie asked Roger after he had inspected one bale. Roger nodded and grinned, his teeth flashing in the dying light.

Nearby, Rudy jammed a branch between two trees and weighed the contents of each accepted bale on a fish scale. When they were finished, only one bale sat apart.

"I'm sorry," Roger said to the grower. "The quality is excellent but it's too wet." The grower gestured his acceptance of Roger's verdict, then the real business began.

Given the uniform quality, the group agreed to bargain collectively, and Eddie watched, fascinated as Roger bartered like a Belizean native until they agreed on the price he knew Roger had wanted to pay all along. He and Rudy exchanged knowing glances about their leader's skillful haggling as Roger counted out the payment to each grower, then Rudy glanced at his watch and sighed.

"We need to get to our meeting in the city," he murmured to Eddie, "so let's put fresh batteries in the flashlights and take one load back when we leave."

"What about the rest?" Eddie asked, frowning. "We don't have time to load it all, right?"

"Maybe you stay with Junior and take care of it and we meet you at Hill Bank later tonight."

"Good idea," said Roger as he approached, "but I want Eddie with me for support and to enhance my image. The growers can help Junior load it up, then he can wait for us at Hill Bank."

"*Thank* you, Mr. Roger," Rudy said in response to Roger's trust in his son. "Junior will get it done right." Roger patted Rudy on the shoulder.

"If I didn't think so, we wouldn't do it this way." Rudy grinned and started toward the weed pile, flashlight bobbing in his hand. Eddie glanced sharply at the growers, then back to Roger.

"Really?" Eddie asked, skeptically. Roger's teeth flashed in the glow of Rudy's flashlight.

"This is not Colombia and we're not dealing with powderheads."

297

"Sorry, man," Eddie said, "I keep forgetting."

"Old paranoia habits are hard to break."

"Yeah, they sure are," Eddie said as they followed Rudy to the pile. "I like this place more all the time."

Hardly a soul stirred as an intermittent ocean breeze spread the dreaded smell of the Belize River throughout the crowded warren that was Belize City as they arrived at Carlos Weatherton's house. Roger got in the back seat with Eddie as the big man approached. The suspension sank under his weight when he sat down, and the car seemed to labor briefly as Rudy pulled away.

Roger and Carlos checked each other out like two strange dogs, circling each other with wary questions, each man trying to sniff out the other's character and intent. Roger could from the start tell by how Carlos spoke that he had a college education and had studied English. He also felt his confidence, competence, and caution and he could see clearly that the man had risen to manage the national airport by competence and force of personality rather than political connections. Roger saw that his own professionalism and focus impressed Carlos, too. Then they got down to business.

"I'm not really involved in your trade," Carlos opened, "but even I have heard of your reputation. People talk, you know. Gillette wants me to make sure it's wise to bring you two together. As the head of our country's anti-narcotics squad, he is a secretive man. He only agreed to meet because he wants to make certain things are clear about your losses last week."

"I'm not here looking for trouble," Roger said, puzzled but also encouraged a bit that his near-bust several days before would be part of the conversation, so he pressed on. "I just want to get an understanding with him. You speak of him highly, but can he be trusted?"

"Like you, Gillette is a man of his word, *Señor Huevos Grandes*," Carlos said evenly, signaling to Roger that he'd done his homework about him. "You can count on whatever he says. He knows you're very active and respected, but he is a powerful man in Belize. He must take due care."

"Well, what's your decision?" Roger asked quietly but forcefully. Carlos looked at him for a long moment, then extended his hand over the seat.

"Let's see what you and Gillette can get done," he said in the same tone. They shook, and Roger jumped to the next phase.

"Is it possible to load a gig at the airport?" he asked. Carlos held up a cautionary hand.

"Nothing is done here without Gillette. Everything runs through him so it is he whom you must ask about such things."

"Good enough," Roger said. Carlos said a quiet word to Rudy and they turned off the main road into a higher-class neighborhood of homes sitting one story in the air on stilts to protect them from occasional hurricane tidal surges.

"This is his street, Mr. Roger," Carlos said. "His house is the white stucco halfway down on the right."

"Okay, slow down and keep driving," Roger said to Rudy, then clicked into scanning mode, peering into the narrow passes between the wooden structures, looking around and watching behind them. "Make several circles so I can survey the situation."

The car looped around the neighborhood until Roger was comfortable, then he directed Rudy to park across the street from Gillette's house and tap lightly on the horn in the quiet night air. Gillette emerged almost instantly and walked down his stairs to the street. He approached the car cautiously until he recognized Carlos, who slid over in the front seat as Belize's anti-narcotics chief got in without greeting.

"Drive," he ordered Rudy, who immediately pulled away from the curb. "You're sure you weren't followed?" he asked Carlos.

"*I'm* sure," Roger interjected, seizing the initiative. The grey-haired Creole turned to look him over and offered Roger his hand—but Roger didn't take it.

"Before we bind any friendship," he said tersely, "let's get something straight. I'm working this country, and if you want to form a relationship, we better come to terms."

Gillette withdrew his hand and studied Roger, then smiled slightly and re-extended his hand.

"I allowed you to meet me for precisely that purpose," he said evenly. "If your credentials weren't as they are, you wouldn't be here. It wasn't until the Tres Legos seizure that I realized the level of your activity. That speaks well for you. Now tell me, how can I help you?"

Roger shook hands with Gillette.

"We're about to do another air shipment," he said, "so what can you do for me?"

"I have sole control of the forces pursuing the drug trade," Gillette said without hesitation. "You tell me when and where you're going to be, and I'll make sure my men are unable to respond to any call. If for some reason things get fouled up and you're taken into custody, I will see to your freedom and exit from the country. This will cost fifty thousand dollars."

Roger looked at Gillette through his sunglasses like a card shark as he digested the proposal and the others looked on anxiously.

"That's a lot of money for not doing too much," Roger countered. "However, to establish the relationship, I'll consider it—as long as any deal we make includes protection for anyone who works for me, and your word we won't be betrayed."

"I let you see where I live with my family," Gillette said smoothly. "That should be proof enough of my word, yes?"

"Perhaps, but I already knew where you lived the day you stole my load," Roger bluffed.

"I'll provide assistance to your workers," Gillette went on just as smoothly, ignoring Roger's jibe, "but make it known they may get arrested just for show if there are too many witnesses, so they must not panic and start talking. Now tell me if you're interested."

"I am, but there's one final thing. I'm told you're looking for George Ramirez. His safety is part of the deal." Rudy flinched at the name.

Gillette frowned slightly. "Ramirez is no good for you, Roger," he said tersely. "Neither is Pete Smith. I suggest you stay away from them both."

"George is a friend of mine," Roger said flatly, "so he's a non-negotiable part of the deal. Otherwise, it's me against you."

They stared each other down for a long moment, then Gillette nodded curtly.

"All right," he said, "but only if you assure me there will be no more gun fights and your men carry no weapons. Too many things are happening now in Central America that we don't need in Belize. This thing is about money, not blood."

"Agreed," said Roger, "and I apologize for the misunderstanding last time. I assure you that will not happen going forward."

"Excellent," Gillette said, and he visibly relaxed. "Now tell me, Roger, when are you planning to do it?"

"Tomorrow at noon on the new highway."

"No way," Gillette said abruptly, his composure deserting him. "No way you can do it there. Out of the question." Roger grinned and delivered the next blow.

"Listen, my friend, you're the one who blew up my runway after you stole my load."

"Isn't there somewhere else?" Gillette asked, composure regained. "What about Progresso or Orange Walk or one of the strips south of here?"

"Sorry, no," Roger answered in a carefully controlled voice. "I'm bringing in a big plane to make up for our losses, so unless you want us to land at International, it's my way and that's the highway." Gillette's eyebrows arched and he drummed his fingers on the back of the seat. Roger could tell the anti-narcotics chief didn't usually have to bargain like this.

"My oh my, you ask a lot, my new friend," he said with a faint smile, "but here's what I'll do. Tomorrow morning, I'll take my men on a surprise maritime strike to San Pedro. That will have us out at sea when it happens, but I want the money up front." Roger shook his head and reached into his knapsack.

"Half now, the rest after the plane's safely out of your airspace." He held out $25,000 to Gillette, who looked at it for a moment, then took it.

"I'll trust it's all here," he said mildly, then said more forcefully: "Now I want *you* to get some things straight. First, nobody approaches me directly. All communications go through Carlos. We have a reason to speak to one another and a code has been worked out. Second, never use my name for any reason at any time. Third, if any of your people get intercepted by my men, they use the word 'Jack' to identify themselves as one of yours. That is a code U.S. agents are using, so it will work for you, too. I personally oversee the important runs and so I can guarantee there's no interference."

"I like that last part," Roger said sternly, though once again the reference to the American government presence there made him uneasy, but it was too soon to probe the topic. Gillette directed Rudy back to his house, then turned to Roger and shook hands with him.

"We will repeat this process tomorrow night for the rest of the money," Gillette said as he got out of the car and walked away without another word.

Rudy dropped off Carlos, then grinned at Roger and Eddie.

"And now I give you a treat," he said. "Dinner at Yuen Woo's, the finest Chinese restaurant in Belize. "They also have phones you can use," he added, winking at Roger.

"Man!" said Eddie, shaking his head in wonder at Roger. "At first, I thought you were way too aggressive, but you sure seemed to know how to work that guy."

"Cops are pretty much all alike," Roger said. "If you act like a mouse, they'll go cat on you and pounce—and if you're all big dog, they want to fight, so you gotta be tough enough that they don't pounce but calm enough that they don't fight."

"How'd you learn to do that?" Eddie wondered.

"Getting inside the head of skydiving students mostly," he said, flashing his famous grin.

Yuen Woo greeted Rudy and his guests graciously and gave them the best seat in the surprisingly elegant establishment. Roger and Eddie were impressed again with Rudy's connections. They ordered a meal and Roger went to clear his messages.

"Tony'll be here on the one o'clock flight," he said, raising his glass, "and the rest of the crew is in place and ready to go." They clinked glasses and drank.

"Okay," Roger said when they put their glasses down, "from now on we call Gillette 'the Razor.' I believe he's playing us straight, but I sure would feel better if we could verify that he and his men really do go to sea tomorrow."

"Why did you tell him we were doing it tomorrow?" Rudy asked. "You told me the plane wouldn't be here until Thursday."

"That way we'll know if he's around the highway, and if he is, then we know it's a set up. When I see him, I'll just say Sugar had engine trouble, which—"

"—is true," chuckled Eddie, "just not this time around."

"I'm more worried about his credibility than if he thinks he's getting the runaround," Roger continued, "and engine trouble saves face for him."

A few minutes later, a small Asian lady brought several dishes, and the four enjoyed a good meal.

As they finished, Yuen Woo returned and bowed.

"May I speak to you privately for a moment, Mr. Roger?" he asked quietly. Rudy was surprised but hid it pretty well as Roger accompanied Yuen Woo into the kitchen—where to his own surprise he found George waiting for him by the cooler.

"George! How did you find me here?" Roger asked incredulously, impressed by his old friend's detective skills no matter what his answer was.

"When I learned Rudy was putting together a large load," George said, "I knew who it was for, so when Buddy saw you at the airport, I just kept an eye on Rudy's car until you showed up."

"Yeah, but how did you know we'd be down here?" Roger wondered. "I know you didn't follow us around the bush." George laughed and smiled knowingly.

"I knew he would introduce you to his big friends, so when you left Orange Walk I just found myself a nice spot along the highway near the city and waited for you to go by, then I came here because Rudy never leaves the city without stopping at Yuen Woo's." Roger smiled despite his displeasure with his friend and business partner, then turned serious again. George got the message. "I know we got a lot to talk about, and I've got some explaining to do, but for now you must know there's an American here looking for you. It's the same one Pete introduced me to who bought our excess. Says he's a friend of a friend."

"Don't know who it could be," Roger said, "but that meeting'll have to wait. There are several things we need to clear up. After our last experience, I decided to pay off the police. With the size of these loads, I had to make sure it didn't happen again. Part of the deal was to leave you alone." Roger's words stunned George for a moment, then he broke into an appreciative grin.

"You're always so good to me, Roger," he said, "sometimes even when I don't deserve it."

"That's to make up for the times when you more than deserve it," Roger said, cracking a slight smile. George smiled sheepishly.

"I know things went bad for us, but it's just the way it happened. I'll understand if you don't want to work with me, but if you need any help,

Manu and I would like to finish what you already paid us for. What do you say?"

Roger let George's question hang for a few tactical moments. That was exactly what he'd hoped to hear, and on top of that, George's skill at both hunting him down and staying undetected not only impressed him, but reminded him how cleanly and efficiently things almost always went when George was involved. But he wasn't going to let him know just how happy he was to have him back.

"Let's do a trial run first," he said, "and go from there."

"Sure, Roger, whatever you think is best."

"All right, here's the gig. I met directly with one of the country's leading officials and I'm still leery about him, so I lied and said the trip was going down tomorrow at noon. He said he'd take his men to the cays, but I don't have a way to verify that. If you could put a tail on them and confirm it, I'd feel a lot better."

"I can handle that, Roger," he said as he flashed his big Belizean smile. "I know right where the police boat docks, and I have a friend who does runs to the islands. A hundred bucks to rent his ship, and we'll be on the pier waiting for them to leave."

Roger handed George a few hundred dollars. "Meet me here at a quarter after ten tomorrow evening. Make sure to get details on everything he does. Our meeting's at eleven and I want to blow him away with what I know."

"No problem," George said, "and if you have any trouble scoring, I know several growers with very good bud."

Roger could see that George felt he was back on the team—and given how unimpressed Roger was with the current buying pace, he was glad of it.

"Bring Manu with you tomorrow night and be ready to shop." Roger slapped George on the shoulder and gave him a big hug. George waved good-bye and slid out the back door. Roger returned and finished dinner with Rudy and Eddie, relieved to be reunited with his main man and now able to see if Gillette really was a man of his word. When they finished eating, they headed back north to rendezvous with Junior.

They stopped along the way at the small village of Rancho Delores, where Rudy took them to a farmer with 300 pounds. Roger accepted half, which they stashed in the bush on their way toward Hill Bank, where they reached just after 1 a.m. They found Junior sleeping in the pickup parked in a cluster of thatched roof huts encircled by narrow trees tied together with vines. The nearby New River Lagoon mirrored the moon's reflection.

"Everything ready?" Rudy asked him after he'd rubbed the sleep from his eyes. He nodded and held up a finger to wait, then walked over to one of the huts and had a murmured conversation with someone inside. A moment later, the shadowy figure of a Mayan man left the hut and disappeared behind a building. He returned a minute later with two other villagers carrying big empty packs and spoke in Mayan to Rudy, then turned to Roger.

"Are you ready for a long hike and do you have something to carry a load?" he asked. Roger nodded and the Mayan led them through their crude fencing system into the bush, their flashlights bobbing in the darkness to follow the dim trail.

They reached a stand of trees 20 minutes later and there under a makeshift tarp shelter tied between the trees was an exceptional batch of 400 pounds. Roger accepted all of it, and they carried it back to the truck, arriving just as the moon set. With nothing more to do until daybreak, they curled up in their vehicles and got some sleep.

The Mayans woke them at sunrise, and they proceeded to a crude floating pier.

"We need to take a boat because there are some stashes we can only get to by water," he explained as the Mayans readied the square-backed rowboat with a 10-horsepower trolling motor bolted to its stern. They climbed in and putted toward the south end of the lagoon.

"I could row faster than this," Eddie muttered as they moseyed across the water.

"Yeah, but then you'd be too tired to haul," Roger grinned back.

"And this water," Eddie observed. "Is it always this dirty?"

"Belize is Mayan for muddy water," Roger said. Eddie grinned and kicked back to enjoy the view. Roger smiled at him; unlike most of the smugglers he knew, Eddie was a pretty regular guy who enjoyed normal things, not just the supercharged part of the business.

The Mayan driver guided his boat to a landing at a wooded section on the opposite shore, and they walked up a swampy trail to a 200-pound stash of good weed. Roger took all of that too.

"There are many more places we need to check by boat," Rudy said on the even slower return trip. "Maybe Junior and I should drive now to Indian Church and meet you there."

"Makes sense," Roger said, and pointed to the Mayan. "He knows where to stop on the way?"

"He's The Man," Rudy said. "He was showing me."

"Good enough," Roger said. "See you in a while."

They unloaded the bales at the floating pier, then left Rudy and Junior and headed up the waterway, moving slightly faster now with the lighter load.

"I know some of the Indian Church growers," Roger said to Eddie, "but I've never seen their fields. I hear they grow some of the best bud in the country, though."

"Well, let's hope you heard right," Eddie grinned.

The journey was remarkably beautiful as they meandered northward, stopping at several points along the way to buy small batches of weed. All of it was good to excellent and Roger rejected none of it.

The waterway varied from wide stretches to narrow passes and the tangled rain forest on either side formed a massive green cathedral overhead. Giant ferns periodically draped the boat like drooping hands, caressing everyone as they passed. It was eerily still as they approached the landing at Lamanai and saw ghostly Mayan ruins poking up above the canopy. They made sure the weed in the boat was well-covered, though they couldn't do anything about its fragrant aroma.

"More temples?" Eddie whispered as the Mayan beached his boat near an old man repairing his own tattered wooden boat by the pier. "Why didn't you tell me?"

"Didn't know we were coming here," Roger explained as his boat driver said something to the old man, who quickly disappeared up a small footpath into the trees. "But this is a good one—the Temple of the Jaguar."

The Mayan led them to a hut surrounded by fruit trees, where they met Rudy and Junior with the vehicles. They walked to the ruins that had been cleared of all jungle and Roger was as awed by it as Eddie. Ancient pyramids and sports arenas loomed around them, dwarfing the crumbling remains of a Christian church that represented a more recent era when Spanish missionaries brought the Holy Word to the Yucatan heathens. The missionaries had abandoned the church when the Indian population dwindled and Spain lost its influence in the area.

Roger walked into the decaying church, admiring its basic design. Remembering Rudy's relative at the other ruins, he dug in the dirt for a few moments, flipped over a stone he unearthed and found a small cross under it. He rubbed away layers of crust between his fingers.

"Hey man," he said to Eddie, "let me see that thing hanging around your neck." Eddie handed over his vine necklace and Roger added the cross to it. "Now you're double protected." Eddie put the vine back around his neck and patted the two talismans on his chest.

"Either that or they cancel each other out."

They left the church as Rudy sent one of the locals into the bush.

"The one you saw repairing his boat is the settlement's elder," Rudy said, "so he was the right guy to talk to." Rudy pointed to a jungle path as three growers appeared, lugging their wares for inspection. Roger checked random bales from each one, and closed a few more deals. Another farmer displayed an impressive sample, and they drove to his stash to inspect the rest. It was 1,500 pounds of freshly harvested colas sitting on and next to a flatbed truck.

"Guess you heard right," Eddie chuckled.

"Ask him how much to use his truck too," Roger said to Rudy, who nodded and talked to the farmer.

"He says to add fifty bucks to the deal and he'll do it," Rudy said. Roger smiled his thanks to the man and they started packing the rest of the load back on the truck. It was then that Roger noticed that every bag was marked with "Grown by the Indians of Indian Church." They covered the load of each vehicle with a tarp, and the now-three-vehicle convoy headed north.

They arrived back at the staging camp without incident, and parked under a canopy of trees next to the large converted box truck that now looked much different. Its shiny surfaces had been wrapped in burlap and the white box camouflaged with branches. Several sheets of plastic lay stretched on the ground, waiting for them to sift through another batch.

Roger showed his men what he wanted done and put them to work sifting out the dirt, stems, and seeds before repackaging the bud. Roger joined in at first to more fully inspect his goods and to just help out; the large haul placed a heavy burden on the men. Eddie also joined in, and Rudy hired the Indian Church grower to help too.

Roger stood back from the processing and watched it go, then smiled again as he watched Eddie naturally managing the operation, getting the men to work more efficiently, yet doing it in a low-key way that perfectly matched their culture.

"Hey man, I think it works best for you to stay here," Roger said to him, "if you don't mind."

"Happy to," Eddie grinned. He stuck a sticky cola near his nose and inhaled deeply. "This beats the heck out of bouncing around crappy roads with a bunch of smelly dudes. No offense."

"None taken," Roger said, "and I agree. You're definitely getting the better part of the deal."

Roger left again with Rudy and Junior to check a stash at Rancho Delores. Roger accepted it and left Junior to load it up and take it to camp while Rudy and he picked up Tony at the airport.

When they got back to camp, Roger invited Tony to go for a walk so he could get the additional cash from him. No one else needed to know how many Franklins Roger would be carrying.

"Did I slow you down?" Tony asked, after they'd completed the transfer.

"No, everything's right on schedule," Roger said. "Tight, but on schedule. We're half way done, and I could use some experienced help loading the plane. You want stay an extra day and give us a hand? It'd be a good way to ensure your investment."

"Nah, man, that ain't in the deal," Tony said, eyes darting nervously to check the bush. "Besides, I gotta be on that flight tomorrow to make some appointments in Tampa."

"Well, if you gotta go, you gotta go," Roger said casually as he picked up on Tony's fear like a jumpmaster getting a first-time student ready to go.

"So how's Eddie working out?" Tony said, changing the subject.

"He's doing okay," Roger said, deliberately lowballing his new assistant's contribution. "Better than the locals anyway."

"He's all right, I guess," Tony said, and Roger could see that the pipe lover at his side had no idea what a class act Eddie really was.

They got back to camp and watched Eddie and the other men hard at work cleaning and repackaging the load.

"Roger says you're working out okay," Tony said to Eddie. "How come you don't work like that for me?"

"Maybe I do and you just don't notice," Eddie said lightly, without looking away from his work. Roger grabbed Tony's arm and steered him away before the conversation went any further.

"Seriously," Tony said to Roger as they strolled away, "he's not—"

"—a bad kid at all," Roger said. "He's a good hand—and hey, look who's coming to dinner." He pointed to Junior, pulling in with the load from Rancho Delores.

"You're late," Rudy scolded as his son got out of the truck.

"Sorry, Papa, but there was some unexpected business," he said, looking squarely at Roger. "As I left, I met several other growers with much weed. I told them I didn't have money, but they gave it to me anyway and told me where to bring the money tonight if you wanted it."

"Good work, Junior!" Roger said with an approving smile. "Let's see what you got."

Roger inspected the load and accepted it all.

"All right, that makes forty-six hundred pounds total," he said. "We still have long ways to go, so let's go to Orange Walk for supplies and more help."

They lucked onto another 900 pounds while shopping and cleaned out Orange Walk. Rudy also learned of a large stash west of town, and they followed the directions through a series of cane roads to a drunken Mexican who insisted there was "lots," but would only take one American because the others would get nervous.

"Don't go, man," Tony said nervously. "I think it's a setup."

"Maybe in Colombia," said Roger, ""but probably not here, and we don't have time to waste."

He passed his excess cash to Tony and waded into the bush with the drunk. They climbed over a small ridge and onto a drivable lane. The drunk walked a weaving gait for a couple of minutes, then turned into the jungle. Roger constantly scanned for an ambush then, to his relief, they came upon two peasants—but to his dismay, they had just three moldy bales of junk, so Roger left angrily without a word, leaving his tipsy guide behind.

Just as he stepped back into the lane, a British Harrier roared over the treetops, startling Roger, who settled slowly back into the bush until it disappeared. As he jogged back to the others, the jet made another pass from the other direction, and he detoured into the bush until it went by.

When he rejoined his companions, they were already in their vehicles waiting to roll. He jumped in the wagon and for once Rudy drove fast.

"You think Razor set us up?" he asked Roger while he kept his eyes on the cane road.

"Maybe," Roger shrugged, "but that'd be a weird way to do it."

"You better tell me what the fuck is happening!" Tony demanded from the back seat. "I didn't come here to lose my money and get busted." Roger turned a stern gaze on him.

"Relax," he said flatly. "The Brits control those, not the Belizeans. I don't know what that was all about but I don't think it has anything to do with us."

"Like hell," Tony snapped, clearly rattled. "You expect me to believe that pilot was just fucking around having fun?" Roger looked at him stonily, then laughed.

"No, I expect you to know that as a *fact*, man. You know as well as I do that's exactly what pilots do, especially fighter pilots in the boonies with nothing to do."

"Maybe we even screw up *his* deal," Rudy offered. "Those things, they land like helicopters, right?"

"Right, so maybe we actually saved him from a bad deal," Roger said, shaking his head. "That stuff was worse than the paraquat weed."

Their banter calmed Tony, and he slouched quietly in his seat as Rudy bumped over the rough road. Roger kept his eyes on the edges of the road, hoping either he or Rudy was right about the pilot, and that Gillette hadn't sent a ground crew along with the jet. He also pondered what to do with Tony before they next met with the anti-narcotics chief.

Another American face would help Roger make an even bigger impression on Gillette, but the risk was opening a new door for The Snake to exploit. Then Roger remembered that he was on his retirement run, so it wasn't a risk at all. When this gig was done, he'd never again have to worry about what Tony or any other smuggler was doing.

He turned to Tony. "Tonight I'll take you to a meeting with the top cop in the country and then you'll know exactly what's happening with your investment." Tony nodded gruffly at this news, but he couldn't hide his elation. Roger turned his eyes toward the road again knowing that The Snake was already thinking of ways to jump his connection. So be it.

They wasted the rest of the day chasing false leads, and he became impatient with Rudy as the sun dropped toward the horizon, and they drove away from yet another rejected stash and headed south to meet Gillette.

"I don't care if we have to search the Maya Mountains or go all the way to Punta Gorda," he said harshly, "we're gonna be done by tomorrow!"

"Please, Roger," Rudy begged, "you know not everyone who talks can back up what they say. Just give me a little more time."

"I have no more time," Roger said coldly.

"And you don't have any more fucking sources," Tony snarled from the back seat.

"Tell me he's wrong," Roger said quietly. Rudy darted a pained glance at Roger, then watched the road again for a long moment before shaking his head.

"He is not wrong, Roger," he said miserably. "I am sorry." Roger let him wallow in his apology for several moments, then patted him collegially on the shoulder.

"Don't be sorry, man," Roger said soothingly. "You did pretty well considering how big a job I gave you."

"But what will you do now?" Rudy wailed. "I have failed to fill your plane."

"Don't worry about that," Roger said, flashing his famous grin. "I always have a Plan B." Rudy glanced sharply at Roger and frowned.

"You talk to George again, yes?" Roger nodded and Rudy sighed. "Then I guess it was good you didn't listen to me about him."

"Oh, I listened, all right," Roger said, "but when he chased me down yesterday after things were already going slow, I had to take the chance."

Rudy nodded his understanding and turned his attention back to the road. Roger knew Rudy was disappointed in himself as well as with Roger's decision to work again with George, but he clearly accepted it. *A good soldier he is*, Roger thought. *It's a shame I met him at the end of my dealings here, not the beginning.*

They stopped at Rancho Delores to pay for Junior's haul and discovered that the enterprising growers had brought in even more bales and Roger quickly bought another 500 pounds. They loaded it into Junior's truck and sent him back to camp with instructions to meet them.

"You were right about your son," Roger said as they got back on the road. "He is a good boy—a very good boy."

Rudy beamed at the compliment and by way of thanks, he stepped on the gas. Roger laughed and nodded his appreciation at the gesture.

As planned, George and Manu were parked on the street near Yuen Woo's when Rudy, Roger and Tony arrived.

"You guys go grab a quick drink," Roger instructed as he got out of the car. "I'll come get you when I'm done." Then he walked over and got in George's truck.

"So how'd it go?" he asked as the three of them exchanged handshakes and smiles.

"I'd say your top official is a man of his word," George smiled.

"Call him the Razor from now on," Roger prompted. George nodded.

"Well, the Razor left for San Pedro at six a.m. with eight men and then to Cays Chapel."

"Then he called his office about one-thirty," Manu said. Roger arched his eyebrows, impressed. Manu laughed and patted a huge pair of binoculars on the seat.

"And they came back after three p.m." George concluded.

"Great work, guys," Roger said, smiling. "That's really good news."

"And more good news," George said. "I can take you many places to fill your needs, but the Cayo District is plentiful right now. I also ran into the gringo who's looking for you and he says he has a ton of primo weed and that you both have a mutual friend. He'll be at his villa in Belmopan tonight if you're interested."

"We'll save that for later," Roger said, not wanting to commit to any deal or even meeting with an unknown gringo—especially not now. He didn't need complications like that no matter how big the potential upside. "For now, go link up with Junior until my meeting's over. You know that closed repair station on Dean Street?"

"Near Albert," Manu said knowingly. Roger nodded and got out of the car.

"One more thing," Roger said to George. "You'll be working with Rudy the rest of this gig, so I trust you to be professional, all right?"

"You got it, Roger," George said solemnly. "He will be my new brother." Roger nodded approvingly and George drove away into the darkness.

A few minutes later, Rudy was driving Roger and Tony to pick up Carlos for their meeting and with each passing block, Tony grew more nervous.

"Why do you call this guy 'the Razor'?" he demanded.

"Because he's a dangerous but useful tool," Roger said, wanting to make sure Tony gave Gillette the proper respect, "and because that's his weapon of choice. One wrong move and he'll slit your throat."

"*Sí, señor*," Rudy added, picking up on Roger's intent. "He has killed many men with his razor and they never see it coming until it's too late."

This information made Tony more nervous, which pleased Roger. The last thing he needed was for Tony to be his usual loud-mouthed, obnoxious self.

They picked up Gillette the same way they had the last time and Roger quickly introduced him to Tony.

"This is Steve," he said, "one of my financiers. He wants to make sure his investment's properly protected."

"Understandable," Gillette said smoothly. "These are not times for putting your assets at risk. It is a pleasure to meet you."

"Same here, man," Tony said, then Gillette smiled sardonically at Roger.

"I was happy to hear from my office that nothing unusual happened today," he said. "I assume things went smoothly?"

"We didn't do it today," Roger said bluntly.

"What?"

"In fact," Roger said, smiling grimly, "I never was. Today was your test." Gillette was startled, then angry, then almost smiled.

"Very careful of you, Roger," he said with a hint of admiration in his voice. "So. Did I pass?"

"Well, let's see," Roger said casually. "Nine of you left at six. First San Pedro, then Cays Chapel, then a one-thirty-ish call to your office to tell them you were coming home empty-handed. That was a touch of class, so yes, you passed."

"I am impressed with your intelligence," Gillette said, relaxed again, "though you're not the only American who's impressed me this way. I won't bother asking how you learned all of that, but if you're satisfied with my credibility, what's the real schedule? I do have a department to assign."

"Thursday at noon," Roger said simply, wanting to know more about the other Americans, but not wanting to reveal his ignorance. Gillette nodded in approval.

"Then, since I passed your test and with your blessing, I'd like to keep my schedule of working the region around the highway tomorrow night. Will that be a problem?"

"What's the story with the jet buzzing us today?" Tony blurted out before Roger could reply. Gillette frowned and glanced at Roger, who gave him a "you know how twitchy some of the money guys can be" shrug to cover for Tony's bad manners. Gillette looked tranquilly at the agitated cokehead.

"Probably a British training mission," he said evenly, "and you need not worry. They aren't permitted to do anything but report to us. Since Guatemala still considers Belize a stolen province, the British are keeping some jets here for a while to discourage them from acting on their claim. This has worked to our advantage. The negotiations are very favorable, and we expect a treaty very soon."

Tony visibly relaxed at the straightforward answer, and Roger turned the conversation back to the business at hand.

"I'll go along with your plans but our paths may cross, so let's go over that one more time."

"No guns, stay calm, and keep quiet except for the code word 'Jack.' We are very serious about our work at night so it could be very tense at first, but if your men act like professionals, they will be treated as such. Shall I plan on seeing you Friday to conclude business?"

"That won't be necessary," Roger said and handed him the remaining $25,000. Gillette pocketed the money and gave Roger a long, respectful look.

"It seems that everything I have heard about *Señor Huevos Grandes* is true," he said, extending his hand to seal the deal. They shook hands earnestly. "If this goes as well as we hope, I can see a long and prosperous future for both of us."

"As do I," Roger said just as earnestly and respectfully. He liked Gillette and felt a twinge of regret that he would not be working again with this elegant man.

"How can you be serious about your duties and work with us at the same time?" Tony demanded, teeth grinding, and Roger knew he was thinking more about putting a pipe into his mouth than he was the words coming out of it. Gillette and Carlos, however, picked up only the rudeness and the accusation. They looked at Tony coldly.

"You should know how it works," Gillette said almost sadly. "Ours is a poor country, dependent on the powerful to be allowed our sovereignty. Our mission is not to die imposing on our own people the policies and troubles of the powerful but to make a living for our families. Your level of activity contributes much to the prosperity of our people, so we stop the many smaller loads to satisfy our overlords and give cover to our own politicians. Thus do we improve the lot of our people and keep our government intact by deterring popular unrest without violence. And as long as our people are happy with their government, the foreign aid keeps coming. It all fits together to support the agenda of the world's wealthy."

"Really?" Tony sneered. "You're telling me this operation is big enough to contribute to your country's prosperity?" Roger and Carlos glared at him, hoping he'd shut up, but Gillette waved off their worry and smiled indulgently at the uptight American.

"Yes, you are," he continued, gently. "As I said, Belize is very poor and your money is absolutely a force to be reckoned with." He nodded matter-of-factly in Roger's direction. "Just as importantly, he not only treats the people fairly, he helps them often in ways that go far beyond being a fair businessman." He stopped and smiled warmly at Roger.

"I told him about Rosa," Rudy said proudly.

"I had heard the story," Gillette continued, now looking back at Tony, "but not who did it—and when Rudy told me, that was when I decided that your associate here was a man with whom I wanted to do business. So yes, he—and by extension, you—are very much contributing to the prosperity of Belize and we thank you because what we most fear is being caught in a situation like Nicaragua, where many innocent people die and all the people suffer because your government played games by placing Somoza in power and then allowing him to be overthrown. What is the real purpose for all this? Now the country is in turmoil. Tons of weapons arrive, and tons of drugs ship out. In Belize, we wish to avoid the violence, so we do as we do in order to increase our prosperity and keep the peace so we can make it as hard as possible for your government to create problems here too."

Roger shifted in his seat and started to interrupt, then decided not to. Gillette was on a roll and everything he had to say was good information for the future—except, Roger reminded himself, that he had no future in Belize if this man kept his word and his gig went off without a hitch.

"The Soviets took advantage of the resulting unrest and supported insurgencies," Gillette went on, "so the U.S. sought allies against the expansion of communism and was willing to support abusive dictators in that quest, so the brown guys ended up doing most of the dying on both sides. Argentina, Peru, Bolivia, Colombia, Venezuela, Panama, Salvador, Honduras, and Cuba. We see this also in the Middle East, with Islamic extremists taking on the role there filled here by the communists. The world will pay the price for a long time to come, and I hope only that, through what little I can do, Belize will not pay as high a price as have so many others."

"Yeah, well, whatever, dude," Tony said, "but what I—"

"Thank you, *Razor*," Roger interrupted forcefully, and Tony paled as the name reminded him of their earlier conversation. He glanced fearfully at Gillette.

"Hey, man, I'm sorry, I didn't mean any disrespect," he said clumsily and held out his hand. "Seems like you got everything under control." Gillette shook hands graciously.

"Thank you very much," he said, "and thank you for helping Belize to prosper."

"Sure thing, man. Happy to help." He sat back and tried to disappear into his seat. Roger and Gillette traded knowing glances.

"Steve hasn't spent a lot of time studying great power politics," Roger said, covering the awkward moment, "so thank you for explaining. And as agreed, we'll be on the highway Thursday at noon."

"Best of luck," Gillette smiled, "and hopefully I won't see you until your next visit." They grinned at each other and the meeting ended.

Rudy drove the Belizean officials home and smiled as he stopped at a once-stately and now somewhat worn-out building.

"This is where the British officers pass the time between flights," he smirked at Tony. "Many very nice young ladies tend to their needs, if you know what I mean."

Tony grinned for the first time since he'd been there and slapped Roger on the shoulder.

"Thanks for taking care of your old buddy, man," he said. "Looks like you got everything in hand, so I'll see you back in the States."

"Okay, brother," Roger said as they shook hands. "Have fun doing all those things I don't do." Tony laughed and disappeared into the building.

"What an asshole," Rudy said as he put the car in gear and headed for the repair station to meet the rest of the crew.

"Yeah, but one with money," Roger said, "and remember, we also got Eddie out of the deal."

"Yes, Eddie is a good man, Roger," Rudy said. "Reminds me a little of you."

"Thanks, man," Roger said, "and you remind me a little of George at his best, so you guys be cool to each other, okay?"

"No problem, Roger," Rudy grinned. "I take back every bad thing I said about him."

"Good," said Roger.

They met George, Manu and Junior in the dirt parking lot of the closed repair station, then proceeded down the Western Highway to the Cayo District. It took them more than an hour to get there and then George found only another 1,000 pounds throughout the course of the night, 2,000 pounds short of what they needed.

"Maybe now it's time to meet the gringo, yes?" George suggested, as they took a break on a side road, bleary-eyed, dirty and hungry. The eastern sky started to lighten.

"Do it," Roger said, and George drove them quickly through the prosperous university town of Belmopan to one of its nicer neighborhoods just as the sun was rising. Their dirty, heavily-laden vehicles looked out of place but there was no one up and about yet so they passed unnoticed.

George parked on a side street, then walked around the corner and knocked on the door of the nearest villa while Roger and the others waited with the loads. He came back two minutes later and waved for Roger to join him.

"Victor, I'd like you to meet Roger," George said to a muscular, square-jawed man with short brownish-black hair and a professional, almost military bearing. Roger didn't recognize him, and he watched his eyes carefully as they shook hands.

"Nice to meet you," Victor said, then looked over his shoulder toward the street. "Probably be a good idea for you to park your rigs behind the house."

"Thanks," Roger said. "You took the words right out of my mouth."

"And when you get done with that," he said to George, "take everyone in the guest house. They can clean up a bit and I'll have the cook bring you some grub." George nodded and left to take care of that while Victor welcomed Roger into the house. They sat down at the kitchen table and the cook served coffee, then went back to the kitchen.

"I've been trying to meet you for a while," Victor said. "I was told you had a hit-and-run operation, and he was right. Every time I thought I'd caught up, I was told you had already left."

"George tells me you're a friend of a friend," Roger said, feeling uncomfortable with this stranger talking so familiarly about him in this way. "Is that true?"

"In more ways than one," Victor said easily, "but let that rest for now. If we decide to do business, I'm sure you'll understand."

"All right," Roger replied just as easily, to mask his growing alarm, "then we need to make that decision so we can get out of town before traffic picks up. Show me what you got."

Victor left the room and returned with a full garbage bag of beautiful colas. Roger marveled at the unusual quality.

"You have a ton that looks like this?"

"Probably more," he said matter-of-factly, without a hint of boast or bravado, "but listen, since you're already loaded, you better get going. This is stashed north of the city, and I can't get free until later, so how about you meet me at the Sand Hill Tavern tomorrow evening?"

"Where the old and new highways join together?" Roger asked. Victor nodded and extended his hand. They shook to seal the deal and Victor looked out back at the dirty caravan.

"It's best if you only bring one truck."

"Sure thing," Roger said, "and I'll try to wash it." Victor smiled slightly and gave the idea an emphatic thumbs up. Roger left feeling better, especially because the pickup point was close to his camp. Maybe this gig would end up being his retirement run after all.

They departed as the sun began casting its morning light.

The day revealed Cayo's distinctive landscape as they left town and drove back to camp. Unlike northern Belize, Cayo had lush rolling hills dotted with occasional farm plots scratched out of the jungle. Stoic Mennonite barns accented the swells of green with their Old World look.

They turned off the Western Highway onto the Burrell Boom Cut to save time and avoid driving near Belize City, then linked up with the Northern Highway just north of Los Lagos.

They arrived without incident at the camp, where Eddie quickly organized the other workers to unload the latest acquisition, then gestured for Roger to join him over at the seven-thousand pound mountain of processed weed stacked higher than their heads. Roger sat on a bale and smiled at it.

"Good work, Eddie," he said admiringly. "Looks great." Eddie pointed to a separate, much smaller pile of five bags. "Check out those."

Roger leaned over and opened one of the bags. It was stuffed with nothing but dust and seeds. He glanced at Eddie, dismayed.

"What is this, five hundred pounds?"

"Six," Eddie said unhappily. Roger held up a handful and let the debris sift through his fingers back into the bag.

"Well, that's what happens when you're in a hurry," he said. "Still, I can't believe we bought *this* much junk. No sense carrying back something we can't really sell, but I didn't figure on losing *this* much." He sighed and looked over at the unload operation. "Why don't you make sure they're dialed in, then take a break. I can see by this pile you haven't had one yet."

"Thanks, Roger," Eddie said. "Don't mind if I do." He walked over to talk to the workers.

Roger walked around to the jungle side of the weed mountain and settled himself into a comfortable nook among the bales, then started planning his next move.

The unexpected high payment to Gillette had seriously depleted their funds and what they now had wouldn't fill the plane. It was enough to recoup their investment but not enough for a retirement run. If he took advantage of Victor's high quality supply, though, he'd have the record breaking scam he'd planned all along; he just hoped he had the cash to make the deal. He fell asleep among the sweet-smelling colas trying to work out the math in his head. On the other side of the mountain, Eddie set the crew to work sifting the new batch, then found himself a soft spot and embarked on his own power nap.

Roger woke refreshed just before noon and saw Eddie already back at it. He cleaned up from two day's worth of backcountry dirt, then had George drive him to Orange Walk.

"Nice to be in the clear again," George said. "I missed my family and it's very hard to hide this truck!"

"Well, I hope you stashed the Enforcer until I'm outta here."

"Oh yes, Roger," he said sheepishly. "She is not even at my house. I'm so sorry I didn't listen to you from the first about that."

When they got to Orange Walk, they stopped at a phone where Roger left a message for Mickey—"Trish is looking forward to the party"—then they went shopping for food and other staples for the crew while they waited for Mickey's response. When it came on schedule in exactly the form they wanted to hear—"Sally is ready to party,"—they used the balance of the afternoon buying ten gallons of white paint and finding two 55-gallon drums of aviation fuel. They returned to the new camp with the fresh supplies, then left after sundown to make their final purchase.

Roger didn't want to take any chances this close to the gig, so he and Rudy followed Manu and George in their truck. They met Victor behind the Sand Hill Tavern and climbed into his Land Rover, leaving the conspicuous station wagon behind.

He led them dangerously close to civilization, to the international airport road, and down the dead end road to within half a mile of the terminal, then parked behind a large cement block building and entered through a loading dock.

To his surprise, Roger saw that the weed in the building was his; the neatly cubed bales they'd lost to the police at Tres Legos were unmistakable. He frowned at Victor.

"How did you—"

"A friend of a friend," Victor said, smiling. Roger looked again at the pile and smiled grimly.

"Can't believe I gotta buy back my own product," he muttered.

"Fortunes of war," Victor said, "and, really, I'd rather it didn't shake out like this, but the way I look at it, we had to buy it ourselves and since we can't ship it all, better for you get the rest than someone else. So instead of playing games, just tell me what you have to spend."

"Give me a minute, would you?" he asked, and walked away with George even before Victor had nodded his assent.

"What do you think?" he asked George.

"Top quality and we know we won't have to sift it," George said.

"You mean, we already did," Roger said wearily.

"Don't remind me," George said, "but at least we get it back, yes?"

"Yes," Roger said and slapped George on the back, "so let's make a deal."

He told Victor how much cash he had left and what he needed to keep for his crew and the remaining expenses. Victor pondered for several moments, then stuck out his hand.

"Deal." They shook and Victor smiled. "By the way, there's not two thousand there." Roger's eyes narrowed and Victor grinned. "There's twenty-four hundred." Roger laughed.

"You ought to be a comedian," he said appreciatively. Victor winked.

"How do you know I'm not?" They both chuckled at that old standard of the smuggling business—how little they actually knew about the lives and backgrounds of the people with whom they did so much handshake business.

Victor said he'd babysit half of it while they loaded the first half into George's truck and raced back to camp, stopping at Sand Hill to retrieve Rudy's car. They unloaded quickly and got back on the highway to get the rest. Then George saw the eerie but familiar image of several flashlight-waving men on the road ahead.

"Here we go again," he said to Manu, reaching for a radio, "but this time we do it differently." He keyed the radio. "Hello, hello, cops ahead! I say again, cops ahead."

"Ignore them," Roger replied instantly from Rudy's car a quarter mile behind them. "Hold back until we catch up to you, then just drive through and keep going and make sure you don't hit anybody! We'll follow you and stall them, then meet you later at the place."

"Okay, will do."

George slowed up until Rudy was right behind him, then they both sped past the checkpoint.

"Yep, it's the cops all right," Roger said to Rudy as they roared by, then watched over his shoulder as the men scrambled into Jeeps to pursue. "At least they didn't start shooting," he chuckled, then looked to see sweat pouring from Rudy's forehead. "Chill, my man, it'll be cool." He keyed the radio. "Hello hello, keep going. We'll take care of this."

"Okay okay," came the answer, then Roger stashed the radio in a bag with some other incriminating stuff, watched for an identifiable tree, then had Rudy slow down while he tossed the bag into the roadside bushes.

"All right, go ahead and pull it over," he said calmly, trying with his voice to soothe his companion's jangled nerves. "Now we find out what the Razor's all about."

Rudy nervously screeched his wagon to a halt and moments later headlights lit up the inside of the station wagon and they heard booted feet, jingling military equipment and shouting voices.

"Hold your hands outside the window," Roger said, then did the same with his own. Still, he heard the unpleasant sound of submachine gun bolts being charged and pistol hammers being cocked.

Two men on each side pointed their gun muzzles at their heads while a third opened their doors.

"Get out and get down on the ground," said one man sternly and with great authority but without anger or cruelty. A good sign, Roger thought as he carefully complied, and the voice seemed vaguely familiar.

As Roger laid down slowly on the ground, he saw Gillette holding a .45 automatic with an extended clip as two other police officers searched the car.

"What is your business in this area?" one of the door-opening officers asked Roger.

"Jack," said Roger resolutely. "We're looking for Jack."

He saw Gillette frown and do a double take. He apparently hadn't recognized Roger or their muddy wagon in the darkness. He looked closely at Rudy, then gestured at his men to get back in their vehicles.

"Go back to the checkpoint," he said. "These aren't the ones we're looking for."

And with that, Gillette holstered his pistol, his men uncocked their weapons and they all vanished into the darkness, leaving Roger and Rudy still lying on their stomachs outside their car. Rudy sat up and laughed.

"I'll be damned," he said. Roger stood up and got back in the car as if nothing had happened.

"Come on, let's go." Rudy jumped into the car, they backed up and got the bag, then went back to the airport stash building and met up with George, Manu and Victor.

"George says you had a little adventure on the way back here," Victor said with a grin.

"Not much of one," Roger deadpanned. "They mistook us for someone else for a couple of minutes. It's all good now."

"Indeed it is," said Victor as George and Manu loaded the last of Roger's repatriated bales into the pickup bed. He extended his hand one more time. "Been a pleasure, Roger," he said as they shook again. "Don't be a stranger next time you're down this way."

"Done," Roger said, smiling to himself at the idea that, after this gig, he really wouldn't be down here again.

They made it back to camp without any more adventures and after adding the last 1,200 pounds to their mountain, Roger collapsed onto the nearest bale and grinned at Eddie.

"Stage One complete," Eddie said.

"Now for the easy part," Roger said, flashing his famous grin. "We don't let it out of our sight until it's on Sugar Alpha and we watch her gear retract."

# CHAPTER FIFTEEN

———— ⊶⊷⊶ ————

## THE RETIREMENT PARTY

With the acquisition phase complete, Roger shifted gears into Phase Two—what he called "DC-3 school." He had his work crew arrange bales in a semi-circle of seats around Weed Mountain for a pre-op briefing. He did this before every flight to make sure everyone was on the same page, but he knew from Rudy's own lack of knowledge about aircraft operations that he could safely assume no one on this crew had done an airplane gig besides Eddie and him, so he wanted to conduct a thorough briefing.

He started with an overall view, sketching a DC-3 diagram in the dirt with a stick, then adding a map of the highway section they would use, complete with the curves for the road blocks. Then he used his stick as a pointer, with Rudy standing next to him to translate, even though most of them spoke at least some English. He wanted to make sure they understood every word.

"The aircraft will land from the north, which is this direction, then slowly taxi up and stop at the quarry road," he said, then watched their eyes as Rudy translated. When he finished, Roger banged the stick along the forward edge of both wings on the DC-3 drawing.

"The area in front of the wings is the Death Zone. The propellers on the engines will kill you instantly and *you cannot see them*. So do *not* go in front of the wings *for any reason*." He paused while Rudy translated.

"I will tell the pilot where to stop," he continued, "and I will park him so the plane door is even with the truck." While Rudy translated, Roger looked at Eddie. "Your job is to help the co-pilot re-fuel as soon

324

as possible in case they have to make a quick departure. The co-pilot will hand out four containers of oil, and we'll have one of the fifty-five gallon drums on each side of the pavement to top off the mains. Just do what he tells you and when that's done, fill in where you're needed."

"Got it," Eddie said, "and if it's okay with you, I want to hear the rest of this so I know the whole show."

"That'll be great, man," Roger said with a grin. "Sure is nice having a good hand along."

Roger then assigned each man a position for the loading, with himself inside to handle the stacking and three others inside to pass him the bales in a bucket-brigade system. He delegated Rudy to supervise the men throwing the bales from the truck through the door, and for his cousin Armando to back the truck gently up to the threshold.

"When the plane stops and I open the door, my three assistants board with me," he said to Rudy, Armando and Junior, "but Armando, you must *wait* until I signal you to back up because there will be several empty fuel drums we need to throw out before we can load. All right?"

"Yes, Mister Roger, I understand," Armando said, focusing intently on Roger.

"Now keep in mind," Roger continued to all of them, "the engines'll be running the whole time so it'll be very loud and there'll be a strong wind, so it will be confusing and hard to communicate. Everything that comes out will blow behind the tail, and I want you guys, Armando and Junior to gather it all up. This is a professional operation—we don't leave evidence. Pile the trash way off the road and when the truck's empty, load it in there. All right?"

"Yes, Mister Roger," said Junior. "No one will even know we were here."

"All right," Roger said, "one more time. Rudy, I'll give you the backup commands. Junior, you sit in the cab and relay your dad's commands to Armando. Armando, *go slow*. Take your time and make sure you don't hit the plane. Say it to me."

"Go slow, take my time, don't hit the plane," Armando repeated.

"One more time the last part."

"Don't hit the plane." Roger grinned and patted Armando on the shoulder.

"Just keep saying that to yourself as you back up and you'll be fine," he added. "All right," after you're all in place, keep the bales pouring in unless we tell you to slow down. Got it?"

"Got it," Rudy said.

Roger walked over to the workers he'd assigned to inside duty and shook hands with each of them.

"Hermes," he said to the biggest one, "since you're the strongest, I want you to take the bales when they come in the plane and throw them as far forward as you can to your brother." He looked at the man next to him. "Francisco, when you get them, you do the same. Try to work out a rhythm with each another because it'll go easier that way. We'll have to move them sixty feet at first, then less as we fill it up." He looked at the final man. "Ted, the pilot and I will grab the first few bales and stack them behind the cockpit seats. Then you start carrying them to us so we can arrange things properly. We want to put the heaviest bales and most weight in the front. All right?" The men all nodded soberly. "Final thing. Don't work too hard, and don't go too fast. This is a long race not a short one, so pace yourself and let me know if you need a break."

Roger sent the inside crew off to eat and rest, and turned his attention to the remaining three of his ragged but increasingly well-drilled crew. He went over their instructions with them, and deliberately left Rudy out of the conversation so that they'd pay closer attention, going over each Indian's duties until he could recite each step back to Roger without hesitation.

When he was satisfied with their answers, he organized a simulated loading and critiqued their work, then had them repeat it until their efforts were almost as coordinated as a Freak Brother 10-way launch. Almost. When he was satisfied, he dismissed his loading crew for the night and turned his attention to the roadblock team: George and Manu, plus two of the sharpest Indians, Jose and Fernando. He picked up his marking stick again and walked with them to his highway map.

"Jose, Fernando, the north will mainly be sympathetic growers," he said, pointing out the location of their roadblock, "so I want you to pass out cold beers and ten-dollar bills. If they start complaining, give them another ten. We want to make it a big happy party on that side because when we're finished, we have to leave that way and we need a friendly path to get through. All right?"

"*Sí*, Mister Roger," they said together. "We will get it done." He nodded his approval and turned to George and Manu.

"Our biggest risk is from the south," he said, "because that's where the police and army are, and there's no culvert to keep people from

326

driving around the roadblock. If anyone gets through, they could block the runway and keep the plane from taking off—which means your job is second only to the pilots, all right?" He looked at them sternly. They nodded. "That's also why I'm putting you two there," he went on, "and the more vehicles you can pile up, the better the blockade. If the police come, it's up to you to see they pay more attention to you than getting past you and going up the road."

George and Manu traded glances, then grinned at Roger.

"We will give them an adventure that will keep them busy all day," George said confidently. Roger nodded and then they worked out some basic radio codes, and he sent them over to Weed Mountain to get some rest.

Roger found his soft spot on the back side of the mountain and went over his plan again and again, looking for holes, thinking if he'd missed any tricks. He couldn't think of any, but he realized he was distracted a little by the nearly full moon that brightly lit the jungle. Smuggler's Moon, it was, and he smiled as he thought of the boys at The Ranch being able to work under that moon when the load arrived tomorrow night. He also remembered that his father had jumped under that same moon the night before D-Day, from a C-47, the military version of the DC-3.

He glanced at his watch. Less than an hour before Sugar Alpha's planned departure from Ohio, where Jeff and Billy were no doubt freezing their butts off as they got the old girl ready to roll. He walked around the front of the mountain and found Eddie.

"George and I are going to Orange Walk to confirm the launch. Get as much sleep as you can, all right?"

"You woke me up to tell me that?" Eddie joked. Roger chuckled at the jest and climbed into George's truck, waking the snoring Belizean when he shut the door.

"Let's roll," he said. George smiled and started the engine.

In Hamilton, Ohio, Sugar Alpha was fueled and idling on the tarmac when Roger's confirmation came through on schedule. Jason drove Mickey from the hangar to the plane and Mickey saluted Blind Jeff, who saluted back, then advanced the throttles and taxied to the end of the runway. Moments later, it rolled.

Mickey held his breath as the heavily-laden old airplane slowly gathered speed, then broke free of the ground, both engines humming steadily, and skimmed low over the rest of the runway in ground effect as it accelerated.

"Hell of a pilot," Jason whispered at Jeff's airmanship.

"That's why they call him Blind Jeff," Mickey said proudly. "He can feel an airplane better than any man alive." They watched the big bird disappear into the darkness, then Mickey frowned at the dashboard. "Is there something wrong with that fucking heater?"

Inside Sugar Alpha, Jeff puffed away as he held the big wheel between a thumb and forefinger, feeling her for the change that told him to reduce power and trim her for the climb to cruising altitude. A few moments later, Sugar sent her message and he slowly eased the throttles back and adjusted other controls as though they were part of his own body. Then he slapped Billy Bob on the shoulder and grinned around his cigarette.

"She's purrin' like a kitten, pardner," he said. "Tell our buddy on the ground we'll see him tonight."

"O-*kay!*" Mickey exulted when he received the coded message as they sat in the idling car inside the hangar. He pumped his fist and Jason grinned. Mickey checked his watch. "Now, on to the next airport." Jason drove out of the hangar at headed for Columbus so Mickey could fly to Tulsa and hook up with the ground crew.

At sunrise on Thursday morning, the crew tore down the camp and loaded up the big truck. Roger directed them to load the fluffiest bales first so they'd be the last off the truck and last onto the airplane.

"Harder to drive with the heavy weight in the back," Rudy protested.

"And impossible to fly that way," Roger explained. "You want the least weight in the tail or she won't even get off the ground." Rudy pondered that for a moment, then nodded his understanding.

Blind Jeff had switched to internal fuel after he'd leveled out at cruising altitude and now, over northern Georgia, the big rubber tank behind the seat was half empty.

"Okay, pardner," he said to Billy, "time to start cranking the organ grinder."

"It's gonna be cold as fucking hell back there," he complained. "Why can't we use more from the wing tanks?"

Jeff smiled patiently around his cigarette. "Long trip across the pond and that's a pretty poor place to learn she ain't nursin' off our bottle." Billy's eyes bulged with the shock of understanding.

"Fuck," he said flatly. "If I'd've done that when I flew my gig, I wouldn't have ended up being shark bait."

"Funny how that works, eh, pardner?"

"No shit," Billy said, and slid between the seats into the cabin, making sure he didn't bump Jeff's cigarette as he went. Moments later, Jeff heard fuel pouring into the rubber tank as Billy cranked the hand pump on the first of the 55-gallon fuel drums.

As the last bales were loaded on the big truck, Roger sent scouting vehicles in each direction to report on police activity. Twenty minutes later, both vehicles were back, their spotters waving upraised thumbs out the window, and moments after that the big truck heaved onto the highway and started its seven-mile journey to the gravel quarry.

Roger had already sent some of the crew ahead to set up a defensive perimeter and chop out a cozy spot for the truck. When the truck arrived, he took a few minutes to do one more practice backup with Rudy, Junior and Armando.

It was a good thing they did; with real obstacles around them, Armando was a little twitchy on the controls and skinned some bark off a tree when he stopped an instant too late. Roger went up to the cab and leaned into Armando's face.

"You do that to the plane and we're screwed," he said coldly. He let that sink in to the terrified young man's brain, then punched him lightly in the shoulder. "So next time . . ."

"Be more careful," Armando said. Roger nodded and held up a finger.

"And the way you be more careful is to *relax*. It's easy if you relax, all right?"

"All right."

"Good man," Roger said. "Now get with Rudy and Junior and put as much of this chop on the truck as possible. Cut more if you have to."

Next, Roger took Eddie, his roadblock teams and some of the loaders back to the highway, where he had them all watch as he repeated his earlier measurements, pacing the distance to obstacles on each side of the highway, re-figuring all of the dimensions both for his own peace of mind and so that they would all understand better what exactly would be happening—and why. He checked his watch.

"All right," he said to the loaders, "we have about three hours to get this runway ready, so let's cut every tree and trim every branch that's inside the wing clearance area."

The loaders went to work and Roger took Eddie and the two roadblock teams up the long straightaway and around the large gentle curve to the strategic choke point on the north end, where Roger showed them the best spot to place their vehicles and they reviewed the plan one more time.

On their way back, Roger stopped a thousand feet from the northern bend, where Eddie and he painted several chevrons on the blacktop, then drove a half mile further down the road and painted a three-foot-wide white strip across the highway to mark the touchdown point. There was almost no traffic, so the task went uneventfully, but the few cars that passed streaked the fresh paint with their tires.

They dropped Jose and Fernando off to help the loaders with their tree trimming, then went to the south curve. Roger had just started blocking out their vehicle positions when another Harrier roared down the middle of the highway 25 feet over their heads with an ear-splitting scream. They all ducked and covered their ears and Roger watched the jet bank around the corner and disappear.

"Holy shit," shouted George. "Are we busted?" Roger stared after the plane, remembering Gillette's words about the British rules of engagement, and his own aviation experience.

"Pilots," he muttered. "Always giving me a heart attack one way or the other."

"Yeah, like you didn't do the same thing a few months ago," Eddie said, grinning.

"Huh?" Roger frowned, puzzled.

"I heard about Rosa, man," Eddie said admiringly. "First thing anybody says about you, man—*Señor Huevos Grandes*."

"Except for her family," George added. "They call him *Don Corazon Grandes*."

"Fits even better, man," Eddie said softly, bowing his head slightly. "Chief Big Heart."

"Anyway," Roger said, changing the subject, "I hope that was just another yahoo jet jock scaring the monkeys. At least he was low enough that he probably couldn't even see into the quarry when he went by."

"He'll know what those markings on the road are, though," said George.

"Don't remind me," said Roger, and they went back to work planning their most critical ground operation.

Sugar Alpha had left U.S. soil and crossed into the Gulf of Mexico about 8 a.m., the candy cane-colored plane adorned with eight-foot-high Firestone letters on wings and fuselage gleaming brightly in the warm sun.

"Man, are we lucky to have weather like this," Billy said as he peered out the window at scattered puffy clouds that accented the deep blue sky. Jeff lit another cigarette and exhaled forcefully. The smoke bounced off the windshield and drifted back into their faces. Billy wrinkled his nose at the smell.

"Well, pardner," he said, "if we're really lucky, it'll turn to crap with lots of thunder and lightning so we ain't such an easy radar target on the way back." Billy chuckled and shook his head.

"Man, you think of everything, don't you?"

"Try to, pardner," Jeff said. "Easier to stay alive and out of jail that way."

As Sugar Alpha's estimated arrival time approached, Roger put everyone in position, still hoping that the latest Harrier episode was as innocent and unconnected to their activities as the first one had been. He tried to soothe his own nerves by repeating to himself what he'd said the day before to Tony.

He stood with Eddie on the side of the quarry road wearing fatigues, dark glasses, and skin-tight black gloves. He noticed that Eddie was bare-handed, so he pulled a pair of batting gloves from his pack and handed them to him.

"No sense leaving your prints all around," he said. Eddie nodded and put on the gloves without comment.

Then Roger thought he heard the lumbering sound of distant radial engines. He cupped an ear in anticipation. Eddie grinned.

"That's not it," he said. A moment later, Roger discovered that the sound he heard was only the rumble of bad tires on an approaching truck. They melted into the bush until it passed, then Roger checked his watch.

"Any time now," he said. "Any time."

Blind Jeff had masterfully navigated the Gulf to the Yucatan Peninsula with only a compass. When the shoreline appeared in the distance, he grinned at Billy, who had pumped all the drums dry and now sat again in the right seat.

"Land ho!" he announced, smiling like Columbus discovering America. They hit the peninsula at Cancun and passed over the isle of Cozumel before they received a weak radio signal from Chetumal. Jeff dropped down to 200 feet and flew over the water until he got to Belize, then followed Roger's directions to the north side of Orange Walk.

"Our pardner sure knows how to lay out a flight plan," he said admiringly. "I'd say it's time we give him a call." Billy nodded and keyed one of the handhelds.

"Someone lookin' for a date with Sally?" he asked.

"Say again, Southern Star," said Roger into his radio, thinking it was George who had called.

"I say again, is someone lookin' for a date with Sally?" said a voice that Roger suddenly and happily realized was not George. He heard the engine noise in the background and adrenaline rushed through his body.

"You betcha!" he said. "The party is rocking!"

"Copy that," Billy said formally. "We're ten out of O.W."

"Copy ten," Roger said and spoke into his ground radio. "Close the north door. I say again, close the north door."

"North door closing," came the prompt and clear reply. "Last car through was two minutes ago, a blue pickup truck with two guys in it."

"Copy blue pickup," Roger said. The truck passed him within a minute and he turned to Eddie. "That's your cue. Good luck, man." They shook hands and while Eddie directed the loading crew to roll the fuel drums to the highway shoulders, Roger called George.

"Close the south door when the blue pickup goes by," he said.

"Copy blue pickup," came George's quick reply. Roger gestured to Rudy to have Armando move the truck into position.

"South door closed," George said.

"Copy south door closed," Roger answered as Armando stopped the truck gently. He searched northward for Sugar Alpha's familiar outline and found it just above the treeline. He smiled and took a deep breath, reveling in the rush of it all. This was living!

"Okay, we got you," Billy said. We're two out lookin' right down the alley."

"Copy two out and we have you in sight," Roger answered. "Be sure to make it a straight-in. No go arounds."

"Copy straight-in only," came Billy's reply as Eddie rejoined Roger.

Time stood still and so did the crew as they all watched in amazement as Blind Jeff wafted the massive machine toward the narrow highway.

"Damn," said Eddie in wonder. "Doesn't look nearly that big at the airport."

Sugar Alpha seemed to hang motionlessly in the air as Billy lowered the flaps and dropped the gear. Jeff lined her up perfectly on the narrow road, and stuck the mains to the new asphalt with a gentle squeak and a puff of white smoke. The tail dropped gracefully and Jeff taxied the proud bird down the road, main wheels tracking perilously close to the soft shoulder on either side.

"Excellent job, man," Roger said appreciatively on the radio, as he walked onto the highway to guide Jeff to his stopping place.

"Anything less, pardner, and we'd be picking trees out of our teeth," came the sardonic reply.

Sugar Alpha's wings barely cleared the nearest trees and dragged through some of the taller bush. The engine roar vibrated everyone's teeth as Jeff taxied closer and Roger tried to will its wheels away from the shoulders as he guided the plane to a stop. He and Jeff traded big grins, then Roger's faded as he saw Eddie come toward him so fast he almost forgot about the propellers. Roger frantically gestured him clear of the invisible death and moved toward him.

"The plane scared your inside loaders!" he shouted above the engine roar. "Only the three guys at the truck are left." Roger glanced under the wing at Rudy, who gestured helplessly. "Want me to go round them up?" Eddie asked. Roger shook his head and ducked under the wing, pulling Eddie along so he stayed a safe distance from the props.

"Screw it! We don't have time."

They reached the cargo door as it dropped open. Billy handed out the oil to Eddie, then hopped down.

"Make it like a pit stop," he shouted to Billy over the prop blast and engine noise. "I need you guys to help inside as soon as you're done." Billy saluted, and he disappeared under the belly with Eddie.

Roger jumped aboard and started flinging drums out the door beyond the horizontal stabilizer, trying to make up for the lost help. He grabbed everything that wasn't fastened down and threw it into the prop blast—the retaining bands that held the barrels in place, the control locks, everything. Jeff walked casually down the sloping cabin, puffing a cigarette, clearly in a relaxed mode after his intense landing.

"You call this a runway, pardner?" he asked, not noticing Roger's frenzied actions. "I've eaten noodles wider than this." He chuckled and looked out a window at one wing. "The green stains on these white wings are gonna match the brown stains in Billy Bob's shorts, don't you think?"

Roger ignored him as he waved the truck back then signaled Rudy to stop. Rudy signaled Junior, and Armando stopped perfectly within two feet of the fuselage. Rudy set rocks on either side of one rear tire, the bales started flying. Roger caught the first one and heaved it forward without looking. Unfortunately, Jeff was lighting a fresh cigarette and didn't see it coming and the 50-pounder hit him square in the face and knocked him flat on his back.

"Get out of the way!" Roger roared as Jeff rolled onto all fours as more bales flew over his head and started groping around on the floor.

"Gotta find my glasses, pardner."

"Forget your glasses and help me! Sugar scared half our help into the jungle, so we're short-handed."

"Can't fly without 'em, pardner," Jeff said calmly as he kept looking. Roger froze in his tracks, then gestured for the unloaders to hold up for a moment and scanned the floor for the fragile wire rims, hoping they weren't buried under the weed. Roger found one shattered lens and mangled frame with the other lens still in it and handed the pieces to Jeff, who got out of the way and put them in his pocket just as Armando climbed inside.

"Rudy said I should help," he said. Roger glanced at Rudy and gave him a thumbs up, then turned his attention back to Armando.

'Stand about there," he directed, pointing out a spot. "When I throw the bales to you, you toss them toward Jeff and he'll arrange them."

Armando nodded and Roger turned to see that the doorway was full of bales. He tossed them to Armando, then helped him lug the pile to the forward cabin.

"Don't be steppin' on my fuel system now, pardner," Jeff cautioned the young man, "and leave me five feet on either side of it."

"Sorry, Jeff," Roger said. "This stuff is too bulky for that. Just show me what you gotta have, and let's fill 'er up." Jeff complied by standing over his precious hoses and valves like a mama grizzly protecting her cubs—a mama grizzly that smoked like a chimney.

"This'll do," he said. Just fit 'er in around me and we'll be good."

With sweat pouring down their faces, Roger and Armando packed bales into every available inch around Jeff. When they finished and turned back to get more, Roger discovered that Billy and Eddie had finished refueling and were now slinging bales deep into the fuselage, Eddie at the door, Billy 20 feet inside. With Armando filling the last link in the chain, Roger resumed his original job of packing the bales together like a puzzle until they had only a narrow aisle down the middle.

Then he started filling the aisle to keep the load from shifting on takeoff and Billy balked.

"Hey, man," he almost whined, "you gotta leave us an escape path."

"How much is left?" Roger shouted to Eddie.

"A bunch!" Eddie shouted back.

"Let's add more on top," Roger said, deferring to Billy's concern.

They tired and their pace slowed, but still they worked. Roger saw Jeff lounging in the cockpit, smoking and trying to fix his glasses, but he didn't even consider asking him for help; Jeff needed to stay as fresh as possible for the long flight home to a nighttime landing in a hayfield with no lights.

The load hit the ceiling on both sides, so they filled in the aisle to chest height.

"Dude, please leave us a crawl space at least, wouldja?" as Roger added more to the aisle pile. Roger glanced at Eddie, who just shook his head and gestured that they had still more to load into the small remaining space.

"Yo Jeff," Roger shouted up to the front, and his pilot squinted through the tiny tunnel at him. "Ten minutes before liftoff."

"Okay, pardner," Jeff said. "Billy, come on up front and let's get ready."

"In a minute, I gotta help leave a tunnel."

"Kid," Jeff said evenly, "if we go down, our only hope is the ol' can opener anyway, so come on, let's go."

"But shouldn't I check the CG and—"

"Enough, Billy Bob," Jeff said sharply, using his co-pilot's insulting nickname, "get on up here and let 'em do what they gotta do."

"Thanks for your help back here," Roger said warmly to soften the blow, "we'll take care of it from here." Billy looked at him with fear in his eyes, then climbed through the narrow space into the cockpit, while Roger and Eddie filled the empty gap to the top.

"Man," Eddie said, "She's packed so solid that if she crashes, she won't even bend out of shape."

"Yeah," Roger added with a black death grin, "she'll just burn like one colossal doobie." They laughed for a moment, then looked out the door and saw ten more bales still on the truck.

"You gotta be kidding," Roger said, "we still got five hundred pounds left." He turned and surveyed his remaining space.

"What do you think?" Eddie said, wondering how they could possibly fit that much weed into that little open area left by the door.

"I wanted to keep this area clear for CG purposes," Roger said, talking more to himself than Eddie, "but like Jeff said, we gotta do what we gotta do."

"Good thing Billy's not back here," Eddie grinned, then gestured for Armando to toss them the next bale.

At the north roadblock, Jose and Fernando presided over a party. The score of drivers stopped there had left their vehicles and were drinking beer together, laughing and telling stories. Each new arrival received a $10 bill and a beer, and most joined the party.

Things were not so friendly on the southern end. There, George and Manu faced several furious businessmen that he knew from Orange Walk and who weren't interested in beer or money but in getting through. He would placate one with his story of a terrible accident ahead, and of officials flying out the dead in helicopters, but as soon as a new person showed up, they would all get agitated again.

"The hell with you!" one said finally. "I will just go around you. You can't stop me." He got in his car and started the engine. George and Manu traded glances and knew they had to act quickly. Manu jumped into the passenger seat, turned off the engine, yanked the keys from the ignition and jumped out of the car.

His action prevented the car from going around, but it was still too late. The driver of an olive drab, military-looking bus right behind him saw his opening and gunned his vehicle around the roadblock onto the grass. It tipped high up on two wheels as the downhill side sank into the road berm, but it miraculously stayed upright and the driver steered it back onto the highway and all four wheels and disappeared around the corner. George jumped into his own truck and started the engine, then shook his fist at the assembled drivers.

"I will ram the next man who tries to go past me, so just stay put! It will only be a little longer." His threat, along with the near-crash of the bus, settled down the crowd enough that no one else tried to run the roadblock.

"Man," said Manu, "now I know how those cops feel when we run their checkpoints!" George smiled grimly but he kept his eyes on the crowd.

Roger had filled every nook and cranny with the remaining half ton. The size of the load amazed him. It even filled the bathroom and cargo space in the tail. Never had he seen a DC-3 stuffed to capacity; he couldn't even stand inside—and he still had one bale left.

"Can she still take off?" Eddie asked as he marveled alongside Roger.

"Oh yeah," Roger said. "We're still way under gross. It's a matter of space, not weight because there are no seeds or dirt weighing down the bales." He studied the situation, then grinned at Eddie.

"Not leaving it behind," he said, "so move the truck, then we'll shove it in." Rudy and Junior stood on one side of the air stairs, Eddie and Armando on the other. Roger placed the bale on the door and grabbed hold of the door edge.

"All right," he said, flashing his famous grin, "on the count of three. One . . . two . . . *three* . . ." they all pushed together and, like shutting an overstuffed suitcase, they held the door closed long enough for Roger to throw the latch. They took a brief moment to admire their work, then Roger pointed to the clutter around the door.

"Load that stuff in the truck and get it clear of the plane," he ordered and everyone jumped into action. Satisfied, he ran around the wing into Jeff's field of vision feeling completely exhausted, but he felt better the instant he saw him slouching nonchalantly in the cockpit, elbow sticking out the window, mangled glasses perched precariously on his face, one finger of his right hand holding them in place. Roger gave him a smart salute, which Jeff returned with a smirk—but rather than running up the engines, he calmly pointed his cigarette down the road.

Roger followed his point and his mouth fell open as he spied the approaching bus. He thought about driving the truck ahead of Sugar to clear the way, but he knew he'd never get around the wing—so instead he calculated the distance to the bus and deemed it enough to try, and waved Jeff onward. His pilot stayed put, so Roger gestured more emphatically down the road, this time adding a one-finger salute for Jeff.

Jeff grinned broadly at that, tossed his cigarette out the window and slid it shut. Roger ducked back under the wing and out of the way.

Inside the cockpit, Jeff grinned at Billy, who sat rigidly in his seat.

"I don't want to crash again, man," Billy wailed. "Twice is more than enough!"

"Relax, pardner," Jeff chuckled. "We're a hell of a lot bigger than they are. Now hold my glasses in place, wouldja?"

Billy reached across the cockpit and awkwardly held Jeff's broken glasses in place. Jeff's freed right hand eased forward on the throttles and Sugar Alpha's big radial engines thundered into full roar, kicking up a blinding storm of dust and debris, peppering the ground crew with stinging particles. They shielded their eyes from the gale as Sugar reached full power and Jeff released her brakes.

Roger knew Jeff would lift the tail level with the nose as soon as he could to lessen the aerodynamic drag and, right on cue, he did. He hoped they would clear the bus as he saw Sugar Alpha pass the abort point and he saw her wheels lighten. Roger saw the bus screech to a stop and its occupants pile out of the doors. They ran off the road into the bush just as Sugar lifted off and her gear retracted—and then stopped climbing three feet off the ground. Roger felt sick and unconsciously started running towards the impending wreck—then stopped short and smiled grimly.

"Ground effect," he said out loud and waited to see if Jeff could pull it off.

Inside Sugar, Jeff looked past Billy's arm at the looming bus, feeling his co-pilot's rising tension.

"Relax, pardner," he said, "just keeping her on the cushion to build speed faster."

Billy didn't respond; he sat frozen, one hand on Jeff's glasses, the other helping Jeff keep the throttles maxed out. Then Jeff chuckled.

"Guess those bastards didn't wanna play chicken after all. Look at 'em scatter!"

The bus loomed larger in the windscreen, and at the last moment Blind Jeff pushed slightly down on the wheel and then back up a little more and used the air cushion to bounce the plane up and over the bus.

"See how I did that, pardner?" Jeff said as if he'd just demonstrated a loop to a private pilot student. Billy sagged in his seat and his arm fell limply to his side. Jeff grabbed his mangled glasses before they fell off his nose.

"You crazy motherfucker," Billy muttered.

"Most likely," said Jeff, "now I gotta set my glasses down for a piece here while I trim her up, so make sure I don't fly into any hillsides for a couple of minutes, will ya?"

Billy sat up abruptly and started watching out the windows.

Down below, Roger shook his head in joy as Sugar Alpha blasted down the road and then climbed clear of the jungle. He keyed his radio.

"Dude, did you really have to cut it that close?"

"Just thought I'd teach 'em a lesson about driving on a runway," came the laconic reply. "Figured it'd help slow 'em down from comin' your way too."

"True enough," Roger said. "Thanks and *bon voyage*."

Roger quickly forgot about the airplane whose fate was now out of his hands and turned his attention to the end game on the ground. He saw his crew finishing the site cleanup and getting aboard their vehicles, so he keyed his radio again.

North gate, south gate, let them through. I say again, north and south, let 'em through." Then he jumped aboard the truck and they headed north, refreshed by the cooling breeze of their passage but still dead tired and dirty, hungry and thirsty.

Roger and Eddie looked at each other soberly, then grinned, then laughed out loud and slapped hands to celebrate as a line of cars flowing south passed on their left. At the site of the former roadblock, they found a group of peasants still partying. They happily waved bottles of beer and cheered them on as they passed.

"One step closer to freedom," Roger said, as they turned into their camp to hide the truck until things cooled off. Roger and Eddie climbed into Rudy's station wagon and drove to Orange Walk, where Roger stopped at a phone.

"I left Sally at the party at one-fifteen and she was looking *good*," he said to Mickey's message machine. Then they went to Rudy's house to guzzle water, shower and change while Junior burned all of their loading clothes.

"Thanks for everything, Rudy," Roger said as they embraced. "Couldn't have done it without you."

"I look forward to our next adventure together," Rudy said, holding him at arm's length.

Then Roger embraced Junior.

"You became a man in the last three days, son," he said, looking him in the eyes. "I'm proud of you and I know your dad is too. Remember all that you have learned."

"Thank you, Mister Roger," Junior whispered, and his eyes grew moist. He wiped them quickly, but Roger smiled.

"It is a mark of manhood when you can cry at such things," Roger said, and smacked him hard enough in the shoulder to stagger him slightly. "See you around."

George then drove Roger and Eddie south and by late afternoon they were sitting in George's truck near the airport, waiting for their final flight to the States.

"I want to make sure you understand," Roger said to George. "I don't have any hard feelings. In fact, after dealing with Rudy, I realize how good a man and manager you really are and I look forward to seeing you again. You really know your business, but when the first gig went bad, Rudy was there for me and I gave him my word, so things worked out the way they did. Always remember, one man doesn't make it alone; it takes a team that can work together. If you always treat your people right, you'll never regret it."

"Roger, why do you speak like this?" George asked, frowning. "It sounds like you're dying." Roger put his hand on George's shoulder and smiled sadly.

"Not dying, just getting to the end of this business."

"No, you're just tired," George protested. "You have a great thing going here. You had to work day and night to put this load together. You wait. You will feel differently with a good rest, my friend. You will see."

"Maybe," Roger said, "but nothing lasts forever, and a wise man gets out when times are good. Someone I respect very much once said we can go until we get caught, or pick a point and quit. I like the last option best, and when I do quit, everything I leave behind becomes yours. The trade is coming to Belize. If you keep your group together, you'll have the best operation in the country."

"I appreciate all that," George said, humbled, "but without a connection like you, one I can trust, it'll never be the same."

"Well, I haven't finished yet. I still have at least one more commitment to honor."

"Another big one like this?" George asked, his eyes shining at the prospect.

"No, the logistics are too complicated for that," Roger said, shaking his head. "No. It'll be something we can do out of Progresso, fifteen hundred or two thousand pounds."

"Is that ours?" Eddie asked, pointing to an inbound jumbo jet. Roger checked his watch and nodded. George drove them to their usual drop off point at the terminal traffic circle and they climbed out of the truck. After Roger shut the door, he leaned through the window and smiled at his long-time business partner.

"Always remember, my friend, never let money interfere with your morals or forget how humble it was before we met."

"I will remember, Roger," George said, and they shook hands again. Then the two Americans entered the terminal and George drove back to Orange Walk.

Sugar Alpha had angled across the Yucatan Peninsula after leaving Belize and hit the Gulf near the Bay of Campeche, then crossed the 500 miles of water between them and landfall somewhere near the Texas-Louisiana border.

About two and a half hours after last seeing land, they approached the ADIZ boundary and, instead of identifying themselves, Blind Jeff gave Billy an advanced lesson in evasion. He dropped below the tops of the off-shore oil rigs and skimmed the waves, cruising under the radar.

As the sun touched the horizon, they dodged occasional obstacles and spotted the scattered lights of civilization right on schedule. A dark band of rain clouds along the coast helped cover their entry and, as rain spattered the windscreen, they zoomed over a line of trees. They were back in the States.

"Man, are we lucky to have weather like this," Billy said, recalling his words on the flight out. He grinned at Jeff, who now looked kind of silly with his broken glasses duct-taped to his nose. Jeff lit another cigarette and exhaled forcefully. The smoke bounced off the windshield and drifted back into their faces. Billy wrinkled his nose at the smell.

"So far, so good, pardner," he said, "and if we're really lucky, we'll lose these squall lines and have CAVU all the way to the Ranch." And with that, he pulled back a bit on the wheel and climbed to a less stressful cruising altitude and grinned at Billy. "No sense playing tag with the trees any more. If we show up on anybody's radar now, we're just ordinary domestic traffic."

When Mickey got to the Ranch around sunset, he'd left the Bushman by the entrance as lookout, then discovered to his satisfaction that Mike and Dave had already scouted the area again on foot, looking for any changes or unusual activity. He placed them at opposite ends of the field to operate the runway flares, supervised the placement of the lights, reminded them to keep one eye shut when they lit them to save half of their night vision, then parked at the anticipated stopping point.

They waited at their leisure in eerie silence. Even the moonlit night seemed to hold its breath, the stillness broken only by Mickey's occasional radio checks. Mickey stayed alert, but Dave and Mike rested as much as they could, dozing between radio calls.

"Sally . . . party . . . minutes," said a faint voice on Mickey's radio speaker. He checked his watch; it was 9:30 p.m., right on time for their scheduled 10 p.m. arrival.

"Copy Sally's coming to the party," he replied. He keyed his other radio.

"Nap time's over, boys," he said, and started going over his pre-landing checklist in his mind.

At one end of the field, Dave ripped loose the Velcro of his black gloves and refastened them as tightly as possible, then smeared streaks of camouflage paint on his face and tightened his butt pack. On the opposite end, Mike readied his flares and flashed a red beam to confirm that he was set. Dave mirrored the signal a moment later. Mickey saw them and keyed his radio twice in quick succession. They were ready.

"Ten minutes out," came Billy's call after they'd waited for what seemed to be an hour. Mickey made sure his 100,000-candlepower spotlight was near at hand and its cigarette lighter plug in clear sight. Dave took a deep breath and peered around him at the black and white moonscape, searching for enemies he wouldn't see until it was too late anyway but doing it because at least it gave him something to do while he was waiting. At the other end, Mike took a deep breath too and resumed his semi-napping state, building up his energy for the whirlwind of action that would commence in a few minutes.

"Five minutes out," came Jeff's voice over the radio, the change from Billy signaling that the wild ride was about to begin.

Mickey's adrenaline surged as he heard Sugar Alpha in the distance and estimated her location.

"You're about two miles east," he radioed.

"Copy two miles," answered Blind Jeff.

Mickey listened to the radial rumble fade back to silence as Sugar continued on without changing course. Much to Mickey's relief, the silence lingered; no one was following her. He keyed his radio.

"Sally's coming to the party alone, see you soon."

"Copy," came the clipped reply.

Mickey plugged the spotlight into the cigarette lighter as soon as he heard Sugar rumbling again and peered into the moonlit sky trying to see her. He thought he saw blue exhaust flame but when he blinked and looked again, it was gone.

"Hit me one time," Jeff's voice drawled over the radio and Mickey flicked on the 100,000-candle power light.

"How 'bout that," Jeff chuckled. "Right on line."

Mickey stared above the treeline two fields downrange of the landing area and saw Sugar Alpha's whiteness shining grey in the moonlight, two points of blue exhaust flame flickering on each engine.

"Come to Daddy, Sugar," he whispered to himself. "Come to Daddy."

Inside Sugar Alpha, Blind Jeff pulled back the power a bit and keyed his radio as they descended toward the barely visible ground.

"Let me have another blast." A moment later, a point of light flared from the middle of their target field. "Give me a notch of flaps," he said without looking at Billy.

Billy reached between the seats and held down the lever until it read ten degrees. Jeff bled off more airspeed by holding their altitude.

"Gimme another notch," he told his co-pilot and as Billy again held down the lever, Jeff keyed his radio. "Okay, man, light 'er up!"

Down below, Mickey felt his heart race as he keyed his ground radio. "Light 'em up now. Light 'em up *now!*"

Dave and Mike fired their flares and tossed them inside their jerry cans, Mike carefully keeping one eye closed as the burning magnesium cast out great pools of light, exposing their outlaw operation to any passersby. Dave forgot until he looked away from the flares and saw nothing but spots and darkness.

"Dammit!" he hissed.

Mickey's temples throbbed as he watched Sugar Alpha grow bigger in his field of view, oddly silent as it wafted in on idling engines.

"Lookie there!" said Jeff as he saw how perfectly they were lined up. "Now ain't that pretty." He reached up with one hand and pressed the duct tape holding his mangled glasses in place to make sure it would hold if he landed hard.

Billy remained silent, staring at the ground that filled the windscreen from the steep, gliding approach, hand poised near the flap lever.

"Full flaps," Jeff said. Billy instantly toggled the lever and Sugar slowed and pitched down even more steeply as the fully-dropped flaps bit into the air. "Okay, pardner," Jeff said with a warrior's smile. "Here we go."

Dave stood at the runway threshold, blinking into the night sky and willing his eyes to recover from the flare, when Sugar Alpha appeared right in front, so low he was sure she'd hit him. He dove to the ground but still felt the wind of her passing ruffle his hair and clothes.

"Fuckin' *A!*" he exclaimed joyfully as he remembered to close one eye and turned to watch the big black silhouette merge with the ground. He jumped to his feet and, still keeping one eye closed, dumped the flares out of the can and buried them in the dirt. When he opened his closed eye, he saw Sugar's tail settle onto the ground, her white skin shining brightly in the moonlight.

"Sure didn't need to put cammo on my face, that's for sure," he said out loud to himself as he grabbed his jerry cans and climbed into his pickup.

Mickey had marked the unload point with a flashlight. Jeff parked Sugar's nose right over it and shut down.

Mike heard the rumble cease. A dog wildly barked somewhere nearby as he threw his jerry cans in the truck and drove to the offload point, where Mickey guided him back into position near the door, then grabbed the latch. It wouldn't budge.

"What the fuck?" Mickey muttered, and tried again. No luck. "Mike!" he hissed. "Gimme a hand."

Mike joined him and pushed on the door while Mickey yanked on the latch. Still no luck.

"Great," said Mike as Dave stopped and climbed from his pickup.

"Help us push on the door!" Mickey whispered urgently. Dave instantly complied and with the added muscle, they relieved enough pressure on the latch for Mickey to turn it.

The door exploded outward and buried them in sweet-smelling bales.

"Holy fucking *shit*!" Mickey whispered triumphantly as they crawled free of the weed avalanche and stood up. They pumped vigorous double thumbs-up at each other for a brief celebratory moment, then got to work.

They filled the pickup in less than three minutes and Dave hopped in the driver's seat so they wouldn't have all of their weed eggs in one transportation basket.

"Don't forget to give the Bushman updates until you're out of range," Mickey reminded him as he cranked the engine.

"Will do, he grinned. "See you tomorrow." Then he bounced slowly across the field without headlights, happy for the Smuggler's Moon light that made it easy to see where he was going. He even spotted the Bushman as he reached the road and accelerated smoothly away from the landing area, turning on his lights and flipping a toggle switch under the dash to reactivate his brake lights.

"Well, let's hope no uninvited guests come to the party," he said to himself as he scanned the road ahead and checked his rearview mirror for any sign of DEA or local cops racing to the scene. A few minutes later, he radioed the Bushman.

"So far, so good," he said.

"Cool," said the Bushman, not one for standard radio protocol.

Back at the landing field, Mike had backed the rented box truck up to the door under Mickey's direction and they quickly hurled bales into it, starting first with the central aisle. Billy and Jeff waited in the cockpit until Mickey had cleared a tunnel big enough for them to wriggle out, Billy came first, rushing out of Sugar to relieve himself near the tail. Then he stood and watched Mickey and Mike until Jeff emerged, the ever-present cigarette missing.

"Let's go, pardner," he said, nodding to the truck as he too peed into the grass by the tail. "Quicker we're unloaded, the quicker we quit being sittin' ducks."

"You got it . . . pardner," Billy said, grinning, and jumped into the truck to catch bales so Mike could stack. When Mickey cleared out enough space to start a line, Jeff climbed aboard and started pitching bales to Billy as Mickey passed them to him.

"This is the fullest load I ever saw," he said to Jeff. "How much is here?"

"Looks like as much as would fit," Jeff chuckled.

"Hell of a landing as heavy as she was. Quiet, smooth, no lights. Fucking slick, man."

"Only way to go if you want to stay alive and out of jail," Jeff said as Mickey passed him another bale.

The four men emptied Sugar Alpha in less than half an hour. First they filled the box truck and Mike left immediately with it. Then they loaded up the other pickup, and Mickey called the Bushman in to drive it away. The moment they closed the door on the van, Billy jumped aboard Sugar and waved for Jeff to follow him.

"Let's go, man!" We don't want to wait another minute!" When Jeff just stood there in the moonlight with Mickey, Billy gestured in disbelief. "What the *fuck*, man? What are you waiting for? Let's *go*!"

Jeff winked at Mickey and looked into the door at his frantic co-pilot.

"Don't you think you ought to oil up them engines before we go, pardner?" Billy froze as he realized that he'd forgotten that all-important step. He disappeared into the fuselage and Jeff grinned at Mickey. "That'll keep him quiet for a few more minutes."

"You tell him you need to sit until the boys get clear before you make noise?"

"Sure did," Jeff said, still wearing his duct-taped glasses, still not smoking, "but he tends to fergit things he don't want to deal with." Mickey chuckled and shook his head, as they watched Billy climb from one fuselage window onto the port wing with two oil containers and tend to the engine.

"How'd he work out for you?" Mickey asked.

"'Cept for the whining, couldn't ask for any better. He'll be a good stick if he ever grows up."

"That's pretty much everybody's verdict," Mickey said as he grabbed a vacuum cleaner from the van. "And when he's done with the oil, this'll keep him from talking too much until you're ready to roll."

They climbed aboard and Mickey vacuumed while Jeff unhooked the remaining tanks and fuel rigging and loaded it into the van. Mickey followed him out with the vacuum and the remaining fuel system parts. When they entered Sugar again, Billy was already sitting in his seat as Jeff and Mickey walked up to the cockpit on the sloping cabin floor.

"Okay, we're done," Billy sniveled as Jeff slid into his own seat, "now let's *go!*"

Jeff ignored him and lit up a cigarette. Billy turned to Mickey just as Mickey pulled a .357 magnum revolver from his jacket and pointed it at Billy's head. Billy froze and turned white.

"Sorry buddy, but Roger told me if we're going to retire after this run, I had to shoot the pilots and burn the plane."

"Oh God, oh God, no, please no, *please*," he begged, staring at the nightmare hole in the chrome-plated barrel. "Please, I'll be cool. I'll forget I ever knew you, I'll forget everything"—he glanced at Jeff—"*we'll* forget everything, right, pardner?"

Jeff just stared at him as he puffed away, then he cracked a grin. Then he started laughing. Mickey laughed too and put away his weapon.

"Jesus fucking Christ!" Billy snarled as his companions whooped at his expense. He stared at them in disbelief. "That is *not* funny, you fuckers."

"Neither is your *whining*, asshole," Mickey said. "We figured that'd shut you up for a minute at least."

"No such luck, though," Jeff said as he got himself under control again. He looked at his watch, then glanced at Mickey. "However, it did use up the time. Been about long enough, don't you think?"

Mickey looked at his own watch and nodded, then shook hands with both of them. Jeff was relaxed and low-key as always; Billy was still keyed-up from his apparent near-death experience.

"Thanks for your fucking excellent work," Mickey said intently. "See you guys in a while."

Mickey was still closing up the cargo door when Jeff started up Sugar Alpha for the last time on his watch. Mickey drove to Mike's end of the runway and parked facing into the field as Sugar taxied back along her landing tracks to Dave's end and swung around.

"Okay, pardner," Mickey heard Jeff say on the radio and he turned on the van's headlights. A moment later, he heard Sugar Alpha roar as she rolled and, with no cargo and light fuel, she was airborne before the unload point and 500 feet above the ground when she passed over his head.

With the engine sounds still rumbling around him, Mickey drove across the field, onto the road, and headed for Tulsa to catch an early morning flight.

About two hours later, Sugar Alpha touched down in Memphis. After her 3,000-mile, 18-hour odyssey, she still had more than 200 gallons of fuel in her tanks. Jeff taxied her to the broker's office on the general aviation side of the field and shut her down for the last time. When they climbed out and shut the door, Jeff slapped Sugar Alpha's snow-white flank and smiled lovingly at her.

"She's a good old girl," he said to his co-pilot. "Hope she ends up in good hands. She sure as hell deserves that."

"Can we go now?" Billy whined, looking over at the main terminal. "I don't want to miss my flight." Jeff paused to light another cigarette, then looked evenly at Billy.

"Not exactly the sentimental type, are you, pardner?" Billy snorted.

"Dude, I'm in it for the money. A plane's a plane."

Jeff shook his head as they walked away from the proud old bird to the broker's office. Jeff stopped at the entrance and looked one last time at Sugar Alpha.

"A plane's a plane, all right," he said without looking at Billy, "except when she's not." He saluted crisply and went inside. Half an hour later, Sugar Alpha had a new owner and Jeff and Billy were each $17,500 richer. The broker drove them over to the terminal and within two hours both men had boarded different commercial jets, Jeff for Indianapolis, Billy for Chicago.

Four days later, Roger put together three briefcases full of cash and chartered a Lear Jet. On the way to the airport, he stopped at Billy's house. They sat at the kitchen table and he listened carefully to the parts of Billy's Sugar Alpha tale that he didn't know about yet, then cut him off when he started complaining about Mickey's .357 prank.

"That ought to be a hint to quit sniveling so much," Roger said soberly. Then he flashed his famous grin and set a briefcase on the table. He popped the latches and showed him big load of Franklins. Billy gasped involuntarily at the sight of it.

"Eighty-two-five," Roger said. "That's your fifty for the gig, plus thirty-two-five for a bonus, plus you can keep the seventeen-five you split with Jeff for Sugar Alpha. One hundred grand total."

"Wow, thanks, Roger," Billy said, his eyes glittering greedily. "A couple more of these and I'll be set for life." Roger slammed the briefcase shut and glared at Billy.

"You said you'd quit when I did. You break your word to me again, and I'll let your imagination figure out what will happen. A hundred grand, tax-free. Most people'll work ten years to clear that much so just chill out and be thankful for what you got."

"But I'm too young to call it quits, man," Billy persisted. "We're on a roll! Why do you want to stop now just when things are getting really good? Hell, I'm ready to get back in the left seat and make some real dough next time. Man, if you coulda seen how Jeff rode the brakes to keep Sugar on the road down there, you'd agree I'm a better pilot."

That assertion needed an hour's answer or none so Roger let it slide and just stared coldly at him. Billy got the message and shut up. Roger knew it wouldn't end there, and he was afraid Billy would become an even worse liability. Like a bad dream, every time Billy did a gig, every time his pile of cash grew, so did his desires—and, worse, his opinion of himself and his skill set. It was probably never going to end, but Roger knew he had to try or have Billy come back and bite him hard later on down the road. He drummed his fingers on the briefcase.

"You keep your word, and you know I'll call you first if something comes up, right?"

Billy nodded appreciatively. Roger held out his hand and they shook.

"All right, then," Roger concluded. "Stay cool, don't flash the cash, get some good investment advice and leave this business alone unless I call you."

"You got it, man," Billy said. He clicked open the briefcase and grabbed a pair of $10,000 bundles in each hand. Roger let himself out as Billy smelled his cash and wondered with revulsion if his idiot pilot would roll naked in it after the he left.

Roger got aboard the Lear and flew to Indianapolis, where he met Jeff in a motel overlooking Weir Cook International Airport. He paid off his pilot the same way he had his co-pilot; fee plus bonus, plus he kept his half of the Sugar Alpha money.

"Thanks, pardner," Jeff said appreciatively. "Mighty generous of you." With business concluded, they went to a nearby restaurant for drinks and dinner and when their drinks arrived, they clinked their glasses together.

"To Sugar Alpha," Jeff said.

"Sugar Alpha," Roger said, and they drank. Roger wiped his mouth and grinned at his pilot. "To tell you the truth, I didn't think you could do it."

"It *was* a pretty narrow runway," Jeff said. Roger finished his drink in one long swig.

"No, I mean doing the whole gig without killing Billy Bob."

Jeff grinned back. "Well, I gotta tell you, pardner, it sure helped my mood when Mickey played his joke." They chuckled at the memory, then Jeff winked. "On the other hand, Billy wasn't nothin' when I consider that you gave me an airplane painted like a neon sign, knocked me half-unconscious after I stuffed 'er on a sliver of road, then ordered me to leapfrog a bus to get home."

"True enough," Roger said, "but I knew you could handle all that—I just wasn't sure about Billy Bob."

"Gotta admit, he did try my patience a few times, but all told, he graded out okay. Like I said to Mickey, kid'll be a good stick if he ever grows up."

"Too bad that's such a big if," Roger grouched.

Their food arrived then, and Jeff lit up a cigarette.

"You remember my buddy Jimmy in L.A. I was tellin' you about?" he asked as smoke wreathed his head.

"Vaguely. What about him?"

"Well, he's been doing a Mexican thing but he's having trouble with quality, so he's not getting much back and what does come back takes a long time. Anyway, I'm finally in a position to invest, and they're short on cash, so I been thinking pretty serious about getting in."

"In how?"

"Now, I'm smart enough to know my skills are driving, not putting projects together, so I wondered if you'd consider helping us pull out of Belize. Sure felt comfortable not worrying about Mexican *federales* and the quality's top-notch. And, of course, it'd be a single tripper. I just want to roll my money big enough to start that aviation company I've been thinking about."

Roger turned to his food as he mulled Jeff's proposal. He already had one commitment to keep, and it might be easy to punch Jeff's gig out along with Tony's—if he actually went through with Tony's. He hadn't made up his mind yet, even if he had given Tony his word. Jeff ate too, waiting patiently for Roger's reply.

"The thing is," Roger said after a few bites, "is that I'm not really looking for work."

"I know, pardner, and I hate asking, especially with all those retirement rumors swirling around."

"Billy never knows when to shut up, does he?"

"No, he don't," Jeff said, "so I know you're looking for an exit and the last thing you need to hear about is a sweet run, but you got a class act going down there so I gotta ask."

The waitress brought Roger his next drink and he stirred it until she walked away.

"The biggest problem I have with doing one more is that it's never just one more. You know how many times I've done 'just one more'? Sugar Alpha was supposed to be the last one—but guess what?" Jeff grinned knowingly. "That's right," Roger said in response, "there's a chance I have some other business to take care of, so if you have your ducks in a row in about a month, it's a definite maybe." Elated, Jeff blew smoke at the ceiling.

"Then let's make it a date, pardner," he said, and extended his hand. They shook.

"So, what've you got going?" Roger asked.

"Jimmy's talking about a Panther Navajo right now and we've got this strip in the Ozarks in the middle of nowhere. I checked it out and it's nice—similar setup to the Ranch, actually. I mean, if you can put it together, great. If not, we can always do a Mexican. I'd just prefer to find a friendlier place and avoid investing in a garbage load if I can."

"Well, it seems as if you're thinking about the right things, so I think you'll come out okay no matter what."

"Thanks, pardner," Jeff said, visibly relaxing. "Means a lot coming from you."

Roger's next stop was Tampa and Tony, who met him at the general aviation terminal in a snow-white Lamborghini Diablo. When he got in the car, he instantly noticed Tony's hypnotic stare and grayish-white complexion and knew he was lost in the "world of the pipe." Tony drove him at high speed to his house, where Roger laid out almost a half million dollars worth of Franklins on the living room table.

"Happy?" Roger asked after Tony had counted the bundles.

"In more ways than one," Tony mumbled and nodded over toward the steaming cooker on the kitchen stove. "I got a sweet little run in from Grand Bahama. Good quality, too. That place is just loaded with coke." Roger listened out of habit; new information about traffic or interdiction efforts never hurt—and, as he expected, Tony rambled on. "The run went smooth, and I should get a call for another when word gets back. I'm also expecting a load in Belize." Roger's eyebrows arched. "Oh yeah, and I got you a Titan."

"I didn't ask you to do that!"

"Yeah, I know," Tony shrugged, "but I couldn't let it get away. It's at the shop right now waiting for the H.F."

"What do you want for it?"

"Well, I was going to use it," Tony said with a knowing, devilish smile, "but I found another one, an Ambassador really decked out— LORAN, H.F., nose tank, the works. If you take it, I'll make you the same offer as before. Just tell me when and where, and I'll deliver it and check out a pilot for you—and you don't need to pay me until you get the first one in. I've got a mechanic looking them over real good; they'll be ready in about a month."

Roger pondered Tony's offer. It was extremely attractive considering that Roger needed a plane to do the load for Tony that he'd promised.

"All right, here's what we'll do. I'm not sure I can use it, but one way or the other I can get rid of it for you. Just call when it's ready and we'll go from there."

As Roger winged his way home from Tampa, he felt himself physically deflate. Now that all the Sugar Alpha accounts were settled, he realized how bone tired his brain was, and his body—and his soul. He dozed off for a while, relaxed for the first time in months, maybe even years.

He slept until his aviator's sense felt the plane start descending, and he awoke with his mind racing. Retirement beckoned, but the promise he'd made to Tony stood in his way. He'd made a deal, and he'd honored every deal he'd ever made. That was the way you got ahead in this business, how you attracted honest, loyal people to work with you, how you lessened your chances of getting busted.

Except none of that mattered anymore because he was quitting. Yeah, he'd made a deal with Tony, but The Snake had burned so many people so many times—especially his long-time friend, Mickey—that maybe it would be poetic justice to blow him off. He knew for sure that Mickey would love it and, besides, Tony had already cleared almost a quarter mil on his investment for doing little more than flying to Belize and back.

Roger had an even better reason to renege on his deal with Tony. He knew Jeanie was truly at the end of her rope and the whole decision really did come down to answering a simple question—Tony or Jeanie?—and that answer was a no-brainer.

Except it was more complicated than that. There was Tony's offer on the Titan. There was the enthusiasm of his crew to bang out more runs. He hated to admit it but he knew Billy pretty much spoke for all of his guys in not wanting to quit yet. From the growers in Belize to the buyers in the U.S., everyone was ready to scam and the insatiable U.S. market would suck up every last cola.

Then again, Roger knew in his heart that he didn't really want to do these deals; they were more of a convenient opportunity that he pondered out of habit, not desire or necessity. The lonely motels, the secret meetings, the clandestine communications—none of it excited or even appealed to him anymore. In fact, he wasn't that happy now, even though he'd just pulled off the biggest, most audacious, most lucrative venture of his career—except for the thought that Sugar Alpha really was the last one, that now he really could spend more time with both his long-suffering wife and his too-often disappointed children, all of whom were no doubt asleep as he pulled into the driveway of his darkened home. He turned off the key and looked at the staring windows.

"I want to come home when the lights are on," he said out loud, and thumped the steering wheel with the heel of one hand. He thumped the steering wheel again. "I want to come home while the sun is still up." He thumped the steering wheel again. "And I want to come home every . . . single . . . day."

He took a deep breath and went in the house, shutting the door quietly behind him so he didn't wake up his family.

Jeanie stirred but didn't waken when he climbed into bed, but tired as he was Roger didn't sleep. He laid awake weighing his promise to Jeanie and himself against the word he'd given Tony, against the obligation he still felt to his incredibly loyal and capable crew, against the help he'd love to offer Jeff for making his retirement dream a reality— and yeah, even against the challenge of doing what he knew no one had ever done before: a multi-ship extravaganza, one plane after another, all coming from and going back to different places like an airline company, the kind of over-the-top gig that would make *Señor Huevos Grandes* not only more famous but absolutely legendary. The kind of scam—

Jeanie rolled over and bumped against him, breaking his train of thought. He shook off his musings like a bad dream and delicately slid out of bed. Jeanie didn't waken. He padded in his pajamas and bare feet first into Missy's room and watched her even breathing for several long minutes, taking in the lines of her smooth face, smiling at the ringlets falling across her forehead. He stroked her hair and planted a light kiss on that dear little forehead, then went to Rook's room, where his toddler son slept on his chest, his arms tucked under him, his little rump sticking up in the air, one cherubic cheek smushed again the mattress of his crib, sleeping so heavily he snored slightly. Roger flashed his famous grin at the incongruous sound coming from the tiny body and watched him sleep for several minutes too before patting him gently on the back and walking back to his own bedroom.

He pulled aside the curtain and stared out the window at the moonlit snow sparkling serenely in the yards and rooftops around his cozy little home, the sight and ambiance of it so alien from the jungles and airports and supercharged atmosphere of smuggling. He sighed and, once more, he climbed into bed without waking his wife.

This time, though, he was ready to sleep because he was all done thinking. He knew exactly what he was going to do. The last thing he heard before he drifted off was the sound of a winter breeze whispering around the corner of his house.

Early the next afternoon, Roger, Mickey, Dave and Mike gathered at Café le Cave for their traditional celebration brunch. This time, though, the meeting held much more significance. This time would be the last time. Gus greeted them at the door and offered them their choice of tables. Roger chose one in the corner of the dark, cave-shaped lounge. After the wine steward filled their champagne flutes with Dom Perignon, Roger held up his until everyone at the table grew silent.

"To Hanoi," he said simply.

"To Hanoi," the rest of them intoned, and they all downed their glasses in one swig.

Then the appetizers arrived and the feast began, with more toasts, much merriment, and many secret smiles because they couldn't talk much about the reason for their party in such a public place. But they talked endlessly about everything else, and they feasted like kings, and when the four young smugglers had downed more than $500 worth of food, $1,000 worth of Dom, and a decadently delightful dessert, Roger tapped a fork against his champagne flute until they quieted and turned their full attention to him, both happy and sad to hear what they knew what was coming.

"Sugar Alpha was the biggest, best and absolutely most outrageous gig we ever did," he said, and held up his glass. "To Sugar Alpha."

"To Sugar Alpha," they all intoned raising their glasses with his. He waited until they had once again drained their flutes and refilled them before going on.

"You all share the credit for working like a team and never getting lazy or sloppy, never getting down when things got sticky, never giving up no matter what. It was a first-class operation run by first-class people and we should all be proud of ourselves."

"Hear, hear," said Mickey, raising his own glass. "To us!"

"To us!" they chanted and drank again. Roger flashed his famous grin, then turned deadly serious.

"There's no doubt we did a first-class job, but *believe* me, a lot of luck went our way, not just with Sugar Alpha but with every gig we've ever done and we better be honest enough to admit it." He paused and watched that sink into the souls of the men around him and he was happy to see from their nods and expressions that it did. "And now it's time to remember that wise old saying. You have two choices in this business: You can pick a point and quit, or you can keep going until you die or go to jail. I suggest that we *all* take the wiser of the two. I owe you guys a lot for your loyalty and skill but right now I feel you owe it me to exercise it one more time: Show me your loyalty by giving me your word that you'll retire with me—and then show your skill by *keeping* it."

There was a long moment where no one moved. Then Mickey slowly raised his still-empty flute.

"Deal," he said forcefully. Mike and Dave raised their empty flutes too.

"Deal," they said in unison. Roger raised his to join theirs.

"Deal," he said. "And if you ever feel tempted to go back, come find me at the DZ so I can remind you of the deal we just made."

They all laughed and pushed away from the table, then walked out the front door of the Cave and said their goodbyes while the valets got their vehicles. Then Dave and Mike left together in Mike's car. Roger and Mickey lingered for a moment while their valets waited nearby.

"What about that load you were gonna do for Tony?" Mickey asked.

Roger flashed his famous grin for the last time as a member of the smuggling club.

"I decided that it was time The Snake got a taste of his own venom."

Mickey looked stunned for a heartbeat, then grinned and slapped his partner on the back so hard Roger almost staggered.

"Fuckin' *A!*" Mickey chuckled. "Now that's a fitting goodbye!" They embraced warmly then separated, smiling.

"Enjoy your island," Roger said.

"Enjoy your family," Mickey replied.

And with that, Mickey tipped his valet a Grant and drove away in his rental car to O'Hare International Airport.

Roger gave his valet a Franklin, climbed into his old green pickup truck and drove toward his cozy home in his comfortable neighborhood in his quaint little town, the home and neighborhood and town in which he would soon spend more time.

Much more time. During the past month, he'd spent four days at home. During the past few years, he couldn't even remember how many holidays, anniversaries, birthdays and special family moments he'd missed.

"Not any more," he said out loud as he pulled into the driveway and turned off the key just as the sun touched the treeline a few yards over. "Not any more."

He bounded out of his truck and up the stairs, beating the sunset into his warm house and spreading his arms wide for the onrush of two delighted children and a shared smile with his equally delighted wife.

"Honey," he said to her with finality, "I'm *home*."